PLUCK

# PLUCK

*The Extraordinary Life and Times of David Schnaufer*

LINDA PAULUS

TLP/Night Owl, LLC

ISBN: 978-0-578-34599-4

For more information, stories and photos visit DavidSchnauferPluck.com

*David and friend T.J. jamming on the porch during the 2006 "Dulci-marathon Day" in Belmont-Hillsboro, Nashville.*
*Courtesy of Kelly Love.*

*To Frank and Edith Schnaufer, who gifted their sons to the world, and to Tom Paulus, who is the universe's gift to me.*

# TABLE OF
# CONTENTS

# INTRODUCTION

C onsider the fugue—a work of music that consists of interwoven and recurring melodies. The life story of Texas musician
David Schnaufer is like a fugue; it entails remarkable confluences of
people, places and events leading to and from David that shaped his
life as he became a catalyst for changing people's limited perception
of the mountain dulcimer. Once David discovered the dulcimer (or,
after knowing the story, one might even imagine that dulcimers seek
out their players), their histories became interwoven so tightly that
man and instrument seem inseparable. David's work in Nashville
made an indelible impact not only on his professional colleagues
but on thousands of people he taught and mentored throughout his
life.

When David passed away, his obituaries in the *New York Times*,
the *Los Angeles Times*, and a slew of other newspapers summarized
his life with only the shallowest impressions: he was a musician who
played with famous Nashville artists and, in the process, brought
prominence to an instrument called a dulcimer. True, yet those
obituaries reveal nothing about the challenges David overcame to
become a virtuoso musician or his impact on the world. They skip
the most interesting aspects of the man and leave many questions
unanswered. How did a Texas high school dropout become a
groundbreaking musician, songwriter, historian, film actor, producer, engineer, instrument builder, a university professor, and an
expert on American roots music? How could a man with no formal
musical education, whom others often described as "elfin," "Amish-
looking," or "frail," play so well that he astonished the most seasoned
music professionals in Nashville? One only has to dig a little to find
people who, fifteen years after his death, still find his loss almost
unbearable. Today, others feel compelled to share stories of David

and follow his teaching and/or playing style; many consider him the most unforgettable person they ever met.

David's life is Joseph Campbell's *Hero's Journey* writ large. His story presents a model for the very personal spiritual and psychological journey that we must undertake in order to create meaning in our own lives. His journey started with a simple idea: he wanted to write songs, and to help him, he found an easy-to-play musical instrument: the mountain dulcimer. Long underestimated and often disdained by professional musicians, it had other ideas for him. It became his life's passion, and the pursuit of that passion as he overcame one daunting challenge after another resulted in a world-class dulcimer musician; at the time of his death, he was arguably the finest who had ever lived.

Synchronicity is evident everywhere in David's life. Both David and the dulcimer shared the same German cultural roots; both are examples of the gifts granted to us by the American immigrant experience. The people, places, and events that shaped first the dulcimer, then David, leave us in a state of wonder and reflection for our own lives: *Where do we come from? Who and what shapes our lives? What will be the wake we leave behind?* For those who don't believe in synchronicity, they'll have to find their own explanation for how David's life unfolded and why his memory is still so vividly cherished by so many people.

Folk musician Jean Ritchie once told the *New York Times*, "I see folk music as a river that never stopped flowing." David's story—part folk history, part biography, and part chronology of the times in which he grew into an adult—is a significant tributary of the American folk music river. The story details concurrent movements across time and place, the gifts of immigrants and the curiosity and energetic dreams of young people. It reveals an historic graciousness of inspiring and sharing, and a treasuring of the best that history bestows upon us that is more relevant than ever today. It's about personal and family struggles and secrets, friends, finding oneself and leaving the world a better place.

If you don't know what a dulcimer is, don't worry. To understand why David's impact on the music world is so compelling, the book begins with an introduction to his instrument followed by a narrative of the small decisions throughout history that led to this man and his work.

I imagine if David were alive today and you, the reader, were to call him on the phone, he'd answer, "Schnaufer here!" Through a brief chat, he would sense an untapped passion within you. Whether that passion had to do with making music or some other endeavor, he would encourage you to pursue that passion with his potent mixture of kindness, wit and hard-earned wisdom. He would throw in some advice, too (but only if you asked for it). If, after making his acquaintance and reading his story you were to decide to make a little room for dulcimer music in your own life, he would be absolutely delighted, and most certainly would jump in to "pick a little" with you.

I hope you enjoy his story.
LINDA PAULUS October 2021

Like things vibrate alike.

—W. A. Mathieu, *The Harmonic Experience*

# MOVEMENT 1:
# ORIGINS

As long as I can remember, and as long as my father could
  remember,
and as long as *his* father could remember, there have been
  dulcimers ...
made and played in our Kentucky mountains.
                              —Jean Ritchie, *The Dulcimer Book*

A mountain dulcimer is a musical instrument. If you've never seen one, start by imagining one of its most common forms: an hourglass-shaped, wooden sound box with a fretboard centered on top of its length. Now imagine three or sometimes four strings running lengthwise down the fretboard. The soundbox includes four holes on top of the box to release the sound when the strings are strummed with fingers or a plectrum, or plucked.

Traditionally, the four sound holes are heart-shaped—the first clue that the dulcimer offers a special relationship to its player. In certain regions, the holes resemble sound holes on a fiddle, an homage to the instrument that provides much of the dulcimer's music. Peek inside one of the sound holes, and you're liable to see a little message for you left by its maker: his or her name, the year of its birth, and its sequence in the number of instruments built by the maker.

The dulcimer will be much less hard on you than you are on yourself, and it has enough history, mystery, and musical potential contained within to keep you enchanted for the rest of your life.

It's bigger than a fiddle, and smaller than a guitar. Traditionally, the owner plays it flat on his or her lap or on a table, ready to softly conjure a lullaby to accompany singing. Or, in skilled hands blessed by more than ten thousand hours of playing to reveal its potential, it can sound like just about anything—" a bagpipe, a guitar, a fiddle, a banjo, a slide guitar, a harpsichord...." Yet "none of those instruments can fool anyone into thinking it's a dulcimer," asserted David Schnaufer.

This instrument sports many aliases, depending upon when and where speakers discuss it: Appalachian dulcimer, mountain dulcimer, lap dulcimer, delcimore, dulcymore, hog fiddle, walking cane...scholars refer to it as a fretted dulcimer to distinguish it from a different instrument with a similar name, the hammered dulcimer.

The dulcimer invites the curious. Sit down—use the tip of your index finger, or hold a pick and close your eyes as you strum across its strings: listen to the transcendent drone that evokes the faint timbre of a bagpipe. Welcome to the world of rhythm! If a new player knows how to hum "Go Tell Aunt Rhody" or "Twinkle, Twinkle, Little Star," with a little bit of experimenting at the lowest end of the fretboard, he or she can play the tune in about ten minutes.

The dulcimer's personality seduces: for many who strum its strings or caress the wood of its body the first time, it is love at first sight and sound. Even those who firmly believe they have no musical talent will detect its voice if they lean in close enough: "Yes, I will make music with you."

A dulcimer resonates deep inside its owner. If it connects with a good heart, the Muse will take note and inspire the player to learn how to summon joy, overcome pain or sorrow, forge a sense of discipline, build character and community. The dulcimer will serve as a leader, a follower, and a lifelong companion on a personal musical journey that has no end as far as it is concerned, only new and satisfying experiences along the way. It's a handcrafted escape for lonely and troubled times, a healer for the sick, a teacher of history, a catalyst for singing, dancing and expressing gratitude, and a companion for mourning.

A mountain dulcimer is a time machine. With it you'll meet up with Napoleon, Leadbelly, Lennon and McCartney, Stephen Foster, set a spell with the Carter Family, dance around with sailors, or join Beethoven as he imagines the finale of his Fifth Symphony. It's a tool to create a song that no one has heard yet...a magic carpet transporting your thoughts and feelings to the future.

A dulcimer is a shape shifter with several branches in its family tree. Its earliest, European ancestors were carefully wrapped, packed, and carried across Europe and the Atlantic as emigrants made their way to the Americas. The descendants of the instruments they carried were birthed one by one, each new version shaped by hand. Across time and space, newly crafted instruments included small changes to help a player express his or her innermost emotions and senses.

Many assert that the dulcimer we know today is the first truly American instrument. When the descendants of a German instrument called a Scheitholt were reborn in the United States of America, they were christened "Mountain," or "Appalachian" dulcimers for their association with the early immigrants who streamed down the Great Wagon Road into Appalachia, the Blue Ridge Mountains, into the Shenandoah Valley of Virginia and beyond.

The dulcimer is a democratic, equal-opportunity instrument. As immigrants made their way into the mountains of the eastern United States, self-taught woodworkers built dulcimers in a backyard barn or shack either for family members or to sell them literally for a song. Often, families passed their dulcimer down generation after generation; sometimes, they were discarded on a woodpile when their owners passed away. The dulcimer's design was and is only limited by the maker's imagination: it can be a humble cardboard kit cut out and packed in a factory for the curious to assemble at home. Or, when money is no object, skilled craftspeople bring it to life with the finest rare woods, intricate insets of mother-of-pearl on the fretboard, and the cleanest tones to ring across a room or a stage.

Despite its evolution as a playing instrument, many musicians and even players grossly underestimated its potential during much of its journey. Professional musicians and serious amateurs were lulled into judging the dulcimer at face value: a simple, even primitive instrument, limited in what it could do. It took knowing and nimble hands for the dulcimer's potential to unfold. As one who had such hands described it, it is "the wild animal of the musical kingdom...living in a sonic wilderness." Rhythm is only the first and most fundamental of its many capabilities.

The dulcimer's voice sings in multiple musical modes. And it plays very well with others despite its simple construction and the limitations of its diatonic fretboard (akin to two and a half octaves of a piano but missing the black keys). In the dulcimer's earliest days, aspiring players learned to play by ear. And sing, of course. They loved to sing alone and together in those times, before electricity, before the radio, before television, and before records or easy access to sheet music.

Just as music involves elements of logic and physics, engineering, creativity, emotion, and spirit, so does the construction of a dulcimer. Some still make or assemble their own dulcimers; today, most purchase them from professional craftsmen and women known as luthiers. The best luthiers design well-crafted dulcimers that deliver pleasing sounds in a controlled, predictable way. This means that the instrument's capabilities have a limit, but that limit depends less on the components of the box and more upon the imagination of those who play the dulcimer to express their deepest emotions.

Thanks to several key people and a long series of often improbable events, the dulcimer made its way into the hands of New York City folk musicians in the forties, fifties, and sixties after a long incubation in Appalachia. In the seventies, the Muse beckoned folkies on both coasts to discover it. Thanks to those happy encounters, young, middle-aged, and old players built friendly rivalries and lifelong friendships as the dulcimer became the center of their communities.

Still, the instrument barely registered in the national imagination. Many in the music business considered it too crude and too limited to be taken seriously as an American musical instrument. However, the dulcimer and its music persisted below the surface in the national consciousness until 1986 when it exploded onto the Nashville music scene as a result of a most unlikely encounter: one Sunday afternoon, seemingly out of nowhere, Texan transplant David Schnaufer showed up at the Nashville door of another Texan, John Lomax III. Driven by an insatiable need to find his and his instrument's capabilities, David arrived after traveling thousands of miles throughout the United States to become worthy of the instrument that may have saved his life. His passion helped propel the dulcimer around the country and, indeed, the world. His chance discovery of a mountain dulcimer at one of the lowest points of his life was a stone thrown by an unseen hand into the cultural pond; the resulting ripples spread to touch thousands of souls, many of whom were not destined to meet him but were just as surely inspired by his remarkable spirit.

## 1560 FUNEN, DENMARK: THE ANGEL

If you are in search of the fretted dulcimer's origins, the world's first dulcimer professor points you to the third largest of Denmark's islands, the future home of Hans Christian Andersen. Step into Rynkeby Kirke and encounter the cool air within the silence. Look up to the ceiling, and you'll discover a series of frescoes depicting angels playing various musical instruments.

Walk slowly and scan these pre-Reformation images until you see a particular angel as he floats through a starry sky. He plays a zither, a long, narrow wooden box with sound holes and strings stretched across the top. It is the earliest known image of the dulcimer's ancestor.

Over time, variations of the zither spread throughout northern Europe. When Germans began crafting their version, they christened it the Scheitholt, named after a large piece of kindling, just the right size for getting a blazing fire started.

(1, 2)

## 1700S EASTERN NORTH AMERICAN CONTINENT, PT. I: THE MOUNTAINS

The geography of "Appalachia" exists. But the concept of Appalachia will not appear for almost two hundred years.

A mountainous terrain exists in the present-day United States and Canada. Two hundred years in the future its lands will become known as the Cumberlands, the Allegheny Mountains, the Blue Ridge chain, and the Greater Appalachian Valley. They will stretch some sixteen hundred miles from the places that will someday bear the names Quebec, Canada to northern Georgia and Alabama. The central and southern highlands contain the seeds of future states that will be known as Maryland, Virginia, Kentucky, North and South Carolina, West Virginia, and Tennessee. Virgin forests exist here, interspersed with occasional wide-open spaces in valleys and plenty of rivers, creeks, and waterfalls. Native Americans of the Cherokee nation use the land freely for hunting. Eventually they feel the incoming trickle of German immigrants; among their personal effects, they carry humble but treasured musical instruments. Most—along with Scotch-Irish settlers from the northern part of Ireland—will settle in Pennsylvania where space is plenty, and land is cheap. Between 1720 and 1770, the trickle turns into a flood: approximately 600,000 Scotch-Irish and 110,000 Germans as well as English, Irish, and French Huguenots will migrate to and through the mountains. They and their descendants will go through plenty before they can call themselves Americans, including a revolution in the second half of the century. In the meantime, they buy up, squat on or claim land, and make their living by farming and hunting. They frequently clash with Native Americans as they encroach ever more on lands that used to belong to everyone and to no one.

(3, 4, 5, 6, 7, 8)

## 1779 NORTH CAROLINA: FORT NASHBOROUGH

Francis Nash, a brigadier general in the Continental Army during the American Revolutionary War, never makes it farther west than present-day North Carolina. His contemporaries consider him a war hero, and he will go down in history as one of ten generals killed in the Revolutionary War between 1777 and 1781.

Four years after the war officially ended, Englishman James Robertson (followed by John Donelson) arrives at a choice spot on the Cumberland River on land ceded by North Carolina to the United States for war veterans. There, he envisions a log stockade for a settlement. Once built, they call it Fort Nashborough to honor the fallen General Nash.

Fort Nashborough's population will grow quickly. By 1796, the territory becomes the sixteenth state of the new United States: Tennessee.

(9)

## 1795 ANNANDALE, SCOTLAND: DAVID'S GREAT-GREAT GRANDFATHER

One Samuel Lee Johnston of Annandale leaves Scotland with his family and takes the long Atlantic journey to York, South Carolina, in the nascent United States. Almost a hundred years later, Samuel's great-grandson, Alver Leroy, will be born in South Carolina. When he grows up, he will emigrate to Texas where, in 1923, Alver's wife Annie Belle will deliver a wee bairn they name Edith Ertte Johnston. Twenty-nine years later, Edith will give birth to David Schnaufer.

(10)

## 1821 TEJAS, MÉJICO: THE SEDUCTION

The northern region of Mexico known to future settlers as "Texas" first comes to the attention of nineteenth-century Germans with the 1821 Berlin publication of an intrepid traveler's book entitled *Reise durch die Vereinigten Staaten* (Travels through the United States). The author writes a glowing report of Mexico, having just won its independence from Spain. He fuels readers' imaginations with his descriptions of a beautiful climate, a rich productive soil, wide-open spaces, intellectual and religious freedom, and even the possibility of building one or more German states west of the Mississippi. More travel books and adventurers follow.

A former German gardener, Friedrich Diercks emigrates to Mexican territory in what will become Austin County, Texas, in the future. In a migration process known as "American Letters," Ernst writes to friends in Germany about the wonders of this territory. His letters convince many readers and their families that all Texas needs is more German laborers; as a result, his new home becomes the nucleus of the growing German Belt. These new immigrants from all regions of Germany stream into Texas: peasant farmers, tradespeople, and intellectuals; Protestants, Catholics, Jews, and atheists; abolitionists and slaveowners; farmers and townsfolk; honest folk and criminals. They differ in dialect, customs, and physical features. German settlements in Mexico all reflect this diversity, and their influence will reach its peak in the 1890s. For a time, the settlers and their descendants will preserve much of their culture and sense of "otherness" due to their relative isolation.

(11, 12, 13)

## 1847 TEXAS, UNITED STATES: THE IMMIGRANTS' GIFTS

Two years after the United States annexed Texas as the twenty-eighth state, a group of homesteaders from Tennessee and Alabama make their way to Texas soil to sink roots. Drawn by its status as a slave state and fertile land suitable for growing cotton, they carry their music with them—including the polka—that will become part of Texas's rich cultural stew of Mexican, Anglo, African American, Irish, Polish, Czech, and French influences. These influences will steadily fuel musicians' and songwriters' imaginations for the next hundred and fifty years. The pioneers name the settlement the "Tennessee Colony" to honor their origins.

(14)

# 1860 THE MOUNTAINS OF THE EASTERN UNITED STATES, PART II: A DIVERSE, RICH STEW

The second half of the nineteenth century sees the influx of diverse immigrants pouring into the cities and the coming of the industrial age. Many White American citizens grow uncomfortable with the urbanization and changing faces of America. Those who are reluctant to embrace or even tolerate such changes look toward nature for solace; they imagine an idyllic past and develop a fascination with the predominantly White inhabitants of the mountains whom they imagine exist in the bliss of a "purer" past.

White popular and scholarly writers present the mountains of the eastern United States as the last bastion of Anglo-Saxon purity in a country awash with immigrants and race "problems." However, contrary to this imagined mountain cultural pastiche, mountain people are not a homogenous group. The Black population of the mountainous areas of the South make up 16.2 percent of the population of the Southern Appalachian region in 1860.

Mountain living conditions are primitive compared to those of urban areas throughout the country. Places such as eastern Kentucky will have no electricity to provide connections to the rest of the world via radio (and eventually television) until 1954. Thus, mountain people—well into the twentieth century—have to contend with how to comfort, soothe, or even entertain themselves in such a challenging place. They resort to its saving grace: a diverse musical heritage that rings out every time someone draws a bow, sings a song, and strums an instrument. The fiddle hitched a ride to America with European immigrants while the banjo, descended from African stringed instruments, made its way via kidnapped slaves. The fretted dulcimer, descended from the German immigrants' zithers, has already begun its changes, the most significant of which entails fixing the zither on top of a larger soundbox. With that change, the immigrant instrument becomes uniquely American.

By 1860 a new interest arises in folk songs, considered the "wild-flower" of the musical arts. Wildflowers were seen as an apt metaphor of nature, a refuge from the turbulent changes taking place throughout the country, triggered in part by the drumbeats of the impending Civil War.

As time rolls forward into the twentieth century and generations pass, the central mountain people live immersed in a little-under-stood but bubbling cultural stew consisting of traditions, languages, and dialects, and values from diverse groups of peoples: early immigrants from England, Ulster, the lowlands of Scotland, two waves of diverse German groups and their descendants, and intrepid White and Black people who lived on a borderland where eastern traditions meet the "Wild West."

(15, 16, 17)

## 1867 THE TENNESSEE COLONY, TEXAS: JACOB SCHNAUFER

Circa 1867, one of Germany's post–Civil War emigrants makes his way to Texas. He is twenty-year-old Jacob Schnaufer, whose last name means "breath." He is the future paternal great-grandfather of David Schnaufer.

Jacob will travel to Texas from Ellis Island by way of the Midwest near Kansas where he meets an American woman named Rosa Karol. Once married, Jacob and Rosa head south to the town of Palestine, Texas. Jacob is a carpenter who heard there is work there on the railroad.

(18)

## 1870 HINDMAN, KENTUCKY: "UNCLE ED"

"Uncle Ed" Thomas and his family live in a rough-hewn log cabin outside of Hindman, the county seat of Knox County in eastern Kentucky. Hindman consists of seventeen houses and a hundred people.

Uncle Ed is exceptionally well-liked by his friends for being warmhearted and friendly with a delightful sense of humor. Uncle Ed is also known for his carpentry skills, which he employs to make houses and furniture such as chests of drawers and pie safes. To make a little more money, Uncle Ed makes his first of at least fifteen hundred dulcimers. Throughout his lifetime his dulcimers will make their way from his own log cabin in a holler to places like New York and London. A century from now, his dulcimer design will play a great part in fueling the largest mass production of hand-crafted dulcimers in the world from a little shop called McSpadden's in Mountain View, Arkansas. There, the dulcimer will continue its evolution with design input from David Schnaufer.

(19, 20)

### A Bit about Uncle Ed Thomas and His Craft

J. Edward Thomas is the earliest dulcimer maker and player that anyone has been able to trace in the United States. Born in 1850, he lived most of his life in the village of Bath, Kentucky, about twenty-five miles from the Richies' home.

Thomas made a little chair and a cart with a frame to hang his dulcimers. He'd push his cart up and down the creek roads hoping to sell his wares by inviting people to stop and listen to him play. He charged about six dollars for a dulcimer if someone could pay; if not, he'd swap a dulcimer in trade for anything the potential buyer was willing to offer.

Thomas made a variety of dulcimers out of walnut but occasionally used maple or birch. According to Douglas

Naselroad, researchers associate at least six different pegbox sizes and styles, five different body depths, and at least four different body shapes to "Uncle Ed." His favorite sound hole design was a heart. A few of his instruments show he decorated the hearts with gold paint, or he would paint the occasional dulcimer with leftover black barn paint. Once he was about to finish an instrument, he would write out his name, the date, and the number of the instrument in ink on a piece of paper and paste it to the bottom inside before gluing on the top. Those who purchased his dulcimers could peek into the sound hole and read his label, and the practice continues to this day by other dulcimer makers.

Today, The Appalachian School of Luthiery in Hindman, Kentucky, offers a five-day course on how to make a dulcimer using Uncle Ed's long peghead 1913 pattern. Students need not have any woodworking experience; the school provides all supplies and expertise needed for their students to create an authentic reproduction of Thomas's dulcimer with its "angelic tone." If you'd like to learn more about the school, visit: Appalachianluthiery.org

## 1892 SOMERSET, ENGLAND: SONGCATCHER CECIL SHARP

At thirty-eight years old and after almost a decade in Australia, Cecil James Sharp returns to England, having had enough of working as a bank clerk.

In England, state-sponsored mass public schooling is in its infancy, and music curriculum is a current topic for development. A devotion to music that Cecil nurtured in Adelaide becomes his passion when he returns home. After a short stint as principal at the Hampstead Conservatoire of Music, Cecil will resign in 1905 to focus on lecturing, composing, collecting, and publishing folk music. Sharp will be driven to rescue old English folk songs by traveling around England, eventually building his folk library to over sixteen hundred songs and texts from 350 different singers. He will use these songs as the basis of his theories about folk music, his lectures, and press campaign to ignite his passion within his audiences.

Sharp's songbooks intended for use by teachers and children quickly became part of music curricula, thereby ensuring that folk songs become part of England's national musical heritage. Once successful in England, his thoughts will turn to America; he will become a "songcatcher": one of the earliest collectors and conservationists of American folk music.

(21)

*What is Folk Music?*

Cecil Sharp defined folk music thusly: "A new folk music is impossible without a complete reversion to a feudal state. This is true, because folk music is the product of an unselfconscious peasantry; a peasantry which refuses to transmit the eccentricities of any individual."

Bob Dylan—an early worshipper of folk musician Woody Guthrie—had his own definition. In response to critics who questioned his authority as an urban musician to write folk music, he responded, "Hey, I'm a folk. I can write this shit."

In 1968 folklorist Bess Lomax Hawes expresses a more sophisticated, succinct definition, one that is closest to what we would call vernacular, traditional, or folk music today. According to Hawes, "Folk style" refers to construction and performance of a song in a manner that is comfortable to a folk group (i.e., a group held together by one or more elements they share in common), such as occupation, geographic location, or economics. She outlines folk music characteristics as the following:

1. Not officially taught; transmitted via word of mouth, learned orally rather than literally. Music is intrinsically absorbed by ear. People still would rather hear a symphony than read it.
2. Variation in performance versions is intrinsic to the nature of folk songs. No standard song exists against which each performance is evaluated. No one way is the best way.
3. A folk song is anonymous, if not in terms of origin, at least in the way people feel about it. The song no longer belongs to the writer, but, in a sense, it has become "my song" to the singer or listener.
4. A song can be a folk song in one context and not a folk song in another context.
5. Folk songs have lives or life histories. Sam Hinton says that we can know a few things about a song at first glance, but, to know it better, we have to know its history.

(22, 23)

## 1894 BEREA[1], KENTUCKY: "APPALACHIA"

The first major attempt to map Appalachia as a distinctive cultural region comes in the late nineteenth century from New Yorker William Goodell Frost. Frost, a graduate of Oberlin College in Ohio and grandson of an abolitionist, makes his way to Berea College at its invitation to become its president. One of his first tasks upon arrival is to understand more about the students whom the

---

1. Pronounced Buh-RAY-uh.

college serves. So he spends two months riding horseback through the mountains to learn about the region and its people.

As a result of his studies, Frost views mountain people as not unlike early New Englanders, having preserved colonial ways, being of patriotic character, and having ultimately supported the Union during the Civil War. In 1895, he writes a report in which he coins the phrase, "Appalachian America" to describe a region that includes 194 counties in eight states.

(24)

## 1900 GALVESTON, TEXAS: DISASTERS OF THE NATURAL KIND

Nicknamed "the Western Ellis Island," Galveston, Texas, is an island city located some fifty miles southeast of Houston. It basks in its identity as the nation's biggest cotton port, the third-busiest port overall, a playground for millionaires, and the second-most-heavily traversed entry for immigrants arriving from Europe.

"An absurd delusion," is how Isaac Cline, employee of the new U.S. Weather Bureau had once characterized the fear that any hurricane posed a serious danger to the city of Galveston. Based partly on his opinion, Galveston city leaders dismiss a proposal to erect a seawall, claiming it a needless expense.

Early in September, Cuban weather forecasters send warnings of an ominous storm heading toward Galveston to their U.S. counterparts, who decide to downplay the news. On September 8, most residents stay on the island, unconcerned by what they believe to be a typical storm heading their way. When the Category 4 hurricane hits Galveston, it slams the area with a fifteen-foot storm surge and winds up to 140 miles per hour, inundating the island. A four-foot wave sweeps across the already-submerged island ahead of the vortex. Out of a prestorm population of nearly 38,000, 8,000 die horribly as Gulf water sweeps them away, or as they are crushed beneath falling buildings and flying debris. The southern, eastern, and western portions of the city are entirely destroyed up to five blocks inland, leaving residents who do survive homeless.

Fifty-five years after this disaster, Kentucky singer Jean Ritchie and six others will sing of the storm in a haunting folk ballad with its refrain, "Wasn't that a mighty day—great god—that morning when the storm winds swept the town?"

(25)

## 1900 TEXAS: GAINS AND LOSSES

Beginning in the early 1900s, Anglo-American culture increasingly penetrates the rural world of German immigrant descendants. Rural depopulation, intermarriage, and modern communications facilitate acculturation to a mainstream Anglo-Texan culture.

As the century unfolds, two world wars and the associated anti-German prejudice snuff out any interest in German folkways and curtail the use of the German language. As a result, German Americans and their descendants leave behind their language and culture, forgetting the old ways to become invested in their new American identities. For many of their descendants, their ancestral heritage will be lost to them. Yet, vestiges of the European (and African) cultures will lie dormant in Texan and Mexican music, waiting to reappear thanks to music seekers who discover them thanks to the songcatchers' work.

(26)

## 1902 KENTUCKY: THE HINDMAN SETTLEMENT SCHOOL

The Hindman Settlement School began as a series of education and recreation programs for local adults and children in eastern Kentucky during the summers of 1899–1901. From the beginning, the

Hindman mission included a positive emphasis on regional traditions and cultural identity. Working in large tents, teachers offer classes in sewing, cooking, housekeeping, health and child care. Hindman staff members organize nurseries, teach Sunday school, and host evening socials for young people and adults.

As Hindman grows, the school hires many young women graduates of colleges such as Smith, Vassar, Mount Holyoke, and Wellesley to teach. They encourage students to develop skills in local crafts such as spinning, weaving, and basketmaking. Mountain music is a central focus as well. One of the school's employees is a Kentucky luthier named Jethro Amburgey who supplies the teachers and schoolchildren with dulcimers. Amburgey borrowed his design from Uncle Ed Thomas.

Many of the teachers eventually return to New York. They will take what they have learned of mountain music with them, helping stoke the kindling that will light a fire fifty years from now: the urban folk revival of Appalachian mountain music.

(27, 28, 29)

## 1904 FRANKFORT, KENTUCKY: IT WILL NOT BE ERASED

The Day Law, proposed by representative Carl Day and passed overwhelmingly by a majority of the state legislature, is specifically aimed at Berea College. In effect, the law segregates both public and private schools in the Commonwealth of Kentucky. The Kentucky court of appeals characterizes the law as a reasonable protection of the public welfare in that [it asserts] "the purity of racial blood...deeper and more important than the matter of choice." The case lands in the U.S. Supreme Court, where justices affirm the right of Kentucky to alter Berea's original charter as long as it provides education to all persons after separation of the races.

Frost is forced to revise the College's mission statement to one of educating "Appalachian Americans," a term he coins to describe

White mountain people only. Berea College moves its Black students to the Lincoln Institute in Louisville, a separate school solely for Americans who were born with dark skin.

One consequence of the law will be to contribute to the erroneous perception that Appalachia is an all-White, native-born population. Although the numbers of African Americans living there are much smaller than in the rest of the South, their cultural contributions are part and parcel of life in the mountains, including their contributions to Appalachian music, lyrics, and instruments. Despite court orders, Black culture's influence on Appalachian music will not be erased

(30, 31)

## 1907 HINDMAN, KENTUCKY: SONGCATCHER OLIVE DAME CAMPBELL

Olive Dame Campbell undertook classical music training as a child in Massachusetts and currently lives in Asheville, North Carolina, with her husband John, a sociologist and employee of the Russell Sage Foundation. He engages in a social project with a goal of upgrading the Appalachian school system, Olive decides to accompany him on his long trips into the mountains. During their trips, she first takes note of the mountain ballads and songs they hear. In December 1907, the Campbells visit the Hindman Settlement School. There, they listen to student Ada Smith sing a version of the old English ballad "Barbara Allen." Afterward, Olive writes:

> Shall I ever forget it, the blazing fire, the young girl on her low stool before it, the soft strange strumming of the banjo—different from anything I had heard before—and then the song. I had been used to singing "Barbara Allen" as a child, but how far from that gentle tune was this - so strange, so remote, so thrilling. I was lost almost from the first note, and the pleasant room faded from sight; the

singer only a voice. I saw again the long road over which we had come, the dark hills, the rocky streams bordered by tall hemlocks and hollies, the lonely cabins distinguishable at night only by the firelight flaring from their chimneys. Then these, too, faded, and I seemed to be borne along into a still more dim and distant past, of which I myself was a part.

Following in the footsteps of Cecil Sharp, Olive becomes one of the earliest American-born songcatchers to collect and preserve songs for posterity. Appalachia draws the Campbells with its imagined cultural purity, untainted by outside civilization.

(32, 33, 34)

## 1915 ASHEVILLE, NORTH CAROLINA: JOINING FORCES

Cecil Sharp began to find it difficult to support himself through his work as a lecturer and writer in England, so he makes a visit to the United States in hopes of finding new audiences. Sharp arrives convinced that America has no folk music of its own. His concern: even the backwoods farmer may have a phonograph with records of European concertos that reflect the spirit of different people and will alter the music of the peasantry. Large audiences come to hear Sharp's lectures on folk music. His trip is such a success that he will stay for two years.

Olive Campbell, having collected over two hundred songs by 1915, travels to Massachusetts to meet with Sharp. He is astounded by her collection. "She has tapped a mine...of the first importance," he writes. "The ballads in question are apparently of Irish, Scottish or English origin...presumably carried to that district by the original settlers and passed down by oral tradition to their descendants and so generation by generation to the present inhabitants."

Sharp and Campbell become collaborators; they travel throughout the eastern mountains, collecting songs. In two years they will publish *English Folk Songs of the Southern Appalachians*, a compilation of 445 songs and ballads with notes. Twentieth-century American pop, rock, country, and folk songwriters and musicians will turn to their collection time and again for inspiration.

(35)

## 1916 HOUSTON, TEXAS: CHRISTIAN AND MAY SCHNAUFER

On October 31, a small group of family and friends gather at the First Baptist Church of Houston to witness the marriage of immigrant Jacob Schnaufer's son Charles (known as Christian) to Miss Mary Emily Cleaver, (known as "May" to her friends).

Christian, a handsome man with black hair and gray eyes, is a skilled carpenter like his father Jacob. Christian works as a railroad car builder for D.B. McKenna in Palestine, Texas, for the International & Great Northern Railway Company. May is also a descendant of immigrants. Her father descended from English immigrants and married Elizabeth Shay whose grandparents were Irish, most likely from Northern Ireland.

Christian and May Schnaufer will have three children over the next six years: Christine, Frank Cleaver, and Glenda Rose. Christian works hard building railroad coaches, but in his spare time, the master woodworker crafts toys and furniture for his children.

(36, 37, 38)

# 1917 HINDMAN, KENTUCKY: THE RITCHIES

Cecil Sharp along with another collaborator named Maud Karpeles travels through Virginia, North Carolina, Kentucky, and Tennessee uncovering a treasure trove of folk songs.

Much to Sharp's continued surprise, these newly discovered versions differ from those he had collected in rural England. Sharp writes down the tunes, and Karpeles writes the lyrics. Together, they collect over sixteen hundred songs, a number of which are uniquely American.

While in Kentucky, the two use the Hindman Settlement School as their home base. There, they meet two young girls, "the misses Una and Sabrina Ritchie." Una is Balis Ritchie's daughter and second cousin to Sabrina. Sharp collects two songs from them, one of which will become especially significant in popular culture—a nonsense song called "Nottamun Town," thought to be about the English city of Nottingham. The Ritchies' version is the first to be published and will become popular in the folk revival on both sides of the Atlantic.

Almost fifty years later, young poet and songwriter Bob Dylan will borrow the tune of "Nottamun Town" for his song, "Masters of War," considered by many to be the most powerful antiwar song ever written.

(39, 40, 41)

# 1922 VIPER, KENTUCKY: JEAN RITCHIE

Una Ritchie's sister Ruth Jean Ritchie is the fourteenth and last child born into her family on December 8. Her father Balis Ritchie teaches school, prints a newspaper, fits eye spectacles, farms, and will send ten of his fourteen children to college. In the evenings, he often plays the mountain dulcimer or the fiddle.

By age five, little Jean sings along and watches closely whenever her father plays music. Singing has always been integral to her family: they sing when they work in the garden, when they pray; on the front porch during summer evenings and around the fireplace in the winter. The living embodiment of Olive Campbell's imagined "Barbara Allen," Jean Ritchie sings during times of sadness; she sings to celebrate, and she sings to connect with the natural world that sustains her. The mountain dulcimer has been within her family for as long as her father and her grandfather can remember.

Over the next few years, whenever her father isn't around, Jean takes down his dulcimer from the wall and plays with it.

(42)

## 1937 BROOKLYN, NEW YORK: "A HAPPY COMBINATION OF HERITAGES"

In the Flatbush neighborhood of Brooklyn, spring welcomes newborn Richard George Fariña, born to his Irish mother Theresa and named after his Cuban father Richard Fariña. One friend will later say that Richard is "blessed with a happy combination of heritages." He will grow up to be charming, clever, creative, and develop an imaginative and fanciful account of his ever-changing personal history. After his death, he will be lauded as a genius, a protest singer and songwriter, a novelist, a serial fabulist, dramatic, impetuous, and cooler than James Dean. Thanks to Richard's chance encounter with Jean Ritchie at a party, he will also be remembered as a dulcimer musician of wide influence among his peers for his unique, innovative approach to playing the instrument.

(43, 44)

# 1938 VIPER, KENTUCKY: JEAN RITCHIE: THE PAIN OF LEAVING HOME

Sixteen-year-old Jean Ritchie has mixed feelings of having to leave her home and family as she anticipates graduating high school and commencing her own life journey. She savors the time left, yet feels torn between wanting the familiar and the new, between staying and going, between the known and unknown. Later in her life, she will write a memory of evenings spent with her parents:

> There was something to do every minute but yet there was a lonesomeness that hung over the hills and made my heart ache. And there was still another trouble, and this one I could name. All my life up to now, I had dreamed and longed and schemed to leave home, to go places like the others, but now that the time was coming near, I hated the thoughts of getting through high school, was scared to death of the time when I too would have to go away. It was like a big Something was pushing me out of the house, down the branch, and off onto the railroad trains when I didn't want to go. I wished I could start getting younger instead of older; I wished I could do something about the calendar so that December wouldn't come and bring my birthday, so that I could always and forever be sixteen.

> The long warm evenings were somehow the saddest of all. We'd get our bit of supper over and the work done up ... Then we'd sit around in the front room ... Dad would maybe take down the dulcimer off the wall and make the old tunes ring proud in the still, forsaken night. Have you ever heard a dulcimer played on a still soft night by a lonesome person?

Jean will leave home after graduating high school. In 1946, she will graduate Phi Betta Kappa from the University of Kentucky with a degree in social work.

(45, 46)

## 1941 HOUSTON, TEXAS: PRIVATE FRANK SCHNAUFER

Three days before Independence Day, the grandson of immigrant Jacob Schnaufer drops out of his third year at business college and strides into the enlistment center in Palestine, Texas, to register for the draft. At 5'10" and 135 pounds, Frank Cleaver Schnaufer is smart, philosophical, single, and determined to serve his country.

In November, just thirty-seven days before the bombing of Pearl Harbor, Frank enlists in the Air Force in Houston. Private Frank Schnaufer, due to his college experience, is assigned to work as a general clerk and sent to Sacramento, California.

(47)

## 1943 SACRAMENTO, CALIFORNIA: THE FIRST SECRET OF FRANK SCHNAUFER

Sacramento is home to McClellan Air Force Base and Mather Field, a training school for flight navigators. The school provides operating support for many critical missions in the Asian-Pacific Theater, including retrofitting the bombers used for Lt. Col. James Doolittle's raid of mainland Japan in April of last year.

Private Schnaufer also has training as a medic—a "pill roller" in soldiers' jargon—so he is alert to health matters more than most. Toward the end of spring, he doesn't feel well; he gets weak and has a bad cough that won't go away. When he starts to feel chest pains and shortness of breath, he heads to sick bay where he is diagnosed with tuberculosis and a collapsed lung.

(48, 49, 50)

*Tuberculosis*

Known as "Consumption," "TB," "Phthisis," and "White Plague," tuberculosis dates back to prehistory. Caused by a bacterium, the popular perception of tuberculosis at the time was one of a shameful, dirty disease due to its prevalence in the lower classes. Doctors in the U.S. and abroad erroneously blamed the patient for the disease, believing it a consequence of inherited physical and moral failings. As a result, sufferers of tuberculosis and their families often felt ashamed and frightened by what the community would say and do if they were to discover a tuberculosis victim among them. Whole families would enter into a conspiracy of silence about the illness.

As mobilization for WWII took place, both equipment and experts who could accurately read x-ray films were scarce. The military estimated that a million men were inducted into the service who would have been rejected if they had been subject to chest x-rays, and approximately one half of those men would harbor active lesions.

A peculiarity of this time: during World War II tuberculosis was more prevalent in troops within the United States than in troops in overseas theaters. Frank Schnaufer was one of the unfortunate who contracted TB while in the service, and his infection will have a profound impact on his future family and children.

(51, 52, 53)

## 1943 SACRAMENTO, CALIFORNIA: THE SECOND SECRET OF FRANK SCHNAUFER

After a significant treatment in the VA hospital for TB and now permanently discharged, Frank leaves the hospital. Edith Johnston, his sweetheart from back home, travels to Sacramento to be by his side. Frank had fallen for the petite, twenty-year-old Edith with her long, thick brown hair, and she for him. They have a lot in common: both come from Palestine, Texas; both of their fathers work for the railroad, and both wish for a family. They are quiet, competent, intelligent people who fit together "like peas and carrots." as they say in the South.

Occasionally, Frank suffers bouts of depression. Edith helps him get through the mental and physical health challenges early in their marriage, but both worry about the oppressive social stigmas of Frank's depression and past illness with TB.

Doctors know little about depression; widespread fear of current treatments is the norm. Starting in the thirties and well into the fifties, the medical establishment turns to institutionalization, lobotomies, insulin-induced comas, electroshock treatments, and malariotherapies for patients who suffer from poorly understood mental afflictions. Perhaps the most famous case that contributed to fears of mental afflictions occurred just two years previously as a result of Ambassador Joseph Kennedy's decision to lobotomize his daughter Rosemary in 1941. The disastrous result was her lifelong severe mental impairment and institutionalization.

Before returning to Texas, Frank and Edith marry. They decide it's best not to talk about Frank's TB or his depressive episodes with anyone—including their future children.

(54, 55, 56, 57)

## 1944 FORT WORTH, TEXAS: EDUCATION OF A FUTURE LEGEND

John Townes Van Zandt is born in Fort Worth, Texas, to a wealthy family whose ancestors include a leader of the Republic of Texas (before the United States annexed it) and one of the founders of Fort Worth. Stories of Townes's life will be recounted for many years after his death by those who knew him well and even those who only met him once. Most of the stories will surround the musician and songwriter; Van Zandt will become a Texas and Nashville legend before he passes away at the age of fifty-two.

Starting in Van Zandt's infancy, his parents employed Frances Edwards as his nanny. While the Van Zandts are regular attendees of their local, all-White Baptist church, every Sunday Frances takes her son Jimmy and Townes across the city to the Pentecostal church where Townes is steeped in the passionate rhythm of Black gospel music. It thrills him.

(58)

## 1944 PALESTINE, TEXAS: THE THIRD SECRET OF FRANK SCHNAUFER

The Missouri Pacific Railroad Shop is Anderson County's largest employer. Like his fellow workers, Christian Schnaufer labors hard and with considerable skill in Subdivision 4, the "Woodmill Mechanics-Coach Builders-Cabinet Makers-Locomotive Carpenters." Once the United States entered WWII, Missouri Pacific made room for the coming and going of troop trains as they pass through the railroad yards for service.

Christian's mind is on his work, on the war, but overwhelmingly on his son, Frank, who was discharged last year after treatment for TB. Edith and Frank's close family never speak of his bout of tuberculosis with anyone.

Christian's happiness with the impending birth of his first grand-child is tempered by his worry for Frank when he reenters the hospital in December due to alarming symptoms of chills and rising fevers, headaches, malaise, anorexia, and swollen lymph nodes. Soon, doctors note a dull red eruption that appears first on the trunk of his body and then spreads to his arms, legs, and face. Frank begins to cough and is soon at risk for bronchitis and pneumonia.

Once diagnosed, his doctors inform Frank he has a disease that is normally seen in the tropics among soldiers fighting in the Asian-Pacific theater of war: tsusugamushi fever. Also known as scrub typhus, this disease is transmitted through the bites of mites. Little known outside of Japan, with the advent of large-scale jungle warfare, scrub typhus became a serious medical problem for troops in the Far East. Frank, however, had never served in the Far East. He had been stationed at McClellan, a major hub for servicemen coming and going from the Pacific. Somehow, either at McClellan Air Force Base or in nearby in Sacramento, a hitchhiking mite bit Frank and infected him.

Recovery will be slow as VA physicians watch over him carefully. By the time of his first son Dennis's birth in three months, Frank will have recovered physically unscathed from the disease and feel well enough to enjoy his newborn son. But his mind often troubles him, and he struggles with deepening depression and concern about what others might think if they ever found out about his bouts with TB, depression, and now this strange tropical disease.

(59, 60, 61, 62, 63, 64)

## 1947 NEW YORK CITY: JEAN RITCHIE AND ALAN LOMAX

After graduating from the University of Kentucky and a year of supervising elementary education, Jean moves to New York City to work as a social worker at the Henry Street Settlement, a not-for-profit social service agency in New York City. The agency's goal is to provide educational opportunities via social services, health care, and the arts for New York City residents, especially those of the Lower East Side. Jean uses her singing and dulcimer playing from her own childhood to engage children in learning. She understands the importance of immigrant history to her musical roots and explains to her students, *You can't possibly understand the music of eastern Kentucky—tales of struggle and kin and heartbreak—until you trace its roots to Ireland, Scotland, England, and Wales.*

In the post–World War II time of Jean's life, folk music is a popular curiosity for sophisticated city dwellers. In the evenings, Jean sings and plays the dulcimer in coffeehouses, quickly winning a following. It doesn't take long for the city's growing circle of folk singers, scholars, and enthusiasts to notice the young mountain woman in their midst with her bright personality and performance skills on her unusual instrument. One of her admirers is Bess Lomax's brother Alan Lomax, a renowned songcatcher as was his father John Avery Lomax.

Often before her performances, Jean shares stories of her family's early interactions with song catchers like Cecil Sharp and with others who visited Appalachia during the First World War. As a result of her family's history and her singing, Alan Lomax will record several hours of Jean's songs, stories, and oral histories in 1949 and 1950 for the Library of Congress.

Jean becomes a regular performer on Alan's radio show "On Top of Old Smokey" in New York on the Mutual Broadcasting System. In 1948, Lomax books her in concert at Columbia University, and she soon appears regularly in live venues as well as on the radio. She shares the stage with popular folk singers the Weavers, Woody Guthrie, and Betty Sanders at the Spring Fever Hootenanny. By October 1949, she will be a regular guest on the Folksong Festival radio show on WNYC broadcast. Her voice and dulcimer playing will eventually reach people around the country, and, later, the world.

One of her performances includes her singing with The New Lost City Ramblers, "Wasn't That a Mighty Day," a song about the Galveston hurricane disaster.

(65, 66, 67, 68, 69, 70)

---

*Who was Alan Lomax?*

Alan Lomax first became a song catcher as a teenager dragging a five-hundred-pound recording machine through the South alongside his father, the pioneering musicologist and song catcher John Avery Lomax (the father of folklorist Beth Hawes Lomax and grandfather of John Lomax III, the latter who will play a critical role in David Schnaufer's life).

When he met Jean Ritchie, Alan Lomax was doing important work in New York City to fuel the burgeoning folk revival. He hosted gatherings, promoted concerts and folk events, recorded folk artists for the Folk Song Archive, and worked on his radio show.

Alan eventually traveled the world to become a leading ethnomusicologist and the subject of the biography, *Alan Lomax: The Man Who Recorded the World.* He often declared that his mission in life was to preserve the music, the stories behind the songs and the vanishing communities that produced them and to protect folk traditions from the homogenizing effects of the modern music business and media. He was an advocate of cultural equity: the right of every culture to have equal time on the air and in the classroom. David and many other dulcimer players, especially those on the east coast, drew deeply from the music well built by several members of the Lomax family.

If you would like to learn more about the Lomax family's conservation work, a good place to start is at the American Folklife Center of the Library Congress: https://www.loc.gov/folklife/lomax/alanlomaxbio.html.

> You can learn more about Alan Lomax at the Association for Cultural Equity website at *http://www.culturalequity.org*.
>
> (71)

## 1950 NASHVILLE, TENNESSEE: "MUSIC CITY"

Disc Jockey David Cobb of station WSM nicknames his hometown "Music City, USA," and the name sticks tight thanks to city promoters and the popular Sunday evening talent show "Music City USA," launched shortly after Cobb's gift of the moniker to his city.

(72, 73)

## 1952 HOUSTON, TEXAS: JOHN LOMAX III

Even at the young age of seven, young Johnny Lomax is aware of his family's role in saving America's musical heritage.

Johnny's father, John II, while not as nationally known as his father John Avery or his brother Alan, also contributed to his father's work to save America's traditional music. John II urged his father to embark on a new folksong collecting trip to raise his father's spirits after the death of his wife. Taking over tasks formerly handled by his late mother, John II organized the tour, handled the driving, and helped in the marketing and sales of recordings. He arranged for his father to speak with publishers and helped him negotiate with various archives to decide which one would ultimately house their collected recordings. After talking with Harvard and the University of Texas, father and son ultimately opted for the Library of Congress.

At six-foot-one inches and weighing in at a muscular 180 to 190 pounds, the former Navy man is an inspiration to his son Johnny. As an adult, Johnny will recall that posture was a key part of his father's fitness regimen: "I can still hear him telling me, 'Head up, shoulders back!" After the war, the Lomaxes settle first in Dallas and finally in Houston's West University Place on Vanderbilt Street.

Johnny's mother had grown up in the small Texas town of Clarksville, went to college in Denton and later in New York. She worked as a successful traveling saleswoman in the 1930s for a gas company, but she gave it all up to become a wife and mother. She is a warm woman who believes that idle hands are the devil's playground. Therefore, she is always busy, always helping others, always doing church work, visiting neighbors, cooking, and sewing clothes for Johnny and his little brother Joe who was born four and a half years after Johnny.

Once he learns to read, Johnny finds books from and about his grandfather, father, and Uncle Alan in their family library, learns stories of their work and travels around the world. He hears plenty of music in their home, especially traditional folk songs. His parents plant the seeds for his appreciation of all genres of music. He is proud that America's entire musical heritage might have been lost forever if not for his grandfather, his uncle, and his father.

When Johnny grows up, he will continue the Lomax family tradition but with a modern twist: He will play a key role in reintroducing traditional music to a new, worldwide audience. Future dulcimer aficionados will have plenty to thank him for.

(74)

## 1952 FRANKLIN, TEXAS: HELLO, LITTLE BROTHER: DAVID LYNN SCHNAUFER

Sometime in January—after seven years of being a one-child family with their firstborn Dennis—Mr. and Mrs. Frank Schnaufer find themselves expecting another baby. The impending birth of their second child provides a much-needed bright spot in their lives. Their firstborn Dennis had contracted polio—one of the most feared diseases in the U.S. at this time—just three years ago. Edith lost her older sister Mary Ellen to TB two years ago. Her mother Annie Belle has not been well, and will also pass away from TB in the near future.

Luckily, little Dennis survived. Now seven, he has grown into a studious, thoughtful boy who is dedicated to his church and looks forward to second grade in the fall.

On Sunday, September 28 at 11:23 in the morning, Edith welcomes her second son at the Hearne Clinic Hospital. Edith is a tiny woman, maybe a hundred pounds soaking wet. Her new baby is also tiny, just six pounds, four ounces when he lands into the world. They name him David Lynn.

Since visiting children aren't allowed in the hospital, brother Dennis has to wait to see his new sibling until his parents bring him home. Dennis's first memory of tiny David is standing next to his crib, watching over the curled-up newborn breathing softly, deep in slumber.

(75, 76)

## 1952 NEW YORK CITY: JEAN RITCHIE

Elektra Records' signing of Jean Ritchie begins her fifty-year recording career. Jean's growing popularity ignites significant enthusiasm for her dulcimer playing among aspiring musicians in the New York music scene.

Early ballads she popularizes include "Go Tell Aunt Rhody," "Shady Grove," "Pretty Betty Martin," and many other songs rooted in Europe and saved by the songcatchers. These songs will become standards of the dulcimer canon.

Jean is also a popular party hostess who loves company, so she brings together diverse, artistic people from all over the city to regularly meet and mingle with each other and sing and play music together. On any given party evening, a visitor might hear Jean singing with Pete Seeger, Odetta, and Doc Watson along with all who feel like joining in.

(77)

## 1952 NYACK, NEW YORK: VINCENT NICHOLAS FARSETTA

Mr. and Mrs. Frank Vincent Farsetta welcome their first baby to the world on December 23 in Pearl River, New York. Because he was due on Christmas Eve, they christen him Vincent Nicholas even though he arrived a day early. Little Vincent's parents are first generation Americans, both of their parents having emigrated from Sicily to make a new life in the U.S.

The Farsettas take baby Vince home from the hospital to a house filled with music, food, and laughter. Vince Sr. had once pointed out his future wife to a friend by stating, "I'm going to marry that woman over there" because "he liked the way she danced." He did marry her. And he still dances with her as they sway to records on the hi-fi stereo in its blond wooden cabinet while their baby kicks and waves his hands in his playpen. That first Christmas, Vince is surrounded by carols sung and records spun as he will be every Christmas as a child. He will grow up listening to his parents' music on the hi-fi record player and on the radio: old-time Italian string music and the occasional opera, Glenn Miller from the forties, Mitch Miller, Frank Sinatra, and Roger Miller from the fifties and sixties. Listening to music, dancing, and laughing will become as natural as breathing.

(78)

## 1953 FRANKLIN, TEXAS: DENNIS AND DAVID

Dennis turns eight in March. He shares a small bedroom with year-old brother David. They have one chest of drawers and two beds to call their own; the second bedroom belongs to their parents, and everyone shares the single bathroom. Edith cooks in the kitchen—pressure-cooked beans are standard fare because money is always tight. The family eats meals together when they can. Sometimes, Frank is gone for extended periods to seek treatment for debilitating bouts of depression.

Other times, as the boys grow, life almost seems normal. David's parents value education, so they read to David before bed. In the evenings, the boys play together in the backyard or watch television. Even though he prefers older fare, Dennis sits next to him when David watches his favorite programs such as *Captain Kangaroo* or cartoons. One of David's favorite characters appears on Channel 13 out of Houston: "Kitirik," a woman in a cat costume, complete with tiny ears and a long tail half-curled behind her.

(79, 80, 81)

## 1956 BILLINGS, MONTANA: TOWNES VAN ZANDT

Eleven-year-old Townes Van Zandt's father gifts him a brand-new Harmony six-string guitar for Christmas. Townes was one of thousands of youngsters who had watched Elvis Presley's September performance on the *Ed Sullivan Show* and became obsessed with rock and roll. "I just thought that Elvis had all the money in the world, all the Cadillacs and all the girls, and all he did was play the guitar and sing. That made a big impression on me."

By the time Townes turns twenty, he'll reveal a more mature understanding of the work it takes to become a professional musician:

[First], you have to get yourself a guitar ... And then you have to blow off everything else. You have to blow off your family. You have to blow off comfort. You have to blow off money. You have to blow off security. You have to blow off your ego. You have to blow off everything except your guitar. You have to sleep with it. Learn how to tune it. And no matter how hungry you get, stick with it. You'll be amazed at how many people turn away.

(82)

## 1956 LA MARQUE, TEXAS: DISASTERS OF THE MANMADE KIND

When David turns four, his family moves again, this time two and a half hours southeast to La Marque, Texas, a small coastal town that lies only nineteen minutes northwest of the island city of Galveston with its beaches on the Gulf of Mexico.

La Marque is a semi-rural, small town dominated by the enormous petrochemical plants next door in Texas City. Chemical plants and oil refineries line the Texas coast, with Houston the third-largest shipping port in the U.S. Business interests ignore any concerns expressed about the environment. Most adults either work in the Monsanto, Union Carbide, or Amoco plants, or they work in businesses that support the plant workers. A chemical-like smell—an odor that is an odd mixture of acrid and sweet—permeates the heavy, hot air. When one petrochemical worker's son asks him, "What is that funny smell?" his father replies, "bread and butter."

The Gulf region between Houston and Galveston is an area with a history of disasters, both the natural and manmade kind. When Dennis Schnaufer was three, citizens were rocked by an explosion on the chemical ship S.S. *Grandcamp*. The explosion and resulting tidal wave injured more than three thousand people, and authorities estimated that between five hundred and six hundred people were killed; the exact number was never determined because of the terrible condition of many of the bodies. Twenty-eight Texas City firemen were known to be among the dead in the seventy-million-dollar catastrophe. It will not be the last to maim or kill workers from La Marque.

The more mundane challenges to daily life include the summer heat. It gets so hot that kids seek relief by lying on the linoleum floors to cool off. Coaches cancel boys' softball games often due to mosquitoes swarming so thickly in the air that the players and coaches can't see each other. Children ride bikes to follow behind the trucks spraying chemicals to deter mosquitoes, just to cool off from the spray.

Frank Schnaufer is fortunate in that he doesn't have to work in the dangerous conditions of the chemical plants. He is an insurance writer, very meticulous with his work. He finds a typical coastal house of the 1950s to rent in La Marque so that they'll have more space for the growing boys.

Frank and Edith crank the metal shutters and louvered storm windows closed whenever they learn of potential hurricanes heading their way during the storm seasons. It is their attempt to keep their little family safe from any storms that frequently bear down on them.

(83, 84, 85, 86, 87, 88, 89)

## 1957 NEW YORK CITY: NEAL HELLMAN

Born and raised in Brooklyn, by fourteen Neal Hellman has grown up listening to music all his life; his mother is a teacher and a classical pianist, and his great aunt Rosie plays the mandolin. His parents send him to summer camps where singing folk songs is always on the menu. Songs like "If I Had A Hammer," "The Sloop John B," and "This Land Is Your Land" are permanently saved in his mental jukebox.

Neal and his young friends are firsthand witnesses to the city's folk boom. They love to go to Washington Square in Greenwich Village on Sundays to listen to musicians such as Pete Seeger, David

Grisman, and many others who play there every Sunday. His dad is a member of the Henry Street Settlement where Jean Ritchie works.

Neal knows nothing of Richard Fariña yet, despite his parents living less than a mile from the Fariña home where Richard grew up. Nevertheless, his exposure to the Greenwich Village scene lays the foundation for future expertise on Fariña and the dulcimer.

(90, 91)

## 1957 LA MARQUE, TEXAS: SKEETER'S BIRTHDAY GIFT

Frank Schnaufer used to play the trombone in high school and enjoys listening to popular music. Therefore, he was very pleased when Dennis started playing the clarinet in the junior high school band. When the family celebrates David's fifth birthday, Frank teaches his younger son to make his own music with a gift of a jaw harp. He shows David—whom he nicknamed "Skeeter"—how to hold the small musical instrument against his teeth and pluck the flexible metal reed with his index finger. By moving his tongue around, and breathing through the harp while he alters the shape of his mouth, David quickly learns how to change the sounds of the twangs he makes as he transforms them into songs. David and his daddy are delighted when he can play his very first song, "Fuzzy Wuzzy Was a Bear".

During the evenings, Frank quietly reads to his son, and occasionally gives David some tips on how to play his new instrument.

Frank and Edith may not have realized it at the time, but their gift to David is much more consequential than would be any other amusing toy. The jaw harp will be his entryway to a profound understanding of and sensitivity to the power of sound and resonance.

(92, 93, 94, 95)

## The Jaw Harp

Around the world, the Jew's harp (or jaw harp) has always been an instrument of country people rather than one of the upper classes. Fred Crane, scholar of the Jew's Harp and the publisher of the first scholarly journal on this instrument, calls it an "aerophone", or wind instrument, and considers it extremely versatile:

It has just one basic tone, but it plays all the overtones of that through the series—the harmonic series, the bugle tones, the sounds that are played by a natural trumpet without valves. The tones get closer together as you go up and eventually you get to a point where you can play a fairly normal scale and you can play all kinds of tunes into it. It is an instrument into which you can play traditional music that sound like tunes to anybody, or you can play all kinds of your own invention, or which may be appropriate for all kinds of music.

Crane calls it "the original synthesizer" because "like an electronic synthesizer, one can do almost anything with it."

Why would Frank select this simple and somewhat obscure instrument for David? One reason: it is relatively easy to play. Another is that any child in America who watched cartoons or TV advertisements would know its sound— whenever a cartoon character runs into a wall or gets hit in the head, listeners hear "*Boing!*" with its long sustain.

If you would like to learn more about the jaw harp, watch this delightful short video explanation and demonstration of its history via a local TED Talk: Jew's Harp, Listen and You Will Hear It: Valentinas & Viaceslavas at TEDxVilnius. You'll find the video at https://www.youtube.com/watch?v=4SpWuseQGys.

If you'd like to learn more about and from Fred Crane, visit *http://www.maultrommelverein.at/wp-content/uploads/2011/12/In-his-own-words.pdf*

(96, 97)

## 1958 LOS ANGELES, CALIFORNIA: "THE DULCIMER IS...NOT FOR THE CROWD"

Charles Seeger, musicologist and father of folk musician Pete Seeger, joins the University of California Los Angeles the same year he publishes his paper "The Appalachian Dulcimer" in *The Journal of American Folklore*. He writes of the instrument: "The Appalachian duylcimer, dulcimer or dulcymore, is known to folklorists as an instrument in fairly general use since 1900, and probably for some before that, by musically non-literate rural and small-townspeople in the mountains and foothills of [Appalachia]....It is made of local woods such as pine, spruce, poplar, hickory, birch, maple, and walnut by rural woodworkers with simple hand tools....I have...never known of a factory made instrument."

He notes that the "A" tuning is the most common, citing his own informants who claim they tune the dulcimer to the same note as the fiddle on the two highest strings on the dulcimer, with the bass string an octave lower, varying sometimes as much as a fourth in either direction. Frets, he notes, are either only under the first two or three strings closest to the player's body: or they run across the fretboard under all three strings.

The common manner of playing the dulcimer, he explains, is for the player to hold it crosswise upon his spread knees, or on a table or chair in front of him "with the peg-stock to his left" for right-handed practice. (He shares at least one exception: he found a woman who played the dulcimer with the butt end in her lap, the back propped up against a table in front of her.)

He describes the typical use of a *plectrum*— a feather quill, index finger, or a guitar pick for strumming or plucking—to coordinate with the left hand that uses any hard, smooth, little stick, piece of bone, or even a fingernail to fret the melody string(s). The left hand frets up and down the fretboard as the right hand strums or picks. Seeger cites one practice he considers unique to a Virginia informant who volunteered that he played with a bow. He also cites the practice of certain players who "fret several strings at once with their fingers." He considers neither practice—bowing or fretting across the strings—traditional in the United States. Finally, he concludes: "The dulcimer is for the individual or the intimate group, not for the crowd; for the night rather than for the day, though in the hands of a skillful player, tunes lively enough for the square dance, ordinarily carried by the fiddle, can be rendered."

Some who are young enough to be Seeger's great-grandchildren at the time of this writing will grow up and fall in love with the dulcimer. Along the way, they will prove much of Seeger's article obsolete.

(98)

MOVEMENT 2:
# CROSSING THRESHOLDS

[Consider] the strange serendipity that life is, the near misses and the surprise encounters and the accidents that make up who we are and what we know .... You will never know what would have happened if you [and those before you] chose one rather than the other way to go.

—Susan Orlean, *Airmail: Taking Women of Letters to the World*

(1)

In 1900, the average American male's lifespan was forty-eight years of age. It was fifty-nine by 1930, sixty-six by 1950, and sixty-nine by 1960.

In 1960, a gallon of gas sells on average for thirty-one cents.

A McDonald's hamburger costs fifteen cents. And fries are a dime.

The Dow Jones hovers around 685, and many think that is too high.

Most married women are introduced formally or credited for their contributions to society by the title "Mrs." followed by their husband's first and last name.

Most Americans are oblivious to events in Vietnam, where between 750 and 1,500 military advisors assist the Diem government to repel the growing insurgency movement.

In 1960, four Black students sit down at a Whites-only lunch counter in Greensboro, North Carolina, and refuse to leave, an act of resistance that helps give birth to the modern civil rights movement.

Cigarettes cost forty cents a pack, and more Americans smoke more cigarettes than at any time in our history. Why? Modern, mass production means you don't have to roll your own cigarettes, and safety matches are widely available. Cigarette habits spread via the mess kits of soldiers during World Wars I and II. In addition, mass advertising is by far the most important single factor for the surge in smokers. If you are a mature American, you smoke Kools, which have a menthol flavor and suggest sophistication. The Marlboro Man appears this year, suggesting that if you want to look like a rugged man, you smoke Marlboros. The Marlboro Man is modeled on the face of Clarence Hailey [Long], a ranch foreman from the Texas Panhandle. There will be no suggestion that cigarettes cause any damage to the human body until the Surgeon General's report of 1965. Inside it, he will tie smoking to deadly diseases.

Dr. Timothy Leary of Harvard University begins his research on the psychological effects of LSD and psilocybin mushrooms, hoping to find a role for them as a potential treatment for mood disorders like depression. Such research on their use for a range of physical and mental health issues will continue at least through 2021.

The counterculture will grow across the decade via student activism and the popular media's focus on the rise of "hippies," people who grow their hair long, practice "free love," and experiment with drug use. In a 1969 Gallup poll, only 4 percent of American adults say they had tried marijuana. Nevertheless, parents use scare tactics to keep their kids away from pot, warning that it will cause acne, blindness, or sterility.

America is a hard-drinking country in 1960. Americans consume oceans of beer and spirits.

Popular Music:

The Beatniks of the fifties will slowly peter out in popularity.

The Beatles are not on U.S. teens' radar yet, and Ringo will not join the group until October of 1960 when he replaces drummer Pete Best. There are no Rolling Stones, no Jim Morrison, no Doors yet, nor a nationally known Janis Joplin or Led Zeppelin.

In the world of mainstream commercial music, "Theme from a Summer Place" from the movie starring Sandra Dee and Troy Donahue is the biggest selling forty-five record. Elvis has just been discharged from the military and releases a new hit single, "Stuck on You." Other commercial hits of 1960 include novelty songs like "The Twist" and "Itsy Bitsy Teeny Weeny Yellow Polka Dot Bikini."

Young listeners all over the United States have grown up with songs either limited to their region's particular style of music or listening to commercial music segregated by race and ethnicity. Now they begin to discover a whole range of music new to them as a result of technological developments aimed at their wallets.

(2,3,4)

## 1960 LA MARQUE, TEXAS: "WITHOUT CHARITY, I AM NOTHING"

While David feels close to his father, he adores his mother. He is certain she is the prettiest mom of them all. She deeply loves both of her sons, but there is something about David being her last child that comes to her mind when she has to decide whether to indulge him or not. When he pleads for a mohawk haircut, she relents and says yes—for just a day. Because he likes collecting, she saves him the occasional buffalo nickel and mercury dime she finds in her change from shopping. She gifts him a small penknife known as a Barlow knife to tuck into his pocket.

On Tuesday, Cub Scout Pack 280 Den Mother Mrs. Frank Schnaufer gets ready to take her eight-year-old son David and five other boys from Den 3 on a field trip. Today they will visit the publishing office of the *La Marque Times* ("Serving the World's Finest People: Our Subscribers'"). Their purpose is to learn how newspapers are designed at the local level to help the boys earn their Business Badges.

Today, the Scouts observe as the typesetter sets up stories and features for the Friday edition: "Amoco Approves Wage Increase" (five cents per hour to salaried employees); "LM Quarterback Club Is Being Organized"; "Man Pays for Expensive Padlock" (to replace the one he broke off a water meter); "The Racing Pigeons Union Boasts Many Members", "Junior High PTA to Hear Calvin." Dr. Calvin will speak on "Why Be a Good Student." The typesetter finishes his work by setting up the "Daily Meditation" from Corinthians I, chapter 13 ("Without charity, I am nothing.")

(5,6)

## 1960 NEW YORK CITY: FARIÑA DISCOVERS THE DULCIMER

After dropping out of Cornell University his senior year, Richard Fariña, considered "one of the writers who drink" by his fellow patrons at the White Horse Tavern, heads to Manhattan one January night. He's a regular at the well-known Greenwich Village watering hole frequented by poets, artists, and folksingers. There he meets Carolyn Hester, a charismatic, talented singer and guitarist from Texas, whose voice, it is said, is so pure you could tune a guitar to it. She is smitten; in six months, they marry. Fariña appoints himself her manager and appears as her poetry-reciting stage partner as the two embark on a worldwide tour. In between Carolyn's performances, they plan Hester's third album, which will include a then little-known Bob Dylan playing the harmonica on several tracks.

Upon their return to the States, Richard and Carolyn attend a party given by Diane Hamilton, the founder of Tradition Recording Company. Hamilton also invites Jean and George Ritchie to the gathering. Jean, now the most well-known dulcimer player in the world, takes her instrument with her for a little music at the party. There, the Fariñas meet Jean. Richard, determined to add "musician and singer" to his résumé, watches Jean take her dulcimer out of its case and begin to play it. He can hardly contain his excitement as Jean explains the folk origins of the instrument. She demonstrates how she strums across all the strings: the treble string for the melody while the middle and bass strings are left to drone. After she hands him the dulcimer, Fariña strums it a few times and knows: he must learn how to play this. Jean assures him that it's simple and easy to play and gives him some tips for getting started.

(7,8)

## What is a "Drone"?

A drone is a low pitched, sustained tone or tones that provide a sound foundation for melodies played at a higher pitch level. Drones produce a captivating sound that pleases most players and listeners.

Many instruments are capable of producing a drone; perhaps the most well known is the drone that bagpipes make. However, hundreds of instruments across the world produce drones. Perhaps the most familiar drone to pop music fans appeared in 1964 with a fortuitous accident. After a recording session of "Eight Days a Week," Beatles band member John Lennon set down his semiacoustic Gibson guitar against an amplifier in the studio and forgot to turn down the pickup's volume. Just at that moment, Paul McCartney plucked an "A" on his bass and kicked off feedback on John's guitar. McCartney, Lennon, and producer George Martin recorded the resulting feedback to use as an opening drone on first six seconds of "I Feel Fine". The opening sound of the song was considered so unusual at the time that notices had to be sent to radio stations to tell them that the odd sound was an intentional part of the song and not some unattended error in the recording.

(9,10,11)

## 1960 LOUISVILLE, KENTUCKY: NANCY LOU BARKER

Nancy Barker is a senior in high school and steadily dating Roy, a banjo player. Roy invites her to accompany him for an appointment with luthier Tom Hale to have some work done on his banjo. While the two sweethearts are in his store, Hale picks up one of the treasures in his shop, an eighty-three-year-old Tom Dieson dulcimer. He shows it to the two young people; Nancy doesn't know what it is until Hale explains it. She is intrigued by the sound it produces when Hale strums it.

Shortly thereafter, Roy buys a dulcimer for Nancy for her birthday. Nancy's mother had grown up listening to dulcimer music in eastern Kentucky, so she recognizes the dulcimer when Nancy brings it home: "Why Nancy Lou, where did you get that dulcimore?" Nancy loves the beauty of the instrument; made out of Birds Eye Curly Maple with an arched bridge and wooden tuning pegs, she can't wait to learn how to play it. She searches for her mother's Jean Ritchie records and starts to listen carefully, reproducing bits and pieces of the music a little at a time. Soon, she gets better and better at linking the pieces all together into songs that fill her soul and make her happy.

(12)

## 1961 LONDON, ENGLAND: FARIÑA FALLS IN LOVE. AGAIN.

Guitar maker Terry Hennessy meets the Fariñas after they arrive in London for a series of performances. Richard envisions this trip as an opportunity to promote himself as an artist, and plays Carolyn's George Emerson dulcimer at the famed Troubadour Club. She later writes, "I taught Richard all that I knew of playing, which I had picked up from Howie Mitchell. Richard once shoveled snow with it when we were lost in a snowdrift in Idaho."

Richard commissions a dulcimer for himself from Hennessy. The first dulcimer Hennessy had ever seen was back in 1950 when sound engineer Stan Watkins (who worked on Al Jolson's *The Jazz Singer*) brought him an Uncle Ed Thomas dulcimer made in 1870 to see if he could repair it. Hennessy's assessment then—that the dulcimer was a crude instrument (it had metal staples for frets)—did not keep him from being intrigued by the rough old box. After some discussion, he makes Fariña an hourglass-shaped dulcimer with a design based on the Thomas design. Hennessy later recalls,

"When Richard played the dulcimer I made, he wrapped his arms around it and wouldn't let it go. He fell in love with it instantly. I had made quite a few dulcimers by then. His was made from a mahogany plywood back and Sapele mahogany sides, with the fretboard made of African walnut. The top was made from a rough Taiwanese spruce used for piano soundboards."

Fariña's commitment to the instrument soon becomes well known among the New York City folk crowd. In his own mind, he can now call himself a folk musician. He wills himself (sometimes at Carolyn's expense) to become a player who influences many other players, especially those on the West Coast who will take the dulcimer in an entirely new direction. His style is known as "contemporary," as far from Appalachia as one could get, but with the same passion poured into his music.

(13,14)

## 1961 LA MARQUE, TEXAS: A GOOD SECRET

Nine-year-old David Schnaufer has grown up listening to his parents' music from the thirties, forties, and fifties, but he also listens to the "hard country" music played by Bob Wills and Ernest Tubb that streams forth from the radio. Edith doesn't allow rock and roll in the house; however, thanks to late-night radio listening, David falls in love with rock and roll via artists such as Little Richard.

He is not the only one in the family enamored with current popular music. When his mother leaves the house to go to the grocery store, his father fires up the record player and pulls out his and David's secret stash of Elvis Presley records. Frank places one on the spindle, turns on the turntable, and places the needle on the edge of the spinning disk. This normally quiet, philosophical man leans back and laughs as he taps the floor with his foot, watching his Skeeter dance wildly around the living room. When they hear the oyster shells crush as Edith turns into the driveway, the two quickly pack up the records and put them back in the closet, keeping a joyful secret for a change.

(15,16)

## 1961 NYACK, NEW YORK: A MUSICIAN IN THE MAKING

Nine-year old Vincent Farsetta mows his neighbor Miss Kessler's lawn to earn money to buy records. Miss Kessler lives two doors down from the Farsettas and is old now, but in her youth she was a dancer who had her big break when she was hired to dance in 1919 for the Ziegfeld Follies of Broadway. To Vince's preadolescent eyes, she's still a beauty even though occasionally her lipstick is smeared. Before and after his mowing, she regales him with stories of being chased for years by Mr. Ziegfeld—she assures Vince that she had never "gotten caught." She also comments frequently on the music she hears wafting from Vincent's house during the summer when the windows are wide open: "I can hear your father singing in the shower!"

Occasionally, Vince's family visits his great-uncle Jim in New Jersey. Jim is his grandmother's brother, and one day when they visit, Jim pulls out a very old mandolin to play. The sound captivates Vince. He listens and watches, fascinated, as the old man's fingers dance across the strings, coaxing the instrument to wake up and sing. Sometimes soft and velvety, at other times bright or woody, the music mesmerizes his young mind.

(17, 18)

## 1962 NEW YORK CITY: A NEW APPROACH

Despite his respect and admiration for Jean Ritchie, Richard Fariña ignores the dulcimer tradition she represents. He claims he never listens to records of other dulcimer players or learns music composed for the instrument. He creates his own, using a chopstick for a noter and a guitar pick to strum a fiery, driving rhythm. He experiments by improvising instrumental versions of "Hound Dog" or "Blue Suede Shoes," sometimes chanting the words of poems he has written as he drives the beat.

(19)

## 1962 HOUSTON, TEXAS: THE JESTER LOUNGE

Behind Byron's BBQ on Westheimer, and about two blocks away from "Sin Alley," the Jester Lounge opens around midnight or 1 a.m. on weekends after other bars close. The only building on that street, the lounge is a small, dingy gathering place for folk artists, beloved by both performers and their audiences and limited to seventy-five patrons at a time. Bartenders do not sell alcohol, and the lounge closes at sunup.

In between their opening and closing times, The Jester is fertile ground for talented musicians and writers: regulars include Lightnin' Hopkins, Guy Clark, and a young Townes Van Zandt. When other artists such as Judy Collins, Barry McGuire, and John Denver pass through town, they, too, work and mingle at the Jester. Even Janis Joplin had sung at Open Mic Sunday there.

Thanks to his love of folk music, John Lomax II occasionally sings *a cappella* at the Jester since most of the traditional folk songs first sung by field hands, prison work gangs, and cowboys on horseback were unaccompanied. His son John Lomax III also visits the Jester—with and without his father—to take in the music and find inspiration for his writing. His mind is a growing encyclopedia of music and music culture. Along the way, he learns what makes a good song, how talented musicians distinguish themselves, and the intricacies of the music business for owners, managers, and artists.

(20, 21)

## 1962 DURHAM, NORTH CAROLINA: MCSPADDEN DISCOVERS THE DULCIMER

Duke Divinity School student Lynn McSpadden never had heard of a mountain dulcimer until his roommate Elliot brings him one and shows him how to play it. Lynn is so intrigued by this unusual instrument and the current folk music scene that he decides to teach himself how to make one. He borrows a friend's instrument made by McKinley Craft of Kentucky to use as a model, and discovers he does a pretty good job at duplicating it, much to his satisfaction.

McKinley Craft had based its model on the Uncle Ed Thomas's dulcimer design. The experience of making his dulcimer is Lynn's first inkling that he has what it takes to become a *luthier;* a maker of stringed instruments such as guitars, dulcimers, violins, and autoharps.

(22, 23, 24)

## 1962 AUSTIN, TEXAS: JOHN LOMAX III

Throughout high school, John Lomax III wondered what the future would hold for him. Given the Lomax family's reverence for education, he never doubted he would go to college. In addition, he has always felt the lure of music. Although exposed to diverse musicians throughout his young life, he resolves that performing will not be for him. Despite his mother's encouragement, he lacks confidence in his singing, nor does he put any serious time into learning to play the piano. Instead, baseball has been his passion growing up, and he is good at it. But once he discovers girls, his interest in baseball wanes.

John's interest in writing does not wane, however, thanks to an encouraging English teacher who was impressed enough with him to nurture his growing talent. He graduates high school in 1962 and enrolls in the University of Texas at Austin as a history major.

(25)

## 1962 LA MARQUE, TEXAS: COUSINS

David's Aunt Glenda, Uncle Kenneth and their two daughters also live in La Marque, and the two families occasionally visit together. Glenda is Frank's sister, and, like Edith, she is a homemaker.

Karen and Gena Fleming live in a different neighborhood and attend a different school than David does, so the cousins only get to know one another through family visits. David is especially fond of Karen (a year older than he is) because she makes him laugh. Yet, he resonates with her sister Gena who is a year younger than David. Gena is quiet and introspective, and, like himself, she is more attuned to the natural world than to society.

(26, 27)

## 1963 LA MARQUE, TEXAS: A PARENTS' SCARE

First, David lost his appetite. Despite his excitement about having joined the tennis team, he became listless enough to skip some practices. His parents and friends at school noticed he seemed kind of sickly. His worried mother kept him home from school a few days, Dennis's bout with polio always in the back of her mind. Then, the stomachaches began, mild at first but they worsened over the course of a week, causing him to miss more days of school. When he spikes a fever that will not come down, Edith and Frank take David to the

Galveston County Hospital emergency room where he is diagnosed with appendicitis and sent to surgery.

Dr. Cobb, the surgeon, finds his case interesting enough to take photos of the incision during the surgery and shares them with the Schnaufers.

When David reappears in school after his multiple absences, he faces piles of work to make up and discovers he has been dropped from the tennis team. He offers no explanation of his absence to anyone, not even to his friends.

(28, 29, 30, 31)

## 1963 CARMEL, CALIFORNIA: *CHILDREN OF DARKNESS*

While working the flourishing folk scene, Bob Dylan and another rising artist named Joan Baez began dating. They toured together for the next few years, singing, writing, and engaging politically via protest music. Twenty-six-year-old Richard Fariña has become good friends with Dylan ever since Dylan worked on his wife Carolyn's record.

On a trip to Europe last year, Fariña had met Mimi Baez, Joan's seventeen-year-old sister. Mimi was in France to study dance. When they met, he and Mimi both experienced a bad case of *amor fou*. For Carolyn, her husband's affair is the straw that breaks the camel's back; she was already tired of Richard's micro-managing her life. She divorces Fariña soon after they return to the States, and Richard marries Mimi in April.

The pair move to a small cabin in Carmel where they compose songs with Mimi on guitar and Dick on the Appalachian dulcimer. They will perform as Richard & Mimi Fariña at the Big Sur Folk Festival next year, and record their first album, *Celebrations for a Grey Day*, in 1965.

One of their original songs, "Children of Darkness" will later be hailed by many young people as a biography of their lives in the mid-sixties. One fan says he wore the grooves out of the record playing it. Others will believe, even in their old age, that it was the best song ever written.

(32, 33)

## 1963 NEWPORT, RHODE ISLAND: JEAN RITCHIE

First staged in 1959, the annual Newport Festival showcases the diversity of American folk music from rural traditions to urban pop music and attracts many of America's finest folk artists—Pete Seeger (son of musicologist Charles Seeger), the Kingston Trio, Joan Baez, and Bob Dylan among many others—along with thousands of folk music lovers. This year, Jean Ritchie joins the first board of directors of the festival.

Later, Jean's son John will recall: "We always had music in our home. The reports we gave at school each year on 'What I Did on My Summer Vacation' were a hit with our teachers." He explains, "The other kids in class would say 'I went to camp' or 'We went to the beach.' My brother and I could say, 'We hung out at the Newport Folk Festival.'"

(34, 35, 36)

## 1964 LA MARQUE, TEXAS: JOHN MACRINI

John Macrini notices the skinny kid after seeing him show up regularly to watch his combo play at the La Marque Teen Club right off Main Street. John plays keyboard with his middle school band at the local hangout where kids come to play pool, Chinese checkers, cards, and to dance to the jukebox on Fridays after school and all day on Saturdays for the bargain price of $1 per year membership. (The White kids that is; there is a separate, "Colored Teens

Club".) The club has its own column in the *Mainland Times*, "The Teen Tattle Teen Club," with news of who's who and what's happening among the adolescent crowd. Macrini's band is popular; they play for the club as well as for the Methodist Youth Foundation and the Catholic Youth Organization's dinner dances. He's used to having younger kids look up to him, and he has noticed this one studying him play the harmonica for a while now.

One night after his set, his admirer tells him that he plays harmonica, too. John invites him to sit down with him. The quiet, friendly boy with glasses grows on John, and he learns his name is Dave. As they talk, they discover they have a lot in common besides the harmonica. They live in the same neighborhood, both like fishing and the same kind of music, ranging from Roy Orbison and Delbert McClinton to the Beatles and hard country.

Soon, the two sixth- and seventh-graders are riding their bikes all over La Marque together. They often ride to the La Marque City park to sit under the trees and play harmonicas, taking turns playing lead and rhythm with their Hohner C-Signatures. Some days they go to John's to listen to vinyl on the stereo hi-fi or the radio with its top 40 radio hits. They play their harmonicas along to the music of the Beatles and of the Rolling Stones, the latter having just completed their first tour in the U.S. At other times, they look for songs to bridge the gap between rock and country, like those on the freewheeling Dave Dudley's *Six Days on the Road* album. They frequently ride bikes to fish in the Highland Bayou that makes its way out of Galveston Bay through Bayou Vista to the park.

Dave is the smallest and shyest of John's friends, but John and his buddies like him for his sense of humor and easygoing nature, and they fold him into their group, stepping up to defend him from the occasional bully at school.

(37, 38)

## 1964 LA MARQUE, TEXAS: YOUR UNIQUE PERSPECTIVE

Many a night Frank and his boys sit outside and study the night sky. Frank has always been fascinated by astronomy; so much so that for years he wanted to learn how to build his own telescope.One evening David and his father sit down together like they often do when David wants to talk about something new he has learned.

"Daddy, did you ever see the Turkish Flag? It's got a picture of the sun covered part way with the moon, and the moon has a star on its edge. Well, that's impossible! You can't see a star on the moon!"

"Well, David, let's think about this a minute. It just depends on where you are in space looking at the moon, doesn't it? It's all about your unique perspective, isn't it?"

David sits quietly for a bit. His imagination takes off to outer space where he positions himself first one place, then another to look at the moon. He reckons his father is right, and he'll remember their discussion for the rest of his life.

(39, 40, 41)

## 1964 LA MARQUE, TEXAS: DENNIS ERIC SCHNAUFER

Dennis Schnaufer says goodbye to his parents and to his twelve-year-old brother David as he heads northwest on U.S. 45, leaving La Marque behind. He is making his way to Southwestern University, the oldest university in Texas. As he drives through Houston, around Austin, and makes his way to Georgetown, he reflects on the life he's leaving behind and the new life about to commence.

Dennis knows he has done his utmost to prepare for his goal of becoming an ordained minister. His high school education consisted of good grades, membership in the German Club, and playing in the high school band. He assumed most of the responsibility for his own spiritual education ever since he can remember. Although his parents are religious, they rarely attended their Methodist church, so Dennis attended church without them much of the time. He tried various Methodist churches, in fact. He respects the Methodists and appreciates their emphasis on education, but he feels the Methodists are too hung up on superficial things like drinking and smoking. Both his parents are heavy smokers, and he feels like he already has enough to worry about with his family without having to worry that their souls are in peril for behavior that other churches overlook. His Episcopalian friends take the Eucharist every Sunday, and they aren't as hung up on the smoking and drinking. He thinks about exploring their church once he gets to Georgetown.

He leaves La Marque with mixed feelings: he loves his family, but there's also sadness for their constant struggles with illnesses and the economic perils that accompany them. Within the last nine years he and David lost their maternal grandfather to chronic heart disease; their maternal grandmother and aunt perished from TB. His father's on and off struggles with depression coupled with the family's ongoing fear of society's judgment about tuberculosis within their family feels overwhelming at times.

He's also uneasy with the changes he senses within David as he approaches his teenage years. David started out a happy child. He was a Cub Scout, always had good grades, and won an award for perfect attendance two years in a row in Highlands Elementary. As he grew, he played in Little League and joined the tennis club. However, Dennis senses recent changes within David that he doesn't understand. He hears things from others, and he worries constantly about him, wondering where he goes every day and what he is up to with his friends whom he rarely brings to the house.

His father's periodic times away from home to seek treatment for depression shaped Dennis into a sober young man. As he grew up, he loved David and felt deeply that it was his duty to make sure his brother stayed on the right path, but it has been a struggle. David doesn't share his devotion to the church, and Dennis worries that he might be making bad choices that will lead to life-changing consequences. Given their age difference, he decides that they are children of two different worlds growing up. It frustrates him that David shrinks from authority, whether it comes from his school or from him. He had grown more and more concerned for his younger brother, trying to protect him from an economic uncertainty that Dennis was acutely aware of in their own home: "You've got a chance to go to college and you should grab it," he tells him during one of their heated discussions. David's seeming refusal to pay him no mind results in mutual resentments on both sides.

Now, Dennis wants to move forward. He has always felt under pressure to be the first to attend to a university, a pressure that at times felt like a burden, but now feels like a gift. He declared his intent to major in religion and minor in sociology at Southwestern, and he will begin his college years with the same firm convictions that he did when he started high school.

Neither brother realizes at the time that Dennis's departure for college is the beginning of both brothers' personal journeys that will include long stretches of separation for much of the rest of their lives. There will be occasional brief reunions, but, from now on, they will be on their own diverging paths, rarely seeing but never forgetting each other.

Once Dennis arrives in Georgetown, he throws himself into his studies. His dedication to reading the Bible in preparation for leading worship services after school will earn him the 1964 Southwestern University Bible Reading prize. He joins the university band, the Student Christian Association, and tries on the fit of Pi Kappa Alpha's "Pike" for his identity in the fall. It's a good fit, so, he pledges to the Alpha-Omicron chapter. Dennis feels comfortable with this Memphis-based fraternity, one of the largest in the world. He likes their mission statement: "dedication to developing men of integrity, intellect, success and high moral character, and to fostering a truly lifelong fraternal experience."

(42, 43)

"California" as a concept first stirs Neal Hellman's imagination at Midwood High School. When his history teacher introduces the gold rush as a topic in class, it evokes the Magic Kingdom of Disneyland in his mind. As music pours out of California via AM radio stations in the Big Apple, Neal frequently listens to Richard Fariña's hit song "Pack up Your Sorrows" on singer Judy Collins *5th* album and becomes a devoted fan. At night he lies in his bed and imagines that California has had a special story for all of America and would have one for him, too.

Soon Neal starts hearing the music of a group of young musicians from Southern California called The Beach Boys. They sing in harmony about surfing, cars, and girls. They turn words into lyrics about a "Little Deuce Coupe," a "409" and a granny from Pasadena who likes to *go, go go*. Their songs tell of their journeys to places with exotic names like La Jolla and Pomona to "Ride the Wild Surf" and to experience the joy of well-tanned beach beauties in paradise. Despite his secret that he has no idea what a

"Deuce Coupe" or a "409" are, he is convinced that both must be essential to a California lifestyle.

Pounding the sidewalks of Flatbush Avenue, Neal invokes the Almighty that someday he will be delivered to the Promised Land of the West. He will eventually get there, but first he'll do a stint as a New York cabbie; then, he'll take hippie buses and hop freight trains, work on the East Coast, and move to Canada. Eventually, he will get to the Golden State and make it his home. He will make music his life's work, and the first of many books he will author will be a Richard Fariña songbook.

(44)

# 1965 CAMBRIDGE, MASSACHUSETTS: THE 6 1/2 FRET

Rick Turner has no idea he will be making dulcimer history this night.

Rick is one of many folkies living in Cambridge, most of whom know each other fairly well: the Jim Kweskin Jug Band with Geoff and Maria Muldaur; Bill Keith, the Charles River Valley Boys, Taj Mahal, Tom Rush, the guys who would go on to be the Youngbloods. The Fariñas live about four blocks from Turner's place on Kinnaird St.

One early evening, Turner gets a call from Mimi: "We're doing Robert J. Lurtsema's radio show tonight on WCBR. Richard has just written a new tune, but he's missing a much-needed note on his dulcimer. Can you put in an extra fret?" "*Hmmm*, yes. How are we going to do this?" Mimi replies, "We'll come by and pick you up; can you put it in at the radio studio?"

"OK!"

The Fariñas head over to pick up Rick. He retunes the dulcimer while in the back seat of the car on the way to the station. Once they arrive, he does a quick calculation of where the desired fret should go, saws a kerf in the fretboard, and hammers in a thin slip of a metal bar to add a fret between the sixth and seventh frets. He makes sure it is level and even with its neighboring frets with the right distance between them. He trims off the fret's ends and hands the dulcimer to Richard. He and Mimi walk to the mics to launch into their tune.

Some fifty years later, Turner will learn that the favor he did for the Fariñas made dulcimer history. Fariña's influence and unorthodox playing make it acceptable for the dulcimer to revise its age-old identity as diatonic instrument without sharp or flat notes. Dulcimers that include a 6 1/2 fret will soon become the model fretting pattern, unlocking new sonic possibilities for the dulcimer and its players.

(45)

## 1965 ARKANSAS: GROWING DEMAND, BIG OPPORTUNITY

After giving several of his dulcimers to friends and family, Lynn McSpadden turned to crafting them to sell as a part-time hobby. He focuses on two traditional patterns for his designs, the teardrop and the hourglass shapes. He earns enough money from his hobby to pay his fare to Scotland to study a year at the University of Glasgow. When he returns home, he makes even more money from his dulcimers thanks to a respectable average price of $85. Between his dulcimer earnings and his work as an associate

Methodist minister, he saves enough money to buy a Cessna plane and take flying lessons.

Lynn soon takes a teaching job in Farmington, Arkansas. However, his interest in dulcimers and their design becomes an obsession, and he spends hours researching the instrument in his local library.

(46, 47, 48)

## 1966 WASHINGTON STATE: BOB FORCE DISCOVERS THE DULCIMER

A young college student in Bellingham, Washington named Robert Force is surrounded by other students determined to learn to play musical instruments and share the latest records. When Force hears a recording by Richard Fariña, he is taken instantly with Fariña's poetic lyrics and topical songs such as "Birmingham Sunday" with its social commentary. The droning sound of Fariña's dulcimer, an instrument Robert had never heard or seen before, captivates him.

Robert bases his personal philosophy in part on Chinese poet Li Po's counsel: "A man should stir himself in poetry; stand firm in ritual, and complete himself in music." Li Po's first two admonitions had always resonated with him, but now, he sees a means of learning to understand the third; the dulcimer will provide him the key to his "completion in music."

Force had recently won $18.50 in a poker game with friends, so takes the album cover of the Fariñas' *Celebrations for a Gray Day* to a local violinmaker. The cover depicts Richard holding a dulcimer and Mimi holding a guitar. Arriving with his poker winnings at Albert Fischer's shop, he points to the picture of Fariña's dulcimer and asks, "Can you make me an instrument that looks like this?" To his surprise, Fischer tells him he has one in the shop. He had already started building dulcimers after reading about them from a plan in an old 1945 issue of "Popular Mechanics." Force hands over his winnings and walks out of the shop with a new instrument that will change his life.

(49, 50)

## 1966 NYACK, NEW YORK: VINCE IMMERSED

As Vince Farsetta turns fourteen, he still shares his father's appreciation of the music from the forties and fifties, but now underground rock grabs his attention. He spends every night with his headphones on, hooked up to his dad's stereo hi-fi radio, listening to the many New York City and college radio stations within range of his home that broadcast the burgeoning rock songs.

To feed her children's interest in music, Vince's mom buys him and his ten-year-old sister Tina Marie guitars for Christmas. Vince takes it upon himself to find a teacher for a guitar lesson. One Sunday when the Catholic church is full, Vince and his mom attend the overflow service in the Catholic school cafeteria. Right before mass is about to begin, his guitar teacher strolls in for the service. "Mom! There's my guitar teacher!" Mrs. Farsetta is shocked by his jeans full of holes. Nobody ever saw jeans like that in their community before, especially in church. Vince decides it's best not to tell her that the whole upper part of his teacher's room where he took his lesson has liquor bottles stacked on shelves. He needn't have felt guilty about not telling her; she was one step ahead of him. The next time he asks about taking a lesson, her motherly instinct kicks in and tells him a little white lie for his own good: "No more lessons ... your teacher moved away."

(51, 52)

## 1966 HOLLYWOOD, CALIFORNIA: BRIAN JONES DISCOVERS THE DULCIMER

Among many things Rolling Stones founder Brian Jones is known for is his fascination with atypical rock instruments such as the sitar, the marimba, and the mellotron. He takes them into the studio to add new and intriguing textures and colors to the Stones' songs. After stoking up on hours of Richard Fariña's music, he decides to play the fretted dulcimer on the track "Lady Jane" for *Aftermath*, an album which will be a key pivot point in the Stones' career, helping take them from a good band to a great one.

Fourteen-year-old David Schnaufer listens to a wide range of music with his friends after school, and especially likes the Stones. When he finally hears "Lady Jane", David is intrigued by the unusual song. However, even after studying the liner notes, he has no idea what a dulcimer is.

(53, 54, 55, 56)

*David's Immersion in Music*

Even before the mid-nineteenth-century Mexican-American War,* Texas was a cultural and musical mosaic. That mosaic resulted from the mix of Mexican, Latin American, and diverse European influences that flowed into the northern-most region of Mexico via settlers and immigrants, and from the Indigenous and Criollo influences of greater Mexico and its neighbor, Louisiana. Musical styles such as Afro-Caribbean rhythms from Cuba and from U.S. slaves whose owners settled in Texas added to the mix, along with marching band, tuba, waltzes, and polka music that German, Polish, and Czech immigrants brought with them as they emigrated to Texas. Starting in the 1940s, Mexican radio station XERF's strong signal and expansive programming helped promote a broad range of artists and musical genres, including swing, country, rhythm and blues, and rock and roll.

The twentieth century also saw the rise of the radio along with the honky-tonks and dance ballrooms where working Texans drank and danced to escape their troubles. They, in turn, shaped Texas music beyond church to include a hard beat and lyrics based on the workaday lives and concerns of the people. The electric amplification of instruments in the thirties continued those changes as well. The blues, dance bands, and country western music all were available to David via broadcast stations from faraway places such as WLS in Chicago and WSM from Nashville.

Given David's birth in 1952, his was the first generation to enjoy the rise of the relatively cheap transistor radio and record albums that brought listeners rock and roll music from across the United States (and, indeed, from around the world), an experience that informed his taste in music for the rest of his life. As an adult, he often mentioned the influence of the Rolling Stones, yet never turned his back on other genres of music; he loved it all. One particular favorite memory he shared with Jan Pulsford, in 2000: "I got to hear Ernest Tubb when I was 15—I ran away from home in a borrowed car and went to Nashville and showed up on a Saturday night and found a huge crowd of people outside the Ryman Auditorium. There was no air conditioning in those days, and everybody was hanging on the roofs of their cars listening to Ernest

Tubb and Kitty Wells, and it was magic. When I got back home, I was in a big heap of trouble ... but that's another story."

A good place to learn more detailed information about the myriad of cultural influences on Texas music is Malone and Laird's classic, *Country Music U.S.A.*, especially chapter five, "The Cowboy Image and the Growth of Western Music," pp. 160 to 217 in the 2018 edition. Also, don't miss Ken Burns's outstanding documentary, *Country Music*.

*The U.S. invasion of Mexico led to a war between the two countries from 1846 to 1848.

(57, 58, 59, 60)

## 1966 CARMEL, CALIFORNIA: A FATEFUL RIDE

Richard Fariña has much to celebrate. He and Mimi are widely admired and in demand among their small but influential group of cultural movers and shakers. The two young musicians and singer-songwriters have appeared in festivals, taught workshops, recorded with musicians like Pete Seeger and Mimi's sister Joan Baez, and are friends with Bob Dylan, author Thomas Pynchon, and much of LA's music royalty. They enjoy plenty of work as backup musicians and have recorded two of their own albums as well: *Celebrations of a Grey Day* and *Reflections in a Crystal Wind*. It is Richard, a friend claims, who conceived the idea of merging folk with rock: "Dick said, 'We should start a whole new genre. Poetry set to music, but not chamber music or beatnik jazz, man–music with a beat. Poetry you can dance to. Boogie poetry!'"

Two days after Random House publishes his first novel, *Been Down So Long It Looks Like Up to Me*, Richard is with Mimi at a friend's house to celebrate Mimi's twenty-first birthday. Later that evening, Richard hops on the back of his friend Willie's motorcycle to go for a spin on curvy Carmel Valley Road. Later, police estimate that Willie, a marine biologist, must have been doing ninety when he failed to make a curve. The motorcycle with its two passengers had rocketed up a five-foot bank, ripped through a barbwire fence, crossed a field and finally stopped when they hit a wooden fence. Willie survives the crash, but Richard Fariña is thrown off and killed instantly.

(61, 62, 63)

## 1967 AUSTIN, TEXAS: MUSIC JOURNALIST JOHN LOMAX III

John Lomax III graduates with his B.A. in History in 1967, and will pursue an M.A. in Library Science two years later. He finds work at a library just north of the Bronx in New York City. However, Texas exerts its pull on him, so he returns to take a position as a reference librarian in Houston. John loves his work researching, learning, and supporting other researchers who need his help. Before long, his interest in young adult literature propels him into the new position of acquisition librarian for young adult material. He settles into a newlywed house on Villanova Street with his wife and new baby, John Nova.

As much as he enjoys his library work, he continues to steep himself in music. He writes music reviews so well that he soon becomes the music editor for *Space City News*, a radical, progressive underground paper founded by veterans of the Students for a Democratic Society. The *News* also advocates for victims of social injustice with headlines such as "Free Carl Lee Otis Johnson," the unfortunate victim of a setup as he sat between two narcotics agents who had lit up a joint and handed it to him. As soon as he took it, they busted him, and Carl Lee found himself sentenced to thirty years in prison. Everyone at *Space City News* agrees that the extreme sentence was because he was a Black man.

Employees of the paper become used to many threats and acts of violence against it, including an arrow bearing the note, "The Knights of the Ku Klux Klan is [sic] watching you" shot into their office one day. Nevertheless, John keeps his head down and writes reviews of new albums by John Lennon, the Who, and emerging local artists' albums.

Eventually John will play an influential role in promoting traditional music in an entirely new endeavor. His imagination, his deep immersion in music history, and his appreciation for cultural importance that has been his family's legacy will help the dulcimer's resurrection and propel its traditional canon of music around the world.

(64, 65)

## 1967 GALVESTON, TEXAS: THEY LIVE TO SURF

Thanks to his friends, Dave at fifteen is on to one of the best kept secrets in the surfing world: Galveston Bay. Teens will either hitch a ride with older kids who already have a car, or volunteer to drive if they have one. David and his peers head to the beach most days after school and on the weekends during fall, winter, and spring (the water is too flat during the summer).The bay is the perfect destination for newbie and experienced surfers alike; they can surf the big waves or experience "tanker surfing", tackling the smaller and smoother waves sent their way as the oil tankers move through the channel.

The first time David learns how to catch a wave and steer a board in, he's hooked. He enjoyed playing baseball and tennis, but he finds surfing the perfect sport in which to lose himself in the high of riding the waves. On the weekends, the teens party after long days in the sun.

Since David's friend John Macrini got his "hardship" license* at 14, John, David, and their surfer friends often cram into his father's '59 Ford Galaxy to head to the bay. Certain unspoken rituals are followed before leaving La Marque: everyone in the car chips in a quarter for gas (usually a welcome deal for the driver since gas is only twenty-five cents a gallon). Somebody volunteers to call in to the local 1400 AM radio station where a recent La Marque High School graduate works who is amenable to providing a surf report by phone. If the waves are good, everyone straps boards on the car roof and wherever else the vehicle can carry them. Before leaving, the boys pass by the local grocery story for a quick search for junk food; they fill the car with cupcakes, chips and whatever else strikes someone's fancy for fueling up. Off they go, frequently cutting the twenty-minute drive in half as they speed ninety to a hundred miles per hour down the freeway, radio blasting, playing harmonicas, and telling jokes ... the teens living intensely in the moment as teenagers do. During the weekdays, they make the most of their surf time; they only have an hour or two before hurrying home to do school-work and eat dinner.

For David, the water underneath the wide-open Texas sky offers him the time in nature that he loves as well as freedom from his worries about his family that he keeps inside. Surfing challenges him to develop the physical discipline needed to harmonize with the rhythm of the powerful waves.

The boys' rituals continue as they arrive at the beach. Grabbing their boards, they stop and stand a moment, close their eyes, and raise their faces to sense the wind direction: the best onshore wind is a southeastern coming off the Gulf that builds the swells; the northwestern offshore winds blow against the waves. When David opens his eyes, he runs to the water, lightly boosts himself up to lie prone on the board, and paddles out. He searches for the sweet spot to analyze the surf for "humps" and "juice": indicators that the incoming waves contain enough energy to give him a good, long ride. Using his intuition, he paddles forward as he seeks the opti-mal spot to catch the building wave before it breaks. Once he senses the oncoming peak, he paddles furiously to turn his Hansen 50/50 board into position. With his well-developed sense of timing and harmony with the rhythm of the waves, he pulls himself up to a sitting position, his legs straddling the board. He awaits his wave; when it comes to him, he uses his core strength to pop up to a crouch and then to a stand. Arms up and out for balance, he homes in on the line of the wave as gracefully as ballet dancer, letting the massive energy that flows unchecked underneath him lift and propel him forward. He shifts this way and that as he rides out the wave to its decay, returning to its origin. It's not unusual to be able to catch ten joyous waves in a row, but the surfers always stay alert for the one that will be The Memorable One, the one that sustains the longest.

Most La Marque parents absolutely forbid their kids to go surfing unless they attend weekly church. An early morning visitor to the 6 a.m. Sunday service at St. Michael's might be surprised to see a gang of ten or twelve young teenagers along with one or two little old ladies in the pews every weekend. By the time the pastor's parting words are still ringing in the air, the boys are hightailing it down the Gulf Freeway.

David's other buddy Terry loves surfing, too, and they often get together with their mutual friends on the water. The first time Terry watched David catch a wave, he was surprised to see the skill with which his slight friend rode the board.

David finds the beach a comforting haven. He lives to surf; his time in the water is his happiest. Occasionally he glimpses joyful dolphins swimming alongside him in the rushing blue-green water, their smiling expressions mirroring his own. Before gathering with others to head back to La Marque, he strolls the beach to collect the scalloped shells that have washed ashore. On the ride back, the boys joke with each other, compliment the impressive rides or share techniques for finding and riding the wave's hollow so that it breaks over them, rather than having to eat the wave if it breaks on them. The break-over doesn't happen often, but when it does, they declare it magic.

David starts smoking Kool cigarettes around the same time he discovers surfing. The Galveston excursions provide him and his peers with ample time to enjoy smoking without fear of being found out. Many of his peers smoke, and La Marque High School provides an area they called the Smoking Circle where students congregate to grab a quick drag. Eventually, the school board decides the Smoking Circle is not such a good idea. After that, kids have to do their furtive puffing in the school bathrooms or outside in the bushes.

*Texas grants hardship licenses to minors between the ages of fifteen and eighteen if they pass a driving test and their family provides documentation to support their eligibility for such a license due to family need.

(66, 67, 68, 69, 70, 71, 72)

## 1967 GALVESTON, TEXAS: DINGBOY

To earn some money, David finds work as a "Dingboy" at Doug's Surf and Ding Repair Shop on Fifty-Seventh Street in Galveston. His work entails sanding down customers' fiberglass boards to smooth out cracks and dents. One morning a number of impressive young guys swagger into the shop to get their boards smoothed out. They're fit, tanned, smiling, and have identical crewcuts. When it comes time to pay, one of them asks David if he'll take a package of primo hash in exchange for their boards.

"Who are you guys?" he asks them. They laugh. "We're the Blue Angels."

(73, 74, 75)

## 1968 LA MARQUE, TEXAS: ON THE THRESHOLD OF THE AGE OF AQUARIUS

La Marque High School students are mostly White, administered and taught primarily by male graduates of the University of Texas. Faculty and staff wear suits and ties every day in their mission to run a tight ship; no monkey business allowed, and academic expectations are high. A minority of boys whose parents allow them to wear long hair tend to get plenty of grief from the administration. Yearbook photos reveal page after page of clean-cut boys and girls:

the girls all wear the same collar, and the boys all wear similar suits and ties in their school yearbook pictures.

Sophomore David Schnaufer's photo in the "The Tiger Tale" yearbook depicts him wearing a suit and tie, thus conforming to the conservative values of the school. However, even though his hair is short on the sides, he indicates a bit of independence by leaving it a bit longer at the top, combed over to the right. He looks in the direction indicated by the photographer, a faint wisp of a smile suggested on his face.

What his class picture doesn't reveal has to do with David's highly sensitive disposition combined with a spirit of rebellion that chafes under the structured sameness imposed by school and his conservative community. He feels increasingly isolated as well. At age five, he lost the last of his grandparents. Despite his resentments of Dennis, he felt the separation deeply when he left for college. Last year, his aunt Glenda and Uncle Kenneth moved from La Marque to Findlay, Ohio; thus, he lost the easy access to his cousins. He feels attached to his home but also eager to escape it. David does not yet know what he wants, but he certainly knows what he doesn't want: he resents authority, and he doesn't like feeling bored.

He struggles with uncertainty about where to go and what to do with his life. The questions "Who am I?" "Where do I fit in?" "What do I want to be?" are felt by many during the teenage years. David and his brother Dennis have lived their formative years with additional stresses caused by family illnesses that they don't understand completely and are never discussed openly with them. For Dennis, his hope and refuge has become higher education and the church. The rhythms of the waves and of music are David's.

The journalism students who work on 1968 yearbook depart from the traditional design of the table of contents. They organize the contents by signs of the zodiac, not surprising, given that many of these nice-looking young men and women have already taken their first steps over the line into the Age of Aquarius even before they graduate high school.

(76, 77)

## "'Confrontation': 1968 Was a Very, Very Tense Year"

In 2020, filmmaker David Hoffman releases a brief, historical video to YouTube that had never been released to the public. Filmed in 1968, Christian filmmaker Ken Addison was interested in finding answers as to why young people—here and abroad—were turning away from established practices and values and, specifically, from their churches.

Hoffman writes: "1968 was another of those very complicated and scary times for many Americans ....The Vietnam War was raging and the country was split on whether or not we should be fighting it. Other issues were debated between the sixties generation (or at least a portion of it) and those who were part of the fifties and ... 'ran the show.' I have deep respect for the work of Ken Anderson, the Christian documentary filmmaker trying to make sense in his own way of the conflicts that existed."

Addison states his goal in the opening of his short film:

"We are in search of young people ... what they're thinking, saying .... Plainly, the revolt [in society] is against the establishment ... the status quo. You're aware of the terminology: hippies ... generation gap ... the SDS. We, of course, focused our cameras on other kids ... the so-called 'silent majority'. But the action is with the protest bloc. They may only be a segment of our society, but they hold the fuses, and relentless fire burns in their hearts. We gotta listen to these kids."

Anderson records young people from widely diverse groups in the U.S. and from Britain, Africa and Asia. One young woman tells him, "They stifle us and put us in little boxes. And we have to get out of those boxes .... one way to get out of it is the alternative lifestyle; quote 'the radical lifestyle': long hair, hippies, dope, all that kind of thing, it's against the establishment." Her companion adds, "... and all of these are just mild distortions of middle-class America anyway."

Another student comments: "...It's pretty obvious what young people are thinking today .... When the structure confines the human-ness of the individual so that it explodes, it can't create, that's the kind of thing that has to be changed ..."

"What drives anyone—hunger, thirst, the need to belong, the need to feel a part of ... the need to be respected; this is what motivates a Black man."

One British young adult contributes his opinion: "It's not only up to young people, but up to ordinary people of all ages to control their own lives for themselves; not allow a handful of politicians and businessmen to control what we think and what we do."

It is this tribe of hippies, protestors, and kids who turned away from the church that frightens Dennis and his parents.

You can watch Anderson's film following a brief introduction by filmmaker David Hoffman at: www.youtube.com/watch?v=blMKmlV6A18&t=484s

(78)

## 1968 LA MARQUE, TEXAS: "YOU'RE A SELLOUT"

Most of the time, David looks forward to his brother coming home during his college breaks. Yet when Dennis does return home, he often sees more and more of a new, surly side to his younger brother. His fears grow about him; he wonders if David may have inherited the depression that plagues his father and others in their family.

These days, David looks at his older brother with mixed feelings. He envies his freedom and the confidence Dennis has always had about his goals in life. At the same time, he resents Dennis's attitude that he knows what's best for both of them. Each frustrates the other with their different choices, assumptions, and suspicions about the other's motivations. During one argument, David slams Dennis for being a "sellout to the system," while, in Dennis's opinion, David makes too many wrong choices in his social and school life. Dennis tells him he is too preoccupied with the petty annoyances he experiences at school, like the time he was chastised for wearing high-top moccasins to class. Tensions ebb and flow between them.

Despite their difficulties, there are times when the two set aside their resentments. While Dennis is home, David—a voracious reader—digs through his brother's college texts, especially the sociology texts. He searches for answers in the books, hoping to find clues to understand the people around him. He wants to understand his father's depression episodes. He's also trying to understand himself and why he can't shake off the feeling he is different from the rest of his peers in school. He resents the heavy-handed, conservative administration that keeps a tight grip on student behavior. He feels restless and frustrated, and there's a growing disdain within him for a system he feels is trying to contain him and prepare him for a life that he is sure isn't for him.

(79, 80)

## 1968 NEWPORT, RHODE ISLAND: AMAZING GRACE

Jean Ritchie tells a story about the '68 Newport Folk Festival:

"The mostly young crowd was rowdy, shouting for more of Arlo Guthrie who had just electrified the place with a new song called 'Alice's Restaurant'. This was the close of the festival and Pete (Seeger) didn't want it to end that way, [so] he pushed me, he literally pushed me out in front of the microphone and said, 'Go! Go finish the festival!' I knew they were going to eat me up. I didn't know what to do. The only thing I could think of was 'Amazing Grace'; I started to sing it in the old regular Baptist way, decorated and slow and high. They just quieted down like someone had poured water on them. By the time I finished, you could hear a pin drop."

(81)

## 1968 AUSTIN, TEXAS: JOHN LOMAX III AND TOWNES VAN ZANDT

John Lomax's frat brother Caddo Parish Stoddard III calls on him to say that they need to go to the 11th Door, a two-story folk club in Austin on the corner of Eleventh and Red River. The club is a popular watering hole for college students. It has a bar upstairs for hanging out; downstairs, featured musicians perform for those willing to pay the cover charge. John agrees to meet up with Caddo, and, when they arrive, they make their way downstairs where some twenty-five people are sitting around the most charismatic singer John has ever seen: "a tall, striking, handsome man with dark hair and copper-colored skin." John notes the clear voice and the cleanest guitar playing he has ever heard. During the guitarist's set, he plays a lot of "talkin' blues, really funny songs" that keep John and Caddo in stitches. In addition, he sings two songs, "For the Sake of the Song," and "I'll Be Here in the Morning," which will become two of John's favorites. He feels a visceral reaction to this singer, just fifteen feet away from him. He tells Caddo, "This guy is as good as anyone I've ever heard, and I've heard a lotta folk people."

After the set, they approach the musician and start chatting. John concludes he is as friendly and funny as anyone could be.

After their first meeting, Townes Van Zandt and John run into each other in Austin from time to time and have some good times together. When John eventually moves back to Houston, he finds out that Van Zandt and his wife Fran live just around the corner from John's parents' house on Vanderbilt. John and Townes visit often, thus cementing a friendship that will find both eventually cutting records together in Nashville.

(82, 83)

## 1968 GALVESTON, TEXAS: THE ACCIDENT

For some young men, it's a challenge to step back from danger when you're sixteen and hanging out at the beach with friends who will try anything to show off. On this particular day, David and friends are high, laughing as they surf the big waves. They fly in on their boards, turn around, and paddle back out to do it all over and over again. There are no leashes on boards yet, so anybody who pearls (gets dumped) has to swim to search for his board. David has had plenty of practice since junior high, so he feels confident in his skill and ability to swim. He usually paddles as far out as he can to ride the waves in without giving it a second thought; surfing is as natural as breathing to him.

Today, however, he lets his guard down and is no match for the dynamic energy heaving the waves underneath him. They slam him off his board into a shallow, rocky area not far from the beach. Despite their state of intoxication, it soon becomes apparent to other surfers that David hasn't bobbed up. The boys jump in the water and find him floating underneath the surface, unable to move his head, his arms or his legs. Panic snaps them into motion as they crowd around to drag him out of the water. David appears paralyzed, so the boys half carry, half drag him to one of the cars, pile in, and head to the hospital.

The ER receptionist looks askance at the teenagers who burst in, soaking wet and clearly in an altered state of mind. By the time the attending doctor gets to examine the patient, David has come to and is able to move again. The physician decides against taking an X-ray. He discharges him and shoos the whole bunch of "hippies" out the door.

David leaves, not realizing he has cracked a vertebra in his neck. He won't think about this incident or deal with the resulting physical consequences until forced to. As years pass, growing pain from the break will first interfere with his ability to move his neck, then his arms and hands. Eventually, the pain will become intolerable. Only then will he discover the bone spurs growing in his neck due to this accident.

(84, 85, 86, 87)

## 1968 LONG BEACH, CALIFORNIA: THE NITTY GRITTY DIRT BAND

A love of folk music draws the young teens to McCabe's Guitar Shop; there they hang out regularly, forming spontaneous jams around an old coffee table. They bathe in southern California's heady music crucible with its sounds of rock, pop, folk, and jazz along with a swirl of country and roots music. Certain young patrons pour through racks of records in pursuit of the latest Doc Watson or Dillards' songs to emulate because it's the sounds of the Byrds and The Flying Burrito brothers, acoustic guitar and banjo, jug and bass that resonates the most within their souls.

Like many kindred spirits, two of these young people—Jeff Hanna and Bruce Kunkel—find other like-minded dreamers: guitarist/washtub bassist Ralph Barr, guitarist-clarinetist Les Thompson, harmonicist and jug player Jimmie Fadden, and guitarist-vocalist Jackson Browne. Once multi-instrumentalist John McEuen steps into the mix, they become "The Nitty Gritty Dirt Band."

They are an unlikely group by Nashville's country music standards; the scruffy, long-haired bunch plays Long Beach's local clubs while wearing pinstripe suits and cowboy boots. But the Muse has given them the nod: within a year they will release two albums and appear on *The Tonight Show* starring Johnny Carson.

Long Beach is some two thousand miles from Music City. However, in four short years, many music critics will pronounce the Nitty Gritty Dirt Band the savior of country music.

(88, 89, 90)

## 1968 PADRE ISLAND, TEXAS: BORN TO BE WILD

Although Norman and David attended different elementary schools, they first met through Little League, Norman on the Rotary White Sox and David playing for the Amoco Yankees. They didn't become reacquainted until last year when they bumped into each other in high school.

Since then they have become tight friends. Like David, Norman lives to surf. If he gets the urge to ride the waves, he doesn't let the lack of a car stop him. He happily hitchhikes with his board to and from Galveston if need be. Both friends love to talk about music, although David's tastes are more wide-ranging than are Norman's. David recently introduced Norman to Johnny Winter's new album, *The Progressive Blues Experiment*, and to Frank Zappa's music. Norman isn't crazy about Zappa, but he is impressed by how well-informed his buddy is, not only about music but current events as well. He talks with authority about last August's riots at the Democratic convention in Chicago and the upcoming trial of the Chicago Seven, the Vietnam war, political activist Angela Davis, and whatever other current topics appear in the news.

The first time Norman walked into David's bedroom, he was struck by the rows and rows of books on the shelves. When he saw his current read next to his bed, *Revolution for the Hell of It* by political activist and counterculturist Abbie Hoffman, he was surprised. Norman knew that parents these days are frightened—even appalled by—Hoffman's radical assertions that society needs to change and make way for psychedelic drugs, rock bands, and sexual freedom. Norman's admiration for his friend grew even more;

"This must be why David is so smart," he thought. "I listen to the radio so I know who Abbie Hoffman is, but, David actually reads his book."

Norman talks about David with his mother, Birdie Bea. "He's a good athlete, an avid reader, funny and can play the harmonica like nobody's business," he tells her. Bea likes David, too, and appreciates how he gives her his full attention and listens carefully as she talks to him about her latest reading of the Bible. He also loves her cooking, so she serves up her shrimp gumbo or chili whenever he stops by.

David enjoys spending time with Bea in her large, organic garden pulling weeds, helping her pick squash, peppers and tomatoes. He talks a little, but more often just listens to her. "My husband built me this brush arbor so the beans can run up and over it," she tells him, pointing to a primitive trellis he had made for her out of tall, thin sticks standing in a sunny spot. She often shares memories from her past. One afternoon she told him of the explosion of the Grandcamp twenty-one years ago:

> There was a big cargo ship on fire back in 1947. My aunt asked me to go with her to watch it burn. I had a strong premonition not to go, so my aunt invited her neighbor instead, and she brought her twin three-year old daughters. They all stood on the dike watching, when suddenly the ship exploded. My aunt survived, but the blast hit her so hard with glass, sand, and debris that she was still able to pull out slivers of glass in her face into her seventies. The blast blew the two little children away and they never found their bodies. Her neighbor survived, but she lost an eye.

David is mesmerized by Bea's old stories, and learns from Norman that Bea has a special kind of spirit. She believes in prayer and in healing; she has dreams that come to pass, and many in her family have the same ability. Norman's aunt, his cousin, and even Norman himself have dreams that contain premonitions or that give information the dreamer doesn't know.

This weekend Norman, David and Terry Theobald load their boards into Terry's van to take the three-and-a-half-hour drive south along the coast toward Aransas Pass to catch the twenty-four-hour ferry to Padre Island. They're excited as they look forward to a weekend of surfing at Aransas Pass. Known as "Saltwater Heaven," it's a natural paradise thanks to the waters in Redfish Bay and the abundance of wildlife found there: redfish, speckled trout, sea turtles, herons, terns, pelicans, and countless other bird species.

Due to a late start, they pull into the beach on Padre Island at 1 a.m. Thanks to the almost complete isolation, there are no sights, sounds, or lights anywhere, just the steady rhythm of waves lapping the shore in the refreshing saltwater air. The three fall asleep in the van.

They wake up early to shouts and laughter as hordes of college kids arrive at the beach on this last Saturday of their spring break. Terry, Norman, and David get up and walk over to an old café to grab something to eat before hitting the water. It's so early, they don't see anyone when they walk in the door except a waitress and the local sheriff at the counter having his coffee. They slide into a booth, and despite the early hour, Norman slips a coin into the small jukebox on the wall. He flips through the songs and selects Steppenwolf's "Born to be Wild." As the song blares out across the small restaurant, the three high school juniors glance sideways at the sheriff, noticing that he already has his eye on them.

The weather is perfect, with the seagulls and pelicans flying overhead, and they just about wear themselves out on the waves that get better and better throughout the day.

When they wake up Sunday, the college students are gone. More of their La Marque friends are due to arrive shortly, so they will have the whole beach to themselves. The swells are even bigger and better than yesterday's, and the weekend spent here will be remembered by all three as one of the most joyful in their lives.

(91, 92)

Last year, Dennis Schnaufer opted to begin using his middle name "Eric" instead of his first name since he felt it was more appropriate to his calling. Upon graduation from Southwestern University, he began his seminary work in Virginia.

He chooses his first summer clinical experience—Clinical Pastoral Education—at Austin State Mental Hospital. He lives in a small apartment on the hospital grounds and ministers to the patients. Throughout the summer, he learns a great deal about depression and its impact on the people who suffer from it and on those around them.

The experience helps him gain insight into his own family's struggles with depression (especially his father's) and the impact on his family of his father's lengthy disappearances for treatment. Over time, he gains enough skills to feel comfortable working with patients who seek him for counseling. He ruefully notes that he has more success building connections with them than he does with his younger brother when they see each other.

After a year at Virginia Theological Seminary and his summer clinical, Eric transfers to the more progressive Seminary of the Southwest in Austin near the University of Texas.

One day, a new theology professor profoundly reshapes Eric's thinking about his role as a church leader. His professor announces to the men under his charge: "My job is not to lecture on classical theology; I am here to teach you how to *do* theology." Coming from the more traditional seminary in Virginia, this new interpretation of theology suddenly resonates within Eric.

His professor explains, "We live in a completely different world than classic theologists did," emphasizing that it was no longer effective to regurgitate scripture or dictate from on high as was the practice a thousand years ago. He continues, "The modern world is changing rapidly due to new discoveries in science, new understandings about the size of the universe and the increasing possibility of life on other planets." He asks his students to consider the implications of this proliferation of knowledge for their work, advising them on ways they can include classical theology in their philosophy, but not limit their philosophy to it. Rather, he encourages them to move beyond the notion that the church is led only from the top down. "You must start with your parishioners where they are, not where you think they should be."

(93, 94, 95, 96, 97)

## 1968 LA MARQUE, TEXAS: A MOST DEVASTATING DISCOVERY

By his junior year in high school, David's parents, especially his mother, are afraid for their son. They don't understand his surfer lifestyle, the kinds of books he reads with their radical ideas, nor do they approve of the music he devours. He is so different from his brother that it makes them worry constantly. Like many parents, they always imagine the worst when he isn't home, and as he grows into his teenage years, he disappears more and more. The distance between them is not helped by his resentment against any attempt by his school, his parents, or his brother to control him.

In contrast to his photo in last year's high school yearbook, this year's school photo shows a young man with a determined resolve just below the surface of his face. Wearing his glasses, his eyes stare with slight defiance at the camera. His strategy in this struggle for control of his life is to keep his private feelings closed off inside himself so that he doesn't have to discuss what bothers him. Yet he's highly sensitive; on the occasions he snaps at his parents, he regrets it afterwards. None of his many friends are aware of his inner feelings or even his individual experiences with one another.

However, David still has good moments with his parents. Occasionally, he goes jogging with his mother. On one particular day he joins her, she has to stop because of a pain in her leg. She feels around the sore spot, and detects a lump.

(98, 99, 100)

## 1969 LA MARQUE, TEXAS: BAPTIZED AND CONFIRMED

As a result of several conversations with her husband and son Eric, David's mother quietly arranges to switch her longtime membership from the Methodist church to St. Michael's Episcopal Church. On the fifth of January, she and David go to St. Michael's to see Reverend Kearby and to be baptized together. David is seventeen, and his mother is forty-six. David wonders why it's so important to her to do this now, but she says nothing.

One week later she returns to St. Michael's with David so that Bishop Goddard can administer the sacramental rite of confirmation to each of them. Again, he goes along to please her, but still doesn't get a satisfactory answer from his mother to his questions, "Why?" and "Why now?"

(101)

## 1969 NASHVILLE, TENNESSEE: JOHNNY CASH AND JONI MITCHELL

After he accepts ABC's offer to host his own weekly television show, Johnny Cash sets his sights on the Ryman Auditorium for the show's home. Built as the Union Gospel Tabernacle by Capt. Thomas G. Ryman in 1892, it serves as a concert hall and the home of The Grand Ole Opry radio show. Now, Cash wants to tape his show at this Nashville landmark nicknamed "the mother church of country music."

However, the Ryman is in rough shape. The building has no air conditioning, and those who sit in the audience section of the hall can look up and see daylight through little holes between the slats in the roof. The first time they wheel a sound crane on the stage, it falls through the wooden floor thanks to the termites feasting for years on the floorboards. The orchestra conductor flinches as rats the size of small cats run across his feet down in the pit. Yet, none of this stops the show. The Ryman is too special of a place, and Johnny has the clout and the television audience—some thirteen million people—to get what he wants, so weekly taping begins.

Cash sees this show as an opportunity to break down some artistic barriers, and he acts on that opportunity. *The Johnny Cash Show*, while firmly grounded in country and gospel music, invites the best pop artists in the world as guests, providing them massive exposure to a new audience. If they are good enough for Johnny, they are welcome into the fold as far as he is concerned.

Bob Dylan and Joni Mitchell are two of his favorite people whom he wants to showcase. Both appeared on his first show. Joni returns for a second time, this time with a dulcimer. She performs her song "California" to the millions who tune in, most of whom are likely seeing a professional musician play the mountain dulcimer for the first time, or at least her nontraditional approach to playing it.

Via that one television performance, Joni Mitchell brings so much attention to this thing called a dulcimer that demand suddenly explodes among young folk musicians. The Mitchell-inspired buzz over the dulcimer will help David Schnaufer find the answer he has been looking for to the question of what to do with his life.

(102, 103, 104)

## APRIL TO NOVEMBER 1969 LA MARQUE, TEXAS: A DEVASTING LOSS

Despite the promise of this year's spring, Frank and Edith Schnaufer feel overwhelmed. At age sixteen, David feels out of their reach.

To make matters worse, Edith doesn't feel well. She hasn't felt well in a while since she found the lump in her leg. She is listless, and losing weight, something her family notices on her tiny frame. She finally decides to visit the doctor. He X-rays her and, there it is, an unmistakable presence on the large sheet of film: wide evidence of metastatic cancer throughout her body. The source is unknown.

In the days that follow, Edith and Frank try to keep their worries to themselves, but Eric learns of the bad news while in seminary in Austin as he awaits his summer clinical experience at the Texas Maritime Academy. The academy, a branch of Texas A&M University, has scheduled him to serve onboard as a chaplain of the *Texas Clipper* ship off Galveston for early summer. After recruits participate in orientation and classes onboard the ship, his work is supposed to continue as the cadets and crew spend the next three months cruising to Europe.

Preferring to keep bad news to himself and worried for his boys, Frank explains little about her condition, but both Eric and David feel a growing sense of dread as their mother gets weaker and needs more help at home.

David helps as best he can. The school administration rejects his request to be allowed to go home to help his mother eat and use the bathroom during the day. David believes it's because they consider him a hippie. Furious, he drops out of school to attend to her.

Whether Edith had ignored her symptoms or not, with metastatic cancer spreading quickly throughout her body, she will still face the same result. At forty-six years old, she will enter the Galveston County Memorial Hospital where she will spend the next five months of her life.

Right before he is supposed to leave for Europe, Eric gets a call from his father to ask him for help. David has run away. He took his father's car and drove off to Florida with a friend where they were picked up by the police. Eric flies to Florida, picks up the boys and drives them back to La Marque. Eric, distraught over his mother's illness and now keenly aware of turmoil at home, feels frustrated and depressed by his inability to resolve family problems. He spends the rest of the summer onboard the ship, ministering to young men, and wondering every day if he will have to fly home at the next port.

By mid-November, Eric is back in La Marque. He's twenty-four years old, in his last year of seminary. His father had called him home to see his mother for the last time. He arrives to find his father and seventeen-year-old brother consumed with grief and dread as they face the inevitable.

On the morning of the 14th, Eric drives to the hospital and braces himself as he enters his mother's room. She is sleeping, as she has been most of the time since she entered the hospital. A nurse comes in to check on Edith, then asks him to step outside. When she reappears at the door, Eric learns that his mother has just passed away.

One of the primary reasons Eric chose to become a priest has to do with his ability to stay calm and do what is necessary in a crisis situation. Honed by years of feeling responsible for his family when his father was gone, and having lived through one family crisis after another, he has learned to push his own feelings aside to do what needs to be done. Eric calls his father first, and next, the Episcopal priest at St. Michael's.

When the Schnaufer men finally return back to the house, a sense of profound, painful grief settles over them. Eric will find some solace in his work. David and his father are devastated. David was always closest to his daddy growing up, but their sorrow is so consuming that they are hardly able to comfort each other. David feels deeply depressed that he did not get to say goodbye to her or to tell her he was sorry for the troubles he caused her. He is filled with such guilt, depression, and despair that he cannot think, cannot process, cannot cope.

At his mother's funeral, David whispers to his buddy Terry that he desperately needs to get to the water. Terry can't wait to get out of the funeral home either. As soon as they can, they leave for home to change clothes, pick up their boards, and head for the bay.

(105, 106, 107, 108, 109, 110)

## 1970 GALVESTON, TEXAS: NORMAN AND DAVID

After his mother's death, David gravitated more and more to the Jordan home. He takes great pleasure in Norman's company and great comfort from Bea's mothering. She goes out of her way to take care of the boy who often seems lost.

Tired of school, Norman plans to enlist in the military for two years and then make up his mind as to what he wants to do with his life. He and David have one last summer together before he heads to boot camp.

Shortly after Norman graduates, David calls him up.

"Hey, I'm going to apply for a job in Galveston, so want to just ride with me?"

During their drive, he tells Norman that a draftsman job has opened up in this company that is going to draw plans for burying cable for Southwestern Bell Telephone.

When they walk into the office, David asks the man at the desk for an application and sits down at a table with others who are there for the same reason. Norman sits down on a couch to wait for him. The company rep walks over to Norman and asks, "Would you like an application as well?"

"No, I'm just here with him," pointing to David.

"Well, you're not doing anything; go ahead and fill this out." He hands Norman the piece of paper. At the top of the form the instructions indicate that he should print all information. After filling the application out, he hands it back to the man in charge who takes one look at it and announces loudly,

"Okay, everybody, you can stop right now; we found the guy we want."

Norman and David look at each other, puzzled. Norman replies, "Hey, I'm not the guy you want; I don't know anything about being a draftsman."

"Well, we can teach that to you, but we can't teach you to print like this. Your printing looks like a machine did it. Do you want the job?"

Norman thinks a minute and decides it sounds better than the job he has now working at a grocery store. "Yeah, I'll take the job."

As the two leave the building to walk back to the car, David bursts out laughing.

"That's the last time I'm taking you anywhere, Norman. You stole my job!"

(111)

## 1970 AUSTIN, TEXAS: ERIC GRADUATES

Eric works in his final year of seminary as he faces canonical exams and his second summer of work with the Texas A&M Maritime Academy. His onboard duties will delay his ordination by several months. He's single and longs for marriage and his own family.

His bishop assigns him to the Church of the Good Shepherd in Tomball, near Houston. His excitement is tempered with concern as he ponders his individual goals and the goals for his new church. He wonders, "How do I fit in to this organization? How can I be an effective leader and make the church better?"

When Eric graduates from Austin's Episcopal Seminary of the Southwest, only his father attends. They make the best of the special day.

(112, 113, 114, 115)

## 1970 TEXAS CITY, TEXAS: ANOTHER DEVASTATING LOSS

Not long after Edith's death, Frank experiences a stroke. And then another. After a lifetime of heavy smoking, suffering from the effects of the strokes and from depression, Frank's health continues to decline. When Norman visits the house one day, he is alarmed by

David's father's appearance. *He looks like the life has gone out of him* he thinks to himself.

Frank concurs when Eric makes the difficult decision to move him to a nursing home in nearby Texas City. Eric sells the house and uses the funds from the sale of the home to help pay for his care. David, still deeply depressed over his mother's death last November, now also faces the loss of his father and his home. Already crushed by his mother's death, he'll find no more solace in the water. He has had to give up surfing thanks to a recent diagnosis of a perforated eardrum; the pain is there all the time, but becomes intolerable every time a wave washes over him.

Eric—acting as their father's power of attorney—starts the paperwork to legally emancipate his seventeen-year-old brother. David now has to find a way to earn some money to live. The complete freedom he often wished for has arrived and will leave him adrift for the next three years, living in his car, scrambling for work, playing harmonica, and writing songs for himself. He visits his father as often as he can.

(116, 117, 118)

## 1970 CELO, NORTH CAROLINA: NEAL HELLMAN DISCOVERS THE DULCIMER

After graduating from Lynchburg College's behavior psychology program, Neal Hellman makes his way through the Blue Ridge Mountains to Yancy County at the invitation of Fergus Pope, a medical doctor whom Neal met at Lynchburg. Pope promised him a job in a start-up program he was planning to provide rehabilitation for physically and emotionally abused children.

Upon finally making it to Celo, Neal pulls into the drive of the Popes' farm, steps out of his blue VW bug, and looks around. He notices Dr. Pope sitting up on a hill in front of the house. As he walks up to greet him, he detects a blue aura around the seated Pope; something is wrong. As he gets closer, he sees that the aura consists of hundreds of small fluttering blue butterflies. Pope looks at Neal. "I'm sorry to tell you this. The locals were dead set against this project—too many longhairs around here for their liking."

Neal is dumbfounded. He's suddenly aware that at age twenty-two, he has no Plan B for his life.

"Since you're here you can stay a while and dream but, in a month or so, you'll have to leave."

Neal asks, "Is there something I can do while I'm here?"

Scratching his head Pope replies, "Well you can paint the roof of the barn if you'd like, but, no, there's not much else to do around here."

Neal decides to make the best of the bad situation. He moves in to the large, old red barn, a stone's throw from the gurgling South Toe River. The next morning, he takes a swim, then begins the first of many hikes around the hills. He befriends several of the artists who live in the area including a retired couple from New York City who live just down the road, Rob and Barbara; Barbara gives him a standing invitation to come over every evening to make sure that he has at least one good meal a day.

One evening, Barbara shows him an unusual instrument she recently purchased from a craftsman named Edd Presnell who lives up on Beech Mountain. "Here," she hands it over to him, "it's called a dulcimer; it only has four strings, and you tune it to an open tuning. I never use it, so why don't you take it back to the barn and see if you like it?"

That night, back at the barn, he plays around with Barbara's dulcimer, picking and strumming, just to hear what he can make it do.

A week passes, then another. Every night after painting the barn, Neal retires inside to pick and strum. Finally, he tells Barbara that he has to have one. He has a few hundred dollars stashed inside his VW he'll use to pay for it. Barbara writes out instructions for how to find Presnell.

Neal is a little nervous about meeting the famous local craftsman given the feelings about the "longhairs" in the area, so he trims his beard and pulls his long hair back before embarking on the long, bumpy ride up to Beech Mountain. He needn't have worried. When he finally gets to the Presnell homestead, he's greeted by a man in his fifties with hair down his back and a beard halfway down his chest.

Presnell shows him around his workshop, and ends the tour by demonstrating the sound qualities of the various wood boards in the shop by tapping on them with his knuckles. Neal opts to order a six-string model with a walnut body and a spruce top. When he finally receives it, he discovers it has an enormous sound box and big, wooden friction pegs. It's loud and hard to tune. Neal loves it.

(119, 120, 121)

## 1970 WINTER HAVEN, FLORIDA: HERB MCCULLOUGH HAS A DREAM

Herb McCullough, an electrician and avid motocross racer, dreams of a career change. After working all day running a motorcycle and dirt bike shop in Winter Haven, he likes to return home, play guitar, and write songs. He knows several musicians in Winter Haven, so he asks for advice. "Head to Nashville," they tell him, so he travels there with his five best songs to see a publisher. He makes the rounds and is told he "has potential," but needs to move to Nashville if he hopes to launch a career. Returning home, he tries to persuade his wife to go with him, but she is dead set against leaving Winter Haven. Herb figures his dream of a songwriting career is over. In 1970, so is his marriage, when Mrs. Herb McCullough instigates a divorce.

By that point, one of Herb's high school friends had moved to Nashville and encourages him to visit. At the age of thirty, with no ties to hold him down, Herb figures he doesn't have anything to lose. He leaves for Nashville with a suitcase, his guitar, and a folder full of songs.

(122)

## 1970 THE UNITED STATES: THE NEW BOOM

By 1970, the beatniks of the fifties have mostly given way to the musicians of the sixties. Many, like the Grateful Dead, have branched out from traditional country music to add rock to their repertoire. However, the Beatniks' values—their sense of alienation, rejection of materialism, and the pursuit of spiritual enlightenment—remain. The baby-boomer hippies slip on those values like comfortable Birkenstocks.

Throughout the coming decade, countless young people will find themselves reflected in current music. On the West Coast, experimentation in sex, drugs, and rock and roll is in. On the East Coast, groups like the Highwoods String Band attract thousands of young, middle-aged, and older people alike to rediscover the great tunes collected by the old song catchers like Cecil Sharp, Dame Olive Campbell, Alan Lomax, and others.

The year 1970 will plant important seeds for a landmark album as a friendship grows between country music banjoist Earl Scruggs and John McEuen of the Nitty Gritty Dirt Band. When the young McEuen screws up the courage to ask Scruggs to record with his band, Scruggs's "yes" will have a profound effect on music lovers everywhere in the coming decades. Jean Ritchie, Joni Mitchell, the lingering influence of the Fariñas, and the rising number of young folk musicians will also make their impact: the mountain dulcimer is about to embark upon another revival and renewal by growing new roots across the country. Young folk musicians infuse the dulcimer with new energy and life as they embark on the most intensive playing of their lives and bond with each other. The seventies will give birth to a dulcimer boom.

# MOVEMENT 3:
# ODYSSEYS

....The seventies, when there was a beautiful period of peace in the culture wars, when politicos, rednecks, and hippies were sharing the dance floor and maybe even an occasional joint, all in the name of love.

—Willie Nelson, *It's a Long Story*

[The professional] understands that all creative endeavor is holy, [but] doesn't dwell on it. He knows that thinking about it too much will paralyze him, so, instead, he concentrates on technique. The professional masters how, and leaves what and why to the gods.

—Steven Pressfield, *The War of Art*

## 1971 LA MARQUE, TEXAS: "YOU OUGHT TO BE A DULCIMER PLAYER"

Always worried about his son's future, his father feels a sense of relief when David tells him he intends to take the state GED test to obtain his high school equivalency certificate and enroll at Sul Ross to study journalism in the fall. Obtaining his diploma is a mere formality for David; his natural intellect, past study habits, and love of reading will enable him to pass the test easily.

While he preps for the exam, he mentions to an instructor that he wants to find a stringed instrument to play to help him write songs. "You know, David," she tells him, "you ought to be a dulcimer player" and she hands him a dulcimer catalogue. He flips through it but isn't sure what a dulcimer is, so he sets the catalogue aside.

(1, 2)

## 1971 MOUNTAIN VIEW, ARKANSAS: MCSPADDEN OPENS A SHOPPE

By 1971 Lynn McSpadden, his father, his brother, and his old friend Elliott from Duke University are making dulcimers above his father's garage in Forest City, Arkansas. They can hardly keep up with the demand and so begin planning for their new company: McSpadden Mountain Dulcimer Shoppe. Lynn has his eyes on the small town of Mountain View in the Ozarks with its nickname, the "Folk Capital of America" due to the great concentration of traditional music and crafts in the area. His intuition will serve him well. However, he assesses the dulcimer as a simple, quiet instrument, fretted with a noter on two strings: "It's an instrument, because of its restrictions, that is not suited to a rock band .... Because it isn't played in major keys, it will probably remain free from corruption."

McSpadden will have to revise this overall assessment of the instrument's potential in the coming years thanks in good part to David's input.

(3,4)

## 1971 BOULDER, COLORADO: BONNIE CAROL

At age four, Bonnie Carol began playing the piano somewhat haphazardly on her own. She would accompany her talented mother on the piano (whether her mother wanted to be accompanied or not). Bonnie grew up on the King Ranch in Texas with a natural talent for music. By college, she knew how to play the guitar. However, music was only one of her many interests in life, so, she opted to pursue a degree in psychology. She moved to Colorado and formed a relationship with an esteemed guitar maker named Max Krimmel.

Max senses the dulcimer is experiencing a new resurgence in interest thanks to the growing folk movement, so he makes a fretted dulcimer for Bonnie for Christmas. With her natural curiosity and music background, Bonnie is delighted with her new instrument and quickly learns to play it, just as Max had hoped.

After funding cuts in the mental health field, Bonnie loses her job working for a state mental hospital. "Maybe you could make dulcimers for a living," Max suggests, and he offers to teach Bonnie to build a dulcimer. The dulcimer isn't just another instrument to Bonnie; but because Max had made one for her, she is intrigued. She takes him up on the offer and discovers she has a talent for it and enjoys building the instrument. She joins Max in his workshop, makes a few instruments, and sells them. Gradually she builds her reputation as a luthier, performer, and teacher; in effect, she becomes one of the rare women in a woodworking world dominated by men.

(5, 6, 7, 8)

## 1971 UNION GROVE, NORTH CAROLINA: A MOST FORTUITOUS ENCOUNTER

Some fifty thousand attendees flow in to the forty-fourth annual Union Grove Fiddler Convention this year. Twenty-three-year-old Robert Force from Seattle and twenty-four- year-old Albert d'Ossché from New Orleans are among them. Each believes he's the only dulcimer player there. Whether it's fate, chance, or blind luck, both manage to find the sole dulcimer builder's booth where they meet each other for the first time. They hit it off with each other and the builder, and they decide to hang out at the booth and play to help draw a crowd so the vendor can sell more dulcimers.

Al has always played sitting down with the dulcimer on his lap, eastern mountain style. He uses a traditional G-G-C tuning and creates rhythm by strumming with his right forefinger. He uses his left thumb as a noter on the melody string. Bob, on the other hand, has devised his own atypical way to hold the dulcimer: he stands and uses a guitar strap to hang the dulcimer in front of him as he would a guitar. He uses his right hand to play with an unusual, highly rhythmic overhand style of strumming. His left-hand thumb braces alongside the fretboard as he chords with his middle three fingers. He tunes his strings to "open" D-A-D tuning.

Al has a musical background in keyboards and an educated mind honed to think and analyze. Intrigued by Bob's style, Al presses him to teach him his new way of playing. Thus begins a twenty-year collaboration that starts immediately with Bob and Al playing as a duet. They will commence cowriting as well, and will publish their seminal book, *In Search of the Wild Dulcimer* in 1974.

Their collaboration will become known well enough among dulcimer players in the rest of the country to put Bob Force within David Schnaufer's sights.

(9, 10, 11, 12)

Sixteen-year old Rick Freimuth is curious. He watches the house on the cul-de-sac three doors down from his own as a new family moves into the neighborhood. Two parents and a lot of kids ... looks interesting.

Newcomers Keith and Mary Young have six children. The couple met at the University of Nebraska in the early fifties where both had been students. Mary, a student in the Food and Nutrition program, was swept away by Keith, an agricultural student who rode a motorcycle and busted broncs for fun. By senior year they married. They stayed in Nebraska until 1958 when Keith earned his master's in agricultural economics. Then they headed east. Keith found a position as a scientist in the Soil Survey Interpretations Division of the Department of Agriculture. There he will begin to make a name for himself as an expert on wetland soils.

Keith and Mary opted to move to this wooded neighborhood in Annandale—named after the River Annan in Scotland—due to its proximity to Washington, DC, where Keith works and because there are lots of potential friends in the neighborhood for their children.

As Rick watches the Youngs haul boxes from the moving van into their new home, he feels the pleasure mixed with anticipation of having new friends close to his age. After a short time observing, he overcomes his shyness and walks over to introduce himself to Mr. and Mrs. Young. He immediately decides they are nice. Fifteen-year-old Scott and fourteen-year-old Phil strike up some friendly chatter, and Rick offers to help carry boxes. He learns they have two older brothers: one is in the army, and the other is a freshman in college who will be home in a few months. Before Rick knows it, he feels part of this friendly family.

After helping all day, Rick finally returns home to tell his mom and dad all about their new neighbors. "Mr. Young is going to work in DC and their oldest son is in the army and their second oldest is away at Penn State and I met two cool kids in the family—Rick and Scott—who are close to my age, and they have two younger sisters and Mr. Young must be a musician because he carried a bunch of instruments into the house. . ."

(13, 14, 15)

## 1971 LOS ANGELES, CALIFORNIA: *BLUE*

Canadian singer-songwriter Joni Mitchell, a waif-like young woman with long, blond hair is well known throughout the United States for her exceptional songwriting and musicianship, due in no small part to Johnny Cash's early acknowledgment of her talent. After a string of successful albums, she makes her fourth, *Blue. Rolling Stone* critic Timothy Crouse outlines the main theme of the album as a chronicle of Joni, a freelance romantic, searching for a permanent love. Her line, "I am on a lonely road and I am traveling/Looking for something to set me free" resonates with many of the young hippies, rockers, and folkies in the world.

Mitchell's primary instrument is the guitar, but for the past two years she has used her dulcimer to help her write songs for *Blue.* She purchased her current, uniquely shaped dulcimer from a woman who was inspired to change careers and become a luthier after dancing in the rain while listening to Richard and Mimi Fariña perform.

During interviews, Joni explains that she didn't know anyone else who played the dulcimer when she bought it. She was told that she should lay it across her lap to play it, so, she approached it like a bongo drum. She developed a habit of slapping it and beating it as she played, adding percussion to her lilting melody.

Crouse concludes his review: "On *Blue* she uses her popular music skills along with purity, honesty and vulnerability to transform what was once folk music...[to] some of the most beautiful moments in recent popular music."

*Blue* is an instant critical and commercial success and peaks in the top twenty in the *Billboard* album charts in September. One result of *Blue's* success: interest in the Appalachian dulcimer explodes, especially among young people in their late teens, twenties, and early thirties.

(16, 17)

## 1972 ANNANDALE, VIRGINIA: KEITH AND MARY YOUNG

A year after Keith Young and his family moved in, Rick Freimuth has become a regular in their cozy home. All the neighborhood kids and teens like hanging out at their house because Keith and Mary don't talk down to them, and their house is always full of guests and music. They're welcoming, and they treat everyone, regardless of age, like equals in the great adventure of living life to the fullest.

The Youngs are strict in one sense, however: no smoking (pot or cigarettes); no underage drinking at their home. Mary checks the boys' eyes when they come in late:

Why are your eyes so red? Why are you so hungry?" They work hard to provide a wholesome environment for their brood and their friends. They make it work, and their home is filled with laughter, teens running in and out, and frequent conversations on worthy topics.

Mary's kindness draws the neighborhood kids like a magnet, and they dub her "Ma Young." The older kids forsake the "Mr. Young" address and call him Keith without dropping the respect. Mary and Keith possess the special quality of having both high standards and high affection for young people. In their home, everyone feels important. Ma Young always has an endless supply of homemade cookies for those who are hungry. At dinner time, she always makes room at the table for one or two more and plenty of lively conversation. Mary's day off for cooking dinner is Sunday; she leaves a buffet of popcorn, cheese and crackers, and pickles for the young people to help themselves to. Keith and Mary's enthusiasm for life and their willingness to take anyone and everyone under their wings nourish the neighborhood kids' energetic minds and spirits.

Rick quickly becomes intrigued by Keith's hobbies as a luthier and his ability to play just about any instrument. Keith, who had made his first dulcimer from a kit he bought in Knoxville, Tennessee, now makes guitars and dulcimers after work to help earn college money for his kids. He invites his bandmates from the Front Porch String Band over at least once a week to jam in his living room while Mary sits in her chair and sews quilt squares together. Acoustic instruments hang on the walls and are propped up in stands all over the Youngs' sunny living room: dulcimers, guitars, an autoharp, a full-size harp, a massive bass, and a piano. David Young (now home for the summer), his brothers

Phil and Scott, and friend Rick frequently pick up an instrument and strum, even when Keith isn't home. Later, younger sisters Barb and Liz will do the same.

Rick and David always gravitate to the dulcimers. As a result, Keith offers to teach them some basic tunes before his regular jam sessions with his band. At first, he demonstrates Jean Ritchie style with a noter so the teens learn how to use the dulcimer as a rhythm instrument. As they follow Keith, they pick up the simple, traditional tunes first, such as "Boil Them Cabbage," "Old Joe Clark," and "Cripple Creek." That's all it takes; they play every chance they get, teaching each other by ear when they are alone,

jamming along with Keith and his band, or with other friends to learn new tunes. The Front Porch band members are delighted by the teens' interest in string band music and enthusiastically support their efforts. Often, family friend Maddie MacNeal and neighbor Ralph Lee Smith stop by and play their dulcimers with the band as well.

Keith begins inviting his son and Rick to his basement workshop to learn the art and craft of making instruments. They study him and the meticulous way he measures each piece of wood for the guitar or the dulcimer. They note the care with which he saws the tops and the backs for dulcimer sound boxes.

After a suitable period of observing, Keith pays them to start cleaning up the sawdust and the shop after each evening's work. When he feels they're ready, he teaches them how to use the band-saw to saw out the smaller parts for the dulcimers he builds and sells. Rick and David decide it's a good deal. They're getting paid for what they would do for free, just to hang with Keith in the workshop.

(18, 19, 20)

---

## What is a "Noter"?

A noter is any short, smooth piece of wood or other material, held in the dulcimer player's left hand between the thumb and first two fingers and used to fret the instrument. Over the years, people have used all kinds of objects as noters to fret strings on a dulcimer, the index finger probably being the first. Players used everything from wooden dowels, chopsticks, popsicle sticks, metal rods, and handcrafted noters to fret. The noter is always placed in the space between two frets, usually in the middle of the space, or closer to the left of the fret to the right to avoid string buzz.

Thanks to Jean Ritchie's influence, most players who began playing the dulcimer in the seventies started by playing with a noter; it's one reason for the dulcimer's reputation as a simple instrument to play. Unlike newcomers to the guitar, those who play with a noter don't have to fret across the strings to play simple songs.

---

## 1972 NEW YORK CITY: WILL THE CIRCLE BE UNBROKEN

By now, twenty-year old Vince Farsetta is a self-taught musician who plays multiple instruments including a pretty mean guitar and a Mali African bass with three strings. He hitchhikes to Morgantown in search of more musical good times and finds plenty of them via the old-timers he meets; their stories, songs and skillful playing are endlessly fascinating to him. When his money finally runs out, he calls home to ask his dad to come to get him.

Upon their return to New York, Vince gets a job at the post office. One day he sees an ad for banjo lessons "in the old time mountain style." He had spent lots of time with fiddlers and banjo players in Morgantown, and concluded that the banjo is a really neat thing. New York is full of guitar and bass players, but nobody is playing the banjo. Vince works at the post office for a few more months and then moves on to work for the electrician's union, saving his money for his next instrument.

One evening, Vince listens, enthralled, to the Nitty Gritty Dirt Band's new triple LP—their seventh—entitled *Will the Circle Be Unbroken*. "I was into the melody and the dancing rhythm; it was almost like a mantra," he will share later. Vince's mind is like a sponge—his head is already brimming with his parents' and grandparents' music; with mainstream and underground rock and roll, and with West Virginia's traditional music. Both the sojourn to Morgantown and the *Will the Circle Be Unbroken* album have introduced him to a whole new musical world in which young musicians play alongside old-time master players to make music together. The album cover itself beckons newcomers to this world with its tag line below the title: "*Music forms a new Circle.*" *Circle* bridges the gap between generations and music cultures inside the heart of a country divided by Vietnam protests, civil rights demonstrations, and Richard Nixon, a president who is about to go off the rails.

Vince immediately connects with the band's sounds and their goal to collaborate with country music royalty like Earl and Andy Scruggs, Roy Acuff, sixty-three-year-old "Mother" Maybelle Carter, Doc Watson, Merle Travis, and many other veteran country musicians. Millions of other music aficionados are hooked, just like Vince. *Circle* soars to platinum level and introduces a whole new generation of young people to old-time music suddenly made fresh again.

Three states south of Vince, in Annandale, Virginia, Rick Freimuth listens to the *Circle* album so many times he wears it out. He and friend David Young can't stop talking about it. Neal Hellman, working as a cabdriver in New York City, loves it. And in Texas, David Schnaufer and buddy John Macrini are transfixed.

(21, 22, 23, 24, 25)

## 1972 TORONTO ISLAND, CANADA: NANCY JOHNSON

Nancy Johnson is used to taking off in her VW camper whenever she has a little cash saved up and the urge strikes her. This summer, the urge sends her to Toronto Island for the 12th annual Mariposa Music Festival. Nancy is one of some 33,000 folk music fans who attend the three-day international event with 151 different concerts and craft displays by more than 200 singers, dancers, musicians and craftsmen.

Despite the crowds, Mariposa is known for its quiet pace and "starless" system where audiences are able to watch performers from close up. Headliners can often be found within the audience to see their favorite performers. Some of the most famous musicians of the day—Bob Dylan, Gordon Lightfoot, Neil Young, and Joni Mitchell—

crash the festival this year and mingle with the crowds to listen to the performers. When invited, some of the pros even run up on the stage to perform themselves. Neil Young leads 4,000 attendees in a sing-along as Joni Mitchell looks on, standing and swaying right next to Nancy Barker, much to her astonishment.

The festival almost ends Saturday due to driving rain squalls that force crew members to unplug the electrical systems. Fortunately, breaks in the rain allow the show to go on and lead to another unexpected chance encounter for Nancy. Climbing a hill, she hears a high, lyrical voice singing "Cool of the Day," a voice that she recognizes immediately from her mother's records before she even sees the crowd of people surrounding her idol, Jean Ritchie. Nancy runs up to watch, enthralled.

Despite all the excitement generated by the unexpected appearance of so many folk superstars, Nancy's most treasured memory of the festival some fifty-plus years later will be standing on that hill, listening to Jean Ritchie singing the old songs of Appalachia. If a fortune teller told her that day that she and Ritchie were going to become good friends, she would have laughed out loud.

(26, 27)

## 1972 WASHINGTON, DC: THE HIGHWOODS STRING BAND FANS

Vince hitchhikes to Washington, DC, to catch the annual Smithsonian Folk Life Festival on the Mall. He's especially looking forward to seeing the Highwoods String Band play this year. Vince gravitates more toward acoustic music these days even as the rock and roll wave washes over the United States. For acoustic musicians, the Highwoods String Band is a must-see.

The band consists of five musicians—two playing twin fiddles, a young woman bass player, and a guitar and banjo player lately out of Ithaca, New York and Berkeley. The first notes of their energetic country music electrify the crowd. The Highwoods' musical brilliance, energy, wit, and old-time repertoire attract an unlikely audience: young folkies and hippies who dig the joyful atmosphere generated by the band and old-timers who come to listen and stomp to the music of their youth. At every Highwoods concert, people can't help themselves but jump up and dance.

The stop in Washington, DC, is just one of many they will make as they travel to major folk festivals across the U.S. (Later, they will tour in Latin America and Europe.) The band also inspires countless others, and they will have an enormous influence on future musicians. For now, they play their hearts out with intense energy, joy, and laughter to engage with their audience.

As he watches the Highwoods perform, Vince feels the impact of their music hit him like a two by four. He loves the whole package but connects the most with the banjo player, Mac Benford. Vince, already a multi-instrumentalist, is well on his way to becoming a banjo virtuoso. Many years later he will get the chance to tell Mac how his playing that day on the Mall changed his life.

Elsewhere in the crowd on a different patch of grass, David—stands on tiptoe to see over the thick crowd, his whole body moving in time with the band. The music and the musicians' witty jokes and wordplay in between their fast-paced set enthrall him.

And, in yet another spot, Rick Freimuth and the Youngs are blown away by the sheer joy of The Highwoods' music. On the way back to Annandale, Keith, his son David Young, and Rick talk nonstop of their reactions to and opinions of every moment of the concert.

(28, 29, 30)

---

*String Bands*

A string band is an old-time music or jazz ensemble made up mainly or solely of string instruments. String bands were first popular in the 1920s and 1930s and are among the forerunners of modern country music and bluegrass bands.

String bands resurged again nationwide in the sixties and early seventies thanks to the folk movement. The Highwoods were not the only string band of this time, but they were wildly popular and inspired untold numbers of young people to play guitars, banjos, fiddles, and basses.

String bands are still alive and kicking. They can be found in many parts of the country by those who know where to look. To learn more, visit: *http://stringband.com*.

To watch the same performance that Vince, Rick, and David saw that day, see Larry Edelman's excellent documentary, *Dance all Night: the Highwoods String Band Story* for free on the Folkstreams website here: *https://www.folkstreams.net/film-detail.php?id=435*

# 1973 HOUSTON, TEXAS: LIBERTY HALL

An appearance by the musician and songwriting pioneer Gram Parsons is a surefire guarantee to pack any concert hall or club. Parsons's work with the Byrds and the Flying Burrito Brothers helped usher in the folk-rock genre as well as the psychedelic era, and he is one of the earliest rockers to embrace country music.

East Coast folk musician Emmylou Harris joined Parsons and his 1973 band, The Fallen Angels, her first tour. On stage and off, the two make a charismatic couple. They exude such an energetic and intense magnetism when they appear live at Houston's Liberty Hall that the Hall's 450-person capacity is strained for all four nights of their performances. Their set list includes "Big Mouth Blues," "New Soft Shoe," "The Streets of Baltimore," and "Six Days on the Road." When they bound onto the stage, the air is electric; they are surrounded by an audience jammed full of rowdy, excited fans who have come to see the new music royalty.

Now twenty-seven and a big Parsons fan, John Lomax III is so transfixed that he attends all four shows, slowly inching his way within the crowd each night to find a space to stand. On one of those same nights, twenty-year-old David Schnaufer makes his way to Houston and pays his $3 to squeeze his way through the door and along the back wall of the standing-room only hall. By the time the show is over, he has made up his mind: he wants to connect up all the country music he has ever heard with all the rock and roll he has ever heard, become a songwriter, and learn to play a stringed instrument. When he stands up for his friend Tim's wedding a few weeks after the show, he tells him all about it: "It was country and as hip as hell!" Later in his life, David will assert that the Parsons show changed his life.

Although none of the four met that night, in another time and place David and John Lomax will form an extraordinary partnership. Emmylou Harris will ask for David to play to accompany her for a television special. Even more astonishing, one day David is going to wear the one-of-a-kind jacket from a famous garment that

Gram Parsons owned. But all these events are in the future, and none of these possibilities likely enter David's mind at Liberty Hall.

(31, 32, 33, 34, 35, 36, 37)

---

*Gram Parsons and Emmylou Harris at Liberty Hall*

You can search on YouTube for "Gram Parsons and Emmy Lou Harris at Liberty Hall 1973" to see longer clips. Unfortunately, the visual and audio quality of these clips are quite poor. Nevertheless, the excitement that Parsons and Harris generated is palpable in both clips.

---

## 1973 FINDLAY, OHIO: THE PURPOSE OF MUSIC

Now solely responsible for himself after his emancipation four years ago, David accepts his Aunt Glenda's invitation to stay with her family for the first time since the Flemings moved to Ohio. Now entering their twenties, David and Gena reconnect and grow closer as friends, given their easy rapport and similar sensitivities and values. Both have grown into highly intuitive young people who share a sense of wonder for the natural world, for music, and for learning, all of which lead to long conversations on anything and everything.

Over the course of his stay with the family, Gena is impressed by David's intellect and how knowledgeable he is about everything, especially music.

One day, Gena gets word from her friend Morgan that he's in town and is coming for a visit. When she describes Morgan to David, she mentions that he is a big fan of singer Gordon Lightfoot. Thus, David is not surprised that during their talk about music, Morgan suddenly asks them if they'd like to hear him sing a Gordon Lightfoot song. "Sure," they reply. Gena is surprised when Morgan asks to borrow a guitar; she knows that he doesn't play an instrument. Nevertheless, she retrieves her guitar and hands it to him. The cousins, curious, settle back to listen. Morgan gives the guitar a strum and starts to sing. "Oops, that doesn't sound right," he laughs, and repositions his fingers to try again. Gena looks at David, then back at Morgan who beams with joy at them as he attempts over and to work through the song. Gena and David keep straight faces, despite the fact that it quickly becomes clear that he is completely over his head musically. When finally he finishes the song, he looks up at the two cousins and exclaims, "I just LOVE Gordon Lightfoot!" Gena and David smile back and nod approvingly.

After Morgan leaves, Gena returns to the living room, wondering what David will say. The two look at each other. David, who has been thinking about music a long time, puts his hand on his knee and grins as he leans back on the sofa. "Gena, I think this man has changed my life! He doesn't care how badly he sounds; he loves what playing does for him. I have to totally rethink what music is about ... is it about skill? Is it about entertaining? Or is it about the total love for music that came out from your friend trying to play? I mean, he couldn't play or sing ... I need to rethink the whole purpose of music."

The two continue to talk about the visit, including their initial reactions to Gena's friend stumbling through the song. They agree that the joke was on them, that Morgan's joy reveals a higher truth worth noting. David concludes their discussion with the lesson he has learned: "Music shouldn't be about impressing other people with your skill; ideally, it's about expressing joy and love for the music itself."

David's thoughts resonate with Gena, and she is deeply moved by his insights resulting from an experience that others might have laughed at. She knows how precious this time is with him and treasures it.

(38)

## 1973 TEXAS CITY, TEXAS: ANOTHER DEVASTATING LOSS

Deeply depressed and missing Edith, Frank Schnaufer hangs by a thread after a lifetime of health problems that have exhausted him. Slammed by successive strokes two years ago, this latest and last stroke on June 5 sends him to a bed in Galveston County Hospital, the same hospital where his beloved Edith passed away four years ago.

A loving son to his parents May and Christian, a WWII veteran, a good husband to Edith, dear father of Eric and David, a deep thinker, a retired and meticulous insurance analyst who was fond of fishing with his late wife, of backyard astronomy, of good books, of dancing with Edith in the living room to Glenn Miller, of reading to and teaching his young sons when he was able, fifty-three-year-old Frank passes away from pneumonia four days after his final stroke.

Eric sets aside plans for his upcoming wedding and calls his aunt Glenda to relay the bad news. His aunt and uncle put David on a plane to return to La Marque. While Eric makes arrangements to bury his father, he worries constantly about the impact on his younger brother. His fear is understandable. At age twenty and crushed with depression over this latest family tragedy, David believes in his heart that his daddy grieved himself to death.

(39, 40)

## 1973 COLUMBUS, GEORGIA: ERIC AND THIELA'S WEDDING

Shortly after their father's death, Eric and David reconnect in Georgia, where Eric is about to marry his fiancée Thiela. During his visit, Thiela gets to know David; she finds him to be sweet and charming, and he begins to feel more and more comfortable with her. Impressed by his large vocabulary and his ability to converse on a wide range of topics, she enjoys talking with her new brother-in-law.

Sensing his depression over the dual loss of his parents, she helps him as best as she can by spending time with him.

Thiela's father is a retired military officer and a lawyer near Fort Benning. Upon meeting David for the first time, he sizes up the long-haired young man. Despite his first impression, he also finds him shy but friendly, easygoing, and interesting.

At the wedding, David wears the suit that he wore to his father's funeral.

.

(41, 42)

## 1973 FINDLAY, OHIO: ON THE ROAD AGAIN

After the wedding, David returns to Findlay where he will spend the remainder of the summer with his extended family. As fall approaches and Gena prepares to leave to study abroad her junior year, David tells his aunt he'll being leaving, too. He plans to return to Texas to find work and a place to live. Aunt Glenda wants him to fly back, but David insists on hitchhiking and asks her to drop him off on the freeway. She tries to talk him out of hitchhiking, but he insists it's what he wants to do.

On the morning he leaves Findlay, Aunt Glenda lectures him all the way to the freeway about the danger of hitchhiking, hoping to change his mind. Once they arrive at the freeway, she pulls off on the shoulder to let him out, giving him one last warning. "No one is going to pick you up!" David expresses his thanks and assures her she has nothing to worry about. She watches as he gets out of the car; before he even shuts the door, a semi driver having quickly sized up the situation pulls on to the shoulder of the road in front of their car. "Bye, Aunt Glenda!" David hollers as he runs off to catch his ride on the eighteen-wheeler.

(43)

# 1973 ANNANDALE, VA. TO IOWA CITY: A DEVASTATING LOSS

Having graduated high school in the spring, Rick Freimuth says goodbye to his good friends over at the Youngs' house. His family's car is packed for Arizona where Rick's parents will drop him off at college in a few days. His mom and dad feel the pangs of letting go of their son even as they are happy and proud of him. Rick is close to his parents: his mom, a music teacher, has been pleased with his playing the dulcimer at Keith's and his bandmates during their weekly jams. She also likes that he has been working with Keith in his workshop to learn how to build dulcimers. Rick's dad has spent a lot of outdoor time with Rick so can't help but feel torn by his upcoming move to college. One of his favorite memories is having brought home a Grumman canoe a few years ago to enjoy the local whitewater opportunities with Rick, and he is acutely aware of how fast time has flown since then. He takes charge of last-minute checks that the doors are locked, and the lights are on timers while Rick heads to the car with his backpack and the dulcimer he made with Keith.

The Freimuths' travel plans include a stop to stay the night at the home of Rick's Uncle Frank and Aunt Mary in Iowa City. After dinner, his uncle listens, fascinated, as Rick pulls out his dulcimer to show it to him, explaining how he came to make the instrument. His uncle's nature is to be intrigued; he is the chair of the Sociology Department at the University of Iowa and the family's historian who wrote their story in the book, *They Came From The Smoky Hill*. Rick's aunt and uncle make a huge fuss over the idea that Rick makes and plays dulcimers. They set up a microphone stand in the living room so they can record him playing as his dad takes photo after photo. By now, Rick is skilled with his rosewood noter, and everyone gets a kick out of his pick cut out from an old Clorox bottle. It's a perfectly memorable evening for Rick, his parents and his aunt and uncle.

Rick finally says good night and hits the sack so he'll wake up in time to make the early start in the morning. He falls asleep to the sound of the adults talking out in the living room.

Early the next morning, Rick slowly opens his eyes to see his father sitting on the bed staring at him, barely able to choke out the dreadful news: Rick's mother had passed away in her sleep last night.

(44)

## 1973 CLEBURNE, TEXAS: WITH A LITTLE HELP FROM JOE AND NELDA

Having heard through the grapevine that a new high school was being built in Cleburne, David hitchhikes to the job site and gets hired as a day laborer. Once he earns a little money, he buys an old bike to ride back and forth to work. As soon as he saves a little more, he buys an old beat-up blue-and-white van to live in. He finds a table to outfit the van to make it livable, using it to serve as his bed at night.

A struggling abstract artist named Joe Hobbs had noticed David walking in his neighborhood, so one day he approaches him to strike up a conversation. As they talk, Joe gets the feeling that despite his young age, David is an old soul. He invites him to his home for supper, and it doesn't take more than an hour before Joe's wife Nelda also takes to their dinner guest; she is touched by his kindness and enjoys his conversation.

Eventually, David finds a run-down rental house where he can stay. He has one chair, a pot on the old stove, and a refrigerator. He sleeps on the floor with a tiny white-and-black-spotted stray terrier christened "Zimmerman"—German for "carpenter"—perhaps a nod to David's German American grandfather and great-grandfather. Zimmerman follows him everywhere, even to Nelda and Joe's.

Nelda and Joe invite him to come over whenever he likes for one of her vegetarian meals. "David, you come over and use the bathroom or take a shower whenever you want to," Nelda offers. He takes her up on it, grateful for Nelda and Joe's hospitality.

One morning when Joe stops by his place, David regales him with a story of how Zimmerman can jump straight up in the air to grab a sandwich off the refrigerator. After he tells the story, he goes to the back door and yells outside, "Rosie! Get your wild armadillo ass back in here!" To Joe's astonishment, an armadillo waddles into the house, and a laughing David introduces them to each other.

(45, 46, 47, 48)

## 1973 CLEBURNE, TEXAS: "IT'S EASY AND IT'S HARD"

As soon as he finishes one job, David searches for another. He works as a day laborer in construction doing everything from cleanup to washing bricks to carpentry. At other times, he works demolition; when people ask him what he does, he jokes that he works in "deconstruction."

Eventually he finds steadier work in the Rangeaire Manufacturing warehouse in Cleburne. As he and coworker Jim Bentley take smoke breaks together, they quickly get to know each other. They discover they share many interests: a deep love of music, nature—one of Jim's many interests is collecting unusual rocks—and songwriting. Soon, the two spend weekends rock hunting along the Nolan and the Brazos rivers together. David particularly admires that Jim is a writer, a poet, and has a massive record collection along with an encyclopedic knowledge of music. David has been dabbling at writing lyrics since his teens, but Jim is serious; he has many musician friends and has composed for some of them.

David is a frequent visitor at the Bentleys' home, a large, turn-of-the-century house, one of the oldest in Johnson County. Jim and his parents do their best to make David feel welcome. Music is on David's mind all the time; he's looking for an instrument to help him write songs. He borrows Jim's guitar, then gets his hands on an autoharp, but neither instrument feels right. Nothing quite works to help him put the music in his mind to paper.

The two friends encourage each other to write. Each works individually after which they often meet in the large back room at Jim's house. They sit across from each other at a small desk, surrounded by tall windows and plants that filter the sunlight pouring into the room. They laugh often as they bend over their writings or have spirited talks about music. Both Jim and David are very private people, yet they are so comfortable with each other they can talk about anything, even their challenges with depression; in fact, both notice that the depression stays at bay when they are together. When they aren't talking about music, they head outside to the expansive lawn to throw frisbees, ride bikes, or head to the Brazos to canoe and search for interesting rocks. Nelda and Joe often join them.

Jim's little boy Aaron is drawn to David whenever he visits. Aaron is about the same age as David was when he learned to play the jaw harp, so one day he asks Aaron, "Would you like to learn the easiest and the hardest instrument to play?" The five-year-old nods his head up and down, so David shows him the jaw harp.

"Why is it easy and hard?"

David kneels down to look at Aaron in the eye: "It's easy, because you can make a lot of noise with it," he laughs. Then, turning solemn, he adds, "It's hard because you have to work at it to make yourself happy with songs you learn how to play."

Eventually, David saves up enough money to rent a small, spartan apartment over a garage. Later, after Jim's father passes away, Jim and his mother Millie invite David to move into their large home. Millie Bentley is charmed by David's polite ways and sense of humor and soon considers him her second son. He settles in for what he expects will be a short time. However, after catching an especially virulent bout of pneumonia, he stays a year. Milly Bentley, worried sick about him, gradually nurses him back to health.

(49, 50, 51, 52, 53, 54)

## 1973 ALPINE, TEXAS: SUL ROSS

After David recovers from pneumonia and saves up more money from his work at Rangaire, he reluctantly admits that his song-writing is not going where he had hoped. He feels he ought to do something more with his life than work temporary labor jobs, so he applies to Sul Ross State University in Alpine, some eight hours drive from Cleburne. David's parting words of encouragement to Jim mean everything to him. "Keep working on those lyrics for 'All the Good Texas Weather Has Gone to Mexico' Jim; you've got a fine song there." The two promise to stay in touch, and, with that, the man whom Jim calls his best friend bids him and Mrs. Bentley goodbye, hefts his backpack, and walks toward the highway where he hopes to thumb a ride.

No longer the clean-cut, clean-shaven David depicted in his high school sophomore photo, at age twenty, the young introvert stands out from most of his peers with his shoulder-length hair, beard, mustache, and large glasses. Every day he wears his shell necklace on a leather string around his neck, a totem from his happier, carefree times when he used to ride wave after wave in Galveston.

(55, 56)

## 1973 HARRISBURG, PA: "... LOST IN LORE AND CONJECTURE"

Chet Hines of Centerville, Ohio, is an ambitious man who makes his living as an engineer at Wright-Patterson Air Force base. His life changed when the dulcimer found him as a small boy living in the Appalachian foothills of Ohio. He had no musical instrument, so his grandpa showed him how to craft a small dulcimer out of slats from an orange crate and then make it come to life. Ever since then his hobby has been building dulcimers. His goal is to produce a copy of every dulcimer currently in existence, so he makes a copy of every dulcimer he has ever seen in homes and museums.

With an awareness of the burgeoning rise in popularity of the Appalachian dulcimer among hippies and folk musicians, Chet began writing a book to help guide them and has just sent his finished manuscript to his editor. Hines is straightforward in his advice to his readers. He asserts that master players like Jean Ritchie (whom he calls "The Grand Lady of the Dulcimore") and others are all in agreement: a player must learn simple tunes that can be sung or hummed along with playing techniques for those tunes. He suggests they fully master these tunes until the strings and fingerboard are no longer a mystery. He adds, "All we are really certain of is that the Appalachian dulcimer was made and played by the mountain people during and following the Civil War." "Other than that", he adds, "the history of the instrument is lost in lore and conjecture."

Chet's understanding of history eventually will be corrected by future scholars including Ralph Lee Smith, Keith Young's friend and neighbor. Another scholar who will correct the record will become the first and only professor of dulcimer at any institution in the world during his lifetime.

(58)

## SEPTEMBER 23, 1973, AUSTIN TEXAS: THE BIRTHDAY GIFT

Like many young Texans his age, David feels the magnetic pull of Austin, home to the University of Texas. He loves to watch the street musicians play near the university campus and whenever he visits, he hits as many music clubs as he can until his money runs out again.

It's his twenty-first birthday, and David is here to visit a friend in the city. While on a stroll down Congress Avenue, some thirty unusual instruments displayed in the window of the J. R. Music Store catch his eye. Intrigued, he decides to take a closer look. He enters and greets the clerk who approaches him. "What are those instruments you have hanging in the front window?"

The clerk explains, "They're called dulcimers. A luthier named Jeff Mink over at Renaissance Instruments in Georgetown makes them. They cost $35 and that includes a couple of lessons to get you started. Want to take a look?"

He removes one of the dulcimers from the window and hands it to him. David gently places it on the counter. Looking first at the clerk and then at the instrument, he draws the tip of his index finger toward him across the strings. The feel of the wood and the seductive, earthy sound that emanates from the strum hits him like lightning. "That's it," he thinks. "This is the mandolin, the autoharp, guitar, steel guitar, and banjo all happening at once." Never mind that it is made of paneling salvaged from an old motel; it will work as an aid to his songwriting.

Thirty-five dollars is a lot of money for David, so he tells the clerk he wants to take a walk and think about it. He walks out the door, but then stops, turns around, and walks back in.

(59, 60, 61, 62)

---

### First Dulcimer, First Influences

Jeff Mink usually built instruments such as dobros (acoustic guitars that contain a built-in resonator). Once on a summer job he had torn down an old motel and stacked the cheap paneling in his mother's garage; he figured he'd think of something to do with the it later. When she threatened to have all the wood hauled out, he decided to make dulcimers out of it, perhaps aware of the growing interest in fretted dulcimers triggered by Joni Mitchell and the burgeoning folk movement.

The dulcimer David bought was unusual to say the least. It did have a raised finger board, but the frets were made out of fishing line wrapped around and knotted, "like a lute" he told a friend, adding "I [understood] do, re, mi, fa, so, la, ti,

---

do because of my [harmonica] playing...but [it] had many strange extra frets..."

David did take two lessons at the dulcimer store to get started; his instructor encouraged him: "Man, you can play this thing!"

David's ear benefitted from two pieces of great timing in 1973: first, Roger Nicholson's *Nonesuch for Dulcimer* had just been released. Shortly after buying his dulcimer, David discovered Nicholson, Britain's foremost fretted dulcimer player. Nicholson had taught guitar in the sixties at Cecil Sharp House, the home of the folk song collector. After encountering a dulcimer at a folk festival at Loughborough University, it became his instrument of choice. It featured a number of Nicholson's compositions, including a requiem for the instrumentalist Richard Fariña. Roger Nicholson was one of the earliest of many to inspire David's playing, and he set a high bar for others, whether the traditional players of the East Coast or the contemporary players out West. "I tried to show all the different styles and sounds you can get with the instrument," Nicholson once explained. These ranged from the baroque to more traditional drone-based pieces, reflecting modal and Eastern influences. Britain's *The New Musical Express* called the *Nonesuch* album "a double triumph, completely contemporary in spirit."

The second piece of good luck for David arrived came straight from Appalachia. A family living a hardscrabble life in Virginia had released their first album of music just the year before that featured the dulcimer. *Mountain Dulcimer Galax Style: Bonnie Russell and The Russell Family,* while light years away from Nicholson's style, became equally important to David's development as a player in the coming years.

Two years later, when David buys his second dulcimer, he will sell his first to a girlfriend. Later, when he begins collect-

> ing dulcimers, he will try to find her to buy it back, but by
> then she is nowhere to be found.
>
> (63, 64)

## 1973 ALPINE, TEXAS: THE EDUCATION OF A DULCIMER PLAYER

Over the next three weeks, during breaks in and between classes at Sul Ross, David explores his dulcimer with an intense focus. He is delighted that he can produce a melody from it as easily as he used to do on the harmonica with friends John and Terry.

David has no understanding yet of the dulcimer's history and is unfamiliar with the traditional songs of Appalachia. As soon as he starts tinkering around, he realizes that it's the instrument he had seen in his GED instructor's catalogue two years ago. And it dawns on him that this must be the instrument he heard on the Stones song, "Lady Jane." Therefore, beginning with what he knows, he starts by mentally binding fret sounds to frets, gradually working out the "Lady Jane" melody. He strums with his right hand, working on one short phrase at a time, over and over, sliding the noter in his left hand up and down the melody string. Without any formal music training, he focuses on everything the dulcimer yields under his hands, listening for sounds and rhythms that resonate and those that don't.

He had tried playing guitar before, so he approaches his new dulcimer with that experience in mind. First, he finds an armless chair to give the dulcimer some breathing room and his arms some freedom of movement. Next, instead of placing the instrument flat on his lap, Jean Ritchie style, he imagines it like the guitar, so he tilts it up slightly by laying the edge of the lower *bout* (the widest part of the soundbox) on his right thigh, letting the top edge lie against the center-right bottom of his rib cage. The problem: with this unusual placement, he has to hunch over uncomfortably to see the fretboard, and his left arm and hand are in such an awkward position that it's difficult to slide a noter all the way up to the top fret. He tries repositioning the instrument, finally settling on a way to brace it so that he can hold it lightly but without it moving: he angles the dulcimer by keeping the lower bout closest to his body while shifting the fretboard down a little toward his left knee. He immediately notices a bonus with this position: the tone is slightly louder and clearer because the soundbox isn't muffled by the tops of his thighs.

The dulcimer teeters a bit when he strums it, so he finds a piece of thin rubber to place underneath the bout that rests on the top of his right thigh. Good; it keeps the dulcimer from moving.

Almost there.

Except his feet don't feel right flat on the floor, so he continues to experiment with positioning his legs. He tries moving his feet in small, incremental positions until he finally finds the sweet spot that works for him: maintaining the angle of the instrument tilted slightly against him and across his lap, he lays his left foot on its outer edge, and places his right foot on top of his left. This new foot position and his open knees form a triangle that cradles the dulcimer. His feet enable him to have a fixed point to balance the whole. He's comfortable, and the dulcimer feels and sounds the best to him. When he sits on a wood chair with a stretcher between the two front legs, he feels even better when he places his right heel on the stretcher and his left foot flat on the floor, toes pointing parallel with the fretboard. With this increase in height, the dulcimer feels perfectly secure.

Within a few days, he can't tear himself away from the dulcimer. He builds toward "Lady Jane," then "Ruby Tuesday," then "As Tears Go By" every morning before his classes. He listens to dulcimer music and explores the instrument again every afternoon and evening when he returns. Again, recalling the guitar, he tries making chords instead of using the noter to see what that sounds like. It intrigues him like a puzzle when he can't get the entire song out at once. He calls Eric. "I don't know what to do with it," he tells his brother during a phone call. "I don't know how to tune it or anything." He hitchhikes to visit Dennis and Thiela in Columbus, eager to show them what he's learning.

Eric knows nothing about dulcimers but does have experience with other instruments including the guitar. He shows him how to tune it with the tuning pegs, and shares some tips he knows from his guitar playing.

At Sul Ross, David's education takes a turn. He finds himself walking up the hill every day to class, but then turning around and running back down to explore his new instrument. He feels compelled to spend every waking minute teaching himself to make music with the help of Jean Ritchie's *Dulcimer Book* and others that he finds. He absorbs what he learns from the books and listens over and over to the Russells' and Roger Nicholson's albums, trying to reproduce what he hears. He's excited and curious to find others who play.

After two months at Sul Ross, the dulcimer has seduced him completely. He leaves college to hit the road and learn everything he can from other players. He is determined to learn how to play it well. His first real accomplishment happens one night while he is living in his old station wagon, trying to tune it himself. Finally, as he turns the tuning pegs bit by bit, he recognizes the sound he is listening for when he picks the string: "Okay, so this is what tuning is."

(65, 66, 67)

### The Harmonica/Dulcimer Connection by John Macrini

Throughout his life, David often asserted, "There's an instrument out there for everyone; you just have to find it." His years of harmonica playing in his youth had a direct impact on his search. So, how did his experience of being skilled on the harmonica lead him to feel the dulcimer was the instrument for him? It turns out that dulcimers and harmonicas have several characteristics in common. David's buddy John Macrini explains: "The harmonica is a good entry instrument to learn how to play music. David and I both had a Hohner C-Signature harmonica: when we blew through the comb, it played a C chord, and when we "drew on it"—sucked air through it—we made a G chord. And if we wanted a D chord, we slid the harmonica all the way over to the bottom note on the comb, and there was the D. Those chords allowed us to play along to just about any rock and roll record or song on the radio."

Since the clerk showed David how to play the dulcimer with a noter fretting only one string while strumming across all three strings, David recognized immediately that the chords were built into the instrument itself, just like in a harmonica. The action of strumming, often directed by teachers to students as an "out-in-out-in" strum even today, shares another similarity to harmonica playing: the rhythmic of blowing and drawing: "in-out-in-out."

John adds, "Another thing the two instruments have in common is that they lend themselves to a wide variety of music genres: rock and roll, folk, country and western, even classical." Once, David shared one of master harmonica player John Sebastian's classical music albums with his cousin Gena, surprising her that the harmonica could be used beyond the typical rock and folk music. Most importantly, David never had preconceived notions about any instrument's limitations.

"He also didn't have to read music or understand music theory to play, either. With enough listening, players who don't read music first learn to play by ear. The notes run in a sequence and correspond to specific pitches within a key."

In other words, David's harmonica experiences primed him perfectly to become a dulcimer player.

(68)

# 1973 GEORGETOWN, TEXAS: CRASH

One day, Eric hears an unexpected knock on the front door. Opening it, he sees David, deathly sick from a major case of the flu. After talking with his brother, Eric believes that he may be on the verge of a nervous breakdown. Despite his focus on the dulcimer, the loss of his parents and his sense of being adrift have overwhelmed him. Eric and Thiela persuade him to stay so he can recover enough from the flu to begin therapy to help alleviate the depression. Once he begins to recover, David, formally drops out of Sul Ross, looks for construction work, and will eventually get his own apartment in Georgetown for the time being.

(69, 70, 71, 72)

# 1973 NASHVILLE, TENNESSEE: JOHN LOMAX III DISCOVERS MUSIC CITY

Having left the library world and hankering for the music business, John Lomax III explores his options. He visits New York and Los Angeles but doesn't feel like either city is a good fit for him. Then he visits Nashville.

Shortly after his arrival, John feels like he has gone back in time to the Houston of the '50s. Nashville has many of the same attributes John knew in Austin: it is a growing state capital, has a regional air center, and is the home of a major university, Vanderbilt. Like Austin, a river runs through Nashville: the Cumberland. He quickly notes an unusual Nashville feature: unlike most cities, Nashville is served by three interstate routes: I-40 (east-west), I-65 (north-south) and I-24 (northwest-southeast). This fortuitous placement joins Nashville to thirteen major cities within three hundred miles. If a 550-mile circle is drawn with Nashville at the center, the circle encompasses twenty-two states. The importance of this placement isn't lost on John who is most interested in working in the music industry; musicians and performers (and the writers who write about them) have relatively easy access to 950,000 square miles of some 80 million

Americans. The 50,000 watt WSM radio carries *The Grand Ole Opry* radio program, and the satellite-fed Music Country Network facilitates business and music promotion within this huge circle.

To John, the move to Nashville makes perfect sense. He doesn't have to leave behind his family's legacy, or his large circle of friends and musician contacts. It means he can utilize his broad and deep understanding of music history and genres to contribute to Nashville's identity as a world center of popular music.

(73, 74)

## 1973 ANNANDALE, VIRGINIA: "WEREN'T YOU AFRAID I WAS GOING TO ROB YOU?"

One afternoon, Mary Young sees a teenager walking down the street with a dulcimer strapped to his back. The hitchhiker stops by their house to ask if he might have a glass of water. He explains he's on his way to a nearby folk music festival. Mary invites him in and fixes him a plate. Shortly after the famished young man finishes his dinner, Keith sits down with him, and the two end up talking until long after dark. Mary asks the visitor, "Where are you going from here? Where are you going to sleep?" He tells the couple he's not sure, so they invite him to stay the night in the extra bed in their basement. But first, Mary insists that he call his mother to let her know where he is.

As Mary serves breakfast the next morning, the visitor asks her, "Why did you let me stay here? Weren't you afraid I was going to rob you?" Keith and Mary just smile at him and send him on his way with a pat on the back.

That young man is one of the first of many, many traveling musicians who will hear about Keith and Mary's hospitality by word of mouth. Young people on their way to music festivals will show up at their door in search of these welcoming people who share their joyful, boisterous home, a warm meal, and a soft bed where visitors can lay their heads. It won't be long before such word of mouth about Keith and Mary Young reaches David.

(75)

## 1973 NASHVILLE, TENNESSEE: AN ABUNDANCE OF OPPORTUNITIES

John moved to Nashville thanks to the exciting feel of the city and the abundance of opportunities in the music business. Two factors facilitate his new life as a Nashville insider: one is his friendship with the talented musician and songwriters Guy and Susanna Clark, both of whom he knew back in Texas and who moved to Nashville two years ago. The other is getting hired by Jack "Cowboy" Clement.

Many of Nashville's musicians and aspiring singers and songwriters find themselves at the Clark home, a central gathering place for socializing, song-sharing sessions, for seeking advice and making connections. It is his considerable writing skills and friendship with the Clarks and Townes Van Zandt that provide John with instant access to this circle of artists making waves in Nashville.

Music producer Jack Clement hires John immediately for his publicity company, Information Services, Inc., right across the street from Clement's studio. John hits the ground running, doing everything from writing artist profiles to creating and sending out tour preps. During the few breaks he has, he walks across the street to the studio to watch Van Zandt record his seventh album.

Townes is now at the height of his career as a preeminent songwriter. He is widely respected in Texas and in Nashville by his peers, although he is not as well known outside music circles as some of those peers. His poetic lyrics and magnetic personality notwithstanding, recognition on the national stage has been elusive in part due to neglect of the business side of his career and dodgy management

His situation is not helped by his battles with his own personal demons. Suffering from manic depression and addictions to alcohol and to various hard drugs, Van Zandt has completed his latest album, *Live at the Old Quarter*, but it hasn't been released because his record company ran out of money.

John listens and he watches. He is dismayed that such a lyrical genius—a composer and musician held in the highest esteem among the tight group of songwriters in Nashville and Texas—doesn't get his music promoted to a wider audience.

(76, 77)

## 1974 COLUMBUS, GEORGIA: RESHAPING EXPECTATIONS

Eric Schnaufer has been assigned a position as the new associate rector of Trinity Episcopal Church in Columbus. When Eric and Thiela move to Georgia, David stays behind in Georgetown.

Trinity is a large parish with a wealthy and conservative congregation. Once again, he faces the challenge of getting to know a new church in order to weigh expectations—his own and those of his congregation—and how to balance the differing expectations to design his approach for leadership. Parishioners expect Eric to lead, but he believes strongly in the need to balance the top-down hierarchy that they expect with his own desire to implement more of a partnership between himself and the parishioners in the running their church. The health of his church requires he make that balance happen.

(78)

The Ozark Folk Center opens in May 1973 with a mission to promote pioneer crafts and songs that predate 1941, the year "Texas Troubador" Ernest Tubb sang the first modern country music song, "Walking the Floor Over You." The Center periodically offers classes in fiddle, guitar, and the mountain dulcimer, a well-beloved instrument in this part of the country. Thousands of old-time music fans head to Arkansas every year to explore the family-friendly Folk Center and the surrounding state park.

Construction stops during the Texas rainy season in April and May, allowing David to hitchhike to Mountain View to take a dulcimer class at the center. After class he strolls down the road to a store he noticed on the way to the center: Lynn McSpadden's Dulcimer Shoppe. Now one of the most successful dulcimer shops in the country, McSpadden's luthiers make fretted dulcimers to sell on site and to ship all over the country due to their quality dulcimers at a range of prices to fit every budget.

Saleswoman Jean Simmons greets David as he enters the store. Jean grew up singing and playing traditional music. After taking just a few dulcimer lessons at the Ozark Folk Center down the road, her playing skills took off. She has many responsibilities at the shop: working the cash register, stocking the gift shop, maintaining the displays, and packing up dulcimers for shipment. When customers express an interest in buying a dulcimer, Jean demonstrates on the first instrument that catches their eye by playing it. She explains that the dulcimer's wood will determine to some extent how the instrument sounds, since the wood that the luthier uses to build a dulcimer helps determine the tone of the music it produces. A dulcimer made of cherry wood, for example, will release a brighter sound than one made of black walnut or maple. So Jean always plays three or four different instruments to help the customers recognize "the one." Since many dulcimers in the store look similar to the untrained eye, it is the sound that helps the potential buyer select his or her instrument; sound is everything.

Jean's daughter Pam works at the shop during summers off from high school and works so closely with her mother that she could also run the retail shop if she had to. Just like her mother, Pam plays the dulcimer and loves the old-time style of music. Whether customers are brand new to the dulcimer or seasoned players, Jean and Pam enjoy helping them all.

Jean offers to help David find "the one" for him. As he studies the dulcimers all around him, he realizes that the dulcimer he bought at J. R. Music was of poor quality—a McSpadden, with its handcrafted body, costs about $80.

Once Jean hands David an instrument to try out, he immediately hears the difference between the McSpadden and his. He notices its gleaming finish and the real frets. Their placement looks much more accurate than those on his dulcimer. As he starts to play it, he feels how much easier it is to fret; all this instrument requires is a light touch. "Action," Jean explains, "is the distance between the string and the fret underneath it. If distance is too high, a player's fingers have to push the strings down too far before they come into contact with the fret. High action makes it awkward to play and slows a player down. When the action is too low, string buzzing occurs during the playing. McSpadden's dulcimers have perfect action.

After trying out various models, he eventually settles on an hourglass dulcimer with traditional heart sound holes. David immediately falls in love with it—the sound and feel are above and beyond what he is accustomed to, and it's beautiful.

As they converse, Jean feels a growing rapport with this thin, scruffy young man with his shy smile and mannered way. David, too, senses she is a kind person inside, and not just because he is a customer. Later that day, he feels the same way about her daughter Pam when Jean introduces them to each other over the dinner table. Pam loves his warm, spunky nature and how easily he makes her laugh.

After dinner, the three sit on the front porch so David can play his new dulcimer with them. In between songs, Jean passes along bits of history of the dulcimer, where the traditional songs originated and stories of the people who carried them on the move from the Appalachians to Arkansas. She teaches him the importance of tone and dynamics (when to play softer in a song, when to play louder), and shows him how to play historic tunes like "Bonaparte's Retreat" and "Ragtime Annie." Jean and Pam use noters to fret, but they notice David is already forming chords on the dulcimer. Jean is always encouraging, so David feels right at home. After spending countless hours with professional and talented players, many years hence he'll assert that "[Jean] is still the smoothest dulcimer player I've ever heard." Before long, Jean and Pam consider him one of their family.

David will return again and again to Mountain View over the next twenty years, sometimes to take classes, and eventually to teach classes at the Folk Center. He and Lynn McSpadden will become close friends and collaborators. David will help Lynn troubleshoot design challenges, and eventually the two will work together to design David's own line of dulcimers. Every time he returns, he lets Jean know he's on his way into town, and she always welcomes him with open arms. It doesn't matter if it is a whole year from the last time they had seen David; the three of them pick up right where they left off at the last visit. Pam grows to love him like a brother. Whenever they reconnect, Jean fusses over David and shares her pride in him and how his playing gets better and better each time they play together. Jean's motherly love for David will last until the end of her life.

(79, 80, 81, 82, 83)


## 1974 WEST VIRGINIA: ALAN FREEMAN

For Brooklyn-born guitarist Alan Freeman, music is his raison d'être: listening to it, analyzing and theorizing about it, and especially performing it in front of audiences. His eclectic tastes range from Belgian-born Romani-French jazz guitarist Django Reinhardt to Doc Watson, the American singer, composer, and guitarist of the blues, bluegrass, folk, country, and gospel; from rising star and dobro master Jerry Douglas to the Grateful Dead. He listens to jazz records from the thirties and forties; swing, Dixieland, fiddle tunes, guitarist and mandolinist Norman Blake, and he loves Fariña's music. He absorbs it all and can call up any musical reference in a snap.

In 1961 he left the New York folk scene to live, travel, and play guitar all over the United States and Spain, making "decent basket money" as he puts it. But recently, someone stole his guitar. Despite his pride at being a guitarist, upon reflection he admits to himself he was never satisfied with his playing. When asked whom he really admires, he replies, "Richard Fariña. I not only really want to sound like Fariña, but to *be* Fariña."

On his way to Colorado to visit friends, he passes through West Virginia where he is captivated by the rich musical heritage of the state. Another Alan—Alan Lomax—once described West Virginia as "the mountain melting pot where the traditions of northwest Europe coalesced between the middle 1700s and the early 1800s ... with the Scots-Irish arrival"

Freeman is transfixed by the descendants of Appalachian pioneers he meets. They still play the fiddle and banjo tunes (the latter first learned by their ancestors from blackface minstrels who had learned them from slaves), British Isles ballads, shape-note songs of the Baptists, and the music of the post–Civil War arrival of African Americans who came to work on the railroads and in the mines. They play bluegrass, country and western music, and swing, all melding under the rubric of "traditional American music."

Freeman never makes it to Colorado; instead, he decides to stay in West Virginia for its music culture. He buys a small farm in Grantsville, "two hours from the nearest four-lane and five miles from the nearest town" in the thickly forested hills outside Charleston, W. Va. When incredulous friends back in New York City ask, "Why West Virginia?" he tells them: "There's no reason to leave here. I've got the best musicians in the world to play with; I'd be silly not to try and play with them, and they let me."

Now without his guitar, he digs through moving boxes to find the fretted dulcimer he bought two years ago on a whim. He assesses it with new eyes and decides it's an instrument brimming with potential for the person who knows what to do with it. For the next three years, he will play it every free moment on his eleven-acre homestead and at festivals and contests. He will grow his family with his wife Carol and cultivate large patches of marijuana in the sunlight between the trees.

(84, 85, 86, 87, 88, 89, 90)

## JANUARY 1975, BANGOR, MAINE: *THE DULCIMER PLAYERS NEWS*

From his RFD2 mailing address Philip Mason issues the first issue of his hand-typed love letter to the "fretted plucked dulcimer" and titles it *The Dulcimer Players News* (TDPN). He writes that his mission is "to provide a flow of information on all phases of the plucked dulcimer, both traditional and contemporary" and promises to provide his readers a trial period of one year to discover if there is interest among all those who "share a love for the dulcimer."

TDPN's first issue consists of seven 8 x 11 1/2 sheets folded in half for a total of fourteen pages. His content includes single-spaced, hand-typed news, discographies, bibliographies, articles on technique, the "new" 6 1/2 and 13 1/2 frets that luthiers are adding to their dulcimers, two songs ("Buck-eyed Jim" and "Cumberland Gap"), a poem ("The Lost Chord"), and a builder's page. Mason decorates the pages with hand-drawn illustrations of sound holes, fretboards, and dulcimer external anatomy. He invites readers to send in four dollars for a year's subscription (one issue per month) and assures them that he will accept no paid advertising. Everyone who has something to say about the dulcimer is welcome to contribute so that future issues will contain subjects of interest to readers. He also confesses he depends on readers' word of mouth to spread the news of his new publication, "Just like the old folk tradition."

Mason courts one of the first subscriptions to TDPN by sending a complimentary copy to Ralph Lee Smith of Washington, DC.

Before becoming Keith and Mary Young's neighbor and good friend, Smith lived for a time in New York's Greenwich Village, the epicenter of the folk revival in the fifties and early sixties. Ralph saw Jean Ritchie perform there, and became so enchanted with the dulcimer that he bought one and taught himself to play. Because he attended that Ritchie performance, Smith's world would revolve around the dulcimer for the rest of his life. He has already begun indulging his passion for researching the history of fretted dulcimers.

Such is the power of this humble instrument.

(91)

## 1975 WEST VIRGINIA: ALAN FREEMAN SETTLES IN

Harry Beall decides his new neighbor is a whole different animal, and he doesn't much like him.

Harry's wife had made friends with the Freemans first, then took Harry over to introduce her husband to them. When they return home, Harry tells his wife he's never going back to that house. "Alan backed me in the corner, his finger right in my face and gave me a whole lecture on his outlook on life. Then he tells me, 'That's the way I think about it, and if you don't like you can go home.'"

"I'm never going back to that house, I tell you."

But Harry, a guitar player and songwriter, does return and learns that that's just the way Alan is; he unloads on you, and, if you come back, you're pretty cool as far as he is concerned. Eventually Harry and Alan become the best of friends.

Harry is more into contemporary folk and rock, but Alan impresses him with his utter devotion to the dulcimer and the wide repertoire of music he explores with it. Alan plays with everyone, all the time: with bluegrass guys like the McCumbers Brothers, the old- time fiddle players who make their way out of the mountains for the festivals, and with any strangers he meets who happen to be musicians. He's good, and he knows it. The old timers overlook his aggressive New York City personality and outsider status. This loud, brash, young Brooklynite is an oddity in these parts——but he's loved for his extraordinary playing and interest in the local scene.

(92)

## 1975 NASHVILLE, TENNESSEE: JOHN LOMAX III

After working with Townes Van Zandt, Cowboy Clement brings another Texan named Don Williams to Nashville to write and record songs. Williams started his career as the lead singer of the country-folk group the Pozo-Seco Singers, and he finds his experience at JMI ("Jack Music Incorporated") a welcome one. Clement created the little independent label to compete with the majors. As a result of Williams's success, JMI is suddenly going strong. John Lomax moves from the publicity department to the record company where he learns more of the music business as he helps Don's career by doing a little bit of everything that needs to be done to promote the singer.

John learns that Jack's blossoming business empire consists of several locations in Nashville. He owns two state-of-the-art recording studios on Belmont Boulevard, Jack Clement Recording Studios, and Jack's Tracks. He owns the publicity company Information Services, and another operation working out of his house. He also rents four side-by-side and back-to-back apartments at a place called the Hobbs House. The Clement world is a beehive of activity, and John learns everything he can about the Nashville music business in Cowboy Clement's orbit.

(93)

## 1975 BANGOR, MAINE: CALLING ALL "FRIENDS OF MODES AND 'DULCIMERIE'..."

Phil Mason sends out the third volume of *The Dulcimer Players News* with a special feature listing over a hundred publications related to the fretted dulcimer that cover a wide range of topics. One of the most well known, newer books on the list is *In Search of the Wild Dulcimer* by Robert Force and Al d'Ossché.

This issue also includes an advertisement that invites readers to attend a new festival that Force and d'Ossché dreamed up. Given the scarcity of festivals dedicated solely to dulcimer players, the two decided to create one. They invite musicians and amateur musicians across the country to attend the "Kindred Gathering," and its heart will be attendees playing with each other rather than performing. Now, they are about to realize their dream this coming August.

Bob and Al's advertisement describes the festival's target audience: "... friends of modes and 'dulcimerie' to be held on the central Washington Coast at an artist crafting guild called Alexander's by the Sea." In keeping with the times, everyone is welcome, and admission is free. They hope everyone will pitch in, and, as it turns out, they will and then some.

(94)

## 1975 NASHVILLE, TENNESSEE: THE MURAL

Artist Thomas Hart Benton has finished his mural commissioned by Nashville's Country Music Hall of Fame and Museum. Opened in 1967, the museum is one of the world's largest and most active popular music research centers and the world's largest repository of country music artifacts.

The six-by-ten-foot mural reflects the various cultures that have contributed to country music as represented by depictions of singers, dancers, a choir, fiddlers, a banjo player, and Tex Ritter on guitar.

An old-time steamboat and a train pass by the dynamic musical groups in the foreground. Prominent at the lower left of the mural is a woman in a long, flowing skirt playing the fretted dulcimer, a bit of irony given that the instrument is mostly unknown and unused in Nashville at this time; few professionally trained musicians know about it, and those who do tend to dismiss it.

Thousands of country music fans will trek to the museum every year and pass by Benton's mural that will be displayed prominently in the grand stairwell. It is Benton's last gift to the world. At the age of eighty-five, he dies of a heart attack as he reviews the mural before sending it off to its new home.

(95)

## 1975 IDLEWILD, CALIFORNIA: ENVISIONING A NEW MEMBER OF THE FAMILY

Doug Thomson had played folk guitar for years and later picked up the banjo. Once, while on vacation at Lake Hemet in Southern California, he stopped by the Mountain Music Store in nearby Idlewild where he discovered the dulcimer. He fell in love with the sound and bought himself one. In turn, he became a luthier and started making dulcimers, fixing people's banjos as a side career and selling his instruments at folk festivals up and down California.

This year, on another trip to a music store, he discovers a Bacon & Day banjo hanging on the wall. The Bacon & Day Banjo Company made high-end banjos during the early twentieth century's Jazz Age and were elaborately decorated with gold plating, engraving, and ebony and ivory. Their quality, flamboyant looks, and exquisite sound meant they were in great demand by discriminating professionals on stage. Their top end model cost $1000 at a time when a worker's yearly wage might be $300.

This particular instrument is out of Doug's price range at $2000. But as a luthier and musician, he can't pass up the opportunity to try it. The banjo yields gorgeous, resonant tones as he plays it, one that stays with him long after he leaves the store. He'll go back again and again to play that banjo for the pure pleasure of listening to it.

On one of his trips home from the music store, a thought occurs to him: wouldn't it be neat if he could make an instrument that combines the best of both the Bacon & Day banjo sound and the dulcimer?

(96)

## 1975 ALEXANDER'S BY THE SEA, WASHINGTON: A KINDRED MEETING

The Kindred Gathering festival will take place in two weeks, so Bob Force is busy taking care of last-minute arrangements when David and his dog Zimmerman show up in an old pickup truck. He wants to ask Bob for his suggestions on playing the dulcimer and is eager to hear a more contemporary style of playing.

Bob and his wife Janette take note of the truck with its stacks of canned beans and a bed that David had rigged up in the back. They invite him to stay at their cabin during his visit. When they sit down to talk dulcimers, Bob invites him to play, but he declines."I'm not feeling well; I have a cold" David tells Bob. "I just want to watch you play." Bob obliges for the next three days. David listens and studies; between Bob's playing, the two spend hours in conversation. In between, Bob continues his work on the upcoming Kindred Gathering. Whenever Bob plays the dulcimer, David closely studies everything he does with his body and especially with his hands. After their sessions together, David walks outside to his little camper to practice in private, trying out the techniques he just observed.

Bob's stories of his development as a player make a strong impression on David. "I played six to ten hours a day every day when I started out," Bob tells him. "I had no money. I was homeless. I kept moving...people put me up. I found people who wanted to hear my songs, and I'd hang out with them and play with and for them.

Or, I'd have a notion to go see someone and I'd hitchhike to their place. I ended up hitchhiking thousands of miles across the country." David absorbs his advice, too: "Whenever you get down to your last five bucks, you spend it on a steak breakfast to keep you going while you figure out how to earn a little more money. Oh, and, if you do buy a car, never pay more than five hundred bucks for it!"

On the fourth morning, David gets ready to bid Bob and Janette goodbye. They invite him to stay for the upcoming festival, but he declines, perhaps out of self-consciousness, or perhaps because he has many more people to meet before he returns to Texas to look for work. But this visit has been enlightening. After leaving, he'll use the techniques he has learned from Bob to help him continue to develop his own style.

Three years from now, David will return to see this mentor at the fourth annual Kindred Gathering in Salem, Oregon. Then, David will teach, and he will play in front of and along with everyone.

(97)

*Bob Force's Playing Technique*

David's visit to Bob Force was one of the pivotal points in the development of his style of playing. He closely listened *and* watched while Bob played for him. He noticed that Bob's left-hand position was similar to the way a musician would hold his guitar: palm up, the three middle fingers slightly curled over the neck, and the thumb curled slightly around the neck. But for his dulcimer, Bob rotated his hand position 180 degrees just above the fretboard. Bob maintained the curled fingers to fret while anchoring his left thumb along the side of the fretboard to guide his hand up and down the board as he played.

David recognized that while his old way of playing gave him a somewhat larger reach, Bob's position gave him more flexibility for making chords. After many hours of practice, the position allowed him to cross his pinky over the ring finger like Bob did to create a moveable barre (i.e., to press a single fret across all three strings at the same time). Using a barre in combination with his middle and index fingers facilitated an even greater number of chord combinations. This new position also naturally tucked in his elbow, allowing him greater range of motion and speed. Finally, Bob's position also enabled him to produce sonic embellishments while playing that David was just beginning to explore prior to their visit.

If you would like to know more about Bob Force, visit his website at RobertForce.com.

(98)

## 1975 WASHINGTON STATE: A KINDRED GATHERING

Seventy-five people from the U.S. and Canada heed the call to the first Kindred Gathering on Washington's Olympic Peninsula. The event attracts accomplished players from across the country including Neal Hellman, Bonnie Carol, and Michael Rugg. Steve Katz undertakes the longest travel: he pulls into Ocean City, Washington, on a Greyhound bus for the first half of a seven-thousand-mile round trip from his home in Worcester, Massachusetts.

Workshops and classes are spontaneous and egalitarian; participants suggest topics to learn each morning; if the interest is there, the class happens. Players cook, hike, and jam together, sharing music and techniques. Health food costs a dollar a plate; otherwise, the festival is free.

Mike Rugg of Capritaurus Dulcimers in California gives a workshop on playing old Irish airs such as "Si Bagh Si More" and "Flowers of Edinburgh"; Bonnie Carol and several others teach as well.

Before and after their two workshops, Force and d'Ossché play and stroll in their standing style with their furious strumming; soon everyone stands to play their dulcimers. On one day, each hour is devoted to playing in a different mode—*Aeolian*, then *Lydian*, followed by *Phrygian* and so on— in order to explore tonalities and moods evoked by each mode. Don Berry indicates the start of each session via a tone on The Dragon, a special xylophone he built with additional sympathetic notes that ring in the overtone series like sitars do.

Saturday evening is reserved for a concert that begins at dusk and won't end until two a.m. Everyone is invited to play three songs; names are drawn from a hat to determine order of playing so no one gets preference for being "a star." This mix of amateurs and pros will become a hallmark of the festival's concerts in the years to come.

When participants aren't playing, they're talking late into the night; the learned Don Berry starts one memorable talk entitled, "The Pythagoras Theory and Divine Harmony and Why the Dulcimer Just Naturally Makes Your Brain Feel Happy." Everyone involved considers this first gathering a success and returns home determined to attend next year's festival, which Bob and Al assure them will happen.

Bonnie Carol, who up until now made dulcimers occasionally to sell, leaves the Kindred Gathering with a determination to make a living as a full-time musician. The Kindred Gathering has "taken my heart," she tells friends. On the ride back to Colorado, she begins planning how to make a decent living focused on her new favorite instrument. She builds more dulcimers, begins writing books and articles, teaches dulcimer playing at the Denver Folklore Center and the Music Association of Swallow Hill, performs on the dulcimer at festivals, and produces a radio show at Boulder's community public radio station, KGNU. She names the show "Dulcimania." When she returns home, she drops all plans to search for a job in psychology. She tells Max and her friends, "Dulcimer players are the people with whom I want to spend the rest of my life."

(99, 100, 101, 102)

## 1976 FRONT ROYAL, VIRGINIA: THE SPRING THING FESTIVAL

While David works in Texas to earn money for his dulcimer trips, Phil Mason sets up the spring edition of *The Dulcimer Players News,* now a larger, quarterly publication. Despite his initial vow not to include any paid advertisements, he reversed his policy to keep up with the rising costs of putting out the magazine.

This year, Phil includes an ad for the renowned Walnut Valley Folk Festival's new "Spring Thing" Festival. And, for the first time, the festival will include a mountain dulcimer competition. Once David sees the ad, he makes up his mind to attend. He can't pass up the chance to meet new dulcimer players and learn more songs and techniques from them.

Nineteen seventy-six will be an especially significant year for Phil Mason and the newsletter. Madeleine MacNeil, good friend to Keith and Mary Young and well known in the dulcimer community as a performer, teacher, and arranger, will marry Phil in June, and their photo will grace the cover of TDPN in the subsequent Summer 1976 issue.

Maddie (as she is known to her friends) becomes assistant editor to help Phil due to the burgeoning subscriptions and the "thousands of things to do" in preparation for each issue. Maddie will continue her own work as a full-time folk singer and musician while working on TDPN. The couple will move to their new home in the Blue Ridge Mountains and Shenandoah Valley area of northwestern Virginia, which they christen "Happy Valley Farm."

(103, 104)

## 1976 WINFIELD, KANSAS: WALNUT VALLEY

Now four years running, The Walnut Valley Association produces the annual Walnut Valley National Guitar Flat-Picking Championships Festival. Since that title is quite a mouthful, many attendees just call it the Flat-Picking Championships, or "Walnut Valley" or simply "Winfield." Held at the Winfield Fairgrounds every fall, many of the best acoustic players in the country attend not only to enter competitions but to play in the countless jams throughout the grounds. Just like in the fall, the association's new "Spring Thing" parking lots resonate with nonstop live music: guitar, banjo, fiddle, autoharp, and mandolin players form jamming groups everywhere; impromptu jam sessions take place all day and most of the night over in Walnut Grove, the campsite where attendees set up tents and small campers for the duration. Old friends connect with new; amateurs connect with master players via their love of roots music and traditional songs. The ever-present mingled aromas of hamburgers, hot dogs, barbecue, and chicken waft through the air, cooked up for the thousands who come to hear the best of the best play at the festival.

Dark rain clouds threaten, but they don't deter David from attending. Winfield calls him with its promise of meeting other dulcimer players who are likely to attend due to the brand-new contest for mountain dulcimer players. It's an opportunity to hear top-quality music for a three-dollar entry fee and a chance to meet and play with other attendees. David, just twenty-three years old, makes his way to Winfield from Texas. Driven to understand what he can do with the dulcimer, he has absorbed everything possible from visiting other players across the United States for the past three years. Yet, despite his hours of playing and his sojourns across the country, he only feels confident playing three songs. He hopes to learn more from some kindred spirits at Winfield.

David hangs out in the parking lot during the rain breaks, playing his dulcimer and shooting the breeze with other players who are milling about looking to join in a jam. A luthier and player named Roger Harris from Oklahoma City walks up to listen to a small group play together. He can't take his eyes off David and is astonished by what he sees and hears. During a break in the playing, Roger introduces himself. David tells him he's only there to play with others in the parking lot. Roger laughs and tells him he needs to go sign up for the contest right then and there. David declines, so Roger, a skilled player himself, turns around and walks to the registration area, determined to enter David in the contest anyway. When he returns, he jokes with David that he has to be in the contest now " because I just signed you up!"

Attendee Jim French is at Winfield this year to complete in the dulcimer contest. A skilled guitar player, he's confident that he is a pretty good at playing the dulcimer, too. He doesn't worry about winning or losing the contest; it's just great fun to participate. Jim loves Walnut Valley; it has drawn him each year since it first started. He signed up for the dulcimer contest as a lark before he heads to graduate school later in the summer. He joins the other twenty-five contestants near the Dobro Stage to enjoy the music while he waits his turn to play.

Each player climbs the stage to take a turn in the first round. As in the other contests, the judges sit in a small trailer a ways from the stage so they can't see the contestants. Instead, they listen to them via microphone hookups to their trailer. One by one the players perform; when it's Jim's turn, he takes his walnut-and-spruce McSpadden dulcimer and bounds up the stairs to the stage. He performs his two pieces to enthusiastic applause from the small crowd and returns to the sidelines to listen to the rest of the contestants.

After all twenty-five contestants finish, he waits for the first cut in the contest. He is only sure of one thing. A guy named David Schnaufer is head and shoulders above the rest. His arrangements of his songs are full of complex dynamics and chordings; Jim has never heard anything like it on a dulcimer.

After an hour or so, when announcements are made Jim finds out that he and David made the first cut. They are two of the five who will perform in round two. Again, when he finishes his performance, he stays to listen as David mounts the stage, the last of the five players in round two. When he finishes, the crowd applauds wildly. They don't need to wait for the judges' announcement to confirm what they already know: that Jim and Dave are two of the three finalists who will play in the final round tomorrow.

On Sunday Jim mounts the stage for the last round, this time in front of thousands of people who are standing or sitting on lawn chairs, drawn by the buzz of his outstanding playing of this rare instrument. Jim finishes, and as he climbs down the steps, he turns and watches David as he climbs the steps after him, smiling as he hears the roar of approval from the crowd. After his introduction, David shows off his fancy finger work with the nineteenth-century African-American Spiritual "Golden Slippers" by playing it blue-grass style. He changes century, genre, mood, and tempo with Howie Mitchell's folk song, "If She's Gone, Let Her Go," creating anticipation with the almost five-second opening note followed by a quick pause before diving into the tune. The audience watches; their bobbing heads, swaying bodies and tapping feet keep time as their frequent whoops and hollers of approval accompany David's play-ing. They are mesmerized by his rapid picking and pristine playing up and down the fretboard. For his last number, David picks up the tempo with his pièce de résistance as he hits the first notes of "Santa Ana's Retreat"; his speed, complex technique, and purity of sound astonish Jim and the audience.

The judges are impressed as well. Jim takes third, and they crown David the Grand Champion in the first Winfield National Dul-cimer Contest. With his red plaid shirt soaked and his long hair and beard wild from the wind, he wears a huge smile as he accepts the three-foot-tall trophy, one hundred dollars, and a brand new Tut Taylor Tennessee model dulcimer. Jim and David pump hands and offer congratulations to each other.

With the abundance of shared joy and affirmation of his skill in this moment, David believes it will be the best day of his life.

(105, 106, 107, 108, 109, 110, 111)

## 1976 KELLER, TEXAS: A MAN ON FIRE

Impelled by a new confidence in himself, David uses his Winfield prize money to help finance more trips to seek dulcimer musicians who are willing to play music with him.

In between trips, he plays every free moment he can get. When he hears or reads about a dulcimer aficionado, the once-shy young man develops a habit of calling up players or and luthiers he reads or hears about to ask if he can visit. When he can't find a way to contact the person first, he often shows up at the door. Utilizing his Texan charm, he introduces himself and asks, "You wanna play some dulcimer?" He hitchhikes out west, then back again to explore the dulcimer's origins: the mountains of Kentucky, West Virginia, Virginia, and North Carolina. He is a nonstop whirlwind, chasing down every dulcimer player he can find to play with in order to learn new techniques and to add more songs to his rapidly growing repertoire. When he runs out of money, he returns to Texas to look for work to earn more money and then starts the process all over again during the next spring rainy season.

(112)

### What it takes to win a championship

David bought his first dulcimer to use it to help him write songs. In order to attain his goal, he was determined to focus on learning techniques and connecting with others every spare moment he had.

Winfield became a pivotal point in his life. His winning the championship not only validated his musicianship but also instilled much-needed confidence after years of feeling rudderless. He would continue to pursue songwriting and arranging music in the future, but, after Winfield, the dulcimer became this central focus, a means for expressing every aspect of himself. In his rootless lifestyle of the time, with no ties to hold him nor center to ground him, the dulcimer helped him find his community with and through other players, and it enabled him to send his own roots into America's soil.

Later in life, David will become friends with Linda Brock-inton, who won the Winfield dulcimer championship in 2000. Below, she provides a glimpse of the kind of work it took at Winfield:

I never played any string instrument before I picked up the dulcimer. For ten years I played four to five hours every day. That's how you get better: by playing every day. I'd pick really, really hard songs, and I'd work really, really hard to learn how to play them. I call it 'thrashin' through it. You pick a song and thrash through it. I don't play with sheet music at all, so I would usually take four measures at a time and keep playing until it was smooth and sounded right, and work my way through the song that way. By the end, I had it memorized. You learn lots of things from that and [after] you get through it, then there's more things you learn by thrashing through the next song you pick. Eventually you get better and you start to see there's lots of repetition and predictable patterns in music. Especially during jams. A lot of people look at the hard pieces and decide not to play them, but I never did. I wanted to get better and keep growing.

Linda has her own channel on Youtube. You can learn more about her and watch her play here: https://www.youtube.com/user/TheDulcigirl

(113)

# 1976 DENTON, TEXAS: UNEXPECTED VISITORS

Mack White first heard talk about David from Jim Bentley, his long-time friend from high school. Mack is in a deep sleep in the middle of the night right before he finally meets this David character he has been hearing about for so long.

Around 3:30 a.m., a loud banging on their apartment door jolts Mack and his wife Carla awake. Mack, now on high alert, gets up to see who is at the door. Hearing a familiar voice on the other side, he opens the door and in stumbles Jim with their mutual friend Brian in a state of high excitement. "It's a new era, Mack! It's a new era!" Mack looks out the doorway just as a short, slight, hippy-looking dude trails in behind them. Mack learns they had done the same thing to this guy before they arrived at his place. A little annoyed at first, David nevertheless has gone along to see what happens.

Jim introduces David as his best friend who works with him at Rangeaire. Jim explains they are drunk and stoned and have an adventure to tell. Now wide awake, Mack and Carla invite them to sit down, and Jim tells their story. "On our way to your place, a cop pulled out behind us, turned on his lights and siren and came after us! So we threw the baggie out the window before he pulled us over! We had nothing on us, and he didn't even make us take a sobriety test!"

He goes on to explain that after the cop left them, Brian started up the car, pulled out on the road, and did a U-turn to look for their stash. "Do you believe it? We found it! It's a new era Mack!" Jim hollers as they fall back into the couch laughing. After a few more stories, first Jim and then Brian start to slump over and fall asleep, so Carla, Mack, and David sit up talking until sunrise. David learns that Mack is passionate about graphic arts, and Carla and Mack learn about David's journey with the dulcimer. It's the beginning of a lifelong friendship between the two men.

Mack, a man of wide-ranging talents and interests, knows his music. Until he met David, however, he had never heard of a dulcimer. Shortly after that night, he will hear David play over at Jim

Bentley's house. He will leave impressed enough to tell the rest of his friends about that experience: "Even though he has only played the dulcimer two years, David is a master player who can play anything."

(114)

## 1976 TENNESSEE: THE SCHILLINGS FESTIVAL

For centuries, lands along the northern rim of the Great Smokies—including Cosby's location—were used primarily as hunting grounds by the Cherokee. Today Cosby lies some twenty miles east of Gatlinburg, Tennessee, in a narrow valley that runs from Allen Grove near Newport in the north to the border of the Smokey Mountains National Park to the south. English Mountain towers above Cosby to the northwest, and Green Mountain rises just over fifteen hundred feet to the east. Everyone who lives in or passes through Cosby is surrounded by stunning, natural beauty.

Lee and Jean Schilling originally conceived of "Jean's Dulcimer Shop" in Cosby as a way to provide local craftspeople with an outlet for their work. Lee is a retired NASA physicist turned luthier; Jean, a luthier and musician, was born and raised in the mountains. Both are gentle, gifted, humorous people. They also happen to be two of the nation's leading exponents of Appalachian music and folklore. Jean sings and is an accomplished player on the fretted dulcimer and the autoharp. She's a folk artist renowned for her detailed nature-themed paintings on wood, and pen and pencil sketches of forest flora and fauna. When they are not traveling to festivals or teaching in other states, Lee spends his days woodworking, marble sculpting, playing the recorder and harmonica, and storytelling. He helps Jean manage their shop while he manages their Crying Creek Publishers and record label, Traditions Records.

Jean and Lee had a dream in mind in keeping with their love of Jean's Appalachian heritage. One of their many projects began in 1968, a spring festival to attract folk musicians, mountain craft people and aficionados. Named The Folk Festival of the Smokies, it is declared "A REAL GOOD EVENT" by the memorably named Dick Tracy in a letter to the editor of *The Dulcimer Players News*. Many of the young attendees dubbed it the "Smoke Festival of the Folkies" as a nod to the ever-present smell of cannabis in the air, discreetly generated out of sight of Lee. The festival is wildly popular and attracts visitors from all around the country despite only advertising by word of mouth.

Due to the success of their first folk festival, this Bicentennial year the Schillings have created a new festival but with a focus on dulcimer players. Attendees who travel to the new festival have to cross a small footbridge over Crying Creek to get to the Schillings' shop door. Once inside, they find themselves immersed in all things Appalachian. Jean sells handcrafted instruments including McSpadden and Folkcraft dulcimers as well as instruments she and Lee make. Shoppers find instrument cases and related merchandise like picks, strings, capos, records, cassettes, and books; they sell arts and crafts and supplies for weaving and woodworking.

The Schillings direct festival attendees to walk outside to the back of the shop and look for the stairs. They find the "stairs" are carved out of a hill so steep that climbers have to grab on to vines and brush branches to keep from falling during their ascent as they pass near the back of an outhouse to finally haul themselves and their gear up to a flat meadow. There, they see the Schillings' hand-built rustic compound in a wooded clearing: the "Folk Life Center of the Smokies." The small complex consists of a workshop and a performance and gathering area that is surrounded by campsites throughout the woods. Those who arrived early are already sharing their music on a stage without lights or a microphone—technology is neither needed nor wanted. As evening approaches, the center's magical air carries even the quietest melodies across the field and woods during the performances.

Among several instructors the Schillings have invited to lead a workshop is thirty-year-old Bonnie Carol from Colorado. It doesn't take long for Bonnie to befriend several newcomers, but two especially stand out. She is charmed by the shy David Schnaufer, impressed with his exceptional playing and his thirst for learning. She also likes his girlfriend Diana White, a skilled classical mandolin player. The three hit it off immediately.

(115, 116, 117, 118, 119)


## 1976 NEW YORK CITY/NEW ENGLAND: *TRES RÍOS*

Before leaving the Schillings' spring Cosby festival, David and Diana agree to meet up again with Bonnie Carol in New York City to do some touring together throughout the northeast this summer. By the time they get to New York, they've christened themselves "Tres Ríos" (Three Rivers) and get busy busking, playing music on the streets to make money from tips they earn.

Classically trained Bonnie appreciates the skill with which Diana plays the mandolin and recognizes the mandolin playing techniques she has taught David. David is impressed with Bonnie's technical competence as a player and her openness with respect to her work as a musician, luthier, and business owner, answering just about every question he asks her. She's also a fellow Texan who enjoys David's slow drawl and mannerisms that are a big part of his quiet persona. They spend many an evening trading stories of growing up in Texas; she is captivated by David's stories of the unusual experiences he collects like songs.

To friends who ask her, Bonnie describes her new friend as someone who "plays the dulcimer all day, every day, alone or with others; it's almost all he does with his spare time." She considers him a great player. The three forge their friendship during the tour. David's interest in Bonnie's luthier work will lead her to invite them to move out to Colorado to pursue performing and dulcimer building together.

(120)

## 1976 NEW YORK CITY: A PRIVATE PERFORMANCE

One night during the wee hours, David finds himself alone on the subway. At one stop, four young African American men enter the same car. They sit down on the bench right across from him and look at him without a word. David looks back. Suddenly the four stand up in unison and, without introduction, they begin synchronizing their body and hand gestures while singing a Doo Wop song just for him. As the train slows down for the next stop, they finish. They file out of the car without a word, leaving David beaming.

(121)

## 1976 NASHVILLE, TENNESSEE: A SILVER LINING

John Lomax was a college student when he first met Townes Van Zandt in Austin, and for the last eleven years they've kept in touch off and on. Despite John's firm belief that Townes is "better than Bob Dylan," Van Zandt has been spinning his wheels as a cult artist, never gaining traction among mainstream music listeners. He still struggles with manic depression, drugs, and alcohol; five years ago, he nearly died from a heroin overdose. To make matters worse, he has a history of bad luck on the business side of being a musician, his preference being the life of a wandering troubadour only interested in writing, touring, smoking, and gambling. As long as he has enough money to own a guitar, get to the next show, and buy some drinks, he is happy. Now, he is holed up in Colorado nursing a broken arm with no prospects in sight.

After putting their heads together, John and mutual friend Guy Clark encourage Van Zandt to move permanently to Nashville where there are better opportunities to restart his career. John's belief in his friend's exceptional talent never wavers, and he is convinced he can help save him from himself. When Townes agrees to the move, John becomes his manager on a handshake.

John throws himself into work on Van Zandt's behalf for the next two years, promoting his client as "America's greatest songwriter." He places an ad in *Rolling Stone* to encourage readers to sign up for the new "Townes Van Zandt Fan Club," hoping for a response of seven or eight people. Instead, he receives over a hundred letters from die-hard fans that confirm his belief in Townes's talents. Many write that his songs had saved their lives.

During his time as John's client, six of Van Zandt's albums are finally released. Lomax and his brother Joe compile *For the Sake of the Song*, a book of Van Zandt's lyrics, sheet music, photos, and essays about Van Zandt to demonstrate that Townes's music holds up equally well as poetry: the lyrics, the phrasing, the meter, and the message can stand alone and still reach the hearts of readers. They don't really even need music, John asserts, because they are so well written.

However, while managing Van Zandt, Lomax finds the beginnings of deeply tangled financial and copyright issues related to previous poor management that will beleaguer Van Zandt for the rest of his troubled life. And a troubled life it is. After just two years of work together, John and Townes will part ways in their business relationship. John is left frustrated by his inability to help his friend and client. All the work that he has done to relaunch him now feels for naught. He did it because he believed Townes worthy of being much more than a cult musician. John is even harder on himself than on Townes for not being able to rescue the songwriting genius.

However, one silver lining arises from this otherwise dark cloud. John now has managerial experience with an exceptionally talented songwriter/musician.

(122, 123, 124)

## 1976 BOULDER, COLORADO: MAKING A LIVING

Bonnie and David spend hours in her small workshop where she walks him through the process of making a dulcimer step by step. He's not a total novice to dulcimer building since he has spent time on the road visiting other luthiers such as Lynn McSpadden. He learns quickly.

The two talk often about what it takes to make a living as a musician. Bonnie, already established as a touring performer, teaches him the business end of their work: she shares booking contacts and booking methodology with him: how to find gigs, keep a schedule and negotiate his fees. The three of them—Bonnie, David and Diana—load up Diana's van and travel to festivals around the country, still performing as Tres Ríos. Sometimes, just Bonnie and David travel in her van and perform together, honing their playing and singing skills together.

(125)

## 1976 NEDERLAND, COLORADO: "ARE YOU FAMOUS?"

David is hired to play the jaw harp in a cat food commercial in Caribou Ranch Studios near Nederland. Caribou Studios is better known as a recording destination for professional musicians than for commercial advertising work. Elton John, Chicago, Earth, Wind and Fire, the Beach Boys, and many others utilize the Caribou to record.

While David waits for his call he wanders the building, taking it all in, trying to imagine what it must be like to be a professional musician who records in such a place.

Two young ladies, also exploring the building, walk over ask him if he is a famous star. "No", he replies. "Oh," they respond, disappointed. They turn around and keep walking.

Neither David nor the girls on the make know it, but they are about ten years too soon with their question. David has a lot more hard work and playing to do first.

(126)

## 1977 KELLER, TEXAS: ROGER HARRIS

Short on cash, David and Diana return to Keller. David finds work in construction again, this time as an assistant roofer. When the day's job is over, he spends every waking minute either playing the dulcimer by himself or jamming with Diana as he refines his control of her mandolin picking techniques. He listens to dulcimer music and other musicians of stringed instruments over and over on his cassette player to train his ear and incorporate new sounds in his playing. He continues to seek out dulcimer people he has befriended whenever he can.

Before they return to Boulder, friend and luthier Roger Harris from Oklahoma pays a visit. Roger tells Diana of the good times at Winfield and how he signed up David to compete. After swapping stories, David shares that he has been listening to albums by the Irish group the Chieftains, especially harp player Derek Bell, a multi-instrumentalist and composer from Northern Ireland. He is frustrated with trying to capture the harp's singularly clear and sustained notes; the slides and movements by his fingers on the melody string keep getting in the way. He can't make the dulcimer duplicate Bell's playing despite countless hours of work. Roger thinks for a moment, and then suggests some techniques for him to see if they will help. They do. David is delighted with the results, and he will pay his friend's generosity forward soon with a new endeavor.

(127, 128)

## 1977 AUSTIN, TEXAS: THE TEXAS CIRCLE

David and Jim Bentley's friend Mack White moves to Austin where he enrolls in the University of Texas to explore his interest in psychology and English. He continues to pursue his graphic art. Whenever David travels to or through Austin, he turns up for visits with Jim, Nelda and Joe in Cleburne, and with Mack, who shares his quirky, unique graphics and comic books with him. David loves them.

(129)

## 1977 ANTIOCH, OHIO: LEO KRETZNER

After a few years of playing dulcimer full time, Leo Kretzner now has his University of Michigan biology degree under his belt. He arrives at Antioch College in Ohio; the College's Glen Helen Outdoor Education Center hired him as a naturalist. After his life in Ann Arbor with its thriving music scene, he is pleasantly surprised to see all the folkies playing banjos in Ohio. Because he is the only dulcimer player in his new digs, the banjo players have a big influence on him. He likes the way his D-A-D tuning gives a lower sound and saves the higher notes up the fretboard for later in the song. His style of playing across the strings works well for jamming with banjo players.

Leo easily settles into his new position. He lives in the dorm with the other naturalists in training (there is a separate house for the women naturalists.) The two houses share one phone. Groups of middle school kids come to stay Monday through Thursday and bunk in cabins. The naturalists lead them in outdoor, nature-oriented activities during their stay at the Center.

One day, Leo gets a phone message that someone had tried to call him, and that caller said he would try again a little later.

A short time later, a colleague hollers, "Hey Leo! Phone for you!" Leo runs to the phone.

"Hello?" He hears a stranger's voice. "Is this Leo? LEO *Kreeetz*ner? *Mah* name is David Schnaufer and *Ah'm* from Texas, playin' dulcimer, and *Ah'm* trying to learn, can *Ah* play with you?"

He had gotten Leo's name and number from somebody while on the road hitchhiking, looking for players. It doesn't strike Leo as odd that he'd get a call like that out of the blue; folk musicians are basically nice people. Most of the time people are eager to learn and eager to share when asked, "How do you do that?"

"I would love to get together." Leo tells him, and shortly thereafter David arrives at the center. After exchanging pleasantries, Leo grabs his own dulcimer, and they walk down by a little creek that flows through the camp. David takes his dulcimer out of his case, they tune up, and then begin playing songs to warm up. David tells Leo he had originally started playing with a noter, but now, Leo notices he is playing in D-A-A tuning and already playing with two-finger harmonies on the first and third strings, leaving the middle string "open", i.e., unfretted.

"Your playing is so considered the way to do it," Leo tells him. But David is curious about Leo's tuning in D-A-D. He is looking for new ideas, and Leo is glad to share what he has learned. "I learned the D-A-D tuning from New England dulcimer teacher Margaret MacArthur; I had the same jolt of surprise as you," Leo tells David. They play, then talk, then play for the rest of the afternoon, taking short breaks in between so Leo can show him the clinic for injured animals. David is transfixed by the owls temporarily housed at the center until they recover from their injuries. When Leo shows him the red-tailed hawk that lives permanently at the center, David stares, fascinated. He is thrilled that the raptor lets him pet his breast.

Later, Leo invites his new friend and another naturalist to eat dinner at the Crying Cowboy in Yellow Springs. Both play their dulcimers while they wait for their meal. Afterward, Leo invites David to stay overnight in the men's dorm, but he thanks him and says he must keep moving. He's heading to West Virginia and Virginia to search for two families: the Russells and the Youngs.

(130, 131, 132)

## On Strings and Tunings by Leo Kretzner

In the seventies Jean Ritchie described her strings this way: for a right-handed player, as the instrument lies on the lap with the pegstock to the left, she refers to the string closest to the player's belly as #1. The middle string is #2, and the farthest from the belly—the bass string—#3. In other words, the strings are placed in order of lightest to thickest away from the player. All of the above is the opposite for left-handed players.

Talking about the strings with other dulcimer players sometimes requires a bit of clarification, however. For example, many players use "melody string" to refer to the string closest to the player's body, because it is often used to playing the melody of a song. But the melody line of a song can be played on any string, so calling it the "melody" string is a misnomer unless the melody line is actually played on that string.

Another common practice: some players refer to the #1 string as the treble string, the middle as the "middle string," and the bass simply as "the bass string." Yet, when Jean Ritchie described her tuning, she refers to both non-bass strings as "trebles," meaning "higher frequency" strings.

Modern players who like to change the tunings on strings to play in other keys often clarify whether they are "starting at the bass string" or "starting at the #1 string" when sharing their tunings with others. For example, imagine an arrangement of "Amazing Grace" that requires strings to be tuned in G-G-C. Since some players name string tunings in 1-2-3 order, and others in 3-2-1 order, she would have to clarify what she means: if the bass is tuned to C, then the higher noted strings #1 and #2 are tuned to G.

Players avoid confusion with each other by picking one string to be the "#1 string." Then they clarify when telling others which string they refer to. I always start with the bass string because it's the lowest in pitch, and the lowest note is always the first in a chord name. So if I want to play "Amazing Grace," I'll ask others to "tune to C-G-G with C on the bass."

(133)

## 1977, VIRGINIA: THE RUSSELLS, GALAX STYLE

Patriarch Roscoe Russell earns a living as a carpenter, makes dulcimers, guitars, and ukuleles on the side, and considers music as necessary as breathing. "Country music is the only kind I know," he'll say to visitors, and he has raised his own children to follow his tradition. His son Roy plays guitar, and his sixteen-year-old daughter Bonnie plays a dulcimer that Roscoe made for her. In these highlands of southwest Virginia, Galax dulcimers are a whole new experience for David.

When he does connect with the Russells and sees their instruments, his first impression is that they look like "pumpkin seeds" that produce a unique sound. Roscoe explains the history: in the region around Galax, dulcimers are for dances and parties, unlike in eastern Kentucky where Jean Ritchie grew up. There, dulcimers are rhythm instruments primarily meant to accompany singing. He points out another difference: his dulcimers have four equidistant strings with frets extending just under the two strings nearest to the player. He or she frets with a finger or a noter on two strings while letting the other two strings drone. All four strings—made of simple wire, like piano wire—are tuned to D above middle C and have a shorter string length than dulcimers outside their region.

The dulcimers themselves have a double bottom, and many of the older Galax dulcimers have feet; they are meant to be played on a table where they best project their volume. He explains that they often have hollowed out fingerboards to enhance the sound as well. Unlike the dulcimers David has seen before, Galax dulcimers don't include the typical heart-shaped sound holes. Instead, they have simple round holes or "F"-shaped holes like those on fiddles, since the fiddle is such an important part of the music tradition in the region.

David is especially curious about their practice of strumming with a turkey feather. Once, after seeing a picture of someone strumming with a feather, he got his own feather and tried strumming with the thick end; "Man, that doesn't work," he thought. The Russells teach him how to do it. They don't play with the thick end of the quill. Instead, they strip off all of the vane on each side of the quill and use the thinner end of the quill to strum. When he tries it that way, he learns that it works perfectly. Unlike modern dulcimers, the old Galax dulcimers never had a strum hollow; with good quill strumming technique, a player uses only the very tip of the quill and doesn't hit the edge of the fingerboard.

Another aspect to the Galax playing style intrigues David: players lean back to play rather than bend over the dulcimer. He studies how relaxed they look; by not hunching over, they are able to slide the noter all the way up the fretboard. Like others, they use their fingers as noters, but with their index finger on top rather than their thumb on top. When they do use wooden noters, they are commonly made out of Mountain Laurel, an especially hard, greasy wood that helps them slide up and down the strings easily.

David learns that the joy of their music belies the Russells' hardscrabble lives as small farmers who live an almost hand-to-mouth existence. He spends the most time with Roscoe and his son Roy, just two years younger than David. He tells Roscoe that it was twelve-year-old Bonnie's playing on *Mountain Dulcimer, Galax Style* that impressed him the most when he first listened to it three years ago. To David, her power and her speed, her tone and her feel for the instrument all contributed to his perception that Bonnie is the consummate player.

(134, 135, 136, 137, 138, 139, 140)

## 1977 ANNANDALE, VIRGINIA: RICK FREIMUTH

Rick Freimuth is home for the summer after his second year at the University of Idaho. He applied for a job at the U.S. National Park Service in Great Falls Park, Virginia, as a river rescue/climbing ranger, so paints the house for his dad and works in Keith's shop part-time while he awaits news about his application. Upon receiving news that he has been hired, he decides not to return to Idaho, and, instead, moves back in with his father for the rest of the summer. He accepted the Park Service position contingent on being able to take time off for "Galax," the renowned festival that will take place just a few weeks after he is to begin his new position.

Rick often gravitates to the warmth of the Youngs' house, diving back into music with the Youngs on his days off. He loves the excitement of meeting the musicians in Keith's "Front Porch Dulcimer Band" every week as well as the many who periodically stop and visit as they pass through the area on their way to music festivals. By now Rick and David Young are skilled players, adept at using their rosewood noters and picks cut out from empty Clorox bottles.

As for David Schnaufer, he is on his way to Annandale to seek out this man named Keith Young he has heard so much about. David learned that Keith is a musician who makes quality instruments and has a remarkable ability to maintain the integrity of any instrument he repairs. Keith also teaches. And he has heard that Keith and Mary welcome musicians in their home. Curious and eager to learn, he finally shows up at their door.

(141, 142, 143, 144)

# 1977 ANNANDALE, VIRGINIA: KEITH YOUNG

Rick Freimuth's first impression of David is how quiet he is. He also notices a shell hanging from a thong necklace he wears; David tells him he found it on a Texas beach. He carries a little pouch made of rabbit fur at his belt that holds his cigarette papers and Bulgar tobacco. Rick watches, fascinated, as the Texan rolls his own cigarettes. Out of courtesy to Mary and Keith, though, he always steps outside to smoke. As David gets to know Rick, he empathizes deeply with him, having lost his own mother at a very young age. The two quickly form a strong bond.

David accepts Keith and Mary's invitation to stay after a congenial dinner, and Mary shows him the bunk bed in the basement where he can sleep. That evening, Keith sits up late into the night talking with David, while in another room, Rick and David Young talk about him as well. They are surprised at his being "so super shy—the guy won Winfield, for goodness sake!"

It doesn't take long for Keith, Mary and the kids to help David get over his shyness during meals and at the frequent potlucks they hold when friends come over. Like his hosts, David treats all the neighborhood kids with respect and good humor, as if they were just shorter adults. Soon Rick and the younger kids declare him the "nicest person you will ever meet" when they introduce him to others.

When David shows the family his collection of jaw harps in their leather case. Keith, the kids, and even Mary have great fun learning to play them. Brothers David, Scott, and Phil quickly absorb his instructions for how to play the unusual little mouth instrument. The three troop down to Keith's workshop to tune them up: a little bit of filing here and bending there makes big improvements, and soon David declares them all masters of the jaw harp.

As days pass, family members share their impressions of their new visitor with friends. He's exceptionally kind and funny with a self-effacing sense of humor. He's quick-witted; when teased because the self-proclaimed vegetarian helps himself to a piece of meat at one potluck, David laughs: "I'm what you call a 'flexitarian' when it comes to good food. Being from Texas, it just wouldn't be right to pass up a bite of beef!" They especially enjoy the songs he spontaneously creates wherever he finds inspiration. Mary tells everyone about an amusing song he sang to her as he was removing his cowboy shirts from the dryer, their metal buttons still hot from the tumbling. "Hot Snaps" soon becomes one of everyone's favorites.

The first time David joins a jam with Keith and his band, everyone notices his unusual way of tilting the dulcimer on his lap. When asked why he holds it that way, he explains that it allows the sound to move outward instead of upward toward his face. Occasionally, he stands and plays in the Force/d'Ossché style with his dulcimer hanging from a guitar strap. The Young family and friends also quickly notice that he can outplay them all. While they are accomplished players of the popular "Jean Ritchie" style, Keith points out to visitors that David uses a variety of strum styles, many of which are more common among guitar and mandolin players. Also unusual, he crosses strings with his left-hand fingers to make chords and partial chords rather than fretting one note at a time on the melody string.

Soon the older boys are copying his way of holding and tilting the dulcimer. They discuss David's pick of choice, one that he special orders from Artichoke Music in Oregon, the only source for this particular type: a triangular Herdim brand shark-tooth pick. That blue pick, they decide, is the epitome of cool, as is the way he moves his head and neck to mark the rhythm as he plays, and the way he places his left foot on its edge with the right foot on top of it.

Keith and Mary invite David to stay for as long as he likes and to work in the dulcimer shop on the weekends. As he often does with those whom he deems special, Keith offers to pay him for his work. David's easy ways and impressive playing mean he is a regular at the jams at the Young house and often helps Keith sell his instruments and accessories at his festival booths.

During one of their nightly conversations, Keith offers David a piece of advice: "Learn as many traditional songs as you can while you're here, David. That way, you'll be able to jam with anybody in this area of the country." David takes his advice. Whenever he's not helping around the house, working in the shop or jamming with Keith and his friends, he can be found sitting on his own in the sunny living room or in the backyard, working on learning new songs or composing. Mary tells Keith she is astonished by the sheer number of hours he plays, never seeming to tire.

Over time, his new friends learn other things about David. He suffers off and on from pleurisy. During these episodes, David feels sharp chest pains that will only stop if he holds his breath. Mary urges him to consult with a doctor. He tells her he sincerely appreciates her concern; it bugs him, but it eventually goes away, He reassures her he will see a doctor, but she worries that he never will.

He also confesses one night to Keith and Mary that he has gout. Similar to his pleurisy, David's gout comes and goes. When Mary probes for details, he describes the sudden, attacks of pain and swelling in his joints, especially the joint at the base of his big toe. It wakes him in the middle of the night and feels like his joints are on fire. Once again, he tells them he doesn't think he needs a doctor at this point, but he promises that if it gets worse, he'll see one.

David will work for Keith off and on again in the coming years. Whenever he travels to Virginia, he passes through Annandale, always welcomed by the Youngs.

(145, 146, 147)

---

*On pleurisy and gout*

Pleurisy is a condition in which the fluid space between the layer of tissue that wraps around the outside of the lungs and lines the inside of the chest wall become inflamed. Normally, these layers act like two pieces of smooth satin gliding past each other, allowing the lungs to expand and contract during breathing. When inflamed, the two membranes rub against each other like two pieces of sandpaper. David's heavy smoking no doubt aggravated his condition at the time, but he later told his cousin Gena that he suspected it was his work sanding surfboards in Galveston that originally brought it on. Nobody wore a mask in the shop, so he was breathing fiberglass dust every weekend he worked.

Gout is a common, complex form of arthritis that can affect anyone, even a young man of twenty-five like David. David's gout was extremely painful according to his friend Rick, and caused Rick some fear when he realized he was only two years younger than David. Gout occurs when a high level of uric acid is found in the blood, so urate crystals accumulate in the joint(s), causing the inflammation and intense pain during gout attacks. There could be any number of reasons for gout, one being the consequences of untreated diabetes.

(148, 149)

## 1977 ANNANDALE, VIRGINIA: DULCIMER SUMMER

David isn't the only player to visit Keith and Mary this summer. Bonnie Carol has a two-week summer job as a guide for a traveling music camp for teenagers who are studying music of the Americas. She accompanies them as they visit musicians, luthiers, and locations throughout the eastern half of the United States.

Bonnie arrives with a dozen boys and girls to the Youngs' house to watch Keith build dulcimers and see a performance by Keith's Front Porch Dulcimer Band. A group of her other friends, including Alan Freeman, make their way to the Youngs', too, leading to much laughter, long conversations and jams.

(150)

# 1977 GALAX, VIRGINIA: THE OLD FIDDLER'S CONVENTION

Every year before the second weekend of August, the population of Galax swells as country and mountain music aficionados from the United States and abroad pour into the small town for the Annual Old Fiddler's Convention. Attendees come from big cities, college campuses, and every other place where traditional music is loved and played. A good number who attend don't play music themselves; they come to listen to some of the best amateur and professional players to be found in the country, and not just on the stages. Like Winfield, nonstop music and impromptu jamming take place everywhere in the camping grounds and on the parking lots.

On Thursday night of the festival, contestants compete for cash prizes that total thousands of dollars. Competitors consist of players of every acoustic instrument; jaw harp players arrive with their instruments in a little case, while bull fiddle players pull into the parking lot with their instruments strapped on top of their cars. In separate guitar, mandolin, banjo, dulcimer, and dobro categories, players compete to win from $45 for first place to $20 for fifth place. Last year, Neal Hellman won first place in the dulcimer competition; Maddie MacNeil Mason took tenth, Keith Young, 23rd; Roscoe Russell, took 26th and Keith's friend Ralph Lee Smith just behind him took 28th place out of the thirty three who competed. Old time and bluegrass fiddlers compete for a top prize of $105 down to $30 for the fifth-place winner.

Rick, the Youngs and Alan Freeman put Galax on their calendar this summer. They wouldn't miss it for the world. David has attended before, but has to miss this year; he's on his way back to Colorado to help Bonnie plan a brand new festival.

(151, 152, 153)

# 1978 BOULDER, COLORADO: LET'S SEE WHAT HAPPENS

After her tour out East, Bonnie and David discuss how playing differs on each side of the continent. The West Coast players tend to be more progressive. Heavily inspired by the late Richard Fariña and influenced by the aura of Force and d'Ossché, they use the dulcimer to explore beyond the traditional noter style of playing exemplified by Jean Ritchie and others associated with Appalachian music. They experiment with new sounds, new chords, and strumming, and write original compositions. The East Coast players—with their easy access to fiddlers, mandolin players, and Appalachian traditions—are just as skilled and dedicated in their own ways. They typically stick closer to the traditional music roots. Bonnie and David speculate: what would happen if the two groups had the opportunity to meet?

She starts planning for a festival in Boulder, Colorado, next year, and selects a location on the grounds of the Boulder Public Library, next to bubbling Boulder Creek. The eight acres of the library's grounds, with its ample lawn and walkways and beautiful spots for spontaneous jams and conversations, are a perfect setting for a festival.

Bonnie and Max live in a house in the mountains above Boulder near the small town of Nederland. During his earlier visit, David noticed a myriad of rabbit tracks in the snow; he nicknamed their place "Rabbit Junction," and the name stuck. Bonnie calls the new festival: "The Rabbit Junction Dulcimer Festival" and tells friends that the goal is to see what happens when the two very different kinds of players come together.

News of the festival starts buzzing across the country thanks to word of mouth and an invitation she will place in *The Dulcimer Players News*.

(154, 155, 156)

## 1978 WEST VIRGINIA: ALAN FREEMAN

By 1978 Alan Freeman is considered by many folk musicians to be the best fretted dulcimer player in America. For two years now he has been like a man on fire usually finishing first or in the top three in every contest he enters. He is known for his brash personality, his high energy, and his five-string dulcimer with an atypical approach to tuning that gives his playing a unique sound.

Alan, a self-proclaimed ham, is driven to express whatever he's feeling when performing in front of an audience: amusement, sadness, joy, or even horror. When he does connect with his audiences, it's a high that lasts as long as the performance, and he can't get enough of it.

The Brooklyn-born Freeman now firmly feels he belongs in West Virginia. He lives for the old-time music player community still alive and kicking in the hills, full of spirit, an "unbroken circle" as he calls it. Freeman tells those who question the wisdom of living in West Virginia that the music is a part of a living tradition rather than something put on for tourists. Like Alan Lomax, Alan Freeman has a deep appreciation for the fundamental musical roots of West Virginia that grew from a mixture of the music of Scots-Irish immigrants and African Americans in the mountainous melting pot; he knows their music is a gift and that he is a direct beneficiary of it.

Friends from his former life consider Alan a "modern hillbilly": he talks rough but has a good heart. He likes to imbibe and smoke his homegrown pot; between these predilections and his tremendous musical talent, he's a regular sojourner to a musical state of altered consciousness.

(157, 158, 159, 150, 161, 162, 163, 164, 165)

## 1978 BOULDER, COLORADO: DAVID BUILDS A GIFT

David works in Bonnie's shop to craft a special dulcimer for his good buddy. He chooses Sitka spruce for the top of the soundbox. Thanks to its stable and even grain, Sitka is a favorite for heavy strumming, light fingerpicking, and everything in between on dulcimers and guitars. He makes the sides and bottom of the sound box out of quilted maple. Quilted maple isn't a distinct species of maple; rather, it's a name for a lovely pattern that results from a growth anomaly in the bigleaf maple tree in the Northwest. For some, it's evocative of rippling water; to others, a patchwork quilt. To everyone who sees it, quilted maple is sublime.

Quilted maple from Oregon is a challenge to work with, but David chooses it for its rarity and the beauty of the wood that he will bring back to life for his buddy Rick Freimuth. As he works every day at his tidy place on the bench, his tools neat and orderly, both Rick and Keith Young are often on his mind.

David works on Rick's dulcimer as meticulously as he does on his music. When finished, he inspects his work carefully and is satisfied with his choices: the soundbox is crafted of the highest-grade wood, and the sound holes are a graceful, unique variation with a heart superimposed over a fiddle-style sound hole. It has exquisite shimmer and beautiful tones. David wants his friend to have the best.

(167)

## 1978 AUSTIN, TEXAS: SYNCHRONICITY

Vince Farsetta is a busy, in-demand musician having the time of his life. Back in West Virginia, he works construction during the day and plays guitar and bongos with his buddies in a reggae ska band in Morgantown. After running into Alan Freeman frequently in the tight circle of musicians in the area, they have become friends. Whenever he can, Vince plays guitar backup up for Alan's gigs and at festivals like Galax and the Bob Evans farm.

For a change of scene, Vince takes up another buddy's offer to hit the road with his band the Good Tones to see if they can make it in Austin. Once they arrive, they spend some time playing outside across from the University of Texas student union. One Saturday, David strolls up to the edge of the large crowd of young people who gather around the Good Tones to listen. Back in Texas for a time to earn some more cash, he stands, watching and processing, hearing much more of the subtleties of the music than the nonmusicians in the crowd around him.

David watches one of the band members with long, curly dark hair in a Good Tones T-shirt pick up the fiddle and play like a man on fire. He recognizes a musical genius when he hears one. This is the second time he and Vince happen to be at the same unlikely place at the same time. He won't formally meet Vince on this occasion, but, in a few short years, the man from Texas and the man from New York City will become best of friends and colleagues.

(168, 169)

## 1978 BOULDER, COLORADO: CLOSE CALL

Rick, twenty-three and a recent graduate from the University of Idaho, hitchhikes back to the university to pick up some personal items he left there before he returns back home to start his new job. On his way to Idaho, he thumbs his way to Bonnie's place to pick up his new dulcimer and stay for a short visit to see David, just back from his trip to Texas.

On his last day, the two head over to Diana's cabin in Nederland, a wild area known for hippies and people seeking alternative lifestyles who live there. Rick has a grand time, talking and jamming into the evening. When it's time to leave, David offers to give Rick a lift to the interstate so he can continue on his way to Idaho. Diana, also fond of Rick, gives him a macrame strap she made for him for his new dulcimer. As everyone says their goodbyes, David and Rick climb into Bonnie's jeep and take off down Boulder Canyon Road.

Their talk of Rick's dulcimer and reminiscing over good times at the Youngs is suddenly interrupted by a loud bang accompanied by a bright flash; David can barely control the jeep as Rick is thrown hard against him and blacks out. David tries to control the swerving jeep as best he can. Suddenly Rick wakes up, pulls himself off of David and hollers "I've been shot!" David swivels his head to see blood everywhere, and joins in the yelling, "Somebody shot us!" Scared out of their wits, they continue hollering as David hits the gas pedal and floors it to get to the Boulder Hospital ER. By the time they arrive, Rick is a bloody mess. David pulls up to the emergency exit, gets out of the jeep, runs around to the passenger side, and pulls Rick out of the jeep. As he supports his friend to keep him steady, he notices a softball-sized rock in the back seat and a huge hole in the canvas Jeep cover. David suddenly realizes Rick hadn't been shot; a rock had sheared off the stone wall of Canyon Road, tore through the roof of the jeep and hit Rick right in the head. The ER doctor takes care of Rick, and David stays with him overnight in the hospital.

The next morning David drives Rick—now sporting a big bandage on his head— to the interstate to hitchhike a ride to Idaho. With his dulcimer case on his back (the one with the reflectors stuck on it for safety), they wave goodbye to each other and promise to see one another again soon.

(170, 171)

## 1979 FRONT ROYAL, VIRGINIA: ON THE COVER

The *Dulcimer Players News* cover for the 1979 Summer issue includes its revised title, having dropped the word "The" in the last issue of 1978. It also includes a Bonnie Carol photo of David whose reputation as a masterful, innovative player spreads wherever he goes. She captures him holding the dulcimer rather than playing it; he looks thoughtfully off to the left, his very long hair pulled back behind his head and wearing his usual V-neck white T-shirt.

By the time the editors send out this issue, David had already sent them his first article on music for publication: he wants to share a playing technique he considers valuable for the Fall issue.

(172)

Phil and Maddie work on the Fall issue of *Dulcimer Players News,* this time featuring Neal Hellman on the cover. With six years of playing under his belt, David feels comfortable enough to have submitted an article about a playing technique he learned from his old friend Roger Harris whom he first met at Winfield.

His writing reflects a generous approach to sharing without a hint of self-aggrandizement. Reading between the lines, it's clear that he considers himself a student rather than a teacher of his instrument. The article is a homage to Roger who shared a picking technique during a visit to Texas two years ago. Harris taught David how to avoid the distracting string noise that can occur while playing and how to keep each note ringing into the next. His pursuit of the cleanest, purest layering of notes has become one of the hallmarks of David's playing style.

If David has any lingering misgivings about having dropped out of school, his "Harris Picking" article should put them to rest. The article reflects not only his musicianship but his interest in history and the appreciation of lifelong learning. It begins with a succinct explanation on the value of Harris's instructions and includes a meticulously handwritten piece of tab so that interested readers may practice the technique. He also includes his arrangement of "The White Cockade," a tune written by the eighteenth-century Scottish national poet Robert Burns. The tune celebrates the story of Bonnie Prince Charlie who plucked a white rose to adorn his hat as a sign of rebellion against the British in his bid to reclaim the throne for the House of Stuart.

"The White Cockade" was the signature song of the minutemen at Concord in the American Revolution and continued its life in America as a popular nineteenth-century fiddle tune. It is one of hundreds of songs that Alan Lomax recorded for posterity in Glasgow, Scotland, in 1951.

David found the song interesting enough to choose it for his first published article for several reasons, no doubt. Burns wrote lyrics and songs in Scottish and in English and was also famous for his amours and his rebellion against orthodox religion and morality.

(173, 174, 175, 176)

## What is "Tab"?

Before tablature or recorded music was created, people who wanted to learn to play a stringed instrument would learn to play by ear. Each time they listened to friends or a family member play a song, they would try to reproduce what they heard. Once records and cassette recordings were easily available, a player could do the same by playing a song over and over to learn it. During the seventies it was very common for players to record each other in jams and in festivals so they could take the cassette home to help them learn new songs.

Most dulcimer tab includes an analog version of the strings with fret numbers. For example, look at the first line of David's tab for "The White Cockade." The three horizontal lines correspond to the three strings of the dulcimer, with the bass string at the top, the middle string, and then the treble string at the bottom of the lines. The zeros refer to an unfretted string. The staplelike image under pairs of numbers suggest that the player strum "out"—away from him or herself— on the first number of the pair, then "in" on the second number of the pair. A single vertical line under the number suggests the player strum out once, but not on the "in" stroke.

Tab greatly facilitates widespread sharing of songs. Many dulcimer players in the 60's and 70's enjoyed the benefits of learning to play by ear, but many also came to embrace tab as a tool for sharing their music with others.

In 1977, Robert Force, Neal Hellman, Michael Rugg, Al d'Ossché, and Bonnie Carol collaborated to put to paper an explanation of how they played to help novice players. Most had never tabbed their music. Friend Baila Dworsky acted as editor because she knew how to sight read, write notational music, and proofread—and she was able to transcribe their music. As Robert Force puts it, "It was right [only] when she said it was and she could play it back to us faithfully as we watched, listened and verified." Together, this group of young people created the first comprehensive approach to mountain dulcimer instruction that included tab in the *Pacific Rim Dulcimer Songbook*.

By the time David's article is published in *Dulcimer Players News*, the growing use of tab will make the dulcimer accessible to countless people around the world, regardless of whether they play by ear or read music notation.

(177, 178, 179, 180)

## JULY 12-15, 1979, BOULDER, COLORADO: RABBIT JUNCTION

News of Rabbit Junction has been buzzing across the country at dulcimer festivals, coffee shops, workshops, and wherever players gather. And now dulcimer players have heeded the call.

Bonnie fulfills her vision of connecting all the major players from both sides of the country on the Boulder Library's beautiful eight acres, just fifteen miles from the Continental Divide. Players show up for the chance to meet people whose names many of them had only read or heard about. Accomplished players such as Doug Berch, Maddie MacNeil, Ron Ewing, and Rick Freimuth from the East attend. Vince Farsetta hitches a ride with Alan Freeman, taking his drums and banjo along as they drive. Many including Fred Meyer, Robert Force, Al d'Ossché, Neal Hellman, Baila Dworsky, and Leo Kretzner represent the western side of the country.

David is renting a house close by that he shares with a few friends. He welcomes Rick Freimuth and anyone else who wants to stay but can't fit into the packed crowd at Bonnie's house. Doug Berch, using a message from Bonnie as a guide, heads to David's house where he is welcomed even though he's meeting his host for the first time.

Like most festivals, there are intensive jams all day and all night. Players learn from each other and share new songs, new licks, new and challenging modes, and useful tips on finger placements to make chords. Players record each other's performances to help them practice when they return home. Indeed, they make over a hundred hours of recordings from the main stage that reflect the wide range of attendees' musical interests: traditional folk and fiddle tunes, Irish jigs and reels, bluegrass, ragtime, contemporary and original songs. Throughout the three-day event, attendees go to workshops taught by volunteers, share songs, and tall tales. David, Bonnie, and Maddie MacNeil are among those who perform during the evening concerts. Break time and late-night conversations range from the practical ("What woods are you building with? How do you get rid of buzz on the strings? How do you get this note or that chord?") to gossip to the metaphysical. During one of these talks, David recognizes Vince Farsetta in his Good Tones shirt; he tells Vince he remembers seeing him in Austin and how much he enjoyed listening to his and the Good Tones' music. To each other's surprise, they discover they were both in the crowd at the Highwoods String Band's concert on the Mall back in 1972.

Nineteen-year-old Doug Berch considers himself a musician who plays the dulcimer as opposed to a dulcimer player. He listens with a keen ear when others play, and his work as a luthier has helped him develop a remarkable sense of sound quality and a deep appreciation for playing techniques. When he hears David perform for the first time during an evening concert, he sits up and takes notice. When David follows a duet with Bonnie with a solo performance of his composition, "Rosie's Arms," Doug is struck by his fluid way of playing. Nothing he does is to show off, not a single note or chord is overdone. He isn't trying to be the fastest gun in the West by doing a showstopper piece. Hot licks are not his thing. He just has the most relaxed, beautiful way of playing the music.

Meals are often communal, but those who drive in with vans do their best to cram friends inside and drive into town to eat. One evening for dinner, several friends head to the Monastery, a restaurant where all the waiters wear monks' robes. David suggests to the group that they could play some fiddle tunes on their dulcimers for tips; the songs are so lively the "monks" begin to dance the can-can with their other customers.

Bonnie's house is full. Once all the late night conversations and jams fade away, her living room is crammed with out-of-town players sleeping on the floor, on the couch, and curled up in the chairs. After a first-day grocery run, Al d'Ossché had left a crate of grapes in the middle of the living room floor for everyone to help themselves. However, nobody wants to eat them after the first night since so many people stepped in the crate in the dark as they made their way to the bathroom.

On the last day, the eighty-five participants join together to sing a final festival farewell: Richard Fariña's most well-known song, "Pack Up Your Sorrows." Afterward, the crowd scatters toward all points on the compass, with promises to return to do it again next year. Many attendees share that they had never heard so many excellent dulcimer players in one place before like they did at Rabbit Junction.

(181, 182, 183, 184)


## 1979 FRONT ROYAL, VIRGINIA: MADDIE MACNEIL, EDITOR-IN-CHIEF

In November, Maddie Mason-MacNeil types her first letter as new editor-in-chief for the *Dulcimer Players News* winter issue. She includes a mention within that "Phil Mason has been devoting his time to other projects lately," a polite way of explaining that Phil's other project for the past year is a relationship that doesn't include Maddie. He has left her, both personally and professionally.

Maddie takes over the work to keep DPN going along with help from friends Keith and Mary Young, Ralph Lee Smith, and their large circle. The Youngs provide the workers, the site for assembling the Fall issue, and many meals to help support their friend who is now inundated with responsibilities. Rick Freimuth and several others join in to help her with regular DPN "collating" parties, and do whatever they can until Maddie can hire more help in the coming year.

Maddie decides she doesn't need Phil's small hand tools, instrument woods, hammered dulcimer plans, bulk music wire or tuning pins, so she offers them to Rick and David Young. Despite their sorrow for Maddie, they glimpse a new opportunity for the two of them, so they accept the gift. They will move to Viola, Idaho to become luthiers and open their own shop, "Bitterroot Dulcimers."

(185, 186)

---

### *How to Build a Dulcimer (Simplified) by Rick Freimuth*

Keith Young taught his son David, Rick Freimuth and David Schnaufer how to build dulcimers. Following is Rick's description of what he learned from Keith.

Select the wood; Keith usually used local hardwoods like walnut, cherry or maple and often a softwood like spruce or cedar for the soundboard. After selecting your wood for the back, sides and soundboard, re-saw the wood to 1/8" to 1/10" thick and sand it smooth.

The wood for the soundboard and back is typically bookmatched. This method allows you to open up the adjacent pieces of one board like the pages of a book; they are mirror images of each other. Glue together the two thin, bookmatched planks edge to edge so each is one thin plank, one for the top and one for the bottom. This method of glue-up produces an attractive and stronger dulcimer that produces a good sound.

The fretboard, peghead, tailblock, and headblock are also cut out of the same wood as the main body of the instrument and shaped to fit for the particular dulcimer by sawing and carving.

Place the sides of the dulcimer on a bending iron and in a jig in the shape of the dulcimer, usually a teardrop or hourglass shape. Glue the head block and tailback to the sides while it's in the jig. Very thin strips of spruce called "lining" are glued to the inside edges of the sides and sanded smooth. This structure provides a better gluing surface and helps support the soundboard and bottom of the dulcimer.

The soundboard and back are cut in the rough shape of the instrument and glued to the sides while in the jig. After the glue has dried, remove the dulcimer body from the jig and sand it smooth.

Cut and sand the fretboard wood to its final size. Saw the fret slots and slots for the bridge and nut with a backsaw in a special jig so the fret placement is correct and accurate. This ensures the instrument will sound in tune with other instruments. Press the frets into the fretboard, trim and buff them; then glue the fretboard to the top of the instrument.

Drill the peghead to accept friction pegs or machine tuners. Glue the peghead to the body of the dulcimer.

Now that the body of the dulcimer is complete, give it a final sanding before applying the finish. We typically finished the dulcimer with a lacquer finish sprayed by can or spray gun. After applying several coats of finish, we buffed and polished the dulcimer.

The bridge and nut can be made of plastic, bone or ebony. Cut each to size and insert them into position. Cut very fine slots into the bridge and nut to position and accept the traditional four strings.

> Mount the friction pegs or machine tuners in the peghead and then string the dulcimer music wire of the appropriate gauges.
>
> You can now tune the instrument and have fun playing "Boil Them Cabbage," "Joellen," "Cripple Creek," "Wellyn," "Shady Grove," or whatever you like!
>
> (187)

## 1980 KETTERING, OHIO: RON EWING

Ron Ewing and David first met at Cosby two years ago; the two met again later that summer while David was touring with Tres Ríos. Last year, David took a bus to visit Ron who was working at a pro bike shop and building dulcimers on the side. Ron likes David with his slight Texas swagger and droll sense of humor, and David loves hanging with Ron; he's a luthier and a talented musician. He's also generous with his time and knowledge. Last year, Ron introduced David to the Irish slip jig, "Drops of Brandy," and David returned the favor by sharing "There is a Rose in Spanish Harlem." Now he is back for more; David's interest in Irish music has grown, especially since he discovered during genealogy research that his paternal great-grandmother was the daughter of Irish immigrants. Later, David will write "Rock Th' Shay" as a nod to another kindred spirit, the great-grandmother he never met, Elizabeth Shay.

(188, 189, 190)

## 1980 FRESNO, CALIFORNIA: JEAN RITCHIE, RESIDENT SCHOLAR

Academic Gene Bluestein wears many hats at California State University: English professor, musician, folklorist, and social activist, and he feels a deep connection to the current folk music revival. He facilitates the Folk Artist in Residence Program at Cal State and has invited his good friend Jean Ritchie to become the Scholar in Residence for the academic year.

Jean continues to perform internationally and tours the United States in concerts and music festivals, alternating mountain ballads with European and contemporary folk songs to show the similarities and differences. Her interests have grown considerably since her first foray into New York City as a teacher.

Jean straddles two schools of thought these days: the first is concerned with Appalachian tradition and identity: preserving folklore, songs, toys and games, foods, and cultural perspectives. The second has to do with political and socioeconomics; its adherents are deeply concerned about exploitation and social injustice in Appalachia. She composes much of her own music now, including protest songs. Jean Ritchie lives and works with a firm foot in each camp and is a national treasure known among her fans as "The Mother of Folk Music".

(191, 192, 193, 194)


## 1980 LIMA, OHIO: "SOMETHING NOTEWORTHY ALWAYS HAPPENS"

A year after Rabbit Junction, Doug Berch hitchhikes from Philly to the Great Black Swamp Festival in Lima, Ohio, where he has been hired to perform. Doug and hundreds of other dulcimer players, fiddlers, saw players, autoharpists, bones players and fans of American acoustic music pour into Ohio State University for a day of traditional music immersion.

Ron Ewing attends and considers it the best professionally run festival: performers and teachers get paid; the classrooms are indoors as is a cafeteria, and there's even a nice auditorium. Over the years, Black Swamp will become a model for future festivals, including one that Kentucky's Nancy (Johnson) Barker is planning as an addition to the Kentucky Music Weekend festival she started four years ago.

When Doug gets to Lima, he finds a pay phone to call for a pickup. His ride arrives, and as he and the driver chat on their way to the festival, Doug suddenly sees David hitchhiking on the road. He asks the driver to stop, and the two friends from Rabbit Junction greet each other with laughs of recognition. Once David hops into the car, he explains that he has left Colorado for good. He doesn't know what's coming next, so he just decided to hitchhike out to Black Swamp to see what's happening there.

Once they get to the festival grounds, Doug gets the okay to have David crash with him and the other performers. While at Black Swamp, Al Freeman, another new pal from Rabbit Junction, hooks up with David, Doug and other Rabbit Junction alumni for jams and conversation.

Doug believes that something noteworthy always happens around dulcimers and around David especially. He tells a reporter who interviews him later that day: "You can throw people with all different kinds of interests into a room with a couple dulcimers, and they'll have a blast. It's just something about the dulcimer."

The unexpected continues the next morning. Doug and David only have three dollars between them when they head to a Howard Johnson's restaurant for breakfast. David has just enough money to order the poached eggs, and Doug has just enough for the scrambled eggs. When the waitress arrives to serve them, she places two plates on the table and tells them, "A guy who ordered the identical breakfasts to yours just up and left, so you two get your breakfasts on the house." Doug and David look at each other and burst out laughing. When they leave the restaurant, the waitress gets a very nice tip.

The next time David attends Black Swamp, it won't be as an attendee. He, too, will be hired to teach and to perform to a massive, standing-room-only crowd.

(195, 196)

## 1980 LOUISVILLE, KY: NANCY (JOHNSON) BARKER'S SURPRISE GUEST

Nancy Johnson, now Nancy Barker, has grown from a teenager in love with the dulcimer and Jean Ritchie's music to founder and director of the annual folk festival "Kentucky Music Weekend." Now, she's in the middle of prepping for an additional festival to be called Kentucky Music Week, which will immediately follow the weekend festival every spring to bring music, food, crafts, and classes to thousands of traditional music fans.

Nancy had first conceived of Kentucky Music Weekend as part of the Kentucky 1976 Bicentennial Festival. This year, she expects fifteen thousand attendees at Louisville's Iroquois (Park) Amphitheater. Kentucky Music Week will take place afterward at the University of Louisville campus. The girl who once stared with awe at Jean Ritchie singing at Toronto's Mariposa Festival now counts Jean as a friend whom she hires to perform whenever she is available.

Nancy is a new mother with a year-old baby, trying to juggle the countless tasks involved in running not one, but two back-to-back festivals. One afternoon, a week before the festivals, she hears a knock on the door and opens it. Startled to see a little long-haired hippy smiling at her, he introduces himself as David Schnaufer, one of the performers and teachers she hired. "I just hitchhiked into town," he informs her. Nancy has interacted with all kinds of quirky musicians over the years as a festival director, but she is swamped with work. To have an unexpected guest the week before Kentucky Music Weekend is unwelcome, to say the least.

David notices the panic on her face and says with his finest and slowest Texas drawl, "*Nowww, Nanceee-loou,* what can *Ah* do to make your life easier?" Nancy gives him a look: "the dishes, and then watch my daughter Jenny Lou so I can get you a place to stay and I can work on Festival business." Without missing a beat, David tells her, "I can do that!" And he washes the dishes, cooks supper, and takes care of little Jenny whom he nicknames "the (Jelly) Bean."

As Nancy gets to know David, her stress basically vanishes. She is struck by how full of love her houseguest seems to be. She feels a kind of bright light around him whenever he walks in to the room. She invites David to stay, offering him her foldout couch for the next week. Thanks to his help and much to her surprise, Nancy finishes all the festival work on time. She loves his stories and the gentle ways he interacts with the Bean. One evening, David proudly shows Nancy his leather case full of jaw harps and plays different songs on several different harps for her.

His performance at Kentucky Music Weekend is a showstopper, as are his standing-room-only classes and performances during the weeklong festival. The time they share since David arrived is the beginning of another strong, lifelong friendship, and Nancy will invite him back to stay at her place every year he teaches and performs. Later in life, when she talks with her friends about David, she will tell them: "He was the brother I never had with a touch of best friend thrown in for good measure."

(197, 198, 199)

## 1980 SANTA CRUZ, CA: "THE INHERENT PROBLEM OF … A PECULIAR INSTRUMENT"

Bob Force and Al d'Ossché agree to talk to a reporter about their preferred instrument's challenge in the world of today's music. The reporter notes their ability to live with little notoriety in Santa Cruz; "Such a state" he writes, "sums up the 'inherent problem' of the modern dulcimer player." He characterizes the dulcimer as a "peculiar instrument" with "typical sounds rooted in the 'hillbilly school of music' of Appalachia with its 'round up the chickens and feed the hogs' themes ... an entertaining but somewhat limited form of aural entertainment."

The reporter finishes his piece, titles it "Taking the Dull out of Dulcimer," and submits it to the *Santa Cruz Sentinel* for publication.

(200)


## 1980 RIO GRANDE, OHIO: THE PASSING OF THE TORCH

This year is the tenth anniversary of the three-day, eleven-thousand-acre Bob Evans Farm Festival, some 120 miles from Dayton, Ohio. It's the perfect time of year—mid- October—with the fields surrounded by cornhusks and falling leaves, the air filled with smoke from cooking fires mingled with the sounds of old-time music wafting in every direction. Thousands of attendees come to experience a taste of rural life of the past, a time when most of them imagine life was slower-paced and simpler. Sipping hot cider, they visit a farm museum to study the vintage tools, or take walks in nature to see milking demonstrations, oxen pulling hay wagons, and a band of Spanish mustangs that Bob Evans imported from the West. Visitors watch hundreds of heritage craft demonstrations, including rifle making, soap and candle making, quilting, blacksmithing, stone cutting, log hewing and shingle splitting, sheep shearing, weaving and log rolling in the pond. They can watch sorghum molasses or apple butter making surrounded by the ever-present smoke and aromas of ham and beans bubbling in big black kettles over hot fires.

And there are contests, too: tobacco spitting and chasing a greased pig that anyone with a sense of humor and an urge to try can give it a go. For music lovers, opportunities abound: clogging and square dancers, fiddlers, guitars, and mandolin players perform and

compete. Ten contests alone are dedicated to fretted dulcimer players with divisions for children, adults, solo players, duets, and so on.

Last year, Alan Freeman was the star of the Appalachian dulcimer contests at Bob Evans, taking first place in most of the contests he entered, including Grand Champion Mountain Dulcimer.

This year, the throngs are packed to see and hear David
Schnaufer. As he hits the strings and rips through "Santa Ana's
Retreat" for the finale, the crowd roars with approval. David takes
first place in every contest he enters, and the judges name him
Grand Champion Mountain Dulcimer Player of the Festival.

(201)

## 1981 WEST VIRGINIA: "THE ONLY THING THAT SOUNDS BETTER…"

After bumping into each other at one festival after another, Al Freeman, keenly aware of and impressed with David's sweep of the Bob
Evans festival last year, invites him to live at his place in Grantsville
to play music and tour together.

David accepts his invitation and makes his way to the Freemans'
little farm just outside Charleston. He arrives to see that the house is
tin-roofed, small and rough-hewn. It consists of two bedrooms, one
large room for the kitchen and living room and an outside pump in
lieu of running water. Alan and his wife Carol have one bedroom;

their two toddlers share the other. At first, David sacks out on
the couch by the wood stove; later, he moves to his old van to sleep.
No indoor plumbing means that everyone

uses the outhouse out back with its interior walls covered floor
to ceiling with Alan's countless ribbons and trophies.

Neighbor Harry Beall stops by to meet David. Harry explains
that he considers himself primarily a songwriter, but he plays guitar
with Alan a couple of times a week. Soon the three are playing two
or three times a week in the evenings whenever Alan and David
back home after working gigs and hitting festivals together.

When Harry's wife asks him what it's like to play with David, he shares his impressions with her; with respect to Alan, Harry notes that Alan has a scary charm. He is strong-willed, and likes being the leader in the jams. Alan is a very strong, fast player who loves nothing more than to tear into a melody, mostly using his thumb on the melody string. He even has two grooves on the fretboard from noting with his thumb up and down the string. Alan usually plays the chord root on an open string. He loves to sing, but Harry jokes with his wife that Alan's singing isn't pretty. It doesn't stop him though; he wails out with a gruff voice on many of his songs. She's not surprised when Harry tells her that Alan makes all the decisions about when and where they play along with all the arrangements.

David, on the other hand, seems a little on the shy side, Harry explains. It's just easier for him to let Alan lead. David is primarily an instrumentalist. He plays with a pick, yet he's softer and more melodic, almost as if he were finger picking. He uses all the strings to play the melody and uses all of his fingers except his thumb* when he chords. He really knows how to embellish a chord progression to come up with a sweet melody. Nevertheless, he and Alan trade leads during jams, and Harry plays rhythm on guitar.

Harry loves hanging around with Alan and David. Both are extremely good-hearted, and there is plenty of pot thanks to Alan's patches planted throughout the eleven acres. David is soft-spoken and a gentle soul, and Alan is generous with his knowledge of music. However, the longer he plays with them, the more Harry worries; Alan, especially, drinks a lot, and gradually, Harry regretfully admits that he finds himself trying to keep up with that part too much.

When asked why he doesn't use his thumb, David tells the story of being picked up by a strange guy in a pickup truck while hitchhiking. He became so uneasy he asked the guy to stop, but he wouldn't. Finally, David grabbed his things and jumped out the door, hurting his thumb on the way out. Ever since then, he hasn't used his thumb to fret.

(202, 203)

# 1981 WEST VIRGINIA: LEO KRETZNER PAYS A VISIT

Al and Carol Freeman want to take a short break from the July heat. Along with David they pack up their tents, instruments, floats for the children, and food in the car. Their destination is the Stonecoal reservoir, a favorite camping spot. When Leo Kretzner calls to say he's in the state visiting his mom, David invites him to meet them at the campground. It suits Alan fine; he often expresses his philosophy: "The only thing that sounds better than one dulcimer is two dulcimers, but once you get three or more it's like someone kicked over a beehive."

Leo drives in for the day. He's not long out of the car when the jamming begins. Leo and David start on dulcimers as Al grabs a mandolin. Leo loves the fiddle tunes and leads off; David and Al pick up the song and run with it. Al starts the next round with a ragtime song plucked from his mental library. On and on they play, taking turns with favorites, new songs and old; between sips of beer and tokes on joints, they play, soaked with sweat from the humidity. By evening they're finally spent. Carol calls them over to eat, and they exchange stories about the good and bad gigs they've had, what their friends are up to, festivals coming up and new songs they are working on. Leo shares his thoughts from his own cover story and interview in this spring's *Dulcimer Players News*. Leo's point of view resonates deeply with David and Alan: "A lot of the shortcomings of dulcimer music until recently has been in the way that most people thought of the instrument. It seems that many dulcimer players had a lower expectation for their music than a guitarist or a banjo player would have had. Anything a banjo player can play, I ought to be able to play. If I can't, I don't think of the instrument as being limited, but that I need to develop a new technique or tuning, or maybe just practice more."

Leo is scheduled to teach a course at Augusta college soon, so as night approaches, he packs up and says goodbye. As he drives away, David and Alan start another jam again. When Al finally decides to hit the sack, David stays up until the wee hours under the stars, softly playing the dulcimer to and for himself.

(204, 205)

## 1982 AUSTIN, TEXAS: MACK WHITE

As a kid, Mack White was always drawing and dreaming of being a cartoonist some day. Now working as a staff member at the University of Texas School of Architecture, he splits his time between working for a living and following his passion: as a longtime underground comics fan, he uses his art and writing skills to self-publish comics he sells through the mail. Occasionally he mails his unique artwork to an appreciative David, or shows him his latest creations whenever David passes through Texas.

(206)

## 1982 WEST VIRGINIA: "THE GUY'S A HIPPY, BUT HE'S A FAMILY MAN"

The police officer sits hidden in his cruiser off on the side of the road, his radar gun on, and his eyes peeled for suspicious characters. David drives by in his latest vehicle he calls "the Stealth," a moniker he bestowed upon it when he bought the old junker. It had so much duct tape wrapped around various parts inside and out that he figured it was there to hold the car together. As the policemen sits, scanning the traffic, he notices a long-haired, shaggy hippy drive past in a rust bucket and decides he's up to no good. He hits the lights and the siren, pulls out, and hits the gas. David, seeing the lights in his rearview mirror fast approaching, stiffens as he pulls over, knowing that someone who looks like he does in this town runs the risk of getting roughed up for sure.

As he hands over his license and registration, he is more polite than the policeman expects. When the officer notices a Beanie Baby stuffed toy on the dashboard, he changes his mind. "The guy's a hippy, but he's a family man," he thinks. He tells him to get home, and sends him off with just a warning.

(207)

## 1982 AUSTIN, TEXAS: "THE PRINCE OF NASHVILLE'S MUSIC JOURNALISTS"

The Barker Texas History Center at the University of Texas sponsors an evening of stories and anecdotes during the opening night of the exhibit to celebrate the patriarch of the Lomax clan. Entitled "Folklorist John Avery Lomax," the exhibit showcases the life of the music pioneer whose work includes publishing the first collection of American folk songs. Visitors can browse original documents, photos, vintage recordings, and artifacts that trace John Avery's lifelong search for American ballads.

Other attendees noted this night include the well-known humorist (and *Hee Haw* storyteller) John Henry Faulk, who speaks on "Ballad Hunters and Story Chasers I Have Known." John Avery's son and renowned musicologist Alan Lomax mingles; so does John Avery's daughter Bess, the well-known and respected authority on children's folklore. Bess and Alan's nephew John Lomax III is there with his family. The next day, the papers will describe John III as "the Prince of Nashville's music journalists."

(208, 209, 210)

## 1983 NASHVILLE, TENNESSEE: THE JUDDS

The fastest rising superstar musical act in Nashville is a mother/daughter duo by the names of Naomi and Wynonna Judd. Their music reflects their intimate experiences of working-class, small-town women gained firsthand in their own long and personal struggles first in Kentucky and, later, in California.

After the two moved back to Kentucky, Naomi began her determined pursuit of a career in Nashville. Finally, RCA signed the pair this year, and the two work on their first full-length album, *Why Not Me* for release next year. The Judds appeal to a wide range of listeners via their blend of traditional country harmony, bluegrass, and Appalachian folk with pop, rock and Wynonna's bluesy lead vocals. Two of the album's songs will earn them Grammys, and the album itself will sell over a million copies.

David Schnaufer catches their song, "Had a Dream" on the car radio, released this year as a single. He is captivated by the tension between their energetic rhythm, their perfect harmony and the story of a broken heart. It's their acoustic sound, however, that resonates most. He has already started making plans to cut an EP record demo to showcase his playing and songwriting skills, and he is determined to play with the Judds. *Why Not Me?* indeed.

(211, 212)

## 1983 NASHVILLE, TENNESSEE: COUNTRY MUSIC TELEVISION

When MTV launched its own music channel in 1981, the network's popularity exploded. Video-friendly artists like Australia's Men at Work had struggled to catch on in America during the first half of 1980. Suddenly, they found themselves selling unexpected millions of albums in the markets that had been wired for cable TV. Before long, many other artists were topping the Billboard charts, too—proof that MTV had become nearly as influential as radio in launching new hitmakers.

Country music stakeholders want a piece of the action, and they get it on March 5th, 1983, at 6:19 p.m. Country Music Television, or CMTV [1] starts things off on a traditional note by airing its very first music video, a mellow clip of Faron Young's "It's Four in the Morning." Just before the song begins, Young asks the female violinist, "Are you ready, lovely?" Andrew Leahey of *Rolling Stone* points out that his question might as well have been directed to a new generation of country fans who wanted to *see*, not just hear, their music.

(213)

## 1983 BOULDER, COLORADO: A MAN TRANSFORMED

Bonnie Carol, who had been inspired both by Richard Fariña's music and Jean Ritchie's instructional book when she first picked up a dulcimer, publishes her own *Dust Off That Dulcimer & Dance!*, a guidebook to the care and playing of the dulcimer. It's an homage to the seventies dulcimer boom and a testimony to her dedication to a lifetime of devotion to dulcimer music that is filled with her photos of dulcimer players.

Part music theory textbook, part tab and method book, Carol's book presents the dulcimer as a contemporary phenomenon. She thanks all who have helped shaped her own musical journey and reveals the indelible stamp that David and mandolin player Diana White left on her life. The book includes several songs they wrote and/or arranged over twenty years ago. She credits Diana with "Have Mercy on the Turtle in the Road" (a title coined by David), "Prizes," and "Growing Rain." She also includes "Santa Ana's Retreat," the traditional song that Diana arranged for David long ago and the one that he played many times in the competitions and contests of his early performing years. She highlights David's contributions for his work on the dulcimer, harmonica, jaw harp, and bones.

---

1. *Later, Country Music Television will drop the "V" from its acronym when MTV sues the network for trademark infringement)

One of the more insightful, original compositions Bonnie penned and includes in the book is entitled "La Marque." It chronicles the transformation of a man who begins life from a place of sadness and woe into a person who has come to know his place in the world and is content with it.

(214)

## 1983 WEST VIRGINIA: "SOMEBODY'S GOT TO DO IT ..."

Alan cut his first album, *Black Mountain Dulcimer* back in 1978, only two years after he picked up the dulcimer. After touring with David, he decides it's time to produce an album together. They have plenty of songs and an impressive sound; David is excited about recording since he'd rather earn money selling his cassettes at the festivals than by working in construction on the side. Based on the immense and enthusiastic crowds they encounter wherever they perform, they feel confident that the market for their music is there.

Pulling in friends for the session work, they record *Hog Fiddler's Fancy* straight to cassette. They list the contents as "A Picker's Dozen," the joke being there are only eleven songs. Alan chooses the songs that best demonstrate their versatility across different traditions and genres.

One of Al's favorite Dixieland tunes, the 1910 football fight song "Washington and Lee Swing," heads the top of the list. Al leads and David plays the jaw harp, a skill that he learned almost a quarter century ago from his father. David sings and plays his Bonnie Carol dulcimer on "Rosie's Arms," a gentle ballad he wrote about a woman across the border in Mexico who gives more than she takes from a man with certain sorrows in his heart. David's voice sounds younger than his thirty-one years, but confident. His clean lyricism reveals a longing for Rosie's company mixed with resignation at the way the world works. He pulls out the jaw harp again for "Santa Ana's Retreat", crediting the version to Diana in the liner notes. He leads on the lively "Texas Quick Step" with the dulcimer and their cover of Ennio Morricone's spaghetti western theme, "The Good, the Bad and the Ugly." Their composition "Viper Moon" shows off their jazz chops. Mexican composer Juventino Rosas's waltz, "Sobre las Olas" ("Over the Waves," often attributed erroneously to Strauss) provides yet another genre. The unlikely mix of tunes even includes the Christmas song "Bring a Torch" [Jeannette Isabella] on the hammered dulcimer and bowed bass.

The list ends with "Whiskey Before Breakfast," a tune originating from the percussive Metis fiddle tradition of Canada. Al's growly voice front and center tears through their rendition, evoking a frenetic songfest at a rowdy pub. The two partners mesh seamlessly on every song. Just as they imagined, the cassettes sell well at festivals and gigs wherever they play. However, it still isn't enough to live on, so David continues to work construction in Virginia on the side; he needs to earn more cash to pay for his upcoming travel plans.

Aware of the resurging popularity of acoustic music thanks largely to the Judds, David knows the time is right to promote the mountain dulcimer as a studio instrument as worthy as the fiddle, banjo, and guitar. For years now, he has tried to reach guitarist/producer Chet Atkins to make the case that the dulcimer needs to be taken seriously in country music. After taking David's calls and messages and reading letter after letter from him, Atkins's weary secretary advised him that if he really wanted country music to take the mountain dulcimer seriously, he would have to do more than write letters and make phone calls. He needs to move to Nashville and take a demo record with him.

When David tells Alan about his plans to leave West Virginia for Nashville, Al doesn't take it well. Alan is a bundle of contradictions: a self-described abrasive, opinionated man, he is part wonderful, part overbearing, part nurturing, but often brusque and obnoxious: a man with a big heart but who frequently rants and complains. David's plans don't sit well with Alan; he likes things the way they are, and he's angry about the split. Alan pushes hard against the idea. David pushes back, pulled by the need to continue his odyssey to spread the gospel of the dulcimer as an instrument worthy enough to join the pantheon of serious country instruments.

Even though David has long been sleeping in his van at Alan's, it doesn't help that five people within the small house has become too much. It's time to go. David is grateful, but he wants more. Arguments continue. David tells Alan he can come with him, but Alan says no. He's perfectly content to stay in his adopted home of West Virginia, playing with the old timers at the festivals and performing in club gigs.

The next time David sees Bonnie Carol at a festival, he tells her: "*Somebody* needs to take the dulcimer to Nashville; I guess it's going to be me."

(215, 216, 217, 218, 219, 220, 221)

---

### David and Alan

Since the beginning of their friendship, Alan was in it for the camaraderie and the most intense playing of his life. His approach to the dulcimer and dedication to pushing boundaries resonated deeply within David. During their four years of touring and performing on the road, David served both as partner and an eager apprentice who never rested on his laurels, despite his own blue ribbons hanging next to Alan's in the outhouse.

Their mutual friend Harry Beall concluded about Alan and David: "I think they were both born for the dulcimer."

When David bid goodbye to the Freemans, he was on the last part of his eight-year odyssey. Through his letters, tapes, and unreturned calls to his hero Chet Atkins, David tried to convey the strong case that the first authentic American instrument is the most country instrument of all, with its long taproot into the earliest folk music of the United States. The dulcimer will not be ignored.

David expressed his gratitude to Alan Freeman during interviews for the rest of his life.

"I learned an awful lot from him, especially about theory. He made me learn my scales and where the chords were— all the stuff I'd been missing." This multi-champion contest winner will always self-assess and will always credit others for their help in shaping him as a musician.

(222, 223, 224)

*1560 Angel playing a zither. This image on the ceiling of Rykenby Church in Denmark is the first known depiction of a dulcimer. David Schnaufer will share this image in a scholarly paper some four hundred years after an artist depicted this angel. Courtesy of Rykenby Church.*

*1821: Nineteenth century German immigrants sent documents like this one ("Travels through the United States") to friends and family back home to convince them to join them in the United States.*

APPALACHIAN AMERICA

*The 1903 map of Appalachia by Berea College president Robert Goodell Frost.*
*Courtesy of Berea College Special Collections and Archives.*

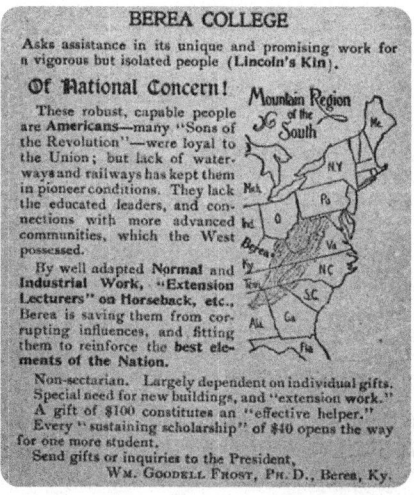

*Robert Goodell Frost's plea for funds for Berea College after coining the term,*
*"Appalachia." Courtesy of Berea College Special Collections and Archives.*

*Christian and May Schnaufer holding newborn grandson Dennis Eric Schnaufer in 1945. Courtesy of Eric Schnaufer.*

*Alan Lomax in 1947 New York City where he did much to promote the dulcimer through his work with Jean Ritchie. The Alan Lomax Collection at the American Folklife Center, Library of Congress. Courtesy of The Association for Cultural Equity.*

*Three generations of Lomax men. A young Johnny Lomax listens as his father John II reads from his grandfather John Avery Lomax's book,* Adventures of a Ballad Hunter. *Johnny will grow up and do his part to promote the dulcimer and its music through David. Courtesy of John Lomax III.*

*1952 Frank and Edith Schnaufer with new son David Lynn Schnaufer. Courtesy of Eric Schnaufer.*

*David toddles while his big brother Eric watches in 1953. Courtesy of Eric Schnaufer.*

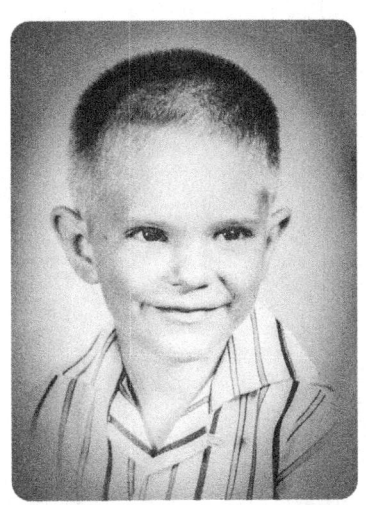

*1957 David is five in this 1957 photo. Courtesy of Eric Schnaufer.*

*Six-year-old Vince Farsetta . While Vince grew up in New York and David in Texas, their lives overlap starting in their twenties; the two musical geniuses seemed destined to meet. Courtesy of Vince Farsetta.*

*1968 David's high school junior photo, the year he dropped out of school to help take care of his mother*

*David in Bea Jordan's garden in 1971 Bea's garden would inspire "Brush Arbor",*
*the song David co-wrote with friend Rick Roberts. Courtesy of Norman Jordan.*

*David and Norman Jordan in the Jordan's garden.*

*Vince Farsetta with his first banjo in 1972. Courtesy of Vince Farsetta.*

*David stands up for Eric and Thiela's 1973 wedding. Courtesy of Eric Schnaufer.*

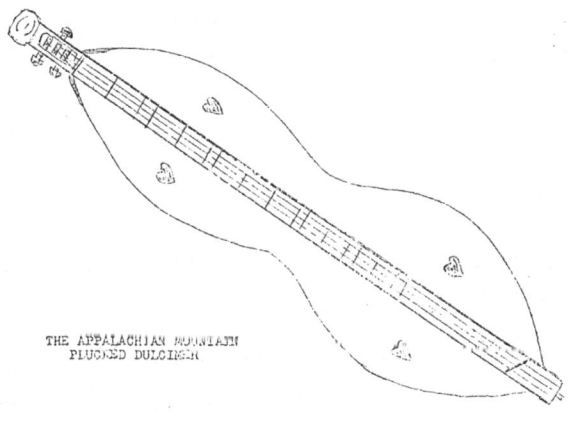

THE APPALACHIAN MOUNTAIN
PLUCKED DULCIMER

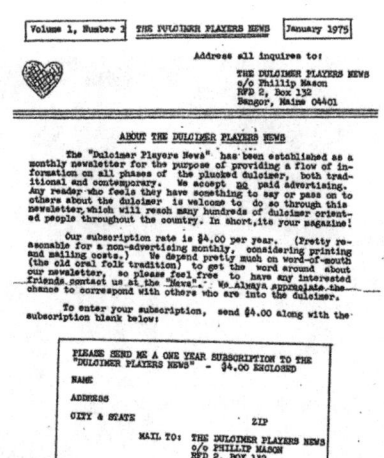

*The hand-drawn and typewritten first cover and first page of the first magazine known then as The Dulcimer Players News. Almost half a century later, Dulcimer Players News is still going strong. Courtesy of Dulcimer Players News/Ashley Ernst.*

*David at Jean and Lee Schilling's first dulcimer festival in Cosby, Tennessee in 1976. Courtesy of Bonnie Carol.*

*Classically-trained mandolin player Diana White taught David mandolins skills that contributed to his development of his unique style of playing. Diana and Bonnie Carol helped David learn to arrange music as well. Courtesy of Bonnie Carol.*

*Forming in 1976, Tres Ríos—Bonnie Carol, Diana White, and David—toured together after meeting at the Schilling's dulcimer festival in Cosby, Tennessee. Courtesy of Bonnie Carol.*

*Al d'Ossché (left) and Robert Force were two of the most unique and influential West Coast dulcimer players. Courtesy of Rick Freimuth.*

*When David first arrived at Keith and Mary Young's home in Annandale in 1977, the neighborhood kids were fascinated by his humble personality, his playing posture and the Herdim pics he special ordered. His Texas belt buckle, and his little rabbit fur pouch helped make him larger than life in their eyes. Photo courtesy of Rick Freimuth.*

*L to R. David looks on while Mary and Keith Young give directions to Jay Round and Cathy Barton, two of the many traveling folkies who passed through their home during festival season in Annandale, Virginia. Photo courtesy of Rick Freimuth.*

*Brooklyn-born Al Freeman made a life-time career on the dulcimer with his unique tuning and music repertoire after moving to West Virginia. Here he jams at Keith Young's booth at the Old Fiddler's Convention in Galax, Virginia. Photo courtesy of Rick Freimuth.*

*Informal jam at the 1977 Galax Festival. L to R: Rick Freimuth (seated); Alan Freeman and Keith Young watch Ralph Lee Smith play. Ralph and Keith were friends and neighbors. Courtesy of Rick Freimuth.*

*Phil Mason, founder of The Dulcimer Players News, and Maddie MacNeil at Galax. Maddie*
*became sole editor in 1979. For the next twenty-seven years, she became an acclaimed*
*performer, recording artist, author, and music teacher. Her friends treasured her, and her*
*contributions to mountain dulcimer history are priceless thanks to her work on Dulcimer*
*Players News, her recordings, her music and her writing. Her collaborations with good friend*
*Ralph Lee Smith helped save and promote traditional folk music. Courtesy of Rick Freimuth.*

*Al Freeman and Keith Young watch David play at Keith's booth during the 1977
Central Pennsylvania Arts Festival. Many players who looked up to Keith jammed
around his booth to help attract customers to his instruments and goods for sale.
Courtesy of Rick Freimuth.*

*Bonnie Carol visited the Youngs during the summer of 1977 while leading a tour
of music students to the East Coast. Here, Jay Round, David and Bonnie jam on
the Young's back deck.*

*1978 David and Bonnie in her Colorado workshop. Bonnie, an expert luthier and musician, taught David the intricacies of dulcimer-making. A year later, Bonnie would create "Rabbit Junction", the national dulcimer festival designed to bring the best dulcimer players from both sides of the country to meet in Boulder. Courtesy of Rick Freimuth.*

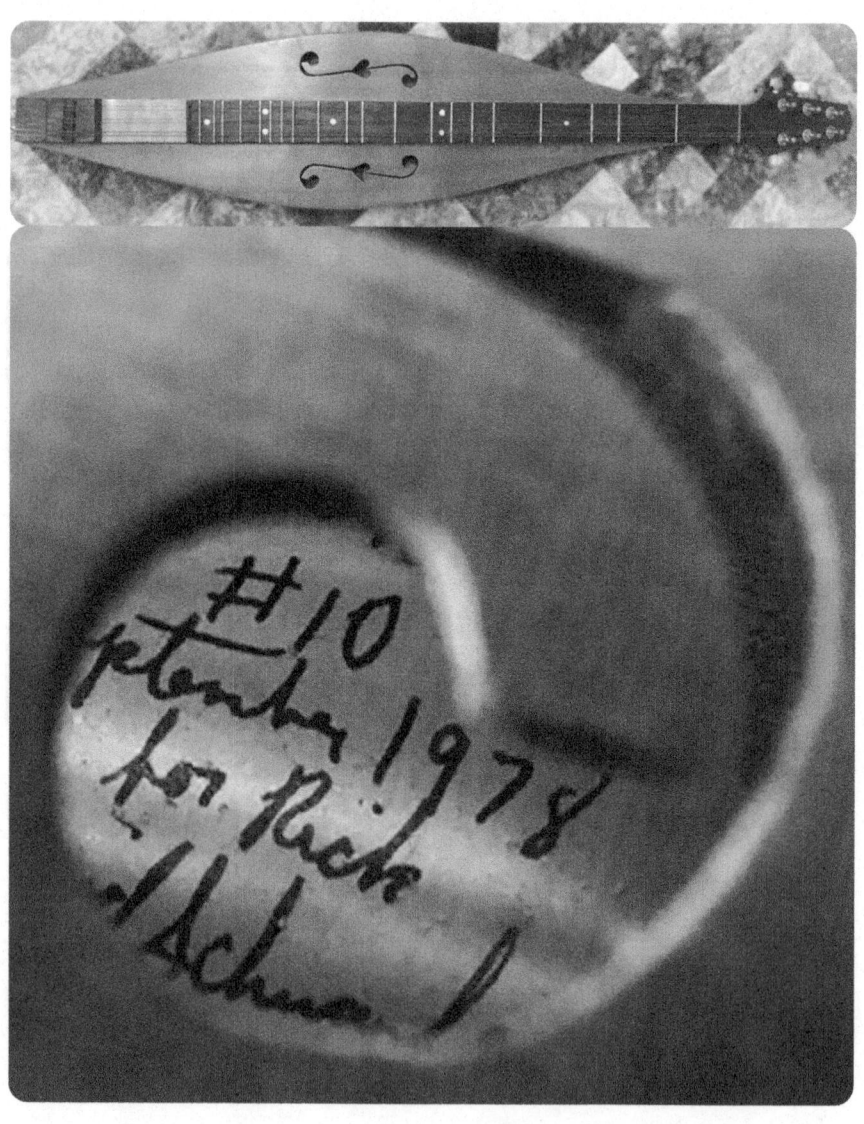

*David learned a great deal about working as a musician and dulcimer-making thanks to*
*Bonnie Carol. He made his tenth dulcimer in Bonnie's workshop for friend Rick in 1978.*
*David's signature is tucked inside the sound hole. Courtesy of Rick Freimuth.*

Bonnie's 1979 Rabbit Junction festival attracted a hundred of the best players in the country for a weekend of learning, performing, jamming and socializing. David is in the front row, third to the right from the center; Vince Farsetta is in the second row, just behind and to the right of the hammered dulcimer in front. Rick Freimuth is seated in second row to Bonnie on the right. Photo courtesy of Rick Freimuth.

*Vince Farsetta at Rabbit Junction. David and Vince finally met each other; upon seeing Vince in this t-shirt, David told him he had seen him perform in Austin. They learned they both had attended the same performance by the Highwoods String Band on the Mall in Washington. Courtesy of Bonnie Carol.*

*David getting ready to perform on stage at the Rabbit Junction festival. Courtesy of Bonnie Carol.*

*Leo Kretzner was working as a naturalist in the serene surroundings of Ohio's Glen Helen Outdoor Education Center when David show up at his door to jam and learn from him. Courtesy of Leo Kretzner.*

*Alan Freeman and David on a camping trip in West Virginia. They were joined by Leo Kretzner on a visit for the day as he was making his way to teach a course at the Augusta Heritage Center in Elkins. Courtesy of Leo Kretzner.*

*Jean Ritchie, the woman who started the mountain dulcimer on its journey through modern time, visits with Neal Hellman, member of the next generation of modern dulcimer musicians at the 1981 Kentucky Music Weekend in Louisville, Kentucky. Photo courtesy of Leo Kretzner.*

*In 1981 David met up with old friends at Booty's Number Two Crossing on the San Gabriel River near Georgetown, Texas. Here, good buddy Jack Masters and David play the jaw harp together. Courtesy of Jack Masters.*

*David at Booty's Crossing. Courtesy of Jack Masters.*

# MOVEMENT 4:
# ARRIVALS

It wasn't magic. It was fucking hard work and paying attention.

—Townes Van Zandt

You shouldn't just play a song. It should be an event.

—David Schnaufer

Vince Farsetta, living in Morgantown since 1973, awaits David's arrival to record a demo for his trip to Nashville. The night before they record, the two catch up with each other rather than talk about what's ahead. David finds much to admire about Vince: he's smart, kind, and often hilarious. He lives and breathes music and is a composer, lyricist, and multi-instrumentalist: clawhammer banjo, guitar, mandolin, fiddle, drums, dulcimer ... it seems like there isn't anything he can't play when he puts his mind to it. Vince performs mountain music, ska, reggae, calypso, rock, and pop with equal enthusiasm and skill. David considers him a musician's musician, a musical genius, and he loves the history as much as David does.

Since they last met up, Vince has been busy developing his own country roots, too, as a composer and arranger. He shares that one of his favorite places to hang out these past few years is a music store in Glenville, West Virginia, owned by a guitarist friend, Frank Beall. (Alan Freeman's next-door neighbor Harry Beall is Frank's cousin.) David knows both Bealls and the store; Alan liked to hang out at Beall's.

Vince shares how fortunate he feels to have experienced Beall's in the seventies when the last of the real mountain people were often found there. "These people had access to tunes going back at least to the mid-1800s." People like Sherman Hammons and his sister Maggie were recorded by the Library of Congress as recently as ten years ago by the latest generation of song catchers. Just this year, the University of Virginia released an LP of their songs that Louis Chappel had recorded in 1947. "I love these really cool old guys who come out of the hills to play at the Glenville festival; it's phenomenal! It's full of all these old-timers who brought all these traditional fiddle tunes."

David sits on the floor, laughing and soaking up the stories that tumble out one after another. Vince recounts his experiences hanging out with Sherman Hammon: "The Hammons were real old school....They grew up in the wilderness and there's a story of Sherman and Burl freaking out when a plane flew over them once because they didn't know what it was and had never seen or heard of anything like that. I got to know Sherman the best and he was quite a character who liked to drink and smoke and gobble like a turkey. He played banjo and could sing songs for hours that were brought over that were kind of naughty, and he would giggle as he sang them...I visited him a couple of times at his house when me and a buddy were on our way to go trout fishing because Sherman lived around some great trout streams in southern West Virginia."

"Sherman's sister Maggie sang old British and Scottish tunes from long ago that she learned from her ma, who learned from her ma, who learned from the ones who came over on the boats. She'd sing them *a capella*. Sherman told me his ancestors had lived in a cave when they first came to the country!"

The two friends continue talking until the wee hours, both knowing that they are part of something very special. They happily feel obliged to continue their chosen traditions; music sings to them from the earth, rising up and settling deep in their bones, then flows out through their fingers and up to the heavens where the muses smile upon two they've made favorites for their having accepted the torch passed to them.

(1, 2, 3, 4, 5)

## 1984 MORGANTOWN, WEST VIRGINIA: ROSIE'S ARMS

David books two days at Kim Monday's Frozen Sound studio in the basement of his home. Kim, a musician and self-taught recording engineer, opened the only recording studio in the small university town four years ago. Monday has hosted all kinds of players in his tiny studio, everyone from the Preservation Hall Jazz Band who happened to be passing through Morgantown, to locals who believe they have what it takes to become famous; most of them don't, but he records them anyway when they ask. Kim has never been impressed by the dulcimers he recorded in the past, considering them ratty, trebly things.

Vince and Alan will record with David; this time, however, David has producer credits in the liner notes. Vince will play bass and electric guitar; Alan will play dulcimer, and Kim's friend Rick Ravenscroft will play drums. Titled *Rosie's Arms and Other Retreats*, the demo contains three additional samples David will showcase besides "Rosie's Arms." First released on "Hogfiddler's Fancy"; "Viper Moon," co-written by David and Al; "Santa Ana's Retreat," this time using his own arrangement rather than Diana's, and finally, "All the Texas Weather has Gone to Mexico," one of his favorites written with Texas buddy Jim Bentley.

Kim's first impression of David upon arrival is that he is the complete opposite of Alan. He's very quiet, even shy, but, once he starts playing, he becomes a whole different man. Kim thinks to himself, "David's playing doesn't even sound like a dulcimer, especially on "Viper Moon" with his clean, jazzy lines." His playing is so precise that Kim thinks he sounds like the best jazz guitarist he has ever heard.

After recording, David meets with Kim's friend Butch Lee, a graphic artist. He and David talk the owner of the local eatery Speedy Gonzalez into letting Butch repaint the front door of the restaurant. Butch hides the current name by painting a new name above the door to suggest the locale is Rosie's Arms. David, who cut his hair short after the recording session, leans against the door with his dulcimer next to him. When his work in Morgantown is finished, he will take his master tape and move back to Texas briefly to earn some more money working in construction to pay production costs for the EP at Boy Howdy Records in Cleburne, after which he will send them off to be pressed in New York. Then he will make his move to Nashville.

(6, 7)

## 1984 NASHVILLE, TN: 1984 NASHVILLE

Close to a half-million people live within Music City and its outskirts in Davidson County. Music is the fifth largest industry here after Banking, Insurance, Medicine and Tourism, but, for many in the United States and in other parts of the world, music is the first association they make with Nashville. The city also is the home of twenty four-year colleges and universities as well as several community colleges and vocational and technical schools. Vanderbilt University and Belmont University are two of the largest schools of higher education. Vanderbilt consistently ranks in the top twenty of America's higher-learning institutions.

Newspaper stories that will appear this year in the *Tennessean*:

Earl Scruggs brand banjos make their debut at the Nashville Gibson Guitar factory.

London band the Clash make a tourist stop to take a photo in front of Tootsie's Orchid Lounge, a famous watering hole patronized by their hero, Hank Williams.

Pulitzer Prizewinning poet and novelist Robert Penn Warren will read to an audience of a thousand people at his alma mater, Vanderbilt University.

Vanderbilt University's Memorial Gym will host Auburn University junior Charles Barkley when he plays against Kentucky.

Later, the Eurythmics will perform there, and by the year's end, Cyndi Lauper will sing there for a packed audience.

The Grand Ole Opry's schedule for the year includes singer Tom Jones; Arkansas governor Bill Clinton will be among several fellow governors and country music stars to appear on stage; movie star Jessica Lange will perform on the Opry stage to re-create Patsy Cline singing "I Fall to Pieces" to promote the film, *Sweet Dreams*. President Ronald Reagan will attend the "the king of country" Roy Acuff's eighty-first birthday celebration, and five days later Neil Young will perform on stage.

Rev. Jesse Jackson holds a presidential campaign rally two days before his primary rival Walter Mondale speaks at Legislative Plaza. Democratic vice-presidential candidate Geraldine Ferraro will also hold a rally on the plaza later in the year.

Russian ballet master and director of the American Ballet Theater Mikhail Baryshnikov will perform at the Tennessee Performing Arts Center.

Gonzo journalist and author Hunter S. Thompson packs in an audience at Vanderbilt's Langford auditorium.

Ray Charles will perform with the Nashville Symphony orchestra.

*The Far Side* cartoonist Gary Larson signs copies of his latest book in Hillsboro Village, a Nashville neighborhood located between Belmont University and Vanderbilt University. The Belmont-Hillsboro neighborhood is located south of downtown Nashville, and in 1980 became listed on the *National Register of Historic Places*. Early twentieth-century bungalows, foursquares, and Tudors line the streets.

(8)

John Lomax III profiles "Music Row" in the manuscript for his upcoming book, *Nashville: Music City, USA*:

> Commercial music made in Nashville is created, published, sung, recorded, mixed, mastered, marketed and administrated in a twenty-four-square block tucked in just south of downtown known as Music Row. This six-by-four block section is home to most of Nashville's music business. All six major record labels have their offices on Music Row, as do several hundred recording artists, publishers, producers, songwriters, agents, managers, publicists, and music executives. It is a tight-knit, clannish town unto itself, suspicious of strangers, even those who have experienced success in the music business in other cities. Normally, newcomers can't make it here on talent alone without doing their time, learning the unspoken rules of the music game, and fraternizing and politicking with those in power.

Despite the low odds of making it here, Nashville is a mecca for musicians and songwriters who look to break into the business. Every year, the city draws thousands of aspiring musicians hoping to be discovered, but almost all fail. Those who fail are people who have spent too little time learning their craft or possess too little talent. They are barely noticed—if at all—by those who know excellence, talent, and uniqueness when they see it, surrounded as they are by outstanding musicians, engineers, songwriters and other business talent at the top of their game.

(9)

## 1984 NASHVILLE, TN: EXCEPTIONS

Mother and daughter Naomi and Wynonna Judd are exceptions to the rule that it's almost impossible to make it relatively quickly in Music City. After their unheard of chance to audition live for RCA Records executives, they signed a contract and became the opening act for the Statler Brothers. The very first time they performed live, they walked out on a stage to face ten thousand people in Omaha, Nebraska.

David set his sights on the Judds. He figures they will know what a dulcimer is since they are from Kentucky. Playing on a Judds record will be his best shot for re-introducing the dulcimer to country music. Nashville producers and musicians need to understand that a dulcimer can contribute to and enhance country music. He wants people to love the dulcimer like he does: as a historical and versatile instrument, as a tool to facilitate composing, and as an instrument for players to express themselves by releasing the music within their souls.

(10)

## 1984 NASHVILLE, TN: THREE NASHVILLE LANDMARKS:

The Ryman Theater: known as "The Mother Church of Country Music", the Ryman is the home of the long-running Grand Old Opry radio show from 1943 to 1974 and currently a concert venue.

Opryland, USA: 406 acres of the most unique entertainment facility in the world. It consists of a twelve-acre musical theme park; the Opryland House, new home of the Grand Old Opry; the Opryland Hotel with, among many other wonders, its two-acre conservatory; the Nashville Network, WSM AM-FM, the flagship broadcasting station of the Music Country Network.

The Parthenon: Chosen to reflect Nashville's nickname "Athens of the South," the full-scale, concrete replica of Greece's Parthenon lies in the center of Centennial Park. This Parthenon was originally built in 1897 to commemorate Nashville's centennial year.

(11,12)

## 1984 NASHVILLE, TN: FINDING WORK

David arrives in Nashville after dark. Consulting a map, he decides a public park would be a good place to stay since he is broke. He spent all the money he earned working construction on producing copies of his demo records, now tucked in a box in the trunk of his beat-up car. He makes his way to Centennial Park to sleep for the night.

The next morning he wakes up disoriented as he sees a huge building outside the car window that looks just like the Parthenon in Athens, Greece.

The first order of business is to find some work, and the best way to find work as a newcomer is to head to the local watering holes where other musicians and songwriters hang out. After asking around, he hears of Brown's Diner, a historic beer and music joint in the Hillsboro neighborhood. He finds the renowned diner and tiny bar inside two paired trolley cars with their shabby exteriors and dim interior, lit mostly by the year-round Christmas lights overhead and the neon beer signs that glow from the walls. Brown's is known for great old-school cheeseburgers and a friendly staff that will serve patrons in the bar or out back on the patio. It is also one of the quintessential hot spots for trading information and networking in a variety of businesses, especially the music business. Everyone from university PhDs to blue-collar workers to musicians like John Prine and Don Everly are often there planning, celebrating or commiserating.

When David arrives, he sits at the bar and orders a hamburger and a beer, soaking up the atmosphere, making friendly small talk with the bartender and patrons on either side of him, the beginning of his networking to find work and learn the lay of the city.

Before long, David's search for vegetarian food leads him to the Slice of Life Bakery at 1811 Division where, at a small restaurant, he makes friends with Haeyung Popkin, the Korean owner. Popkin listens to his pitch for work and is impressed with his considerate manner and politeness, so invites him to play for tips. Popkin schedules him to perform starting Wednesdays 6:30 to 8:30 p.m.once or twice a month. When a delighted Popkin notices that there are bigger crowds on the nights David plays, she adds weekend gigs for whenever he is available. With her red beans and rice always available, she makes sure David doesn't go hungry.

To earn a little more cash, he also works as a dishwasher at the Stage Deli on Hillsboro Road, where he quickly makes friends with the Iranian owners. Neither Popkin nor the owners of the Stage Deli know that David is living in his car; he'll stay there until he makes enough money to rent a place to live.

(13, 14, 15, 16, 17)

## 1984 NASHVILLE, TN: "EASYGOING CHARM"

Music historian and journalist Robert K. Oermann always has his ear to the ground to listen for new trends and talent. Shortly after David arrives, Oermann picks up the beginnings of a buzz about a newcomer to Nashville. He is intrigued by what he hears, so he sits down with David for what will be his introduction to Oremann's readers. The journalist's keen eye and long experience studying people in the music world lead him to quickly jot down the personality traits he perceives as he and David talk:

- whimsical
- elfin
- twinkle-eyed
- instantly memorable
- unique
- dry wit

- aw-shucks personality
- immediately likable Texas drawl
- easygoing charm
- vagabond-artist
- fascinating, natural entertainer
- both innovative and traditional
- a promising songwriter

However, even Oermann, a nationally published expert on music, doesn't know what David knows about the dulcimer. After listening to David's demo record and interviewing him, Oermann concludes his article by asserting that "the dulcimer can be effectively used as a backup instrument."

Despite Oermann's conclusion, David doesn't correct him. He's too polite to contradict his interviewer as well as grateful for the instrument's introduction to Nashville that Oermann will provide. David is content to wait and let the dulcimer "speak" for itself.

(18)

## 1984 NASHVILLE, TN: A MOST GENEROUS FRIEND

In between performing three nights a week at Slice of Life, David heads over to Brown's to learn from others who are already plugged in to the music network. By now, many of the regulars know David and stop by to say hello; they are flattered that he remembers everyone's name. In between visits, he doodles song lyrics and thoughts he wants to remember on cocktail napkins which he neatly folds and tucks into his pocket when he leaves.

One evening a fellow sits down at the bar next to David. After drinking a beer, they start to talk. He introduces himself as Drew Ponder, a regional district manager at CBS Records. Drew, born in Waco, feels an instant connection with David when he finds out that he, too, is from Texas. Drew notices the stacks of cocktail napkins on the checkerboard bar with David's notes on them and the friendly conversations as others stop by to say hello to him. He senses David is bright and well read, and, within twenty-minutes, invites him to stay at his apartment over on Seventeenth Avenue avenue at any time, and even gives him a key to the place: "If you ever need a roof over your head. . ." he nods to him. Drew always has an open door for his friends.

One day when David stops in to say hello, Drew shows him a hole in the side of the door jamb, and sticks a rolled-up twenty-dollar bill into the hole. "Just in case," he says, "you run low on money: take it, it's yours."

(19, 20)

## 1984 NASHVILLE, TN: FIDDLER, MEET DULCIMER PLAYER

A quiet twenty-three-year-old with a ready smile regularly shows up at the Slice of Life on Monday, Wednesday, and Friday evenings to eat a meal and listen to David's music. What attracts this patron the most are the fiddle tunes David plays. One of his favorite songs as a child was Joni Mitchell's "Both Sides Now," and he is captivated with David's approach to the song; he loves the sound of the dulcimer and notices things like the little intervallic refrain between each stanza.

As always, David's friendliness draws people like a magnet, and before long the two find out that they have a great deal in common. The young man is just starting his career as a session musician. He comes into the Slice regularly because he likes health food, and it's the only vegetarian restaurant anywhere near Music Row. Over the course of their conversation, they share their history. Both won their respective national championships at Winfield: David when he was twenty-three, and Mark O'Connor on guitar when he was fourteen. Mark won the fiddle championship twice at Winfield in 1974 and 1977. Kindred spirits, their friendship is born.

Soon one evening, Mark mentions that he is getting signed to Warner Bros. Records as a solo recording artist. "When there's an opportunity, I want to do 'Both Sides Now' as a duet with you; can you imagine my fiddle with your dulcimer?" "Yes," drawls David with a big smile, "Yes I can. I'd like that."

(21, 22, 23)

---

*What is a "Session Musician"? by Mark Miller*

Nashville Producer and Recording Engineer Mark Miller explains: The most in-demand, skilled musicians in Nashville usually self-select to either play live, e.g., backing up an artist, or, if they enjoy the creative side of music, they work as session musicians.

A session musician is someone who performs music in a recording session for a record, CD, or video performance. He or she is hired by the producer or the production company to play music for recording purposes whether for listening or for watching. Session musicians are the "top guns" of the musician hierarchy. Most have a formal music education background since being able to read music and/or understand the "Nashville Numbering System" is one of the many skills critical to the job.

Sessions musicians make big money on the record; with some exceptions, they would be too expensive to go out on the road with a performing artist. It's typical that the musicians whom the audience sees on stage backing an artist are not the same musicians who played on that artist's recording of a song that they later perform on the stage.

Recording sessions are a structured part of the music business. Sessions are typically three hours long and union regulated with a set fee for that session. Any overtime is paid in fifteen-minute increments. Some in-demand musicians do three sessions a day—i.e., nine hours a day—and those musicians are working the hardest of all because they have to stay sharp for nine straight hours.

To make it as a successful session musician requires a keen sense of professionalism, unmatched musicality and creativity, and the deepest understanding of the capabilities of their instrument or instruments. Most are very nice people who enjoy collaborating and creating with others.

(24)

## 1984 NASHVILLE, TN: JOHNNY MEARS

Texan singer/songwriter Johnny Mears grew up in the flattest land in Texas, not far from La Marque, and made his way hitchhiking to Nashville after a rough stint in the Marines in California. The first time he encountered the rolling hills of Tennessee and saw the trees with their jewel-like fall colors, he was stunned. "It was one of the most beautiful sights I had ever seen, better than seeing a rainbow."

"When you don't have a lot to lose, you don't fear a lot," he likes to say, and he is both fearless and where he wants to be as an aspiring singer/songwriter. Unlike his experience at Camp Pendleton, he finds Nashville a hotbed of creative people, fun and adventures, parties, and hijinks. He savors every moment: the camaraderie between the struggling artists looking for gigs and jobs and those who already have steady work; the famous and not-so-famous who crowd into Mack's Diner where everyone goes to eat a meat and three. The next Willie Nelson, the next Kris Kristofferson, the next Dolly Parton could be just around the corner or eating a meal at a table across from you.

Music Row fascinates him. The stately nineteenth-century buildings—all former homes—line the streets in the heart of the music business. Typical renovations included basement recording studios, first floors converted to offices, and attic apartments. No curtains at the attic windows means that late at night, pedestrians will often see inhabitants walking back and forth as they work on their songs.

Everyone is cool. Everyone is friendly. The energy is positive; everyone is happy for anyone who gets a job as a staff writer or scores hit song or a gig. Johnny quickly picks up the vibe that pervades everywhere he goes: "We are all in this together." That feeling appeals the most to him.

He makes friends quickly, one of whom is Drew Ponder. He had approached Johnny after a gig at the Bluebird Cafe, and they became fast friends. Drew is one of those who looks for opportunities for his friends and newcomers, especially those newcomers who need to eat and have a roof over their heads. Drew understands the way things work in Nashville; it's not just what you know but who you know that matters when you hope to get established in "The Business."

When Johnny signs up for a songwriting seminar he meets Bob who is working his way up in management and production; he recently bought an empty Victorian house that needs a major renovation two doors down from Waylon Jennings's office on Music Row. Bob hires Johnny to watch the place. Thanks to this connection, Johnny now lives in and works on Bob's empty building, scraping off lead paint and removing asbestos to prep it for the tradespeople who will come in next to work.

Occasionally, Johnny goes over to Drew's house to socialize and listen to music. They share a love of music, and Drew is a walking encyclopedia of music history. He has a record collection that represents every genre of music and every recording artist, well-known or not. Drew loves to spin the records and the stories behind each one as he places disk on the turntable.

Not long after Johnny's first visit, Drew invites a friend to join them. He introduces Johnny to David, another Texan and recent arrival to Nashville. Pretty soon the three are meeting weekly; David and Johnny catch a bus and head over to their "teacher's," they joke. Sometimes they order pizza or stromboli sandwiches from the little Italian place just down the street for fuel as they eat, listen, talk, and smoke together. Hanging with musicians, talking music and Nashville, reminiscing about Texas, helping his friends...Johnny believes that life doesn't get much better than this. All three of them are keenly aware it's a special time.

"We are on our own paths and journeys, but at crossroads we find each other at the same time. You don't realize you're searching for someone, a kindred spirit. but, if you search, you find one," Johnny likes to say.

(25, 26)


## 1984 RANCHO CUCAMONGA, CA.: CHASING THE ELUSIVE SOUND

Despite working full time for Southern California Edison, Doug Thomson continues to work as a luthier on the side and is still perfecting his dulcimer/banjo hybrid instrument. Still chasing the elusive sound of the Bacon & Day banjo he discovered a decade ago, he has made five different models but isn't satisfied. They sound good, but not like the Bacon & Day paradigm in his mind.

In 1984, he decides to file a patent application with the U.S. Patent and Trade Office for his instrument. To his surprise, his application is rejected for not being an original idea. In 1912, someone had patented a simple, stringed zither, and the Patent Office decided that was the end of that.

A friend tells Doug he could apply for a worldwide patent, but the cost is prohibitively expensive. So, he suggests that Doug continue working on his new hybrid with the goal of being the first to market with it. That way, he can lay claim to being the original maker.

(27)

# 1984 NASHVILLE, TN: VIP KNOWS MUSIC

Vip notices the sound first. He has just sat down to order lunch at Nashville's well-known organic restaurant, The Laughing Man. After he orders, he hears the music from the far corner of the room. Turning, Vip is struck by the appearance and total focus of the guy playing a dulcimer. When he talks to the patrons, he sounds like an authentic country boy, but he has long hair and some kind of granny glasses that remind Vip of John Lennon. He notices that his songs are not obscure old dulcimer tunes; he plays a variety of folk, classic rock and roll, pop, and traditional standards. *On the dulcimer.* His playing is both ancient and broadly modern at the same time. And, to Vip, it all sounds exceptional.

Vip knows music. Vip Vipperman has lived in Nashville since 1978; he is a successful professional music producer, publisher, songwriter, and musician with four number-one songs on four different charts: Country, Gospel, Texas Music, and CMT video charts. Two years ago he won multiple awards for his work with Randy Travis and Trace Adkins, a success that will eventually lead him to many other awards including a Grammy nomination and to work with countless artists ranging from Odetta to Reba McEntire; from Kris Kristofferson to symphony musicians. He will perform on movie soundtracks and as a composer for television shows.

As he listens to David play, Vip becomes an instant fan. When he leaves the restaurant, he leaves David a good tip in the jar. He has a feeling he'll be seeing more of him again.

(28)

# 1984 NASHVILLE, TN: MORNING BIRDS

Easter Sunday morning around 4 a.m., David opens his eyes; it's still dark. He lies in bed half-awake, awareness slowly drawing near. Just as the night begins to give way to the first morning light he hears a single bird start calling to his mate, and then another. He rises up out of bed, reaching for his dulcimer. Determining the birds are singing in the key of A, the fingers of his left hand slide up the fretboard to tune to A. Once he is satisfied, the fingers of his right hand gently search for the best rhythm to compliment the birdsong. He adds some soft fingerpicking across the strings to suggest their fluttering wings as his left hand moves up and down along the fretboard.

By the time the sun rises, he has composed "Morning Birds," a simple, exquisite tune. Apropos for a resurrection Sunday, he closes his eyes as he plays the dulcimer with a gentle, lilting quality that evokes the wonder of a fresh, new morning: tiny bird melodies, perhaps some lightly trickling water, morning light appearing to kiss the darkness goodbye. His new song is soon ready, a depiction of his mind's landscape to share with future listeners.

(29)

## 1984 MORGANTOWN, WEST VIRGINIA: DAVID ON HIS MIND

Alan Freeman hires Vince Farsetta to play on his new cassette, *Old Time, New Time, Rag Time, My Time* that he hopes to sell at his gigs and use as a demo to pitch as a bluegrass album. Vince brings his considerable skills—guitar, banjo, mandolin, fiddle, and vocals—to the session at Frozen Sound Studios. Once again, Kim records Alan and friends as they run through a variety of genres to demonstrate his range, everything from Appalachian songs, rags, and waltzes to a live recording of the Poca River Blues from the recent Stonewall Jackson Jubilee Festival in West Virginia. During a break, Alan asks about David.

Not long afterward, Alan runs into Bonnie Carol at a festival. As they sit and catch up with each other, Alan mentions his former partner. "David's where we all want to be," he tells her. Bonnie looks at him and thinks, "We do?" But she remains quiet on that subject.

(30, 31)

## 1984 NASHVILLE, TN: THE SUBSTITUTE TEACHER

Darrel Ellis moves to Nashville to take a new position as a physician at Vanderbilt Medical Center. As he unpacks the moving boxes in his new apartment, he finds his dulcimer and sticks it under his bed.

Darrel first discovered the dulcimer via his older brother, an investigative reporter in Little Rock, Arkansas. Once, while reporting on McSpadden's Dulcimer Shoppe, he bought a dulcimer there. Later he played it whenever he visited the family. Darrel thought to himself, "He's not usually that good, but he sounds okay on it," so he orders one, too. After messing with it a little bit, unsure of himself, he stuck it under his bed. But he didn't forget about it and occasionally told himself that if he ever had a chance to learn how to play, he would take it out from under the bed and try again.

Shortly after moving in, Darrel sees an ad for a series of five classes for people who want to learn how to play the dulcimer at a local community center near Centennial Park. A lady is going to teach the classes, so he pulls the dulcimer back out from underneath the bed, signs up, and pays his $25.

When he arrives at the first evening class, the woman who was going to teach isn't there. Instead, Darrel sees a "little, gregarious guy" walking around shaking hands with each of the students. He explains that the teacher who was going to conduct the class had to leave to do a gig out in Washington State, so he will be teaching instead.

Under David's guidance, Darrel and his classmates spend the first half hour of the hour-long class learning to tune their dulcimers. When David gets to a lady right before Darrel's turn, he tells her she has a "Hang on the Wall Dulcimer."

"What's that?"

"You hang it on the wall because it won't play well," he laughs, and he goes on to explain that she needs a better-quality instrument.

Close to the end of the class, David asks, "Are there any questions?"

"Would you play a little?" asks Darrel.

"Yes, I will; tell me a song you like." Darrel watches the way he tilts the dulcimer on his lap and thinks, "Man, this guy doesn't even know how to hold a dulcimer." Then, when David starts to play, Darrel sits back, astonished: "This is amazing!"

The following week, a friend who is town for a conference at Opryland invites Darrel him to meet him for a drink that evening. "I can't; I can't miss a dulcimer lesson I have tonight. This thing really intrigues me." However, when he shows up for the class, no one is there. After returning home, he gets another call from his friend.

"Hey Darrel, you know while I was waiting for my drink they had the show 'Nashville Now' on the tv and Arlo Guthrie was on the show. What was the instrument you said you were trying to learn?"

"The dulcimer."

"You know, Arlo Guthrie had this guy come out and said he was the national dulcimer champion."

The following week right before his third class, Darrel asks, "David, did you go out and play on 'Nashville Now' last week?"

David smiles. "Oh yeah, I'm sorry for canceling the class but I just didn't want to turn down the chance to play with Arlo Guthrie in front of two million people."

(32)

## 1985 NASHVILLE, TN: HANK AND PEGGY

Hank, a music engineering student in Belmont University, first hears about David through his friend Peggy, an art student at Belmont. When Peggy tells him about a musician she has seen who has an extraordinary way of playing an instrument called a dulcimer, his curiosity is piqued. Hank knows dulcimers well, having grown up in the Ozarks where he spent a lot of time at Lynn McSpadden's Dulcimer Shoppe. In fact, Hank had bought a McSpadden kit and built a dulcimer for himself before going to Belmont. He gradually gave up on playing it after having decided that it wasn't really a virtuoso instrument and that there wasn't much one could do with it anyway.

Peggy takes him to meet David who supplements his income by working as a bartender at the Villager Tavern, a dark and cozy beer joint in Hillsboro Village. Hank recognizes him as soon as he and Peggy sit down at the bar. He didn't realize that this bartender, a good-natured, affable fellow he had seen there before is the musician Peggy had told him about. David is delighted to swap stories with both of them. He tells them about his upcoming gig at the Station Inn and says he hopes to see them there.

Hank looks wide-eyed at Peggy. The Station Inn is a haven for local and international bluegrass musicians, a 175 seat Club that has hosted the best like Bill Monroe, the father of Bluegrass, and others like Mark O'Connor, Waylon Jennings, Hank Williams Jr., and scores of other top Nashville talent. Hank thinks to himself, "This is a long way in a short time from the eight-table Slice of Life gigs David worked at upon arriving last year."

The first time they sit in to listen to David play, Hank is awestruck; he thinks David seems to be able to play anything on the dulcimer. He jokes with Peggy that—until that night—he always thought that the dulcimer was sort of a gift to those without much musical ability. No more. As they leave, Hank is impressed by this bartender's, and even more so by his humility about his talent. He will never look at him or the dulcimer in the same way again.

(33)

## 1985 GLENVILLE, WEST VIRGINIA: "IT'S THE PORTABLE TRANSMITTER"

Despite how he feels, despite how otherworldly he looks, Vince plays the fiddle at the West Virginia Folk Festival this year. A local news station even films him.

It's a miracle he's there. Shortly before the festival, he was working on a cassette for one of his favorite bands, Leftover Salmon of Colorado. Vince composes music for them, and whenever he gets a chance, he plays with them. After the recording sessions, Vince and lead man Vince Herman of the Salmon were working on a roofing job to supplement their income. As Farsetta stepped off the roof and onto a scaffold board, it broke. He dropped twenty-five feet, hitting the bars of the scaffold on the way down, knocking himself out before he hit the ground and broke his neck. He spent a week in a Stryker bed with his head screwed down tight.

Later, the doctors screwed a halo brace to his skull—Vince tells his friends there was no pain medicine, so he felt like his eyeballs were popping out of his head—"I'm telling you, it was the Spanish Inquisition!"—and now he's locked into the halo with the bars screwed in for three months. He can walk, but he can't turn his head without turning his whole body in the direction he wants to look. Vince, (perhaps short for "invincible") sees the humor in everything, so exploits the situation for all its worth. Right after he leaves the hospital, he learns to ride a motorcycle with his buddy Gary while sporting the big metal halo. He cackles when he tells stories of little kids freaking out at the way he looks. One rainy day he heads to the woods wearing a giant poncho over the halo to keep from getting wet. There he finds the biggest ginseng root of his life, afterward telling his friends that he wonders if there is some good luck connection to the halo. He even wears it when he plays reggae gigs; his fans think the contraption on his head is a harmonica rack.

When he visits his buddy who is a deejay at a radio station, Hall of Fame football player Sam Huff walks in to be interviewed, takes one look at Vince, and blurts, "What the hell is that?" pointing to the large bars and halo.

Without missing a beat, Vince tells him with a straight face, "It's the portable transmitter for the station."

When he shares stories with David during a drive together, the two of them can't stop laughing as they roll down the road.

(34)

## 1985 BLUE RIDGE MOUNTAINS: HERB MCCULLOUGH

Songwriter Herb McCullough started "writin' a lullaby" for his first grandchild Ashley a few months after her birth. As was often the case, he wrote one verse in what he called "stream of consciousness" and then lost the flow for about a year. This time, at a stop during a drive through the Blue Ridge Mountains, he is struck by the lovely sound of music coming from the front porch of an old store across the gravel parking lot. He decides that this is the sound he wants on Ashley's lullaby. He walks over and asks the woman about the instrument she's playing, and she tells him it's a mountain dulcimer. Herb decides that this music is perfect for a lullaby.

He never thinks about where he'll find a dulcimer player: he just acknowledges the gift and rolls on down the road back to Nashville.

(35, 36)

## 1985 NASHVILLE, TN: HANK AND PEGGY

After chatting one night at the bar, David invites Hank and Peggy over to his apartment near the Villager. The three walk toward his place, chatting and laughing. Once inside, David rolls a joint and passes it around. Then David decides to entertain them with a couple of songs on the dulcimer. He sings the beginning lyric of a song he invents on the spot: "Elvis Presley is still alive ..." with a chorus that concludes with "the aliens are coming to take us away!"

Hank and Peggy start giggling; even though Elvis had died eight years ago, recent conspiracy theories about Elvis being alive are rampant in the tabloids. Once he finishes the song, he switches tone by playing an exquisite rendition of the sixteenth-century English tune "Greensleeves" for them. As his left hand moves nimbly up, down, and across the strings, Hank and Peggy's laughter turns to silence. They stare in awe of this rare talent in front of them. As they walk home later, they agree that it was the most brilliant and magical evening in their memory.

(37)

## 1985 NASHVILLE, TN: BRENT MAHR NEEDS A DULCIMER PLAYER

After the runaway success of their first album. *Why Not Me?*, the Judds are back in the studio again to create their second album, *Rockin' with the Rhythm*. David gets a tip from a friend: mega producer Bret Maher is looking for a dulcimer player for one of the Judds' tracks, but he can't find one in Nashville.

David grabs his case and heads over to Maher's Creative Workshop Studio office and makes himself conspicuous. Eventually, the receptionist thinks to ask him, "What are you doing here?"

"I heard you need a dulcimer player for the Judds" he explains. "I'm the one you're looking for."

Maher and the Judds had just about given up hope of finding a dulcimer player at all, much less one with the professional skill they required to play on their track. Nobody in Nashville had ever cut a record that included the fretted dulcimer. Maher agrees to give him an audition, and that's all it takes.

Instead of one track, he asks him to play on three: "The River Rolls On," on the album title song, "Rockin' with the Rhythm," and on "The Sweetest Gift," Maher is so impressed by his playing that he also books him for the next Judds album they've been planning, *Heartland*.

(38, 39, 40, 41, 42)

---

### Who is Bret Maher?

Bret Maher is a critically acclaimed musician, producer, recording engineer, and composer who has worked for years with music artists at the top of their field, ranging from Ike and Tina Turner, Gladys Knight, and Diana Ross to Roy Orbison, Willie Nelson, Kenny Rogers, and the Judds. Maher was in the midst of developing the new "acoustic country sound" with the Judds at the same time that David moved to Nashville. Their work together was a win-win for both.

(43, 44)

---

## 1986 NASHVILLE, TN: "CLOSED – WE'RE AT THE BLAIR SCHOOL OF MUSIC"

Since 1980 David has had steady work as a traveling musician, either as a solo artist or in duets and small bands around the country. Since his arrival in Nashville two years ago, he has played gigs across the city in between his work as a session musician. After playing on three songs from the Judd's *Rockin' with the Rhythm* album, his phone started ringing. He's already booked to do session work next year with Dan Seals, Holly Dunn, and Kathy Mattea and to play once again for the Judds on *Heartland*. And now he is planning his most important performance as far as he is concerned: a showcase for the dulcimer, not as a backup, but as a solo, front-and-center performance instrument.

David goes all out for this show. He rents the Turner auditorium at the Blair School of Music at Vanderbilt University; he loves the room and the perfect acoustics. He makes and sells the tickets himself; virtually every one of the patrons and the staff at the Villager Tavern buys a ticket. Any new patron who shows up that night will find the place closed with a sign hanging on the door, "We're at Blair."

His goal for this evening concert is to showcase all the diverse styles he's adapted to the dulcimer via music from Bach, Beatles, bluegrass music, his original songs, lute music, fiddle tunes, and country classics. He'll include standard songs familiar to everyone to help the audience recognize the sounds of the dulcimer. For how can they appreciate the instrument without knowing exactly what it sounds like and how those sounds make them feel?

(45, 46)

## 1986 NASHVILLE, TN: SATCH'S STUDENT

David's solo dulcimer performance at Blair was a sellout and a complete success, yet David's priority is to keep learning more to stretch both himself and the dulcimer. One night at the Springwater Tavern, another local musicians' hangout, he listens to guitarist Satch Wright perform. David asks him if he'll take him on for some lessons. Despite having little use for organized religion, David does enjoy playing old hymns, so he asks Satch to help him learn the classic country hymn, "Wings of a Dove." Satch also helps him arrange the George Harrison song "Here Comes the Sun" for dulcimer because David would like to pair "Morning Birds" with it. Together they explore some classic popular tunes like "Somewhere Over the Rainbow." Since David doesn't read music yet, Satch tutors him a bit, and the two work tirelessly until David expands his repertoire and is satisfied he gets the absolutely best sound possible out of the dulcimer, no matter what he plays.

(47)

# 1986 NASHVILLE, TN: WALK THE WEST

Paul Kirby, Will, and John Golemon have been playing music together since their grade school days in Hendersonville, a suburb of Nashville. By the time they hooked up with Tramp—who is equally adept at fiddle, mandolin, and guitar—Sam Poland, dobroist and steel guitar player, and drummer David Kennedy, they became a fixture in Nashville's clubs as "Walk the West." On the road, they earned themselves a reputation for packing clubs and concert halls with college students who love their high-energy music. They also got picked up by Capitol Records, and released their first album last year. They went on tour with the Ramones, Cheap Trick, the Smithereens, and Stevie Ray Vaughn. It was a skyrocketing dream for the young band members.

Until it wasn't.

Their management dropped them, not knowing what to do with the group's eclectic blend of their original music, their rock covers, and the occasional country tune. They moved back to Nashville to lick their wounds and rethink themselves as a band.

There's a healthy tension within the group between the hard rockers and Tramp, the latter having grown up listening to mountain music at the crossroads of Tennessee, North Carolina, and Virginia while learning the violin via the Suzuki method. Despite their being dropped by CBS Records, the band is a perfect crucible for Tramp's out-of-the-box thinking to come.

(48, 49)

# 1986 NASHVILLE, TN: LIKE KIDS IN A CANDY STORE

Once Vince's halo is a thing of the past, David invites his buddy to visit so they can talk over some upcoming projects. When he arrives in Nashville, he is like a kid in a candy store, exhilarated with the music that saturates the city. Often thought of as the country music capital of the world, in reality, all kinds of music are heard and played in Nashville: country, bluegrass, rock, pop, Americana, gospel, classical, symphonic, jazz, and blues. Vince decides Nashville needs to be the center of his world: he can't believe all the opportunities for skilled musicians. The air crackles with creativity and opportunity for the best of the best.

After making the move to Music City, he runs into an old buddy, Rick Roberts, another recent transplant. Before long, Vince, Rickie, and David appear around town in local clubs and at city festivals, sometimes calling themselves "Fretilizer"; on other occasions, "The Big Otter String Band"

To supplement his playing and composing income and to feed his creative side, Vince starts a small side business. Music City Graphics allows him to tap into his visual arts side. He teaches himself to hand-block silk screen images on T-shirts, ties, and well-made cotton and linen jackets he occasionally finds at Goodwill. He's drawn to flowers, western images, and musical figures; soon, he has clothes on consignment in various shops, and even a few that are worn in music videos. David is one of the biggest fans of his creations.

The two of them head over one night to the Slice of Life, where David introduces Vince to Haeyung Popkin. Charmed by Vince, she offers him the Friday night performance slot.

(50, 51)

## 1986 NASHVILLE, TN: "JOHN, THIS IS DAVID SCHNAUFER"

John Lomax III is lying back after another busy week, half-dozing, half-watching a football game on a Sunday afternoon in his living room at his Acklen Avenue apartment. An unexpected banging on his door prompts him get up and open it; his friend Drew Ponder stands, smiling. Slightly behind Drew, a long-haired, small man stands, holding a music case. At his first glance at the stranger, John thinks of a gnome.

"John, this is David Schnaufer; you guys need to know each other."

John invites them both in, but Drew he begs off and leaves. As the gnome steps into the room, John asks, "Well, what do you do?"

"I play the dulcimer," David replies. At the time, John is vaguely familiar with the dulcimer through his uncle Alan's recordings of Jean Ritchie for the Library of Congress. He knows Jean uses it as rhythm instrument; she frets with a noter and strums gently to provide background as she sings. Nobody in Nashville uses the dulcimer professionally, and most people outside the folk and dulcimer worlds either have no idea what it is, or they don't consider it a serious instrument.

"Well, c'mon in and play me something."

David smiles and walks in, sets down his case, and opens it. He pulls out his dulcimer, sits down, and checks the tuning. He adjusts it on his lap with a slight tilt, then looks at John for a moment with a slight smile. Then, with unexpected speed and grace, he launches into a flawless rendition of "Steel Guitar Rag," a bouncy Western Swing dance tune that depends on clean and rapid finger work on the fretboard with lightning-fast picking alternating with strumming.

John feels the hair rise on the back of his neck.

David looks downward as he plays. John watches David's face light up as he runs through the tune, his head and body moving rhythmically to keep time. John knows "Steel Guitar Rag" has been mandatory performance material for steel guitar players for decades. But, on a dulcimer? John, by now accustomed to seeing and hearing the work of some of the finest musicians in the world, can't believe this guy in his living room. His eyes focus on David's left hand flying up and down the fretboard while his right hand provides a complex, dynamic rhythm to the classic honky-tonk dance song. It's the kind of performance that John has only personally witnessed in the work of the best sessions musicians.

John will share later that he had rarely ever felt this way in his professional career: stunned speechless.

(52)

## 1984 NASHVILLE, TN: RATTLESNAKE ANNIE

Rattlesnake Annie arrives in town again. "Snake," as she is known to her friends, is a rarity in the music business: a woman who is determined to be fully in charge of her own career. The Tennessee-born singer/songwriter/guitarist and producer—along with her husband Max—spends most of her life on globe-spanning sojourns to collaborate and perform with musicians around the world.

Snake grew up on a farm in the midst of a Black community in the flatland cotton culture near Memphis and has been playing the guitar since she was a child. The very first song her father taught her to play was the "Saint Louis Blues." She learned to pick quickly via the "Dark Night Blues." "Wildwood Flower" and every song that caught her ear through local radio stations, especially those that featured the blues-loving disc jockey Wolfman Jack.

Having just left Spain and due in India in a few months, Snake and Max spend the time between trips by renting an apartment next to Chet Atkins's office on Sixteenth Street. One evening they catch up with old friend John Lomax, who introduces them to his new client, David. Snake takes to David immediately during an impromptu jam session when she starts picking blues riffs and he joins in with her. She knows the mountain dulcimer is a country music instrument, but this guy is something completely brand new to her: a dulcimer player who can keep up with a woman who has the blues in her DNA. Snake had never heard anything like him before.

Although it's clear that David is strong, determined, and focused, Snake senses a kind of fragility within him. She looks him up and down at the end of their visit, concerned that he's too thin; she knows many musicians don't get enough healthy food. When they learn David lives just down the street, they invite him to come over and eat with them whenever he can. Max always has a good stew or other hearty soup on the stove. Soon, David meets them every evening for supper, often emotionally fried after a full day of pounding the pavement looking for work on Music Row. Gradually he opens up to them, revealing his vulnerabilities and sharing his life experiences prior to his arrival in Nashville, always emphasizing that the hard times profoundly prepared him for the challenges of finding work in the music business. Snake and Max like how David seems to feel at home in their safe and comfortable little nest.

Supper around the living room coffee table is always followed by Snake's favorite kind of picking, just she and David experimenting with different kinds of music, but always including the blues.

(53)

## 1986 SANTA CRUZ, CA.: NEAL HELLMAN

Neal Hellman has been on the road six days a week making a living as a professional dulcimer player. He sells his book, *Life is Like a Mountain Dulcimer* along with records and cassettes on the side at his gigs and at festivals through his Berkely publisher, Kicking Mule Records. Since Kicking Mule wasn't great about responding to requests for their albums, Neal talked to owner Ed Denston and made a deal with him not only to sell his own records on the road, but to carry other artists' albums with him to sell. At first, Neal felt it was a win-win for both as the boom in acoustic music rolled across the country. However, the small royalties and personal costs of producing his own work started to grate on him. Neal eventually decides to call Joe Weed, his fiddler friend who has a studio in Aptos not far from Neal's house.

"Joe, I've been thinking about my last albums and have some changes in mind. What do you think about producing my next album?"

Joe, who has played off and on with Neal for a number of years likes what he hears. He believes that Neal wanting to take control of his own music marks him as a musician who wants to make an artistic statement, and Joe is in the same frame of mind. The two put their considerable skills together—Joe, with his background in country, swing, and bluegrass fiddling, and Neal, with his interests in Celtic and Irish music—to create their new label, "Gourd Music." They begin writing and recording their acoustic instrumental debut album, "Oktober County" for a release next year.

(54, 55, 56)

---

### Gourd Music

Neal named his new company "Gourd Music" as a nod to the fact that so many instruments such the original banjo, sitar, and the kora were originally made from gourds. Neal worked nonstop since he started touring in 1981; he sold a lot, and he learned a lot. Due to his gregarious nature and his raconteur's ability to tell a good story, many people enjoyed working with him and selling for him. Gourd Music became a success because Neal has all the key attributes to make it so: he is an artist, a musician, a composer and arranger, a distributor, and a label all rolled into one. He serves an important niche market for classical and world music, and today his reverence for preserving historic music has meant that his productions can be found everywhere from movie soundtracks to Shaker museums to the collections of people who love diverse, classical, or soothing music.

After his early publications, *Life is Life a Mountain Dulcimer,* he authored *The Richard Farina Songbook, The Dulcimer Songbook*, and many other books that reflect his interest in world music. Neal continues to work hard to this day, teaching hundreds of dulcimer students secrets of playing he has accrued over a lifetime.

> If you would like to see the kinds of music Gourd offers and listen to samples, visit Gourd.com

## 1986 NASHVILLE, TN: MARY LAWRENCE

Mary Lawrence Breinig volunteers for the Nashville Symphony Guild to promote classical music in the local schools. During a chat with a fellow Guild member, they share thoughts on their favorite music. Mary Lawrence's friend tells her she loves the haunting sound of the dulcimer. "What is a dulcimer?" Mary Lawrence asks.

(57)

## 1986 RESTON, VIRGINIA: NEW HISTORIES REVEALED

Ralph Lee Smith, good friend and frequent jamming companion with Keith Young and Maddie MacNeil, publishes his first book, *The Story of the Dulcimer,* through Jean Schilling's Crying Creek Press. The book is a survey of the fretted dulcimer's historic folk origins and evolution.

Smith had been a young musician back in 1957 Greenwich Village, the cultural crucible of the post–World War II folk-music revival. He heard Jean Ritchie sing and play her dulcimer there; from late spring to early fall, every Sunday afternoon, people gathered in Washington Square to play folk music and sing. Ralph, started playing fiddle tunes on harmonica; songs such as "Mississippi Sawyer," "Grub Springs," and "Forky Deer" were brand new to him. On a visit to a shop in the Village, he paid $30 for a dulcimer made in North Carolina. He later wrote, "The dulcimers took my breath away! "

Ten years after buying his first dulcimer, Ralph's interests grew beyond playing to include collecting, cataloguing, and analyzing the dulcimer's evolution to answer a question that had fascinated him from the start: "Where did this instrument come from?" Three years ago, L. Allen Smith (no relation) released his book, *A Catalogue of Pre-Revival Appalachian Dulcimers* while Ralph's research and writing was well underway *The Story of the Dulcimer*.

Ralph loves sharing his own collection of instruments and his growing expertise on dulcimer history. He will write many more books and in 1993 will head his own column, "Mountain Dulcimer Tales and Traditions" in *Dulcimer Players News*. His writing for DPN as a regular contributor is a perfect touch given that he was the person who first encouraged publisher and editor Maddie to play the dulcimer. He will continue writing his column until the age of ninety-two.

Ralph's and L. Allen Smith's books contribute much to readers' understanding of dulcimer origins and how the instrument evolved. One of those readers is David Schnaufer, who for some time now has been fascinated with the same questions that started Ralph on his search for answers: "Where did this instrument come from, and how did it change as it was carried across America?" David is equally curious about the players and how and what they played.

(58, 59, 60)

## 1986 GATLINBURG, COSBY, AND NASHVILLE: MARY LAWRENCE

Mary Lawrence hears live dulcimer music for the first time at a craft fair in Gatlinburg, Tennessee. She and husband John stop at luthier Keith Medling's booth to admire the lovely wooden instruments— John had built a harpsichord, so he has an eye for quality craftsmanship. As Medling plays a song for them on one dulcimer after another, John notices her beaming as she listens. He buys her a dulcimer for an anniversary present. When she and John return to their home in Nashville, Mary Lawrence sits down with the dulcimer and the little booklet that comes with it, and tentatively attempts to pick out songs like "Twinkle, Twinkle Little Star" and "Ode to Joy." She doesn't feel like she knows what she is doing. Impatient with herself, she sets it aside in a closet.

(61)

## 1986 NASHVILLE, TN: PICKERS

By the end of their stay in Nashville and just before the trip to work in India, Snake calls her good friend Vip Vipperman to invite him to join her at a party and picking session at the apartment on Music Row. Vip brings his old 60s Guild guitar. When he walks in, Snake introduces him to her close friend David, whom Vip recognizes immediately as the dulcimer player he met at The Laughing Man restaurant.

Rattlesnake Annie is brilliant at connecting talented people, and just about all of her favorite people crowd into the apartment this evening to find a place to settle and do what they love best when in a room with fellow musicians: jam, drink, carouse, and talk shop during breaks in playing. She is pleased that both Vip and David get to play together this night; Vip is a blues player at heart, and she tells them both she's glad David will be in good hands after she and Max leave soon for India.

As it gets later and later, the crowd dwindles until Snake, David, and Vip are the only ones left. They continue picking well into the night. Several times David remarks that he loves the sound of Vip's old Guild and how well it blends with his dulcimer.

Later, Vip reflects on their evening together. He concludes that David is more than a musician, he is an artist determined to realize his vision to make the old-time dulcimer relevant in modern acoustic music. They often run into each other on "campus," i.e., Music Row, and they, too, develop a friendship built on mutual admiration and respect. To neither's surprise, it won't be long before they will see each other again; next time, it will be in the recording studio.

(62, 63)

## 1986 NASHVILLE, TN: WANDA

Wanda O'Guin works as a psychiatric nurse at the Baptist Hospital. During a trip to Opryland, she buys a "Plincket," a kind of mini-dulcimer with nylon strings tuned to the key of "C." She teaches herself to play the list of songs that come with the Plincket and is surprised how fun and easy it is to pick out a tune by ear. She takes it to work with her to show her coworker and friend Nanette. Nanette likes it as well, and the two of them begin talking about getting a dulcimer. Nanette orders a standard-size dulcimer from luthier Enos Yeager in Alabama and drives there to pick it up. Once Wanda gets to play it on their next break together, she's hooked. She is intrigued when Nanette tells her that—just like her Plincket—she doesn't have to read music to be able to play it. Wanda decides to order a dulcimer from Yeager, too. "My sister is taking lessons from a lady named Sandy, " Nanette tells her. "You want to learn how to play?" Nanette gives Wanda Sandy's phone number.

Once she gets her dulcimer, Wanda starts lessons. As she learns to play the beginner songs on her new instrument, she falls in love with it. One of the earliest songs she learns to play is "Grey Cat on a Tennessee Farm," a simple nineteenth-century fiddle tune.

She also discovers there are dulcimer festivals throughout the year and begins to attend as many as her schedule allows. Her favorite is close to home: the Three Rivers Dulcimer Festival in Waverly, Tennessee. She soon becomes skilled enough on the dulcimer that she gets others excited about it, too. Wanda feels like the dulcimer has opened up a whole new world to her, and every chance she gets, she plays.

(64, 65)

# 1987 NASHVILLE, TN: WALTZ OF THE WATERS

The first time he heard Townes Van Zandt in Texas, David recognized the sheer talent of the songrwriter/guitarist. Thanks to their shared Texas origins and Lomax connections, they have become good friends. When Townes suggests they write a song together, David agrees. Townes is one of David's favorite songwriters and poets, known for his reluctance to cowrite music with others. They dip into their well of Texas memories to start composing a sweet fiddle waltz they call "Waltz of the Waters," based on a short poem that Townes had written:

*Waltz of the Waters*

> There is a call where rivers collide
> The fall of the fish, where the deer stand watch
> The blue of your eyes, the blue of the stream
> The sky in my heart, Tell me what do they mean
> The days we're apart, Tell me what do they mean

The resulting melody is so pretty that they agree it doesn't need lyrics; other musicians will just enjoy playing it as much as they do. They set it aside, planning to finish it after composing a second part. They both are busy, and the song will sit for several years, waiting to be recorded.

(66, 67)


# 1987 NASHVILLE, TN: HERB MCCULLOUGH

Every day at Jack's Tracks, John Lomax meets the usual circle of friends for their 9 a.m. coffee klatch: an hour of shooting the breeze, joking, trading stories, and information before they start their respective days. This morning John's new client David stops by, so John introduces him to the others: producer Jack Clements, recording engineer and producer Mark Miller, and Herb McCullough who had signed with Clements as a songwriter. When John told his friends he had a new client, Herb had asked, "Who the heck is David Schnaufer?" John sketched in the picture for him: David started playing a dulcimer at twenty-one, won the Winfield National Dulcimer Championship three years later, was making a living traveling all over the country playing this obscure Appalachian instrument and teaching, and there was enough growing buzz about him in Nashville that musicians were looking to work with him. At that moment, Herb remembers his trip the year before in the Blue Ridge Mountains and thinks, "Here is the dulcimer player for my lullaby for Ashley!"

David arrives and as John introduces him to Herb, they immediately click. Herb admires his wizardry with the dulcimer, his gift of storytelling, and the fact that he has started teaching lessons. He is impressed; David's interest in teaching others to play stems from his desire to teach everyone to love the dulcimer. David admires Herb's songwriting skills and easygoing, laid-back personality. Herb holds himself to high standards; that means a lot. The two can't stop talking with each other as they swap stories of how they came to Nashville.

Later, after leaving the studio, an unexpected thought pops into Herb's mind: "that David is an old soul ... a fellow traveler of mine for the last 10,000 years."

(68, 69)

---

### "Recording Engineers" by Mark Miller

Mark Miller and David will work together on every record that David will make with John Lomax.

"My job," Mark shared, "was to make sure that everything performed in the studio is recorded properly—back then, on a tape machine. To record well you have to know what an instrument sounds like and be able to present it in the most optimal way possible while ensuring that every sound is true to the instrument."

Mark is a living example of why education in the arts is so important for school-age children. Even as a child, he loved going to the symphony, and at age seven he saw "Peter and the Wolf." The fact that the instruments became the characters in the story fascinated him. He chose to learn the guitar as he grew a little older, but thanks to his "Peter and the Wolf" experience, he loved all kinds of instruments and immersed himself in music. The Beatles were a big influence on him during their first U.S. tour in 1964, and he saw them live in Indianapolis.

Even though his parents weren't musicians, they loved music and encouraged his interests. As a teenager, he had an early stereo system, and much like David, Vince, and Rick in their teens, he would lie in bed every night and listened to music. "The Late fifties and the sixties were an incredible time for music: Motown, the Memphis soul sound of Stax Records, the California sounds, and the British wave," recalls Mark, "it was heaven for music lovers. Even Tom Jones, a favorite of my friend's mother, had some of the greatest musicians ever backing him." Today, Mark plays golf with Peter Sullivan who produced Tom Jones.

So, how did Mark end up in Nashville? "I pursued songwriting for years. I also played guitar for other artists and through those connections I met the fantastic Allen Reynolds who produced Crystal Gale and Don Williams. In between gigs I was painting houses to keep my kids fed, and playing in Allen Reynolds's girlfriend's band. One day Allen invited me down to the studio and said, maybe we can find you something at the studio to do. So I went down and paid attention. I apprenticed under Herb Allen, John Donegan, and Garth Thundis, the studio engineers who were there when I got there. They were so generous to show me everything. Back then that's the way it was. I had already been to New York and Los Angeles, but I thought, "Nah, this is where I want to be." By a couple years later, I was recording records for Allen."

Good recording engineers understand sound, microphone placement, and when and how to utilize effects to enhance sound, such as reverb and echo.

"You can't be a recording engineer without having had exposure to many musical instruments because you never know what is going to come through the door—like a dulcimer!"

(70)

## 1987 NASHVILLE, TN: A MATCH MADE IN HEAVEN

John Lomax had signed David as fast as he could get the paperwork together. He sees him as a calling rather than just a client. John now shares David's passion: to bring the dulcimer into the fold of country music. Once he listens to David's *Rosie's Arms and Other Retreats*, he decides he wants to promote David not only as a musician but as a songwriter, too. He puts David on a $400 per month retainer so he doesn't have to work as many part-time side jobs; it will give him more time to do session work and write songs.

John gives Herb McCullough a call after their meeting at Clement's; "Herb, would you be interested in writing with David?" Herb agrees to work on whatever David wants to work on, but he also keeps in mind the start of the lullaby for Ashley.

A week later, Herb knocks on the door to David's Music Row apartment. David opens the door, greets him with a bow and a handshake, invites him in, and pours him a cup of coffee. "Play me a song," Herb tells David, and so he plays him "Morning Birds," the piece he wrote back in 1984. Herb will later tell his wife Joanne that he was blown away by the gentle beauty of the piece. David finishes, laughing: "Okay, your turn!" So Herb picks up his guitar, plays, and sings the one verse he has for his granddaughter Ashley's lullaby. They start working on the song, trading ideas for lyrics and music. When Herb comes up with the line, "Moon beams love to life," David tells him "I don't get it; '*Moonbeams* love to life?'"

"No", Herb replies, "it's moon *beams* love to life!"

David starts calling him "Herb the Verb" and they both crack up laughing. They feel like old friends before their cups are empty, and within an hour, they have turned the verse into a song they title, "Starry Lullaby." They sing it and play it, David on the dulcimer and Herb on his guitar, tinkering with it until it feels right to both of them. By the afternoon, they've put on the final polish; it's finished.

"Herb, you know, I believe this song will someday reach thousands of grateful listeners," says David as Herb gathers his things to leave. By then, Herb just feels lucky to have survived more than ten years in the songwriting and music business "wars," so he smiles, nods, and thanks David with a hug. Before he leaves, though, he wants to ask David something.

"Why do you have a poster of Chet Atkins on your living room wall?"

"Oh, that's my 'Wishing Wall,'" he replies. I want Chet to play on my dulcimer record. I used to have the Judds up there, and now I have a Judds platinum record award over there on that other wall. I'm going to put Emmylou Harris on my 'Wall' next."

When Herb shows up at David's place the next week, Emmylou's photo is on the Wall. Chet Atkins has offered to play guitar on David's first album.

(71, 72)

## Chet Atkins

David had written to Chet Atkins for years hoping to plant seeds about the importance of the dulcimer.

No single country musician achieved the renown and respect of Chester Burton Atkins. His enormous influence on country, rock, and jazz musicians from Jerry Reed to George Harrison and Duane Eddy to Earl Klugh lasted more than a half-century. The guitarist became one of Nashville's early "A-Team" of session musicians, recording with everyone from Wade Ray to Hank Williams and Webb Pierce. He also appeared on the Grand Ol' Opry as a solo act. Atkins eventually took charge of RCA's Nashville studios and eventually became an RCA Vice President, responsible for Nashville operations.

As rock began to roll over country record sales, Atkins's production skills flourished. He was determined to increase sales by making country records appeal to pop and country audiences. Atkins, along with Owen Bradley at Decca and others, began to produce singers backed by neutral rhythm sections. He replaced steel guitars and fiddles with vocal choruses—a style immortalized as the "Nashville Sound."

In 1973 Atkins was elected to the Country Music Hall of Fame; from 1967 to 1988, he won the Country Music Association's (CMA) Instrumentalist of the Year honor eleven times. In 1982 he relinquished his RCA executive role and left RCA to record for Columbia in 1983. Frequent collaborations with younger players like British rock guitarist Mark Knopfler reflected Atkins's desire to remain contemporary.

In 1993 Atkins received a Lifetime Achievement Award from the National Academy of Recording Arts and Sciences (NARAS), placing him among such musical greats as Louis Armstrong, Ray Charles, Leonard Bernstein, and Paul McCartney. In 1997 Atkins won his fifteenth Grammy for his

1996 recording of "Jam Man." Fortunately, there are plenty of audio along with video recordings of Chet Atkins performing on *youtube.com*, so people can enjoy his virtuosity even today, long after he passed away of brain cancer in 2001.

The fact that Chet Atkins volunteered to play—gratis—on David's first album was a dream come true for David, beyond his wildest expectations.

(73)

## 1987 DONELSON, TN: "BOTH SIDES NOW"

Mark O'Connor is working on the music for his third Warner Bros. release, *Elysian Forest*, named after his newborn son Forrest. Mark has turned the entire first floor of his condo into a recording studio and is getting ready for a session when the doorbell rings.

He opens to see David smiling at him with dulcimer case in hand. It is the first time the two friends actually play together, just the two of them. The wish Mark had expressed to David that evening at the Slice of Life— to play together on "Both Sides Now"—is going to happen today.

When they listen to the finished recording of their instrumental version of the song, the two of them agree: they are satisfied that their exquisite violin and dulcimer playing has given new life to Joni Mitchell's song.

(74)

## 1987 NASHVILLE, TN: A SHARP DRESSED MAN

David once told John's wife and production partner Melanie Wells that if he hadn't become a musician he would have liked to have been a clothing designer. So, when John asks him to pick a look for publicity purposes, David immediately thinks of his buddy Vince's Music City Graphics. Vince had designed a hand-blocked and painted jacket that caught David's eye: made of white cotton and silk-screened with Mexican red poinsettias, it evoked the more elaborate suits that many country music stars like to wear when playing at the Grand Ol' Opry. David's friend Alan Mayor takes photos of him wearing the jacket over a patterned shirt, jeans, and cowboy boots while he holds his Bonnie Carol dulcimer. David chooses the shot of him standing, looking slightly down, with the dulcimer on a small stand on the floor with his left hand lightly resting on the peghead. He orders prints of it for the next time John needs a publicity photo.

Vince and David leave together after the Mayor shoot because David wants Vince to meet Herb McCullough. Vince, already a seasoned songwriter also feels a chemistry with Herb, much to David's delight.

(75, 76)

## 1987 NASHVILLE, TN: TRAMP JAMS WITH THE BEST

With three years in Nashville under his belt, twenty-three-year-old fiddle player Tramp still has one foot in outsider's territory yet one foot inside the music business thanks to his impressive work in the local indie band Walk the West. When an artist friend invites him to one of her legendary parties, he overcomes his shyness and accepts. It's a fortuitous decision because he will have plenty to tell his bandmates later.

"I walk in the door and see a huge circle of musicians I looked up and listened to all my life: Jerry Douglas, Mark O'Connor, Sam Bush, Béla Fleck... all jamming together. I was like, 'What the hell?' I am standing in a room full of the best musicians anywhere! I start in playing, feeling like I am in way over my head, but, at the same time, I am in seventh heaven. I couldn't believe I was right there with them."

"Everyone is jamming like crazy and, suddenly, I notice this guy in the circle playing a dulcimer. He was clearly *not* over his head playing with these guys, but he was playing a dulcimer! I was dumbstruck." Tramp knows what a dulcimer is. His mother played an Edsel Martin dulcimer that had a carving of a girl crying on the scroll. She often played with a noter and a goose quill, and she loved playing the traditional songs. He had a dulcimer growing up in Kingsfort, East Tennessee, where he was steeped in old-time mountain music and bluegrass as a kid while he studied violin via the Suzuki method. He knows the dulcimer canon of songs, especially the beginner tunes such as, "Go Tell Aunt Rhody" and "Boil Them Cabbage". Listening to his mother's songs taught him to play by ear.

As he watches the dulcimer player, he thinks to himself, "Who DOES this? They're changing chords and stuff, but he's not going, 'Oh, no, I can only play in D.' I *know* about dulcimers, and I'm watching him play, and I'm thinking, this guy is badass! I've never seen anybody be able to play a dulcimer in a jam session without having to dictate what key everybody plays in, or to stick to modal things, or explain to them that he can't change chords the same way they do or as fast as they do. He wasn't saying anything about that; he was just playing hard and fast along with everybody else, just like he was playing an acoustic guitar. No special treatment at all for the dulcimer player. It was great! We were playing some really cool stuff; I was just in heaven. All these super pickers were there, and for me, these were all the guys whose records I would listen to before I came to Nashville, and then there is this guy playing the dulcimer and grinning."

"Despite all my idols being there, I just kind of gravitated toward him when things slowed down. During a break, I approached him. 'Hey man, I'm Tramp...what the hell? What's your deal?' We just hit it off, and I tell him I had grown up in the intersection of North Carolina, East Tennessee, and Virginia, close to Bristol where the Carter Family lived. 'When I got to Nashville, I went to work as a fiddler for the Kendalls, a father-daughter duo, and then a cou-

ple years after that I joined Walk the West; we had an uphill battle in the home of country music.'" David listens as Tramp explains:
"Walk the West was the brainchild of Paul Kirby, Will Goleman
and his brother John. We played high energy rock with a touch of
country, and created an alter-ego group we call 'The Cactus Brothers' to sometimes open for us. I would bring in these old fiddle tunes
I had grown up with to try and nudge the group a little more toward
the country side but without losing the sounds that made us unique.
These guys in my band are all straight ahead rock and roll guys,
really good; they could play stuff like "Blister in the Sun" just fine,
but they had no exposure to traditional music. When I first started
trying to teach them, they were all like, 'What? What is that?' We
got dropped by Capitol Records after our first album, so, we've been
working on developing the Cactus Brothers so we can continue our
experiment with the rock/country synthesis. The Cactus Brothers
and Walk the West are the exact same people. Our electric guitar
player brings in his banjo for the Cactus Brothers. We play less rock-
and-roll originals and more country-ish covers; we aren't that different from before. In the mean time, we all live and work in Nashville,
so we've been playing side gigs."

David listens as Tramp continues. "I always loved fiddler Vassar
Clements and the records that would take a fiddle tune and put also
put drums, bass and electric guitar on them; I am a fan of the Dixie
Dregs and instrumental bands like them, and I love Irish rock ... I
love any band that has a traditional fiddler featured but then would
put heavy rhythm sections behind it."

As the break winds down, he and David begin playing some old
mountain tunes, starting with "Blackberry Blossom," just the two of
them on fiddle and dulcimer. "I'm watching him while we play, head
down, long hair, Camel cigarette hanging out of his mouth, looking up and grinning every once in a while, and I'm loving it." Soon,
everybody comes back, first to watch and listen, and then join in to
pick with them.

(77)

## Behind the Action: Aspects of the Schnaufer Style

*By Stephen Seifert and Doug Thomson*

Even at the age of twenty-three, fiddle wizard Tramp was familiar enough with the dulcimer to recognize that David was in a league of his own when it came to his playing style. It was characteristics like these that made his style unique:

David had unusually strong fingers. Even when fingerpicking, the strings sounded out as loudly as if he were using a pick. He tended not to use his thumb or pinky to fret; instead, he relied on his ring, middle, and index fingers to fly up and down the fretboard.

His right hand had the ability to strum with a seemingly infinite variety of rhythms, from the slowest basic strum to arrangements in which he interjects flatpicking or fingerpicking at warp speed. He played smoothly using alternate strumming to keep his hand moving in a rhythmic strum whether hitting the strings or not. He would strum in (toward himself) occasionally on a beat or strum out on the beat; hold for a nanosecond, and do a controlled in-strum with a flourish to it, letting all three strings ring like a drum roll.

David was meticulous about accurate note production from the entire length of the fretboard; he had to be in order to work as a session musician. Luthiers in the 80s tended to measure fret placement starting at the number one fret; David encouraged them to measure from the nut to first fret, then from the nut to the second, and so on. Lynn McSpadden changed his measuring to meet David's standards, as did Bob Mize, another well-known luthier at the time.

Typical action (the pressure required to fret the strings) in the 80s was inconsistent through the length of the fretboard. David expected perfect tonal quality from the lowest to the highest fret and worked with McSpadden and later luthier Don Blom to achieve it.

He used a 26" or a 26 1/2" string length, and used string gauges slightly heavier than most players: .012 for the melody string, .014 for the middle string, and a bronze wound .026 for the bass. The heavier gauge allowed him to get the most volume even when he played gently.

The nut and bridge on his dulcimers had an extra groove to allow him to utilize the higher D string. He tended to use the equidistant four-string arrangement to fingerpick, and played more traditional tunes on the paired D strings in the alternate position.

He often used a capo on the 1st or 3rd fret, and a pickup for plugging into an amp to project the dulcimer's sound so it wouldn't be drowned out by louder guitars.

David tended to use partial chords with an open bass: he fretted the melody and middle string, and left the bass to drone. He loved the drone. He would hold down two or three strings with one finger, e.g., the ring finger with his middle finger on top, thus freeing his index finger to move to two or three frets quickly enough to play the fastest fiddle tunes while maintaining a very clean sound.

He had an array of left-hand skills and techniques that enabled him to vary the arrangement of a song, even on the fly. He created interest by playing the melody all over the fretboard, e.g., at the lower octave on the treble string, on the bass string, and/or both up the neck of the fretboard to the higher octave. His playing tool kit included techniques such scaler slides, hammer-ons, pull-offs, harmonics, string bending, and others he had learned during his work with other studio musicians.

Most importantly, he had exquisite taste not only in music but in his arrangements. He knew what to do when and where, and what not to do when and where. Although he did not read music at this stage of his career, his years of songwriting and his mental music archive gave him an intuitive understanding for how to use dynamics to bring out the best in a given piece.

(78, 79, 80)

## 1987 NASHVILLE, TN: "THE SCHNAUF HAS BROKEN THROUGH THE WALL!"

When Herb shows up at David's apartment this week, he comments on the Emmylou Harris photo on David's "Wishing Wall." David tells Herb that that Chet Atkins had offered to play on his new record. Prominent drummer Kenny Malone would also be playing along with the world-renowned producer and musician Dave Pomeroy on bass, and Cowboy Clement on guitar. Herb throws his head back and laughs: "The Schnauf' has broken through the wall!"

(81)

## 1987 NASHVILLE, TN: "WE NEED SOMEONE LIKE YOU. . ."

Shortly after meeting David, Tramp asks him to come with him to have a talk with the rest of his bandmates. The two take a drive to Belle Meade, just a stone's throw south of Nashville where the band is setting up to rehearse at the Purple Onion Club. Tramp explains on the way, "We need someone like you in the band, someone who knows traditional music. I like rock and roll, I like to be aggressive with the music. But if we add the dulcimer, now we're a string band.

You can play anything we play with a pickup so people can hear the dulcimer."

When they arrive, Tramp does the introductions: the founding bandmates—Paul Kirby and brothers Will and John Goleman—have been playing together since elementary school. Sam Poland plays dobro, and Dave Kennedy is their drummer. The first question everyone raises is "What's a dulcimer?" David pulls the instrument out and plays for them. They sit up and lean forward, impressed. They explain their metamorphosis from Walk the West to the Cactus Brothers and the style of music they're aiming for. Sam explains, "Everybody has tried to classify us as something like 'Ricky Skaggs Meets U2.' I tend to think of us as the Grateful Dead of country music."

As they all talk, David mostly listens. By the end of the meeting, David agrees to think about joining the group. He's about to have the busiest year of his life, so he'll consider it once he gets the upcoming recording work out of the way that John has scheduled. David explains how the normally softer-sounding dulcimer can be hooked into an amp so it can be played along with the electric instruments. He also plays the chromatic dulcimer*, and that, too, can be amped. When the boys tell him they're looking for a manager, he recommends John Lomax.

Tramp is thrilled. With David there, the guys don't seem to object to learning some of the traditional tunes in order to move themselves to the more marketable country side of playing.

Suddenly, Tramp's dream of playing rollicking fiddle tunes with a big band behind him looks within reach.

(82, 83, 84)

*In the days before Fariña had the six and a half fret added to the diatonic dulcimer, the sharps and flats were left out, leaving only natural or "whole" notes. A chromatic dulcimer includes all of the natural notes, sharps, and flats on the fretboard, thus giving the player the most options to play any song.

## 1987 NASHVILLE, TN: *DULCIMER DELUXE*

John and David often head to the Villager Tavern for a beer and to discuss everything from current events, books they've read and music history to strategies for introducing the dulcimer into mainstream commercial music. David explains, "I think most producers think of [the dulcimer] as limited, especially if they've never heard anybody play a wide range of stuff on it. Their response is always, 'I never knew it could make that many sounds.' I know it's something a little different. It's not exactly a mandolin sound, it's not exactly a guitar sound, although sometimes it gets confused with both of them.'"

John knows he's right. Despite his encyclopedia knowledge of folk and traditional music, before he met David, he, too, had a narrow view of the dulcimer's capability. Both of them are determined to fix this situation so that the music world never thinks of the dulcimer the same way again.

David has a habit of using the word, "deluxe" to describe things he likes very much, so he and John decide that the obvious title for their first album will be *Dulcimer Deluxe*.

(85)

## 1987 NASHVILLE, TN: ONLY THE BEST

John, impressed with David's taste in music, leaves the track selection up to him. John will take care of everything else.

First, he creates a new label SFL ("Sounds from Lomax") just for David's work. David. Next, he only wants the best people working on this debut; he knows that most dulcimer recordings tend to be recorded with one mic on tape players in someone's house, the result being a flat, poor-quality recording. He pulls in friend Mark Miller to be the recording engineer and studio director; they'll record at Jacks Tracks, a studio now owned by Allen Reynolds. John asks his friend Bill Johnson from CBS to moonlight and do all the graphics under the pseudonym of "Billy Dakota." Vip Vipperman comes on board to play guitar as does Gove Scrivenor, a master musician on the autoharp. Mark O'Connor happily agrees to play fiddle.

Because they want to show off the versatility of the dulcimer, David includes some traditional dulcimer songs but also selects a diverse list of tunes, e.g., solos ("Last Date," "Somewhere over the Rainbow," and "Steel Guitar Rag"), duos (e.g., "Viper Moon" with Alan Freeman and "Santa Ana's Retreat"); cover songs (e.g., George Harrison's "Here Comes the Sun" paired with his original composition, "Morning Birds"; Bill Monroe's "Blue Moon of Kentucky"). Two original songs David composed with Herb ("Twilight Eyes" and "Mr. Snow") make the final cut for the list.

Chet Atkins not only volunteers to play on the Stephen Foster classic "Beautiful Dreamer" without charge but will also co-arrange it with David.

John is satisfied that they will have a professional-looking and sounding album. By working with Mark Miller in that studio and with those players, he knows they will produce an album worthy of Nashville's reputation for quality recording and production, the first ever for a dulcimer player.

(86, 87))

## Hank Snow (1914-1999)

It's no surprise that Herb and David wrote "Mr. Snow" to pay homage to Hank Snow. The most successful country music star to come out of Canada, Clarence Eugene "Hank" Snow was considered one of the most distinctive stylists, one of the best songwriters, one of the most prolific recording artists, one of the finest guitarists, and one of the most masterful businessmen in the modern industry.

David greatly admired and identified with Snow for a number of reasons: he never turned his back on the classic style that first made him famous. At the same time, Snow loved to experiment outside his comfort zone. In Snow's case, that meant Latin rhythms, jazz, blues, Hawaiian styles, recitations, the mambo, and gospel songs. Snow continually delved back into his early repertoire to resurrect old songs for new audiences. To him, repertoire was a living thing, and his sense of tradition was as sharp and keen as that of any folksinger. Snow became one of the first country singers to see the LP as the basic creative unit, and created some of the first theme, or concept, albums.

(88)

## 1987 NASHVILLE, TN: PLENTY OF SESSION WORK

Vince Farsetta and friends make their way to the Uncle Dave Macon Days Festival in Murfreesboro, a forty-five-minute drive from Nashville. To no one's surprise, Vince takes first place in the Old Time Banjo contest.

With the easy access to festivals and the abundance of performance venues (close to seventy venues a week listed in the *Tennesseean*'s "Showcase" feature alone) Vince listens to and plays more music than he did in his prior thirty-two years. He picks up more and more work as a session musician. He also devotes time to his songwriting, especially for one of his favorite bands, Leftover Salmon. In addition to his Slice of Life gigs, Vince often plays at places like the Grapevine Café and the Station Inn. He, David, and Rick Roberts continue to play as Fretilizer and as the Big Otter String Band to enthusiastic fans.

Vince, David, and their rapidly growing circle of musician friends means they live in a kind of musical whirlwind. David has started teaching private students; he performs in Nashville clubs and frequently travels to conduct workshops and perform in festivals. He has plenty of session work under his belt by now: besides his work with the Judds, he has worked on albums with Rattlesnake Annie (*Rattlesnake Annie*), Mark O'Connor (*Elysian Forest*), Kathy Mattea (*Untold Stories*), Dan Seals (*On the Front Line*), Holly Dunn (*Holly Dunn*), and the Wagoneers from Texas along with several other easy listening collections. And if that isn't enough, he starts playing informally and occasionally on stage with Walk the West and his new friend Tramp.

As for Vince's next gig: he'll play the banjo and guitar as a session musician on David's next project. The cassettes for *Dulcimer Deluxe* aren't even shipped from the factory yet when John and David start working on *Dulcimer Player*.

(89)

---

### *Who was "Uncle Dave Macon"?*

Uncle David Macon, also known as 'The Dixie Dewdrop," was "a proficient banjoist and singer of old-time ballads who was, during his time, the most popular country music artist in America." Artists like Dave Macon and the Carter Family became sources of music inspiration those who followed them.

Macon was the first real star of The Grand Ole Opry, appearing from 1926 until almost up to the time of his death at eighty-two. Macon derived much of his repertoire and stage patter from vaudeville and minstrel shows, but his songs reflected on a wide variety of subjects from political corruption to current events like the advent of the automobile. The Annual Uncle Dave Macon Days Old-Time Music & Dance Festival has been held every July at Cannonsburgh Village in Murfreesboro, Tennessee, since 1977.

(90, 91)

---

# 1987 NASHVILLE, TN: "WE WEAPONIZED THE DULCIMER."

As soon as John and David discuss the plan for David's second album, *Dulcimer Player*, John sets up recording sessions.

*Dulcimer Deluxe* was released as a cassette. John wants to produce cassettes *and* albums for *Dulcimer Player*. He suggests a similar array of traditional, original, and new songs as they had done on *Dulcimer Deluxe* but wants to market this new album not only to David's dulcimer fans but to a wider, mainstream audience. David picks the songs, and John's production sidekicks (Melanie Wells and Mark Miller) return to Jack's Tracks.

David and Herb had recently formed a writing partnership, and four of their songs will be on the new list. David's first and only choice for their singular song, "When Silence was Golden" is buddy Mark O'Connor. David asks his new friend Tramp to play the fiddle on another evocative instrumental he had written with Herb, "O, Pony." Jack Clement himself is onboard to play guitar as is Vip Vipperman again, and Vince will play banjo and guitar. David and Vince surprise John with "Dapper John's Reel," a song they wrote for him. As they record their homage, Vince performs his breathtaking runs on the clawhammer banjo with David on dulcimer.

Every once in a while, the Muse smiles on artists whom she perceives have the right motivation, and the studio is full of people with the right motivation on the day they record "Fisher's Hornpipe," one of the most widely played fiddle tunes in the world. Tramp and his Cactus Brothers come to the studio to record on what may be the first ever rendition of "Hornpipe" led by a dulcimer. Right before they start with the warmup, there's a feeling in the air that something special is about to happen.

John and Melanie often listen in the control room with their eyes closed during recordings to focus on the sound; however, this time they don't close their eyes. Once Mark cues David, he starts off with the electrifying opening strum that grabs the attention of everyone in the studio and stops them in their tracks. They are about to witness a once-in-a-life-time live performance.

When David and the Cactus Brothers finish the reel with a perfect flourish, the room is dead silent; everyone is speechless. Suddenly, laughter and applause break the silence. Because this take was supposed to be a warm-up, Mark had recorded on two tracks only; as they listen post-performance, they know that this very well could become David's signature song. Typically, warmups are not saved, but for some reason Mark had saved this one. Subsequent recordings, while excellent, don't reach the transcendent experience of the initial recording. Mark's capture of the best take on a warmup is almost unheard of in recording studios; the only way he will be able to describe listening to the recording later is to pronounce it "a blast of enervating energy." John immediately imagines what to do with the song besides including it on this album: he adds "Fisher's Hornpipe music video" on his must-do list.

The Hornpipe isn't the only impressive recording, however. David's rendition of the Hank Williams classic, "I'm So Lonesome, I Could Cry" has a similar effect on Mark and John, ensuring another a music video.

The once shy David is nowhere to be seen in the studio now. He feels completely in his element, surrounded by trusted friends; a dream he birthed and nurtured that now overlaps with theirs. Thanks to John's music business savvy, sensitivity, and appreciation of David's talent, the experience is much bigger than he ever could have imagined the day he bought his dulcimer in Austin, and he knows it. He savors every single minute.

(92, 93, 94, 95)

---

### The Hornpipe

A hornpipe is both a wind instrument made out of horn made to accompany dancing, and a centuries-old dance associated with sailors that was typically performed by one person. Scholars and writers over the years have posited many different origins for the name "Fisher's Hornpipe." Most

---

agree it first appeared in the latter half of the eighteenth century, but few agree on the original composer. Songcatcher Alan Jabbour recorded Henry Reed playing "Fisher's Hornpipe" in Giles County, Virginia, in 1966 for the Library of Congress. Whatever its origin, the tune became widely popular in a short span of time. Along with "Rickett's Hornpipe," it is one of the most the most popular hornpipes played in the Southern Appalachians throughout history.

(96, 97)

## Mix Master Mark Miller

"The best studios I've worked in are the studios that feel comfortable and have a good vibe because that's where musicians feel the best, so they relax and play well. Some studios look like a dentist's office; I don't like that. I want the studio to feel like a home. So when musicians come in, I'll offer them a Coke, let them have a cigarette, encourage them to get comfortable, and they'll usually start tuning up. I play them a simple version of the song I want to record so they get a feeling for the melody, the structure. The music is never written out. We use the Nashville Numbering System on a chart so they can see the song's chord structure instead.

With respect to recording equipment, normally we have a big tape machine that has twenty-four tracks on it, or forty-eight, whatever you want; each instrument is recorded separately on a different track. If someone makes a mistake, you can go in and fix one note, or ten notes, or take that instrument out and put a new track in."

Miller goes on to describe how typical sessions worked at the time he worked on *Dulcimer Deluxe* and *Dulcimer Player*. "The musicians start playing, and these people are so good that often by the second or third time they've got the song down. I encourage all of them to improvise because, together, they are trying to figure out the best way to make the song work. It's very collaborative.

In a way, everyone in that room is acting as a songwriter because they are all contributing to create this song. You don't record every time because they're learning the song, so normally they might play it through a few times, and it might be an hour before you turn on the tape machine. Once I think they've got something that works, I'll say, 'Hey, let's put one down.' Then they'll stop and we listen to it and talk about it, everyone chiming in to make suggestions on how to make the song sound its best. It's a pretty amazing process."

In this case, Mark recorded "Fisher's Hornpipe" live to tape the first time David and the Cactus Brothers played it: "It's exactly what everyone heard when it went down." Because he recorded it directly to two-track tape, i.e., left and right stereo, he explains, "I couldn't fix anything because it was only supposed to be a warmup. That's how it was cut. When they hit the last note, I realized it was mixed and done. That almost *never* happens. That's one take, you hit, and you're done. There were seven guys recording on that cut. To get it all right the first time was a damn miracle. It's fun when it happens. David's performance was fantastic. That recording is when we weaponized the dulcimer."

"'Cutting a track' means recording it. We took a lot of time making the dulcimer sound as unique and as good as it could. David would come over in the evenings to try different microphones, trying to get the biggest sounds for the dulcimer's voice. Later, I had friends who used to "tune the rooms" with that cut to make sure the speakers sent out the right frequency. They would use David's recording to do that, a real compliment to our work together.

"'Mixing' happens once you get all the music elements on separate tracks. You have to put together the tracks to make them sound like songs on a record. For example, you want all the elements of the song to make sense: you lower down the drums and put any vocals in perspective. Mixing David's music was simple because there wasn't a lot of instruments. Today, I could spend a week or more on a song if there are sixty or seventy instruments on it.

"Mastering the cassette, vinyl or a CD has to be done as well, because you don't normally cut songs in the sequence the consumer listens to on the final record. So, you want to put the songs in a meaningful sequence. You have to open well and have a great song at the ending. You level out the recordings to have the same volume; you determine the space between the songs; you assemble the record, and then you have it."

(98)

## 1987 NASHVILLE, TN: FLAWLESS

Once John releases *Dulcimer Deluxe*, close to three thousand orders pour into his mailbox even before the cassette and album for *Dulcimer Player* are released. It's an astonishing number for an instrumental cassette of a relatively rare instrument, due largely to the extraordinary quality of the production along with John's nonstop promotion of his client. He pours through *Dulcimer Players News* to familiarize himself with the growing dulcimer world and the opportunities and vendors it delivers to his fingertips. From John's point of view, it isn't even necessary to reach out to radio for airplay; David's promotion of the cassette at his many gigs and festival performances continues to increase demand.

John taps his friends across the country who live anywhere near a festival or workshop on David's schedule to host him at house concerts, a small but mighty venue that raises even more money and sells even more cassettes to people who wouldn't normally attend a folk festival. Music stores like McSpadden's Dulcimer Shoppe, Jean Schilling's store in Cosby, and Neal Hellman's Gourd Music in California snap up as many cassettes as John will send them since they know David and his impact on his audiences.

Whenever David returns to Nashville from his periodic road trips, John catches him up with the stellar reviews that he incorporates in his press releases to journalists across the country. One particularly satisfying notice is a review from *Country Song Roundup*: "Not only is [*Dulcimer Deluxe*] flawless in its musicianship, it quells the rumor once and for all that the dulcimer does not belong in country music."

(99, 100, 101, 102)

## 1988 NASHVILLE, INDIANA: A GOOD TIME TO BE AN ACOUSTIC MUSICIAN

Neal Hellman is on tour again, this time with Gourd Music's new vinyl album and cassette, *Oktober County*. Everywhere he travels he stops in local stores that are potential vendors for the album. Once he plays sample tracks, he usually sells between five and ten cassettes at each spot thanks to fresh sound of the contemplative music.

During a stop in Nashville, Indiana he sees a high-end gift shop, the Olde Bartley House. He talks to the owner to see if he would be interested in carrying his cassettes. The owner laughs and asks him if he knows he's in Brown County, whose nickname "October County" is due to the magnificent fall leaf colors that attracts tourists in the autumn. As they chat, he places an order with Neal, but it won't be his last.

In one season the Old Bartley will sell ten thousand dollars' worth of "Oktober County" cassettes. It's a good time to be an acoustic musician.

(103)

## 1988 WINCHESTER, VIRGINIA: A TIP OF THE HAT

Doug Berch, two years after his double win at Winfield in both the national hammered and fretted dulcimer categories, joins *Dulcimer Players News* as music editor. He prepares arrangements that featured players send in to be published along with their articles. He also works with editor Maddie MacNeil on her new "Performer Profile" segment she designs to help her readers learn more about players and how they approach their work.

The Fall issue includes reviewer Mitzie Collins's report on *Dulcimer Deluxe*. She notes that the entire cassette "superbly demonstrates the wide range of musical styles possible on the instrument and David's own extraordinary technique and musicality ... [and is characterized by] remarkable clarity and fidelity of sound ...."

The Fall issue also includes a quarter page ad placed by John Lomax that features the Alan L. Mayor photo of a short-haired David in jeans and Vince's silk- screened jacket.

David is thrilled to read the review and see the ad, although what he considers the "deluxe" part of the experience has less to do with the outside reviews and more to do with realizing his dream of introducing Nashville to the dulcimer. Chet Atkins's offer to play on three songs on *Dulcimer Deluxe* means that Atkins did it as a gift to David, a tip of the hat to the new virtuoso in town.

(104, 105)

287

## 1988 NASHVILLE, TN: DULCIMER PLAYER DELUXE

John knows they are on a roll, but he's also aware that the days of cassette tapes and players are coming to an end. The new technology wave bearing down on Nashville is the compact disc, popularly known as a CD. Before they even wrapped up the work on *Dulcimer Player*, he and David decided that their third production will be a double CD that combines songs from David's first two cassettes— some seventy minutes of play time—onto one CD. They'll leave behind "Cherokee Shuffle" and "Davy Crockett's Honeymoon" due to space limitations of the CD format. They agree that an apt name for their first CD together is *Dulcimer Player Deluxe*. John also wants to release it as a vinyl record album for the turntable crowd. One could argue that *Dulcimer Player Deluxe* will turn more people around the world on to the mountain dulcimer than any other album in history.

(106)

---

*The Move to Digital Music*

In the late eighties, digital recordings transferred to compact discs (CDs) and rapidly elbow cassettes out of the music stores. The CD format was perfect for dulcimer music since it captures the high transient and dynamic sound of the instrument with exceptional clarity.

CD technology differs radically from that used to produce vinyl records and cassette tapes. The latter are the final product of a conventional analog recording made on a magnetic tape with the sounds being translated into mechanical impulses. For vinyl records, those impulses are conveyed as grooves whose depth and width reflect variances in dynamic range. A record's sound limiting factor has to do with the range of sound the grooves are physically capable of produc-

---

ing. If the grooves are too deep, they will pierce through the record; too shallow, and they won't etch the vinyl. A further limitation is the usage time of the record or cassette. Both formats create friction that degrades the recording with each play over time. In the former, a recording stylus, and in the latter, a track head, over time, will result in unwanted pops, hisses and scratching sounds.

Contrast this old technology with the new in 1988: in digital recording, music is sampled over forty-four thousand times a second and then turned into binary numbers for information storage. These numbers are recorded as "minute pits" in the metallic surface of the CD, which will be read by a laser beam. The sound exists only as a binary code, so there is no limit to the sound it can reproduce and no moving parts needed to play the recording; CDs are read by light. With an expanded song capacity of up to seventy-four minutes, the theory is that they are a perfect package for conveying music and will never wear out.

(107)

## 1989 CINCINNATI, OHIO: STEPHEN SEIFERT

Throughout elementary school, Stephen Seifert's scores on his aptitude tests have confirmed what his parents already know about him: he's enthralled by music and has a gift for working with technology.

Growing up, Stephen loved to talk about the music his great-grandma listened to when she was young. She still liked to sing the old-time songs and often wrote down the lyrics of her favorite songs in a little book. When she got her long braid cut off, she gave him the braid and the little songbook. He occasionally takes out the book and studies the songs within to recall his grandma.

At age ten, he created his own tv news network, and when someone lent him a flutafone, "he played the heck out of it" his mother Nancy tells her friends.

At age fifteen, his cover of "Jump" by Van Halen impressed his dad at so much that he bought him a synthesizer. Nancy bought him an electronic keyboard, but his hands grew so fast he needed a larger keyboard before long. He played in the background for a neighborhood group called Simple Aggression.

Now at sixteen he plans to attend the Cincinnati Dulcimer Society meeting in Norwood, Ohio, after falling in love with dulcimer music while listening to the Russell Cook CDs his mother Nancy had purchased. He walks into the meeting not realizing that Cook's CDs are recordings of Cook playing the hammered dulcimer, a different instrument altogether. After some initial confusion, a club member explains they play the mountain dulcimer, not the hammered dulcimer. She hands him a cardboard dulcimer to see how he feels about this instrument, and shows him how to strum along as they play. He's immediately hooked.

Shortly thereafter, Nancy and Big Steve take Stephen to a Nashville, Indiana, music shop and buy him a student dulcimer. Afterward, they walk across the street to a record store and to buy some CDs. When he sees the store carries David's cassettes and CD, he is so excited he runs over to tell his mother that they have David Schnaufer's CDs. Nancy asks, "Well, who is David Schnaufer?"

He pulls his head back and looks at her incredulously: "MOM! HE is a GOD!"

(108)

## 1989 AUSTIN, TEXAS: ALREADY AT THE TOP OF THEIR GAME

Ten years after Rabbit Junction, David and Vince opened for Townes Van Zandt at Austin's Cactus Café last year. On this October evening, they are back in Austin again, this time at Poor David's

Pub. Tonight, the pub is packed, and the lucky audience is about to watch and listen to these two virtuosos at the top of their game as they perform "Sarah," a song David cowrote with Herb McCullough.

David opens the song with the story of a young West Virginia woman in 1911 named Sarah: "The young fellow made her a dulcimer, and she kept it, but refused to marry him. Now I own that dulcimer, and my buddy Herb and I decided to write a song about Sarah."

As he tells his story, Vince sits quietly to his left. As soon as David begins to play, Vince's body starts to move in time to the beat. As the song unfolds, Vince slides in effortlessly on his banjo to accompany him. They play together as if they were one person, as smooth as silk. When they finish "Sarah" they glance at each other with pure pleasure. Next, they launch first into "Spanish Harlem," with Vince on guitar this time, and then into the lively "San Antonio Rose." Afterward, they swap lead roles; Vince plays "Sandy River Belle" on the banjo while David backs him on the jaw harp. Once they launch into the classic "Wildwood Flower," David proves his comment correct when he modestly tells the audience, "You can make a dulcimer sound a little like a guitar, but it's harder to make a guitar sound like a dulcimer." He alternates playing the dulcimer with a Jack Clement guitar sound and then the dulcimer sound. For the rest of the evening, the feelings about their long friendship together that led to this one night in particular are evident by the quiet, shared satisfaction on David and Vince's faces.

Many years later, John Lomax's son John Nova Lomax will pen in the *Houston Press*, "The Schnaufer/Farsetta duo was one of the most amazing things I have ever seen or heard. Each could simultaneously play rhythm and melody. It sounded as if there were at least four musicians on stage."

(109, 110, 111, 112)

## 1989 SHREVEPORT, LOUISIANA: NOT HIS SCENE: STEVEN STUBBLEFIELD

David and Vince are due at Enoch's, a longtime beloved Shreveport institution. Everyone from tradespeople to surgeons to tourists from all over the world crowd in most nights to listen to top Texas and Louisiana musicians. This fall evening the house is packed to see Vince on clawhammer banjo and David on a 1911 McCowan West Virginia dulcimer (plus another he built himself.) The two are bent on bridging the gap between traditional European and mountain music and contemporary music. "I play works that date from the Renaissance and the Beatles to 'Walk, Don't Run' and Cyndi Lauper" he tells the reporter who calls him prior to his appearance.

Shreveport teenager and amateur punk rocker Steve Stubblefield dreams of playing someday at Enoch's. He won't see David this evening; he's too young to enter the bar, and, frankly, this kind of music is not his scene. He'll see David at Enoch's another time, though; on that fortuitous night, their future collaboration will be set.

Tonight, Stubblefield is eight hours and one minute's drive from Nashville, but it might as well be eight thousand miles as far as he is concerned, given his lack of interest in traditional country music.

(113, 114, 115)

## 1989 NASHVILLE, TN: DULCIMER PLAYER DELUXE

As the whirlwind of work in the late 80s continues to carry John and David forward, David finds himself in demand as a session pro in Nashville; his latest work includes a session for Al and Emily Cantrell's song "Riddle for a Fiddle" for their *Under a Southern Moon* album. He has been playing an electrified dulcimer he built himself for playing with the Cactus Brothers in local gigs, always to rave reviews. He draws students like a magnet with his charm and the unspoken way he makes them feel part of his special dulcimer circle. He travels regularly to Mountain View to visit and talk design with Lynn McSpadden for a line of David Schnaufer dulcimer models. He has committed to shoot an instructional video with Happy Traum's company to keep up with the demand for dulcimer lessons. Thanks to John's worldwide distribution of David's music, more people than ever have picked up the dulcimer to learn to play it.

John tells friends that David has pulled off a near miracle: he has made a close-to-forgotten acoustic instrument relevant to a wide audience, and he has done it in a high-tech age that is becoming obsessed with drum machines and synthesizer equipment. John is swamped with orders for the new CD and ships them to vendors including Neal's burgeoning "Gourd Music" where they sell as fast as the new orders arrive. John manages both David and the Cactus Brothers, promotes their music at conventions, sends out press releases to journalists and vendors, writes articles, and does interviews. Next year, David will open for the Everly Brothers on their 1990 tour of the United States and Canada, and John will find time to accompany him for part of the tour.

Also at the top of John's to-do list is planning two music videos to promote David on Country Music Television (CMT) with shooting to begin next year. Whenever they can find a moment, both put their heads together to plan for the next CD, *Dulcimer Sessions*.

In an interview with Michael McCall, Dave shares his reaction to the changes in his life: "I'm thrilled with the success. It's especially pleasing to see the variety of people who like dulcimer music. I've had everyone from young rockers with rooster haircuts to sweet, octogenarian ladies come up and tell me that they love my music. It's great—the dulcimer is an instrument that deserves to have a bigger part in the music we hear. It's the only instrument which originated in America. I'd like to see it recognized more, and get to a place where more people know it and are apt to play it. I think that can happen."

Bob Oermann, who interviewed David five years ago when he first arrived in Nashville, reviews the new *Dulcimer Player Deluxe*: "I'm pinning gold stars on my favorite country records of the year.... Single-handedly, David has revived the dulcimer in Nashville. This 72-minute CD is as intricate and gorgeous as Irish lace...in the past few years he's become one of the most influential new pickers in Music City."

And Judds' Producer Brent Maher in *Nashville Banner Lifestyles* adds: "[David Schnaufer has taken his] instrument and not only perfected it in a traditional sense...he's stepped on new turf. There's a real meeting of the minds as far as self-expression and how [he] plays. There's no blocking from brain to heart to hand. There aren't any limitations."

What most people don't know and David doesn't discuss: he's exhausted, and he often doesn't feel well. Occasionally he lets the voicemail box fill up and ignores knocks on the door as he sits in his room, playing the dulcimer or sleeping.

(116, 117, 118)

## 1989 WINCHESTER, VIRGINIA: THE VERY BREATH OF LIFE ITSELF

Just ten years after his first submission to the magazine on "The Harris Technique," *Dulcimer Players News* celebrates all things David Schnaufer in its Winter issue. His hair cut shorter, David appears on the cover and is the subject of a three-page interview within.

David shares how proud he is to have played with top-tier Nashville musicians and to have appeared on TV shows like *Nashville Now*, adding that such performances have opened up a new audience to him beyond the folk gig circuit. He tells the interviewer, "You should be able to play the dulcimer with any instrument in the world—grand piano, kettle drums, an orchestra, whatever....You should use the instrument to play what you want to play, rather than limiting it to only one style of music."

All of the public David Schnaufer is on display in the article: the musician who earned two platinum albums with the Judds is the same person who shares that he always wanted to play "San Antonio Rose" but couldn't. So he took lessons with Satch Wright, his electric guitar player buddy, to learn it so he could include it on *Dulcimer Deluxe*. He wanted to take "Steel Guitar Rag" to a higher level, so taught himself how to use a chromatic dulcimer, an instrument still rare at the time. He expresses gratitude for all the support he's felt from the musical community. But perhaps the most important aspect of David that the writer captures is a single line that would be easy to overlook, buried as it is in the middle of the interview: "For Schnaufer the musician, the dulcimer provides the very breath of life itself."

One could easily make the case that the reverse is true as well.

(119)

## 1989 LOUISVILLE, KENTUCKY: ORPHAN'S PICNIC

Nancy Barker's teachers for this year's Kentucky Music Weekend and Week include David along with his old friend Maddy MacNeil. David and Maddie first met at Rabbit Junction, and then later got to know one another through Keith and Mary Young in Virginia. People who know them both think they are much alike: soft-spoken, talented, generous people for whom music means everything. The two friends especially look forward to seeing Jean Ritchie whom Nancy invited to perform this year. Nancy tells David about calling up Jean to invite her: "Jean answered the phone herself!" Nancy is tickled that Jean told her to hold on when she called; she had to turn over the chicken that was frying on the stove.

David makes another new friend this year, master guitarist Duck Baker, whom Nancy had invited to teach guitar classes. A highly regarded fingerstyle guitarist, his repertoire, like David's, ranges from old-time mountain music and bluegrass to blues, gospel,

Celtic, and ragtime to swing, modern jazz, and free improvisation. David often attracts kindred spirits, so he and Duck begin an easy friendship. David learns that Duck isn't shy about his abilities and that he is very focused on his music. His reputation is one of being uncompromising; he cares only about being a successful interpreter of the music. He also knows a little about the dulcimer from his work for Kicking Mule Records in the early seventies. Its catalog consisted primarily of guitarists, but they added dulcimer music in the mid-seventies thanks to the influence of Force and D'osshe's *In Search of the Wild Dulcimer.* Duck tells David he always liked the deep and serious sound of the dulcimer. While he liked listening to all the dulcimer teachers at KMW, he appreciates David's playing because he is so different. He plays all the right notes and fills in melodies in simple ways, but it doesn't sound like what any dulcimer player would do. "I feel like you are still rooted in something very traditional" he tells David.

As usual, David stays at Nancy's home for the duration of the festivals. When the week is over he gives Duck a lift to Nashville where he has lined up some gigs. On the way south out of Louisville, David points out a sign that always has struck him whenever he has traveled to Louisville: "Orphan's Picnic," with an arrow pointing away from the highway. "It's meaningful and evocative" he tells Duck; "it's both happy and sad; we should write a song about it." He doesn't reveal why he considers it particularly meaningful, and Duck doesn't ask. Nevertheless, the two will stay in touch and write a song entitled "Orphans Picnic" that David will cut for his next album with John Lomax.

(120, 121, 122, 123)

## 1989 NASHVILLE, TN: FOR THE LOVE OF HISTORY

David tells his cousin Gena that once, at a festival in New Harmony he had five or six old dulcimers sitting out on a picnic table. While he was talking and playing a lady strolled over to look at his collection. "Boy, they have sure come a long way from back in those days" she remarked to David. "Well, I wish I could agree with you ma'am....The old dulcimers are delicate in many ways," he explains. "The wood is dry, and they are hard to keep in tune because people used wooden friction pegs to tune the strings. But their sound springs forth from the earth."

His growing appreciation for the old instruments and their histories gradually compelled him to go on excursions—sometimes alone, sometimes with friends—to hunt for them. At times, people who find an old dulcimer in an attic and hear about David will gift it to him. If he finds one he likes that a collector wants to sell, he will use whatever money he can scrape together to buy it.

(124)

## 1989 GATLINBURG TO NASHVILLE TO COSBY: THE MUSE ALWAYS WHISPERS

Mary Lawrence hears David Schnaufer before she ever sees him. On a trip to East Tennessee she stops at Schilling's music shop to look around. During a chat with Jean, Mary Lawrence mentions that she lives in Nashville. "Here is a CD of David Schnaufer," Jean says as she hands Mary Lawrence *Dulcimer Player Deluxe*; "he's a really fine dulcimer player who lives in Nashville. You will enjoy this CD, maybe you can meet him someday." Intrigued, Mary Lawrence buys it and plays it in the car on the way home. She has never heard the dulcimer played with such driving, infectious rhythm and can hardly contain her excitement. When she gets home, she listens to the CD again and again.

Often, in the back of her mind, over the next year, a little voice whispers to her: "You know enough about music. You ought to be able to teach yourself how to tune that dulcimer and play it." When she finally gathers the courage to try the dulcimer again, she takes it out of the closet and uses with the little instruction book to try again. Suddenly, she breaks a string. Taking the broken string in hand, she drives over to Cotten Music and tells the gentleman behind the counter, "I need one of these because I broke it!" After listening to her tale of woe, he gives her a piece of advice. "You need to take lessons from David Schnaufer, he lives right over there," pointing toward Belmont Avenue.

She thinks, "Sure, I just call the guru of the dulcimer world and say, 'I'd like to have a lesson.'" It takes her a few weeks to gather her courage to call, and it takes a few more weeks for David to return her call because he is out on the road. But he does return her call.

On a gorgeous, sunny fall day, she heads to the address David has given to her for her first dulcimer lesson, a basement apartment directly across from Belmont University. She knocks on the door, a little uneasy, not knowing what to expect. When David swings open the door—"Welcome!"—her uneasiness melts away instantly.

She suddenly has a sense that all is right with the world thanks to this journey she is about to begin with this musician who has a friendly twinkle in his eye.

Thirty years later, she will still remember the very first song he teaches her this day—"Morning Has Broken"—and she considers it an apt metaphor for her lifelong dulcimer journey.

(125, 126)


## 1989 NASHVILLE, TN: ANOTHER WISH COME TRUE

David's Wishing Wall doesn't let him down when it comes to Emmylou Harris. Since seeing her sixteen years ago at Liberty Hall, he has encountered her several times in Nashville, but this gig is going to be special. She, along with several other musicians—Chet Atkins, Kris Kristofferson, Ricky Skaggs, Willie Nelson, Hank Williams Jr., Randy Travis, Dwight Yoakam, and Waylon Jennings will appear on a PBS television tribute, "The Hank Williams Tradition." Emmylou asked for David to accompany her on stage at the Ryman to back her as she sings "May You Never Be Alone."

Director Jim Brown Jim will be busy: in addition to directing, he and his director of photography will move back and forth to shoot the pair on three 16 mm cameras. In order to show off the historic building with its balcony and the huge stained- glass windows (which he has lit from the outside), Brown decides to flip the performance with Emmylou facing the back wall of the stage. He creates an intimate scene by having David sit across from her, close in profile with the Bonnie Carol dulcimer on his lap. Both wear jeans, and Emmylou wears a dark flower-print jacket to contrast her femininity with David, who wears his shell necklace, a denim shirt over a black T-shirt, and a cowboy hat.

Jim had worked with Emmylou before and found her lovely and cooperative. Meeting David for the first time, he is impressed with him not only as a musician but as a person. After the initial shoot, they listen to every take. Once Emmylou picks one she likes, Jim does a playback with it and films a couple more takes MTV-style where Emmylou and David sing and play along to the previously filmed and recorded track. When they finally finish, Jim asks John Lomax to take a picture of him talking with his performers.

Later, David will later tell his friend Bob King what a big moment that was for him. "I'd sure like to play a courting dulcimer* with Emmylou Harris!" he laughs.

(127)

## Courting Dulcimers

Courting dulcimers are a somewhat rare type of fretted dulcimer that incorporates two fretboards placed opposite of each other on a single, large soundbox so that two players can face each other to play a song together on the same instrument.

> Legendary performer and luthier Howie Mitchell wrote that it was also known as a "twicimer."
>
> (128)

## 1989 NASHVILLE, TN: "BMI CORDIALLY INVITES YOU..."

BMI's invitation invites the recipient to a reception and performance. Thus, the Nashville music establishment embraces David in celebration of the newly released *Dulcimer Player Deluxe*. *Music Independent Magazine* will award the CD "Independent Country Record of the Year" and David "Independent Artist of the Year." The National Association of Independent Record Distributors will make the CD a finalist for "Best Country Album" while rave reviews continue to pour in to SFL from around the world.

Part of David is happy with the success. But privately he tells Vince that he has grown to hate the schmoozing part of the music business. He prefers the "music part" but knows he needs the "business part" to make a living.

(129, 130, 131)

## 1990 CARTHAGE, OHIO: STEPHEN SEIFERT

David is on his way to perform at the Old Time Music Store, and seventeen-year- old Stephen Seifert can hardly contain his excitement. He and his parents all love Schnaufer's music and are on their way to see him perform.

Stephen has been playing the dulcimer for about a year now. He's a good player with an excellent ear thanks to his dedication to playing and his years of listening to a wide range of music genres. Ever since he first listened to *Dulcimer Player Deluxe*, his mind has been full of questions, all under the rubric of "How does he do that?" The young dulcimer player has come to study his hero tonight to learn from him.

The venue is small; the audience doesn't mind being packed in because they know they are in for something special. The Seiferts consider themselves lucky to be able to sit and watch him this closely. As he and his parents look for three seats together, Stephen is full of anticipation; maybe he'll get some answers to his many questions tonight.

Stephen sees both an electric dulcimer and an acoustic dulcimer ready and waiting to be fired up. David will play solo tonight. When he finally enters and sits down, the audience bursts into applause. After greeting the crowd, he picks up the acoustic dulcimer. Stephen leans forward to listen and watch with a level of intensity and analysis beyond his years. He knows this might be his only chance to understand what this man is doing to make the dulcimer produce these incredible sounds.

He notices that David's dulcimer is strung differently than his own. David's has four equidistant strings. "Maybe that's how he does some of the coolest stuff," he speculates. "He tunes or retunes in between each song; that's pretty impressive." Occasionally David clamps down a small device on the fretboard, sometimes at the third fret, at other times, the fourth, and checks his tuning before each new song. Stephen wonders what that little clamp is for. He notes that David likes to change tunings for various songs and watches David's hands with intense focus: the right hand strums for some songs; for others, he uses a pick, for others, he mixes both. Sometimes he fingerpicks for a softer sound. His fretting is amazing. Unlike the ladies and gents in the Cincinnati club, David's left hand clearly has mastered the fretboard, never lingering too long in one place as it chords across the strings and plays up and down its full length. Both hands perform quickly and slowly, softly and loudly as needed, as if they had a mind of their own. His ability to embellish songs astonishes his admirer.

By the time the performance is over, some of Stephen's questions have been answered, but he's anxious to learn more before the artist slips away. He makes his way out to the front porch, his parents trailing behind him. Outside, David is surrounded by admirers chatting and laughing with him. Stephen stands as close as he can get to his hero where he studies him: "He looks cool. He looks like someone in a book, like some kind of folk character. Oh, boy, he smokes; that can't be good." The first opening Stephen gets, he steps forward to pepper him with questions, seeking confirmation of his best guesses made during the show. He asks him about his tuning:

"I'm tuned to D-A-D-D on the acoustic dulcimer," David replies, smiling at the young man.

"And sometimes you were using other tunings; can you tell me what they were?"

"Sometimes I tune the melody string down to a C; and for some songs, I'll tune the middle strings to a G."

Big Steve, listening as well, asks David about that clamp. "What is that?"

"It's called a 'capo.'" David replies. "It holds all three strings down at a given fret. Musicians use it as a way to change the tuning." Shortly after that exchange, he bids everyone a goodbye, and with a little wave, he's gone.

(133)

## 1990 NASHVILLE TO MAINE: "YOU JUST HAVEN'T FOUND YOUR INSTRUMENT YET."

Nova Lomax, John's son, hops into the car with David as he turns the key to start on his upcoming tour. John thought it would be good for his son to go on tour with David to keep him company, and Nova agreed. So nineteen-year-old Nova, who considers David his older, wiser brother, is thrilled to have him all to himself for a week.

David first caught Nova's attention when he heard about David and Vince going head to head with his great-uncle Alan Lomax at the Lomax family reunion last year. John had invited the two artists to entertain the extended Lomax clan and to join in the festivities, so they planned for a mixture of traditional and contemporary songs. After their performance, the venerable Alan loomed over the two musicians to chastise them for playing traditional songs with traditional instruments "inauthentically." Vince suspected that Alan was more unhappy with their long hair than with their music. Alan continued to lecture the two on the need for "purity in the folk process." Vince, impatient with the lecture, stepped up. "Dude, what are you talking about? This is our interpretation of the song!" he shot back. When it became clear that there would be no meeting of the minds, David and Vince moved off while the rest of the family began singing sea shanties.

Nova heard all about the argument from David. As he listened to the story, he felt an instant bond with the iconoclasts; to Nova, they are kindred rebels against his great-uncle's unspoken tyranny within his family. Nova started hanging out with David every chance he got.

By the time of their drive together, David has had a profound impact on Nova's worldview. His young friend is impressed that David never resorts to pat answers; he accepts almost nothing he reads or is told at face value; he has a novelist's eye for detail, and never feels it is wrong to change his mind after a long think. When Nova bemoans the fact that he tried and failed to play the trumpet and the harmonica, and—even worse coming from his family—he can't sing, David relieves the pressure on his shoulders by telling him, "You just haven't found your instrument yet. There's an instrument out there for everyone." Nova comes to believe that it's his flexibility of thinking, his open mind combined with his drive to grow and explore the world around him that makes David one of the most valuable forces in his life. And Nova tells his friends: even more than the Jesuits at his school, David taught him to question everything and to find beauty almost anywhere or in anyone.

(134, 135, 136)

## 1990 GALAX, VIRGINIA: RUSSELLS REDUX

Heading north on their tour, David and Nova make a side trip through western Virginia to visit a former girlfriend and spend a day and a night at the "Old Fiddlers' Convention" at Felts Park. The highlight for David will be reconnecting with the Russells. "They're one of the first families of traditional musicians," he explains.

David loves the earthiness of their music and its power to physically move the listener. "Bonnie did *Mountain Dulcimer Galax Style* when she was 12 years old!" he tells Nova. "It's all noter and quill music in the D-D-D-D tuning. That record, to me, stands up as one of my primary influences because of the energy of it, the natural quality of the music. It's the only dulcimer recording you can dance to; I wanted my music to feel like Bonnie Russell's music did."

When they arrive in Galax, the Russells instantly absorb them into the clan. Nova hangs around guitarist Roy, and David sticks close to Bonnie. Despite the common knowledge that the judges have a decided bias in favor of local players, David enters the festival's dulcimer competition. He finishes third playing "Blue Moon of Kentucky," nothing to feel slighted about at that level of competition. Even Roscoe Russell and Alan Freeman have placed lower, and Bonnie herself will place nine out of ten next year. But he jokes with Nova, "Yep, one year I finished third behind some old man who couldn't finish "Red River Valley!"

That evening, they drink moonshine and smoke weed with the Russells while the men in the family serenade them with a litany of old songs. David and Nova laugh uproariously while listening to the clan's attempt to sing the chorus of the African American spiritual, "Babylon's Fallen": "Babylon's fallen, fallen, fallen; Babylon's fallen to rise no more." Whenever one of them sings out of tune or makes a mistake, the rest jump on him, "Aw fuck it man, you done screwed this up, now we gotta start all over! Okay, here we go..."Babylon's fallen, fallen, fallen; Babylon's fallen to rise no more."

Later on, David heads to the car to sleep while Nova lies down on a bald knob on the ground. As he runs through his experiences this day, he has a sense that he has experienced something uniquely authentic that has changed little, if at all, going back to the start of the country and the European traditions that still whisper in the ears of the hill people who play their heritage. His great-grandfather John, his father and great-uncle Alan come to mind; they certainly would understand his feeling.

(137, 138, 139, 140, 141)

---

## Living and Dying History

Washington Post writer Lelia Cox makes the case that Galax, Virginia "may have a better claim to being the country music capital of the nation than does Nashville." Country music has been in this region for two hundred years since Scotch-Irish settlers crossed the Blue Ridge. Here, country people use the English language with traces of Elizabethan exactness. They pick a descriptive word as precisely as the notes they produce on a banjo.

David's interest in the history of the Russells, other old-timer players, and the dulcimer (as well as his own family history) has grown unabated since he first met them in 1977. On this trip with Nova, he wanted to revisit Galax because their dulcimers represent a unique branch on the dulcimer family tree. He is keenly aware that time is running out; the old-timers who know the early history of dulcimers and the songs played on them are few and far between.

(142, 143)

## 1990 PLYMOUTH, NEW HAMPSHIRE: "YOU CAN KEEP YOUR MONEY."

This evening David is scheduled to play a show in Plymouth. While he and Nova eat dinner at a vegetarian restaurant beforehand, the banter between them is lighthearted. David gets a kick out of Nova wearing a coonskin cap made out of rabbit fur he had bought in North Carolina; his young buddy's independent streak and sense of humor remind him of himself at that age.

David is due on stage in twenty minutes. As they push their chairs from the table to leave, the sudden screaming of a woman and the sound of popping halts them. A man runs into the restaurant shouting, "Everyone hit the floor, there's a guy out there killing people!" The frightened customers scramble under their respective tables, whispering to each other until they hear the sirens. David tells Nova to stay inside, and steps out to asks another bystander what had happened. "This guy shot his wife in the head with a high-powered rifle just as she was walking into the therapist's office; then he shot himself!" When David returns inside, Nova notices that he is extremely shaken up; he had seen a piece of scalp blowing down the street, tossed over and over by the wind.

David drives over to the venue where he is supposed to play, and the club owner asks him, "Okay, you're going on at 7:15, right?" "Nope, not going on at all," David tells him, "You can keep your money." David and Nova quickly get into the car, stop to buy a quart of beer, and light up a joint once they're on the road heading toward Maine. After an hour of silence that feels like ten to Nova, David turns to him and jokes, "Nova...that's how the Yankees won the Civil War, man...they just don't give a shit about people."

As they cross the border into Maine, both feel an immense sense of relief at leaving New Hampshire behind.

(144, 145)

MOVEMENT 5:
# METAMORPHOSIS

If you don't make mistakes, you aren't really trying.

—Coleman Hawkins

If you're lucky enough to be creative, then create. You have to have something in you that makes you want to make something, and have the nerve to allow things to happen. If you don't do anything, nothing will happen. If you do things, you can't tell what will happen. And if you do it, do it with care and passion, and be nice along the way.

—John McEuen

## 1990 NASHVILLE, TN: A WORLD AUDIENCE OF STUDENTS

While John is busy planning David's upcoming shoot of his "I'm So Lonesome" music video in May, David gets a call from Happy Traum. Born Harry, but nicknamed "Happy" by his parents, Traum mingled with the folkies in the fifties and sixties in Greenwich Village, then jumped into the musician's life. Traum was the first to record Bob Dylan's "Blowin' in the Wind" and worked as a session musician on many subsequent Dylan recordings.

Traum eventually turned a side passion for teaching into the business of teaching. After recording himself, he turned to other noteworthy musicians, including Pete Seeger, Doc Watson, and many others at the top of their profession. In 1984 Traum created "Homespun Tapes" with a mission of convincing musicians at the top of their game to teach their techniques on video for anyone who was willing to pay $49.95 for a peek at how the pros do it.

After Happy watches the PBS Hank Williams special, he immediately reaches out to David. Even though Happy had already recorded Jean Ritchie, he didn't feel his catalog would be complete with him. Once David's tape is available for sale, Traum is satisfied: he has both Jean Ritchie, the woman who brought the mountain dulcimer out of the mountains and introduced it to the world, and David Schnaufer, the man who reimagined the dulcimer and popularized it for thousands who wanted to learn to play an instrument. Customers can choose to learn from one, the other, or both.

(1, 2)

## 1990 NASHVILLE, TN: MOSES

David first heard about luthier Michael Scrivner through the professional musician grapevine. Michael, nicknamed "Moses," made his way to Nashville to work at Sho-Bud Guitars, a local manufacturer of pedal steel guitars since the late 1950s. There he learned to make and repair guitars, and eventually opened his own shop in the garage under his apartment near the Belcourt Theater.

Moses's shop was known not only for his repair work for many of the key pickers in the city, but also for being an informal hangout for friends. Some younger, troubled kids always tended to be around; they liked Moses because he befriended them, gave them advice about life, and didn't hesitate to sell them certain substances.

David knows a thing or two himself about dulcimer building, so last year he began collaborating with Moses to design a custom dulcimer for himself. David wanted it to be perfect in every way, from the build and design of the body to the fret height and the sound quality. He wanted a clarity of notes and a sustain that would serve him equally well from the first to the eighteenth fret. David had helped Lynn McSpadden eliminate the potential for string buzz on his dulcimers by suggesting the "zero" fret placed in front of the nut to provide enough lift to the strings so they would not wear down the slots in the nut and cause the strings to touch the first fret. This dulcimer would include the zero fret. The Koa Dulcimer would have bookended back panels, a Bonnie Carol–style bridged fretboard, meticulous abalone purfling, an abalone "Lone Star" embedded in the pegstock, and a small, single star above the bottom left crescent moon sound hole. The custom-designed Baggs pickup ensured it would work for David in every performance venue. Of exceptional quality, it cost David almost two thousand dollars for the exquisite instrument, a huge sum at the time. Moses also built a hard case in order to protect it from the rigors of airport luggage handlers.

David is so pleased with it that Moses agrees to collaborate by making more to market under David's name. These were not meant to replace the Schnaufer models in production at McSpadden's; this design would become his signature instrument for high-end buyers. John sends out notices to fans that two more are available for $2,200 including the custom-built case. There is only one problem: after Moses made the first Koa Dulcimer, he began to lose interest in building the same quality and precision into subsequent dulcimers.

Over time, David gets more and more frustrated with Moses's work. He doesn't mind the freewheeling atmosphere at the shop, but he expects professional workmanship when it comes to his instruments.

When an Illinois customer contacts David to complain about the odd arrangements of frets on her $2200 "David Schnaufer" dulcimer that she just received, he is livid. Moses had passed it off as something he added to allow her to play blues chords, but David knows better and is mortified at the idea that such an instrument was sold under his name. Their collaboration on dulcimers ends. David and Moses maintain a friendship, but David finds Dan Blom, a talented Nashville luthier to work with him on customizing his instruments.

(3,4,5,6)

## 1990 NASHVILLE, TN: SYNCHRONICITY

The "I'm So Lonesome I Could Cry" project is John and David's first conceptual music video. They conceive the story line as homage to one of David's favorite musicians, Hank Williams, who died on January 1, 1953, just three months after David was born. It will include a nod to an icon of David's generation, the late folk-rocker Gram Parsons. Parsons made a huge impact on David during the long-ago 1973 Liberty Hall concert in Houston, and passed away the same month David bought his first dulcimer.

Melanie Wells owns an invaluable, one-of-a-kind jacket that happens to fit David. Part of a famous suit made for Parsons in 1969 by the renowned Manuel Cuevas of Nudie Tailors in Los Angeles, Cuevas embroidered the suit for Parsons to wear on the front and back cover of the first Flying Burrito Brothers album, *Gilded Palace of Sin*. Cuevas hand-sewed a number of striking images across the sequined jacket, not the least of which is a large red rhinestone crucifix on the back surrounded by rhinestone rays. Other images Parsons requested included nude women on the lapels along with marijuana leaves and poppy flowers. The entire suit was designed to reflect Parsons's thoughts on the synergy of rock and country music, urban and rural environs, and the path of his own life as well. David will wear the jacket in one shot from behind him, the embroidered crucifix linking Williams and Parsons.

Williams's classic song has been covered countless times, but this is the first time fans will hear and interpret its meaning via the plaintive yearning of David's dulcimer. For David, the loneliness expressed in the song is not for a long-lost love, but for Hank as musical icon.

John's goal is to celebrate the country music tradition of the last forty years by associating David with Williams's genius. He taps good friend Greg Crutcher to direct since he is well known in Nashville for his creativity and high-end production values.

Greg and his team at Dream Ranch Pictures will set the stage not only at Mt. Olivet Cemetery in Nashville but also at the Williams grave site in Montgomery, Alabama. John, who at one time worked at the Country Music Hall of Fame, knows right where to go to find a Williams recording from an old "Health & Happiness" radio show for the beginning voiceover portion of the video: the Hall of Fame's Library and Media Center. Because they plan to shoot in the evening, John secures a donation of a dozen lanterns from the Coleman Company to provide the perfect lighting for the mood at the cemetery vault.

In exchange for $250 dollars plus five copies of the finished work, the Estate of Hank Williams grants John's SFL label the right to use eight rare photographs of Williams. Greg will film these projected images on diaphanous fabrics and Williams's tombstone to suggest his ethereal presence. He purchases a pair of white doves to represent Hank's spirit for a one-shot opportunity to film the doves' release as part of the story line.

Coincidently, the shoot is scheduled for May 26, Hank Williams Jr.'s forty-first birthday. The evening shoot will take place just ten miles from the Starwood Amphitheater where Hank Williams Jr. performs that night at the same time as Crutcher films.

The video opens with David playing on the steps of the Ryman Theater followed by a wide, horizontal image of him walking in profile toward the cemetery. Crutcher utilizes 16 mm film to capture the rich, waning light for the evening shoot, and the scenes are lit to perfection by the film crews' judicious placement of large 4K lights and the Coleman lanterns. The song ends with what will become one of David's most recognized notes.

When the video is completed, Crutcher sends it over to John. He and David couldn't be more pleased at their first video experience. They declare it to be the perfect piece of art to take the dulcimer into the new age of television exposure via the TNN and CMT networks. The video will be in steady rotation on the latter for five months and gain airplay on seventy-seven additional outlets in the U.S. and Canada.

For David, his first music video will be his most personal: John asserts "David is going to make a lot of noise on a quiet instrument."

(7,8,9,10)

## 1990 NASHVILLE, TN: "DOESN'T IT BOTHER YOU?"

For six years now, Darrel Ellis has been taking lessons with David whenever the two of them are in town the same time. Darrel has really grown to love the dulcimer, their friendship, and thinks there is nobody better at teaching.

At the end of one their lessons, he asks him, "Doesn't it bother you to be so good and teach people who are so bad?"

"No, Darrel, it doesn't. It's all good...I enjoy seeing my students get to take such pleasure in the instrument."

(11)

## 1990 NASHVILLE, TN: VINCE AND DAVID, WORDS AND MUSIC

In 1979, the Country Music Hall of Fame and Museum began the *Words and Music Program* to support language arts skills in the schools. The program pairs professional studio and symphony musicians with students to guide them through the lyric-writing process. Vince began volunteering to work with students in 1987, and when he tells David about it, he, too, volunteers.

David is assigned to work with Sharina Smith and Kelly Wiggins from nearby Madison. The girls wrote a simple set of lyrics for their proposed song, "Colors," which celebrates the diversity of people and cultures across the land via the metaphor of colors from holidays and life: the red and green of Christmas, the black and orange of Halloween, Valentine's Day red, and the blue sky. The last refrain concludes, "It takes all colors to make this town/Colors/so many colors/Sisters and brothers/so many colors,"

Using the dulcimer, David walks the girls through the process of creating a melody and chords to fit their lyrics. He is so excited about their mix of evocative lyrics with his delicate slow blues and country melody line that he deems it worthy of recording. He explains that the three of them are co-songwriters, and they will share equally in any of the royalties that the song earns. Some of those royalties will come from his next album *Dulcimer Sessions* on which his friend, Texas chanteuse Toni Price will sing their song. The children are thrilled when they hear it will be released next year.

(12,13,14)

## 1990 DONELSON, TN: OLD TIME STRING HEAVEN

Mark O'Connor asks David back to his home studio to record an "old-time track" he has written for his upcoming album *The New Nashville Cats* for Warner Bros. Mark named the track "Traveler's

Ridge" for the area where he had this house built, and he has invited an elite group of Nashville musicians who can play old-time style and who fully represent that genre. The entire project, he explains, is a celebration of Nashville's best musicians.

Today O'Connor serves as his own recording engineer. He'll play the fiddle live close to the console in his control room. He places the microphones and runs the cables for each musician. Grandpa Jones's daughter Alicia Jones Wall will play hammered dulcimer in his living room with the high ceilings. David will play in the foyer next to her so Mark can keep the dulcimers' levels somewhat together. Gove Scrivenor (who played autoharp on *Dulcimer Player Deluxe*) is in one of the bedrooms. Mark Schatz will play old-time banjo, Roy Husky on bass, Randy Scruggs on the guitar, and Sam Bush on mandolin round out the pickers down on the studio level.

When they finish, everyone agrees it was old-time string heaven. Mark and David decide that even though they preferred playing slow music together, it was great to fun to finally jam on a real fiddle tune and record it.

"Traveler's Ridge" will become a much-loved cut for the Grammy and CMA-winning album that will set the course for Mark O'Connor's own dazzling solo career.

(15)

## 1990 NASHVILLE, TN: *DULCIMER SESSIONS*

Full of confidence driven by the ongoing, enormous success of *Dulcimer Player Deluxe*, John and David plan the next album. Again, it will include part cover songs, part old-time traditional music, and part David's original material. Just as he had promised his two young friends from middle school, their song "Colors" will appear on the album with David playing the tune fingerpicking style, arpeggiating the chords on the longer held notes. Just as in their previous sessions, world-class musicians will record with David.

For the CD cover, John wants an image that evokes a traditional connection between David and country music. He recalls a famous black and white photograph of champion fiddler Uncle Jimmy Thompson and WSM Music Director George D. Hay as they waited backstage to appear on the first Grand Ole Opry show in 1925. (That night, Hay was debuting the show as the "WSM Barn Dance"; two years later he named it the Grand Ole Opry.) With photographer Jim McGuire, they'll re-create that image for *Dulcimer Sessions* with John and David standing in for Hay and Thompson.

The two spend half a day at McGuire's studio to set up for the shot. Despite his status as one of the top photographers in the city, McGuire had always loved David's music and shot all of his photo work for his previous albums at a rate far below what he is used to asking. This time he repeats the favor again. John and David take their places in the photo, with John at the left looking down at some papers to suggest a setlist. David, formally dressed in old-time clothes, sits in an old chair on the right in a traditional pose of a dulcimer player. An old-fashioned microphone and another dulcimer on a stand are between them. McGuire clicks the shutter as David looks up at John. (However, he does tilt the dulcimer up and out, a deviation from the traditional Appalachian position.)

Everyone whom John invites agrees to record. Vince will play fiddle and banjo on "Juley Calhoun" with David, a song they cowrote. David's Texas friend Santiago Jiménez Jr. brings his outstanding accordion playing on board for "Santiago's Shottis," a nod to the Czech, German, and Mexican roots of Texas. Because he manages both David and the Cactus Brothers now, John plans for the Brothers to play on several cuts. John also reaches out to other big names who agree to play: Mark Knopfler of Dire Straits; Albert Lee, the world-class English guitarist known for his fingerstyle and hybrid picking technique; and the renowned Sandy Bull who plays guitar, pedal steel, banjo, and the oud. Both John and David admire Bull, an important influence on everyone from Patti Smith to the Beatles.

Mark Knopfler of Dire Straits plans to come to the studio to play on a track, a real nail-biter for John. David wants Mark to play acoustic guitar on the Everly Brothers' "All I Have to Do Is Dream," and he wants to record it live. John worries that Knopfler, accustomed to playing electric guitar and recording in studios with massive forty-eight- track recording consoles, the latest technology for overdubs and other complex procedures, will feel this session is small potatoes. To make matters even more stressful, the day before they are to record Knopfler, Mark Miller, co-producer and recording engineer, gets a call to work on an Emmylou Harris session over at Jack's Tracks. John scrambles to find another engineer, and manages to get Knopfler's session ready to go on very short notice. What will Knopfler think of this last-minute session?

John worries for nothing. Knopfler drives to the studio by himself, walks in with a guitar, and without an entourage: "Hello, I'm Mark," he greets everyone. Mark had agreed to do the session work for the union rate provided that John pays Mark's fee to his favorite charity, an English children's fund. Remarkably, part of his agreement to play includes that the producers not feature him more prominently than any of the other players. David has found another kindred spirit.

(16, 17)

---

*Santiago Jiménez Jr.*

Santiago Jiménez Jr. is a seminal figure in Tex-Mex border music as a singer and accordion virtuoso of *Conjunto* music, and was much esteemed by David.

Like the dulcimer, *Conjunto* music is an original North American creation. When nineteenth-century German, Polish, and Czech immigrants settled in the Mexican region of the Rio Grande Valley, they brought popular forms of dance music such as the polka, waltz, schottische, and mazurka along with the diatonic button accordion, all of which were already known in Mexico. Thanks to the larger immigrant communities in Texas, they became permanent features of dance music in southern Texas and northern Mexico culture. *Tejanos*—Texans of Mexican descent—quickly adopted the accordion for their own dance music and built a musical group that would come to be strongly identified with their regional culture. This group is called simply the *conjunto*—literally, *combo*, or *ensemble*.

The younger brother of the more well-known Flaco Jiménez, Santiago followed more closely in his father and grandfather's musical style by performing a more traditional *Conjunto* sound than his brother did. Like David, he is known for his great humor and quick wit. Like David, he has dedicated a good portion of his life to both playing and preserving the music tradition of his forebears. In 2000 he became a NEA National Heritage Fellow; in 2015 President Barack Obama awarded him the National Medal of Arts. Santiago has been nominated for three Grammys.

(18, 19, 20, 21)

## 1990 NASHVILLE, TN: CLOSE CALL

Whenever he is in town, David performs regularly as a soloist at Merchant's historic downstairs bar in the evenings.

David's buddy Neal Hellman is in town, and tells a friend:

You won't believe what happened to me this week. I'm in Nashville promoting Gourd Music at the annual NAIRD* Trade Show that I usually attend to wheel and deal. I pitch Gourd's music to domestic and foreign music distributors, radio, and occasionally to retailers. There are workshops and panels all geared to the music industry. It's intensive but a lot of fun.

Anyway, I'm staying in the Opryland Hotel and two nights ago I get a call from my friend, David: "C'mon," he says, "I have a gig at Merchant's on Broadway; come and sit in with me." He borrowed a six-string dulcimer from his friend Darrel for me to use. Anyway, we did a set and then another set. It was great to see him again, but it was getting late, and I had to be up early to work the Trade Show, so I told David I had to go. "C'mon, don't be a wuss ... stay and play." "No, no; I've gotta go."

The next day, David called me and teased me for not staying: "You should have stayed, man!" Five minutes after you left, Emmylou Harris and Dire Straits guitarist Mark Knopfler came down the stairs to buy the dulcimer players a drink."

*National Association of Independent Record Distributors

(22,23)


## 1990 THE UNITED STATES AND CANADA: THE EVERLY TOUR

By the summer of 1990, David is a musical Johnny Appleseed, traveling to as many destinations as possible to spread the sound of the dulcimer: Kentucky Music Weekend in Louisville, a concert in Charlotte, North Carolina, the Spring Dulcimer Jamboree in Mountain View, Arkansas at the Folk Center, and back to Nashville for the Summer Lights Festival in June.

Starting in July, David's desire to introduce the dulcimer to the world takes him to his biggest audiences yet: he performs his thirty-five minute opening act for the Everly Brothers' twenty-two stop tour. His dulcimer plugs in to massive speakers so that tens of thousands of audience members in football stadiums will hear him. He walks confidently onstage intent on showing the dulcimer's range. He set list is sprinkled with old and new favorites: "Wildwood Flower," "Jesu, Joy of Man's Desire," to "Spanish Harlem," Stephen Foster's "Beautiful Dreamer" and "Colors."

John and Melanie join him for part of the trip. Melanie, who has always felt somewhat protective of David, notices that David tends to eat oddly. When the three of them meet in the mornings, he orders nothing for breakfast but banana pudding. He tells her not to worry; that's all he wants to eat.

One reviewer proclaims that David is a delight to listen to since he can make the dulcimer sound like a guitar, a mandolin, a harpsichord, and a dulcimer. The other, perhaps unfamiliar with traditional music, pronounces his playing impressive but his song list forgettable.

Neal Hellman manages to catch up with David when he and the Everlys are in California to perform at the Mountain Winery in Saratoga. The two would meet to play to play a short set on the square in Los Gatos early in the afternoon before driving to the Winery. Later, Neal, who knows his music, has one word for the Winery's show: "great."

(24, 25, 26, 27, 28)

## 1990 FROM VERMONT TO TEXAS: WHIRLWIND

In the fall, David hits the ground running on his own tour after working the Everly Brothers whirlwind. He performs and intersperses workshops from Vermont to Boston; Saratoga Springs (with his friend Susan Trump) to Dublin, Ohio, and then back home to Texas where he plays at the Black Cat Lounge, Antone's and the Waterloo Ice House; at La Zona Rosa and the León Springs Café with Santiago Jiménez Jr.

While in Texas, he swings by to visit old friends Jim Bentley and Mack White. Jim had been struck with melanoma a few years ago but is now in remission. All three friends are profoundly happy for the reunion.

(29, 30, 31, 32, 33, 34)

# 1990 MT. HOLLY, NEW JERSEY: THE CARTYS

Back in 1979, Mary and Richard Carty were sitting in the backyard of their home, when the sound of unfamiliar music drifted over the fence from their neighbor's yard. Afterward, the neighbor explained that it was mountain dulcimer music. For the Cartys, It was love at first sound. Off to Sears they went to buy a dulcimer, and it changed their lives forever.

Today, they are the center of the New Jersey dulcimer world as members of the Greater Pinelands Dulcimer Society, founders of the Sunday Circle Dulcimer Band, and owners of Pinelands Folk Music Center. Both Cartys teach classes on how to play the dulcimer every spring and fall at a local junior college.

Mary and Richard first met David in Louisville through Nancy Barker at a Kentucky Music Weekend. Mary and her friends from the Pinelands Club travel to Louisville every year to take and teach classes for the Music Weekend, and Mary has a booth in the vendor area to sell her unique and intricate handmade baskets. Mary and Nancy have become like sisters, and Mary is the only person besides Nancy who has attended every one of the Kentucky festivals since they started.

Once the Cartys got to know David, they invited him to hold a workshop and perform a concert at their folk center in Mt. Holly. During his weeklong visit, he stays with the family. They all love David for many reasons, not the least of which is how crazy Mary and Richard's sons are about him. At age twelve and fourteen, they—like David— are nature lovers. One afternoon, Mary watches David and her older son out in the backyard; David promised to show him a special "trick" to attract raccoons.

"You have to get a fifty-cent piece and a nickel. It has to be those two denominations, or it won't work" he tells him.

"First, you rub the nickel with the fifty-cent piece like this," he demonstrates; "then, alternate rubbing and tapping the nickel like this," demonstrating as he makes a kind of chippy sound from the two coins.

Sure enough, to her son's delight, a raccoon pokes his head out of the nearby bushes. Later, he shows her younger son how to make a tiny, working flute out of the tubular part of a pumpkin vine by slicing off the two ends with his pocketknife and making a hole in the top of the tube.

David also encourages them to follow their own interests, having invited their younger son who plays the nose flute to join him on stage for a duet of "Old Joe Clark" at KMW.

During the evenings in Mt. Holly, David and the boys splay on the floor to flip through the family's encyclopedias together and discuss whatever the two boys find the most interesting.

David also loves to sit and watch Mary weave her intricate baskets. One day he shares that he and Diana White had made baskets back in the seventies when they were on the road. When they made a sufficient quantity they would take them to the famous Greenbrier Hotel in West Virginia. The gift shop would buy their baskets to sell in the shop.

On one of his visits with the Cartys he learns that he and Richard share the same birthday, September 28. From this year on, they'll exchange birthday cards every year.

Mary's grandmother Myrtle lives across the road from the Cartys, and David had always promised to visit her. This time, even though he is late and has to leave, he grabs his dulcimer to walk over for a quick visit to Myrtle's to play for her.

After playing, he chats a little with her: "What was the most impressive thing that ever happened in your life?"

She tells him, "I got the right to vote. I saw the inventions of the car, telephone, radio, but the most important thing that ever happened to me was when I got the opportunity to vote."

Before he leaves Myrtle's, he gives her a signed photo: "To Myrtle, with love, from David."

(35, 36)

## 1990 BOONE, NORTH CAROLINA: "SHE'S ALL MINE!"

During one of his lessons with Mary Lawrence, David tells her about an upcoming Appalachian State Dulcimer Workshop in Boone that he will attend as one of several dulcimer instructors. The workshop is a weeklong annual affair with teachers for beginners, advanced beginners, intermediates, and advanced players. "You might want to go, too, Mary Lawrence, and take some classes there. You'll have a good time."

Often, the instructors go out to lunch with the students. On this day, David drives his well-used car to the restaurant. He finishes a few minutes before the rest so he can return to the university and prepare for the afternoon class. The rest of the participants follow him outside after paying their bills. Everyone gawks as David pulls out of the parking lot, his rust-bucket creaking and belching noises and smoke out the exhaust pipe. He rolls down his window; laughing and waving, he shouts, "Three more payments and she's all mine!"

(37, 38)

## 1990 NASHVILLE, TN: JOHN MCEUEN'S INVITATION

Before his upcoming tour with The Cactus Brothers, David has a recording session scheduled that will be especially meaningful to him, one that will bring him full circle to an important early influence.

After thirty years with the Nitty Gritty Dirt Band, cofounder John McEuen took leave of the band. A virtuoso on banjo, guitar, fiddle, mandolin, and slide guitar, John has long had an album in mind that he'd like to create: a homage to Appalachian music. Ever since his work on the *Will the Circle Be Unbroken* albums, his heart is full of traditional acoustic music. He already has a slew of original tunes that would work perfectly for such an album.

During the last year and a half since he left the Dirt Band, his brother Bill has been nudging him:

'When are you going to make that album?"

"What album?"

"The one you should be making. You know everybody in Nashville: call them."

Agreeing with his brother that the time is right, John starts his new project by donning the producer's hat. One of his original compositions stems from a trip he made to Maybelle Carter's home to deliver her Grammy Award to her for her work on the second *Circle* album. During his visit, Maybelle shared her family's Friday night traditions: "Oh, people come out here around suppertime, start showing up around six or seven o'clock, one by one, or two by two, and we'll end up with a house full of people playing music." John had turned Maybelle's memorable story into a timeless, gentle but lively instrumental tune, "Friday Night at Maybelle's." Her story was so evocative that he penned the song in thirty minutes.

Nashville-based David Hoffner is the first to get a call from his friend John who explains his concept for project to him. John is counting on Hoffner to get recommendations for Nashville musicians. He tells Hoffner that he wants a dulcimer player for "Friday Night at Maybelle's." He isn't sure when the idea popped into his head; he just feels the dulcimer would be right for the song. Hoffner tells him, "You have to hear this guy David Schnaufer; he's amazing." He sends John some of David's music. When John listens to the cuts, he is astonished and calls Hoffner back. "David Schnaufer took an instrument that many people hang on the wall and put a flower in one of the holes to create something outstanding! This guy is great!"

When McEuen gets to Nashville, he arranges for five days of practice at a hotel before he moves everyone into the studio to record. He has assembled a who's who list of string players and percussionists, every one of his musicians at the top of their game: along with himself, David Hoffner on keyboard and David Schnaufer on dulcimer; Sam Bush on Mandolin, Earl Scruggs on banjo, Vassar Clements on fiddle, along with David Grier on flat-pick guitar. John knows this will be a first-rate production; (indeed, eight of the songs would be recorded in one take; the rest would be overdubbed). The project, titled *String Wizards*, is a riff on the nick-name that many people have called John.

David enters the recording session quiet and focused. No doubt he is thinking back to the early seventies when he, like Vince, Rick Freimuth, David Young, and so many others were inspired by McEuen and the Nitty Gritty Dirt Band. Back then, before discovering the dulcimer, he could hardly have imagined that someday he would record with McEuen on his album.

Later, John tells Hoffner that the sad part about his work with David was that their time together was too short. He was so good that his recording work for the "Friday Night at Maybelle's" session took just under two hours from start to finish. "I didn't get to spend as much time with him as I would have liked. David knew exactly what he was going to do, and he did it." John adds that he felt lucky to have him as a performer, and he hoped his contribution to *String Wizards* would serve him well.

As for David's part, he feels the same. As he leaves the recording session, he recognizes McEuen as a kindred spirit in many ways. McEuen shares the same reverence for traditional country music; he is witty and wise, easygoing, and unexpectedly humble and kind.

(39)

## 1990 NASHVILLE, TN: WEARING DOWN AND OUT

By the end of the year, David looks back on multiple memories from each place he has traveled to this year to perform solos and with the Cactus Brothers, conduct workshops, visit old friends, and to be "on" for his tour with the Everly Brothers: Two of many highlights for him include his work for John McEuen on *String Wizards* and opening for friend Mark O'Connor at Nashville's famed Bluebird

Cafe. Every time he returns from the road, he works with his many Blair and private students.

His ongoing success and respect from his peers are welcome, but he's exhausted much of the time physically as well as mentally. David has always been a highly sensitive person who worked hard to overcome his introvert nature. Whenever he travels, he returns to Nashville to a voice mailbox full of messages. It's getting harder and harder to summon up the energy to listen to them, much less return calls. Friends who drop by often knock on the door, but he's too exhausted to answer.

Besides the exhaustion, he has had go to the emergency room near his apartment two different times in order to have a doctor look at recurring skin breakdown on his feet. They aren't particularly painful, but neither do they seem to heal. The ER doctor who attends to him reminds him that the ER is for emergencies only, and refers him to his family physician. *I can't afford one, that's why I'm in the ER!* Schnaufer thinks but says nothing.

(40)

## 1991 HENDERSONVILLE, TN: HAPPY ANNIVERSARY

The couple welcome their guests to their home to help them celebrate the occasion of their twenty-third wedding anniversary. Their house is packed with family and friends, most of them musicians. They drink, eat, play music, and sing with those who have known the couple for a long time and with a few who are newer friends. Singer Charley Pride, bluegrass legend Bill Monroe, and guitarist Norman Blake are already there when David and John ring the doorbell.

Later, David will tell friends that Johnny Cash's party was one of the highlights of his life. But before then, David sits between Cash on his right and Bill Monroe, the father of bluegrass music, on his left in the innermost circle of the pickers who are present. Johnny and Bill, as well as June Carter Cash right behind David, smile with pleasure as David shows them what his instrument can do.

(41)

## 1991 WINNIPEG, CANADA: WINNIPEG FOLK FESTIVAL

Knowing that Cactus Brother dobroist Sam Poland is close to David, John Lomax approaches Sam to ask a favor. "I'm a little worried about David," he tells him, "he can't drive all over the country and perform, too; he gets too tired. Would you consider driving for him? He's up performing and teaching at a National Dulcimer Symposium in the Adirondacks at Blue Mountain Lake this week, and afterwards he needs to get to eastern Canada and then over to Winnipeg for two more festivals." Sam agrees, so he packs some things and takes off in David's old blue Oldsmobile. He drives all the way from Nashville to Blue Mountain Lake to pick him up. The two then travel to eastern Canada where David is scheduled to perform with some Canadian bands. Afterward, they leave and drive the two-day trip on the Canadian Highway to the Winnipeg Folk Festival where they will meet up with Townes Van Zandt and Guy Clark. It will be David's last festival of the trip.

Halfway to Winnipeg, they stop at a little motel. During breakfast, the two friends eat in silence; the waitress asks "Are you okay? You don't seem to be talking much."

"We don't need to talk," Sam jokes, "we can read each other's minds." David nods and smiles.

Sam and David arrive at Winnipeg's enormous festival, the largest audience David has faced since the Everly Brothers tour. As he heads toward the stage, he runs into Guy Clark and Townes Van Zandt who have been looking for him and who also will perform. David introduces Sam to both his Texan friends and then takes the stage. This time, the rave reviews of his performance will come with the recognition of both his repertoire and his exhilarating performance.

After the show, a local socialite invites David and Sam to a dinner party. Sam is struck by the large reception for David; the crowd treats him like the star of the party. The hostess and all the other women surround him, eager to hear him tell them the story of the dulcimer, which he does with as much pleasure as if telling it for the first time.

Sam leaves the party a little before David to get some sleep. At their hotel, the elevator doors open up to reveal Townes and Guy Clark again. Townes sees Sam. "Hey, Sam, you gamble?"

"Nah, not much".

"How about with Canadian money?"

"Nah, I've heard about you two riverboat gamblers. I'm too broke to gamble ... not even pitching quarters!"

(42, 43, 44, 45)

## 1991 NASHVILLE, TN: ELLEN AND BILL

It was John Lomax who first introduced David to Ellen. Her first impression of him was of a quiet and unassuming man, yet, both incandescent and magnetic in the gentlest way. As she has gotten to know David over the past few years, she and her husband Bill believe that David "mirrors the dulcimer itself."

Ellen and Bill—while not musicians— count many musicians within their circle of friends. At one time, she had been fiddler Mark O'Connor's publicist, and now she serves on the Board at Vanderbilt University's Blair School of Music. They often invite many of their friends over on Sunday for chili suppers. Ellen and Bill have become good friends with David and enjoy having him visit whenever he is in town. To their delight, he occasionally stays over for a day or two. They love having him because he fills their house with great music, good conversation, and laughter.

Ellen is also good friends with Judy Massa, the longtime music director of Voice of America radio. Thanks to the ongoing country music boom, Judy had decided to run a worldwide essay contest based on the question, "What Does Country Music Mean to Me?" The top prize is a trip to Nashville during the annual Country Music Association Fan Fair festival in the fall. Judy had received three thousand entries from all over the world; the winner was Zhou Zuo-Ren, a twenty-three-year-old international business student and broadcaster on the Shang Hai People's Broadcasting Station. He and his wife have traveled to Nashville with Judy and two "handlers" from the PRC—the Chinese Communist Party.

Judy calls Ellen. "They're not going to let him out of their sight, and he's not going to get a chance to see how Americans really live; can you help?"

"Well, why don't we invite them to a backyard cookout?"

"Oh my goodness, that would be perfect!"

As soon as Ellen gets off the phone, she calls David to invite him over and to bring his dulcimer so that Zhou (nicknamed "Willie" after Willie Nelson for the duration of the visit) could meet him.

When her guests arrive, Ellen is glad that she invited David. No one else notices, but Ellen knows him well enough to see that David is down, so this get-together will be a good distraction for him. Ellen understands the vicissitudes of the music business: one day you're busier than you can ever think possible, the next, the phone isn't ringing for you, and younger players new to the business are eager to take your place. For many artists, the pressure can be crushing at times. Even though David has no competition in the city as a dulcimer musician, he, too, goes through his ups and downs. He has had moments of unexpected opportunities and wonderful success and then periods when there are long stretches between session work that find him living in his car or experiencing other types of homelessness when the money dries up. A significant part of his unenviable income comes from his workshops at dulcimer festivals and sales of his CDs. Often, festival directors assume he is wealthy because of his work with other famous musicians, so they ask him to work for them for free. Little do they realize the reality of his income situation: he pays his own gas and living expenses while on the road. Many pro musicians feel similar pressure, and it can easily lead to mental anguish when they can't count on a steady income or even if they'll ever work again. Ellen is keenly aware of this side of the music business and feels fiercely protective of David, doing what she can to keep his spirits up when his seem low.

During the get-together, Ellen does her best to make sure he and "Willie" spend some one-on-one time together amid the other guests. When David picks up one of his dulcimers and begins to play, Willie listens for a moment, and suddenly beams as he asks, "Dulcimer ... dulcimer, is that the instrument that was on the third cut of the ..."

David lights up, "Yes, that was me."

Later that evening, Ellen shares with Bill what happened: "So, at this really low point in David's life, this young man from halfway around the world comes over, and knows who David is and what a dulcimer is because of him. It was a palpable moment, you could feel it; you could see David glow and get his mojo back!" Ellen hopes that David understands he's not operating in a vacuum; he really changes people's lives.

(46, 47)


## 1991 NASHVILLE, TN: "JUST DO YOUR THING AND MAKE MUSIC"

Artist Joni Bishop has just moved to Nashville and so finds herself exploring the city whenever she has a moment of free time. Joni is an accomplished guitarist and drives to a music store in Green Hills Mall to look around. She sees an unfamiliar stringed instrument on the counter and can't resist giving it a strum. "The tone," she will later tell her friend Adie, "just blew me away. It had three strings and was an hourglass shape. I just fell in love with the sound." As she explains the experience to her friend, Adie tells her, "You need to talk with David Schnaufer."

Joni calls David. "Sure, c'mon over for a lesson" he tells her. When they meet, he spends most of the time talking to her about the history of the instrument. Then they work on a bit of music together, assessing her approach to her new dulcimer. By the end of their hour lesson, Joni feels the peculiar sense that she has known him all her life. Later, she shares her impressions with Adie. "I didn't know his background, but I knew I could trust him. He was so generous and caring, and it was obvious he had a big heart."

When they meet for her second lesson the next week, she starts by showing him how she practiced the song he had asked her to work on the previous week. David laughs as he tells her, "Get out of here. I was just playing my own way last time. I don't want to cramp your style teaching you all these formalities." No longer as teacher to student, but artist to artist, he encourages her to use the dulcimer to express herself. "Just do your thing and make music," he advises, giving her the freedom to play it her way.

Joni doesn't know it yet, but it won't be the last time she'll play the dulcimer with David. She'll take his advice to heart and learns to play so well that, in the years that follow their first meeting, he'll invite her to his performances to play onstage with him. She'll also start performing at his old stomping ground, the Ozark Folk Festival. She will become good friends with his Ozark "family," Jean Jennings and her daughter Pam.

(48)

## 1991 HENDERSONVILLE, TN: DIAGNOSIS

Sam Poland and David are on their way back to the city after a visit to a music store in Hendersonville, a suburb of Nashville. As David drives past a school, Sam notices that he is awfully quiet. Even more alarming, he has a fixed stare that feels odd. Sam looks over at the speedometer; they're clipping along at 30 mph. "Dave, do you realize you're speeding through a school zone?" David snaps out of his stare and glances at him, "No, sorry. I had no idea."

It wasn't the first time Sam had become concerned about his friend. David never had to leave a gig, but he and the rest of the band could tell at times that he didn't feel well. He'd come in pale, or a little bit disoriented. Often after a gig, he would have to go somewhere private and quiet to rest.

Most people who know him well also have noticed that something isn't quite right. Always the most popular teacher during his annual visit to Kentucky Music Week, Nancy Johnson sensed a new lethargy in him. This year she watches, worried, as he drinks an awful lot of water and soft-drinks in an extra-large cup, all day. He also tends to be hungry all the time, unusual for such a thin man. Nancy and her friend Debbie discuss it and agree to keep a close eye on him. Debbie begins to prepare little care packages for him of snacks like peanut butter and tuna to boost his energy, and both Debbie and Nancy urge him to see a doctor.

Vince has been worried for quite some time, too, and had been insisting he see a doctor He threatens to take David himself if he doesn't go. For a while, David dismisses everyone's concerns with little jokes. Nevertheless, friend Herb McCullough finally tells him enough is enough and drags him to a country doctor he knows. The physician takes one look at him and diagnoses him as being diabetic.

A test confirms it. Later, David tells Sam all about it, laughing. "That that explains everything; hell, I just thought I had been in a bad mood the last year and a half!"

(49, 50, 51,52,53,54)

## 1991 FRANKLIN, TN: "WE'LL PARTY AND SHOOT A MUSIC VIDEO."

Some one hundred friends, family, fans, coworkers, and artists act on the invitation from John Lomax, David, and the Cactus Brothers to show up for a very special party: "We'll feed you, party, and shoot a music video!"

Greg Crutcher is back to direct; he, the Brothers, and part of his crew from Dream Pictures are on their way to the a local family's barn to film the video's live performance scenes after having filmed the B-roll earlier in the day. Among the waiting crowd are the farm's owners and their junior high school guests from Northern Ireland, there for the summer as part of a project that brings Catholic and Protestant kids to the U.S. to participate in team-building work. Nova Lomax, wearing his Spicoli-inspired Baja surfer shirt, hitched a ride with his father and takes in the setting and waits, ready for the party to start.

The crew working at the barn have already moved their RV over to the side and out of sight of the camera lens. A stage large enough to hold the band stands in front of the massive barn doors. Crutcher's crew places the Coleman lantern from the Hank Williams shoot around the stage. Other crew members set up the enormous 4K lights with their daylight color temperature to illuminate the stage when the natural light is gone. They've also placed lights inside a second story hayloft door where David will be filmed as he kicks off the music. Inside the large door below the hayloft Tramp will pose, waiting for the dulcimer cue with one leg on the door jamb, his fiddle perched on his thigh.

Once David and the band arrive, they take a short break to change their clothes. One of the crew starts a bonfire some ways from the stage where the guests will dance. Everyone listens to Greg's last minute instructions and moves into position; David, upstairs with his legs dangling out the window, can barely contain a grin. On the ground below him, Tramp looks up at his buddy, waiting to rip into the fiddle at the moment he hears the dulcimer's cue.

As the pied piper energy of the familiar opening strum calls the rest of the band to come together, Crutcher shoots David grinning from the loft window as he hits the opening strum of "Fisher's Hornpipe." Tramp immediately echoes the dulcimer opening on his fiddle. Cinematographer Matt Coal and director Greg work so well together they read each other's minds as to where to point the cameras next—young, middle-aged, and old, men and women, folkies and families, teens, and small children, some tiny cloggers, another senior clogger, and a gothic young man sporting an extreme mohawk haircut— all spontaneously erupt in a joyful dance the second they hear "the Hornpipe." Minus the film equipment and the modern clothing, it's an event that could have taken place any number of times throughout U.S. history.

As the spirited music's energy flows around and through the exuberant crowd, someone passes a Mason jar full of moonshine to Nova. It's the perfect touch, he thinks, for the magical scene. For an hour, the film set has turned into an authentic, exuberant country hoedown. And "the Hornpipe" will earn the Cactus Brothers their contract with Garth Brooks' Liberty Records.

(55, 56, 57, 58, 59, 60)


## 1991 NASHVILLE, TN: AWARD WINNERS

The Cactus Brothers rendition of "Fishers Hornpipe" was so spot on that actual filming of the barn dance scene had only taken an hour. In post-production, Greg synchs the music to the film-rendered-video and impresses David with the seamlessness and quality of the resulting audio. Lead singer Paul Kirby's girlfriend Elizabeth, lovely in a minidress and cowboy boots, was filmed in a languid walk toward the party with the setting sun behind her left shoulder and an old silo on her right. Crutcher uses her walk for the opening shot of the video. He'll overlay a recording of the field crickets and cicadas chirping around her as she walks.

During their color processing work, the colorist dials down the saturation on Greg's B roll from the pasture performance to render it in black and white. He selectively adds a few touches of appearing and disappearing color to instruments and clothing for effect. The film editor juxtaposes cuts of this pasture scene with the color scenes of the evening barn dance for interest.

David and Tramp's mutual admiration and affection is palpable both on stage and throughout the video; the synergy between all the band members and their fans is as authentic on the film as in their live performances in concert.

Greg submits the earlier Hank Williams music video at the ten-day "Worldfest 1991," the Houston International Film and Video Festival and the largest of its kind in the world. David's "I'm So Lonesome" video wins the Bronze Medal, competing against 3,500 entries from 47 countries. John Lomax, the Cactus Brothers, and the creative wizards at Dream Pictures are over the moon; aside from their own satisfaction at a job done exceedingly well, this professional acknowledgment contributes to David's reputation and sales and to Dream Pictures as serious contenders for future work.

The "Fisher's Hornpipe" music video will enjoy a five-month run of sixty-three plays on The Nashville Network, the most for any instrumental video in the Network's history. The wildly popular video will also accumulate 182 plays on Country Music Television and win the "Best Independent Video" award by *Music Row Magazine*. It will inspire countless people to pick up the dulcimer and learn to play it. It's a testimony to the exceptional work and talent of everyone involved that, thirty years after the barn concert, the video is as fresh and as entertaining to viewers on YouTube as it was to television viewers in 1991.

(61, 62, 63, 64)

## 1991 WINFIELD, KANSAS: TWENTIETH ANNIVERSARY

David reconnects with Jean Jennings and Pam to attend the Walnut Valley Festival's Twentieth Anniversary celebration. Nashville is well represented at the festival with performers such as David, Mark O'Connor, the Dixie Chicks, John McCutcheon, and others.

Upon his return to Nashville, David meets with a new student who wants to start dulcimer lessons. When she learns he had just come back from Winfield, she asks, "Oh, were you competing in the dulcimer contest?" "No," he laughs, "I was judging it!"

(65, 66)

## 1991 NASHVILLE, TN: A NEW ROUTINE

David jokingly asks Sam to be his, "Stab-in-the-Heart Guy" in case he ever passes out when he is together with the Cactus Brothers. He shows Sam his glucagon kit, a case with a syringe and a vial of glucagon, a drug that he can inject intramuscularly if his blood sugar ever suddenly drops dangerously low. He explains to Sam that if something happens to him where he can't inject himself, or if he should suddenly go unconscious, Sam should inject him immediately in the deltoid muscle at his shoulder or in the upper side of his thigh. He always lets Sam know where the kit is in case of an emergency when they are traveling. During their gigs, he sets the case on his amplifier to be in close reach.

David injects himself with insulin every day before a meal, sometimes several times a day before he eats. He doesn't like it, but he does it, and gradually learns to develop a sense of how his physical feelings correspond with his insulin levels. Nevertheless, sometimes during practice with the Cactus Brothers, he will have to sit down, or leave to go home and go to bed.

David acknowledges his diagnosis but doesn't want to talk about it with anyone but Sam and his student Darrel, a physician. "You've got what's called 'Brittle Diabetes,'" Darrel tells him. You've got to take very good care of yourself: get exercise, eat a low carb diet. Quit the smoking." David listens quietly, taking in the enormity of his situation. Everyone soon understands that he has been diagnosed with diabetes. Nancy Barker and Debby Grizzell redouble their efforts to make sure he gets everything he needs when he's at Kentucky Music Week while Mary Carty takes David his special diabetic lunch before her own.

He can't seem to quit his lifelong habit of smoking, but he becomes more careful with his diet. He starts walking whenever he can. The one good news: he notices that he doesn't have any more problems with ulcers popping up on his feet.

(67, 68, 69, 70, 71)

---

### Brittle Diabetes

David was diagnosed with a dangerous form of Type 1, adult-onset diabetes known as "Brittle" diabetes, a term used to describe a particularly difficult-to-control diabetes. People who have brittle diabetes are more likely to experience frequent, extreme swings in blood glucose levels that cause either hyperglycemia (too much sugar in the blood) or hypoglycemia (too little sugar in the blood).

Brittle diabetes has a number of potential causes. Psychological issues such as stress, depression or other issues, or inconsistent digestion as a result of nerve damage account for most cases. Stress can lead to acute and/or temporary insulin resistance in which the body does not respond to insulin, leading to unpredictable rises and drops in blood sugar levels without warning. One consequence: the distinct, daily challenge when David must assess the insulin dosage he needs.

David never could be sure where, when, or how he contracted diabetes. He could have inherited it; his paternal grandmother was diagnosed with adult-onset diabetes later in life. Another known cause of brittle diabetes is from a severe viral infection. David had had several severe viral infections over the years. Finally, Ellen Pryor was right: professional freelance musicians can lead very stressful lives due to extreme schedule demands and their inability to rely on a steady paycheck. Any or all might have been contributing factors to his diabetes.

(72, 73, 74)

# 1991 NASHVILLE, TN: SUDDENLY

David stops by the shop to tune up a dulcimer that he plans to give Darrel as a birthday present the next day. He wants him to have a twenty-inch-long, one-octave "dulcimette" so Darrel can take it with him when he travels. Moses christens the dulcimette a "cherub dulcimer" because it includes a cherub image on it, but when David arrives, he notices Moses sanding off the cherub's face and hands. "What are you doing?" he asks Moses. "Darrel will know" is all Moses replies.

After David leaves, Moses calls Vince to ask if he'd come over the next morning and work on a dulcimer that needed some repairs. Vince occasionally does work at the shop on the side. He gets a real kick out of Moses's dog Tony since Moses swears the dog can talk; to prove it, he makes everyone listen to Tony when he says, "burrito."

The next morning, nobody answers his knock, so Vince lets himself in. He runs upstairs to see what's going on. Moses is still sleeping, his arm tucked under his head. Vince heads down to the shop to start work.

After an hour, Vince decides it's time to wake up Moses because there is a lot to do. When he returns upstairs, he is struck by the silence. Walking over to the bedroom, he peeks in the door to see Moses in the same position he left him, his arm tucked under his head. Then Vince notices that Moses had vomited a great deal; it suddenly hits him that Moses is dead. He was forty-five years old.

Later, as they discuss what happened, Darrel is as surprised as David was by the removal of the cherub. He has no idea why Moses sanded it off.

(75, 76)


# 1991 NASHVILLE, TN: THE PARTING GLASS

This December 1 evening, a week after Moses passed, his friends hold a funeral benefit at the renowned 12th and Porter Club to life the parting glass and perform to help pay his last expenses on earth. Vince promises to finish the instrument work that Moses left pending: some eighteen unfinished dulcimers and some other instruments to repair. Townes will be at the benefit, John Prine, Vince, John and Nova Lomax, and a host of others who knew him. Vince and Nova will be pallbearers. Despite their earlier falling out over a botched dulcimer that Moses had sold under David's name, David will play "Wings of a Dove" for his spirit and to help fill the hat.

Michael Moses Scrivenor will be remembered as a multi-instrumental musician, luthier, and purveyor of certain illegal goods in demand; his circle of friends will bury him in a musician's gear case.

(77, 78, 79, 80, 81)

## 1991 NASHVILLE, TN: HAPPY NEW YEAR

By the last day of 1991, John Lomax looks forward to the new year. He anticipates nothing but more success. *Dulcimer Sessions* is about to be released; he now manages both David and the Cactus Brothers, a most fortunate situation as far as he is concerned. Their work together will continue to expose David and the dulcimer to a whole new audience and music genres. And David's music will continue to shape the Brothers' repertoire. At the end of an otherwise boisterous set in a Nashville bar, Herb and his wife Joann watch, astonished, while the crowd gets very quiet as David leads the Cactus Brothers into "Starry Lullaby." The audience listens to every word until the finish; then, they erupt into thunderous applause. Afterward, Herb exclaims to Joann, "You could have heard a pin drop!" They both agree: the experience was one of life's sweet moments.

(82, 83)

Once *Dulcimer Sessions* is released, John turns his attention back to the Cactus Brothers. He convinces Jimmy Bowen's Liberty Records to sign the group. "Walk the West" is put to rest, and "The Cactus Brothers" take their place. David, who often had played with the group in regional gigs, is now officially a new member.

John leveraged the contract with Liberty Records on the basis of twenty-two demo tracks the Brothers recorded, all in one day, at Jack's Tracks. The band owes that good news to producer Allen Reynolds's daughter. She persuaded her dad to let her boyfriend, lead singer Paul Kirby, and the band into the studio to record.

The Brothers, meanwhile, need a place to rehearse and store their instruments and stage props. They find an affordable house with a basement off I65 at the Harding Place exit, the last house on a side road going north toward town. Despite the railroad tracks out back, they consider the house and location perfect for their purposes. Using their advance money, they rent the house and promptly christen it "Fort Cactus." Tramp and bass player John Goleman move in, and the rest of the band and friends stop by frequently to hang out, practice, or party. Visitors often see abundant cars parked out front, or hear the shots ringing out back where the guys and their friends shoot targets for practice. Anyone who wishes to stay can usually find their choice of several couches to sleep on.

David and Tramp spend a lot of time playing together at the Fort. One day, David shows up with a large box for Tramp. As he opens the box, Tramp sees stacks of T-shirts and several pairs of pants.

"Tramp, I'm givin' away all my clothes to you," David drawls. "I'm going to wear this outfit every day for the rest of my life."

Tramp scans David up and down, taking in the picture of David wearing an old fashioned, long-sleeved shirt, suspenders and jeans, and the plain, black boots. To top it off, he's wearing a straw hat.

Finally Tramp blurts out him, "You look like the Amish, David!" They both burst out laughing, and even though he didn't ask for the clothes, Tramp thanks him. "Looks like I'm getting some cool T-shirts!"

(84, 85, 86)

## 1992 NASHVILLE, TN: MARK WAIT

Mark O'Connor has a standing invitation to Ellen and Bill Pryor's Sunday evening chili suppers, and tonight she introduces him to Mark Wait, the new incoming dean of the Blair School of Music at Vanderbilt University. Wait, a noted concert pianist, will soon move from the University of Colorado to Vanderbilt; he will arrive in Nashville at a good time for academics. Although Blair is small with only nineteen faculty members, Wait agreed to take the position as dean in great part because he sees its potential as a large force for both music majors and nonmajors and for scholarship in the heart of Music City. Wait is a people person, an intellectual with a curiosity about the world far beyond his comfort zone. He enjoys thinking out of the box. He looks forward to taking charge at Blair where he sees the future of music in chamber music, in unusual combinations of instruments, and in mixtures of musical genres. He is unafraid to cross boundaries and even ignore them when warranted.

Later, Ellen takes Mark Wait to the Station Inn to hear Mark O'Connor play. Wait, impressed by Mark's personality and virtuosity, hires him to teach fiddle music for a new folk music program he plans to start at Blair.

(87, 88)

## 1992 NASHVILLE, TN: STRING WIZARDS

After watching one SFL dulcimer release after another result in booming sales, John is disappointed with the early sales of *Dulcimer Sessions*. He gets wind that "dulcimer purists" don't like the CD's mix of old-time traditionals mixed with pop music. Also, all his creative thinking about the cover goes unappreciated. Most music fans don't share John's knowledge of Nashville music history, so the cover homage to Thompson and Hay is over many people's heads.

David has no time to think about it between preparation for the upcoming tour with the Cactus Brothers and his work with his students. His session work on Mark O'Connor's recently released *Nashville Cats* and John McEuen's *String Wizards* is more than gratifying; reviews are glowing for both. One Chicago reviewer of *String Wizards* describes it as "a quirkily brilliant artistic package ... [it] employ[s] the aid of a small but impeccably chosen collection of instrumental geniuses young and old (i.e., Sam Bush, Jerry Douglas and David Schnaufer on the one hand and Earl Scruggs, Vassar Clements and Josh Graves on the other...)."

Such reviews have not escaped Johnny Cash. He asks David to work on his upcoming album *Return to the Promised Land*.

(89, 90, 91)


## 1992 LAWRENCEBURG, TENNESSEE: THE DREAM

One afternoon David flips through a catalog of vintage instruments and stops at a page containing pictures of some long, rectangular antique instruments labeled "Tennessee Music Boxes." He immediately recognizes that they are a type of dulcimer. Once long ago, he had stopped at the Casey Jones restaurant in Cosby, Tennessee, and they had one hanging on a wall. It was the first Tennessee music box he had ever seen.

Shortly afterward, he has a dream one night about a Tennessee music box. In the dream, he's browsing in an antique store near Lawrenceburg, Tennessee, where he spots an old music box on the wall and buys it.

The next morning, he hops into his car and drives straight to Lawrenceburg, about an hour and a half south of Nashville. He stops at the first antique store that feels right to him. As he enters the door, the clerk asks, "May I help you?" and, just as in his dream, he replies, "It's right over there," pointing to a primitive Tennessee music box that hangs on the wall; "That's what I came for." David walks over and studies the circa 1880 box like a tracker would study the ground for signs of someone who had previously passed his way. His experienced eyes look for the tell-tale signs: a bit of fiddle rosin around the bridge tells him this instrument had been played with a bow. The box shows nicks, scratches, and wear, and signs of once having been played a great deal. The frets on the box are made of fence staples, and the bridge is made from old snuff cans. The tuners are made from old eye screws. He turns and looks at the clerk, smiling, and tells her, "I'll take it."

When he returns to his apartment, he mulls over which string material and gauges would work for this box. Sitting on the floor, he strings the box, tunes each string, and draws a bow softly across them. The real sound of the nineteenth century, a sound that mesmerizes him, slowly rises and fills the room. He detects echoes of a hurdy-gurdy or a bagpipe with its mournful, drawn-out deep breaths. He bows the strings slowly this way and that, again and again, exploring the sounds the box will yield to him.

As he draws the bow back and forth, he senses he is waking the box from its hundred plus years of slumber. The low and slow sounds call forth the old players to rise out of the sound holes, like wispy smoke that results when someone blows on the embers of a dying fire.

(92, 93)

---

### Tennessee Music Boxes

When asked to imagine a mountain dulcimer, many picture the traditional, double-bout wooden instrument with heart-shaped sound holes. But that dulcimer has another member on its family tree. Nineteenth- and twentieth-century farmers and woodworkers in southern Tennessee made music boxes with crude materials they had on hand to produce an instrument with a different design. They mounted a fretboard on a very large, rectangular soundbox cavity. The increased size resulted in unique, earthy sounds with a tonal fullness beyond that of its slimmer dulcimer cousins. Many of the boxes also had short legs to lift the soundbox off a table. Multiple holes drilled in the soundbox increase the resonance. Occasionally, they feature painted designs, most well faded by now.

These Tennessee music boxes started to appear around 1870. Playing and construction techniques were passed from generation to generation through the 1940s, after which they began to disappear.

For a closer look at good examples of these rare instruments, visit *http://www.artsinmcnairy.com/tennessee-music-boxes.html*

## 1992 MIDLOTHIAN, TEXAS: PURE COUNTRY

The tagline to the film states: "Bright Lights. Hit songs. Country's biggest star. He'd trade it all to find the kind of love he'd only sung about." The Warner Bros. movie *Pure Country* is about to commence filming in Maypearl, Texas. The Cactus Brothers have been hired to play the role of a honky tonk band, and today they are driving to Midlothian for their first shoot in the "Western Kountry Klub," a historic dance hall. Everyone is excited by the opportunity to be on a real film set that will feature their own songs. However, David gets disappointing news: instead of playing his dulcimer in the film, he will have to act in the role of a piano player.

The Brothers will perform two songs written for them: The "Cactus Line Dance" for the scene in which lead character Dusty meets the girl of his dreams, and "I'm Gonna Right a Great Country

Wrong." They'll also perform their most popular song (cowritten by Tramp, Paul Kirby, and Gary Scruggs), "Crazy Heart."

While he's in Texas, David takes time to visit his buddy Jim Bentley who had suffered a bad bout of cancer a few years ago. Jim is still recovering from nerve damage from a recent surgery but beams when David walks in the door to visit. The two old friends pick right up from where they last left off, swapping stories, joking and laughing, and recalling favorite old times. Jim's son Aaron, now a teenager and well steeped in music thanks to his father, listens in awe while David plays the dulcimer for them. "That's not real," he thinks; "It's impossible that anyone could be that good on an instrument."

(94)

## 1993 FORT WORTH, TEXAS: MACK WHITE

Over the years, Mack White would send David copies of his artwork and comics. Once he hooked up with the Cactus Brothers, David would pass the quirky art to the band members. Everyone decides that Mack's art would be perfect for their posters, including his three-eyed Billy the Kid that began as the black-and-white cover for Mack's *Surreal Western Comix*. David and the band begin using it as a poster, then a mascot, dubbing it "Billy the Id." Mack will colorize it to use on their first album to be released this year.

Liberty Records hires Mack to pen the first edition of *Cactus Comix* for a promotional giveaway. Band members had worked together on a story line with a plot designed to amuse their fans: invaders from the planet "Drab-A" attempt to steal American icons like the Texas Alamo along with Nashville's Ryman Theater and Tootsie's Orchid Lounge (the latter the band's favorite bar). The "Casket Brothers" save the world, and they turn into "the Cactus Brothers."

(95, 96, 97)

The Cactus Brothers begin their first tour with shows in 70 cities and 35 states plus Cancún, Mexico. In between performances they'll make side trips back Nashville for gigs, festivals, and television tapings for shows like *Talk of the Town*.

The band practically sells itself. Fans watch them on the wildly successful "Fisher's Hornpipe" video thanks to its significant airtime on VH1 and CMT. Their catchy cover of "Sixteen Tons" earns legions of new fans (and new kinds of fans, as does their work on *Dulcimer Player Deluxe*). The release of the *Pure Country* film follows the pattern. Everywhere they travel, they leave rave reviews in their wake, especially after their first album *The Cactus Brothers* hits the stores: "Many of the tracks drive and swirl with a force and density almost never heard on a mainstream country recording ... They play country with the passion of rock and the precision of classical. Musically, it's like witnessing a country string orchestra." Mack White's unique art gets plenty of attention, too; one reviewer cites *Cactus Comix* as "the buzz of Fan Jam" in Fort Worth. A giant backdrop of Mack's quirky "Billy the Id" hangs on stage to frame the band. They are something fresh and new: "Scruffy but fun; they project a seductive masculinity infused with a sense of humor and energy. Their eclectic roster of songs stands with one foot in rock and the other in tradition."

As they launch the tour, everything is looking up, and everything seems possible.

(98, 99, 100, 101)

# 1993 JANUARY THROUGH JULY, 50 BOOKINGS:

*Tallahassee, Nashville, Memphis, Knoxville, Nashville, Lexington KY, Nashville, Huntsville, Monroe, Shreveport, Dallas, Nashville, Grand Junction, CO, Santa Fe, NM, Sacramento,CA, Cancun, Nashville, Seven Springs, PA, Eau Claire, WI, Nashville (January through July, 50 bookings)*

As the tour rolls on, David and Sam Poland often retire early after their shows. The two musicians are ten years older than the rest of their band, and they have a lot in common: both are no-nonsense types of men, and both grew up in similar cultures, Sam in Northeast Louisiana and David in Texas. After their gigs, Sam and David prefer sitting together talking or watching old Westerns on TV in their room. They've outgrown the hard-partying-after-the-show stage that their younger bandmates enjoy with local musicians and fans. Having just entered their forties, they jokingly refer to themselves as the "old farts" in the group.

The tour produces experiences that help David expand his playing skills. He experiences the excitement of screaming, adoring fans, many of them college-age women and men. During their May gig at Monroe, Louisiana's Enoch's, psychedelic rocker Steve Stubblefield is in the audience along with Tim Bryan and several other friends. Steve and Tim are impressed by the Cactus Brothers' music, but astonished by David's playing. Steve is already familiar with the dulcimer; when he was little, his grandfather had built one from a McSpadden kit for Steve's mother. His mother even played David's tapes in the car on their vacations. But he had never heard a dulcimer on fire in a rock band like this before.

David is one of the earliest dulcimer musicians to amplify the dulcimer with a pickup since Rolling Stone Brian Jones, and also one of the earliest to play an electric dulcimer. His work on the dulcimer's new identity as an amplified rock instrument would be practically unrecognizable to the earliest dulcimer players of Appalachia, yet, in truth, it is just one of the latest versions of its centuries-long evolution as a folk instrument.

(102, 103, 104, 105)

## 1993 AUGUST THROUGH SEPTEMBER, 29 BOOKINGS:

*Nashville, Alexandria, VA, Chillicothe, OH, Nashville, Rockingham, NC, Knoxville, TN, Topeka, KS, Rockford, IL, Huron, SD, Ames, IA, Stevens Point, WI, Green Bay, WI, Chicago, IL, Minneapolis, MN, Columbia, MO, Lincoln, NE, Lawrence, KS, Boulder, CO, Steamboat Springs, CO, Jackson, WY, Salt Lake City, UT, Sweet Home, OR, Portland, OR, Seattle, WA, Eugene, OR, Prineville, OR.*

The Cactus Brothers' catchy music video of their cover of Tennessee Ernie Ford's classic "Sixteen Tons" includes a short scene of band members loading up their gear and props at Fort Cactus. Another shot reveals inside the van as it rolls down the highway. One of the Brothers jokingly tries to strangle lead singer Paul Kirby. The shot may be an unintended, subliminal acknowledgment of a growing stress and strain within the group on the grueling tour.

David finds touring an unexpected challenge for a number of reasons, beginning with his diabetes. He makes light of the disease at first, asking his fellow passengers to read his dextrometer as he checks his blood sugar levels to see if his numbers prediction matches the readout on the meter. Nevertheless, he feels more unwell as the miles pile up.

With six bandmates and their sound man packed in the Chevy van, his mind begins to question the wisdom of joining the band. The band hauls their equipment in a pull-along trailer with long periods of driving; there's no room for the quiet time to think that he often craves. Decisions about where and when to eat are often reduced to squabbling. Due to the pressures of getting from one gig to another, they frequently resort to fast food, which causes David to struggle to maintain his diet on an even keel. The arguments in the car over who gets to choose the radio station each leg of the tour annoy him, as does having to unload, set up, perform, break down, and reload all the equipment themselves.

Yet, there are many high points. While performing in Seattle, David gets a welcome surprise when he suddenly sees his old buddy and mentor from the Nature Center, Leo Kretzner. Leo attends the show and catches David's eye with a wave. After the show, the two old friends catch up with each other. Leo is living in Seattle now with a wife and young baby at home, working full time as a research biologist and playing dulcimer on the side. He tells David that before coming to the club, he was skeptical about his work in a rock band, afraid David would end up doing too much thrashing around and not have the space to do finer playing. Now that he's heard the band, his misgivings are gone.

"The Cactus Brothers are really good ... you are well-perceived! I'm not worried any more—you, my friend, are clearly not devolving by any means by playing the dulcimer and the jaw harp with the band; you're just doing it in a different setting. It's reassuring!" Leo tells him.

David laughs, and tells him he is a little worried about Leo living in Seattle.

"They're really into heroin in Seattle, you better stay away from them." he teases. "You know how they count off time in Seattle?" He demonstrates a *tap tap tap* with his index finger on the vein inside his elbow. "You don't want to go out like that, Leo."

(106, 107, 108)

## 1993 COAST TO COAST: THE COMMITMENTS

The 1991 comedy-drama film, *The Commitments*, set in Dublin, Ireland, tells the story of Jimmy Rabbitte, an eager young musician who assembles a group of talented working-class singers and musicians to form a soul band. The members' commitment to his cause is strong; however, as personalities take over, the bandmates' commitments to each other start to wane. Tensions grow as the lead singer enjoys demeaning his bandmates a little too much. The oldest member of the group has dubious tales of a lifetime of playing with the best of the best in America; he promises a visit to their club gig by his friend Wilson Pickett, a visit that could be their big break. Desperate to get his bandmates to recommit to their dream, Jimmy invites several journalists to attend the band's next show where they will perform Pickett's song, "In the Midnight Hour" in honor of Pickett who has promised to attend the gig. Pickett doesn't show, however, and their performance ends with the bandmates physically fighting with each other over this last straw. Jimmy pronounces the band over, and leaves the club in frustration to walk home. As he walks in the dark, Pickett's limousine pulls up next to Jimmy, and his driver asks for directions to the club, but it's too late. In the film's closing monologue, Jimmy explains that the band's members have since gone their separate ways, with many of them continuing to pursue musical careers.

If David had seen the award-winning film, it might have resonated. For a while now, he has developed a growing resentment toward lead singer Paul Kirby. Due to his heavy drinking, Kirby frequently turns into a bully—even on stage, in front of the fans—to berate his bandmates for what he imagines as their flaws. David finds brief solace from Kirby by rooming with Sam and by his unsullied friendship with and admiration for Tramp.

He says nothing about his frustrations to John when they return to Nashville. They have two months to rest, and then they will head out for a second, five-week tour.

(109, 110, 111)

## 1993 ATHENS, OHIO: LINDA SACK

Linda Sack had always loved music. When she was five years old in her English childhood home, she was strumming her mother's auto-harp and singing English Christmas carols with her siblings. After her family moved to Michigan, she studied piano and violin for a decade. She became competent with both but not content with playing either one.

Linda moves to Ohio in the spring to do an internship. She feels stuck and alone in the rural environmental until she strikes up a friendship with Liz. Linda is fascinated that Liz plays five instruments, so she tells her she's looking for a new instrument to learn. Liz suggests she try the mountain dulcimer. Linda had seen a dulcimer just once; her former roommate had a very pretty one hanging on the wall in their apartment. Liz orders her a dulcimer to be delivered to Linda before she moves to Nashville in the fall.

Eventually, the dulcimer made by a woodworker arrives at her doorstep. Linda decides it's not the best quality, but it's good enough to start with. She buys a Jean Ritchie book and takes a dulcimer class where she learns to play the children's song, "Go Tell Aunt Rhody."

(112)

## 1993 FRANKLIN, TENNESSEE: THE REFERRAL

One evening after her move to Nashville, Linda takes her dulcimer with her to the "Bluegrass Along the Harpeth" festival, a popular acoustic gathering for musicians, arts and crafts people to play, dance and shop in Pinkerton Park on Friday and Saturday.

Linda meets another dulcimer player, Sandy, and they hit it off immediately. Sandy tells her she has been playing for six years, and offers to teach Linda. She also invites her to join her when she plays for patients at the Vanderbilt Medical Center on Tuesdays. "I wanted to learn so badly that I brought my dulcimer when Sandy was playing for patients; later, she ended up teaching me some songs at her house. She's helping me build my repertoire" she tells a friend.

Linda learns Sandy has a musician friend named David who plays and teaches the dulcimer. She started as his dulcimer student, but now volunteers as his assistant. She runs his fan club, does his bookkeeping, keeps his schedule, and assists him and his manager John Lomax in every way she can to help David's career. She suggests Linda consider taking lessons from David because "you have so much passion for learning to play the dulcimer."

When Linda takes her first lesson with him, she shows him her dulcimer; "It's pretty," David tells her, "but I think you're going to need a different one. Let's look at some McSpaddens." He pulls out their catalog. "See what you think about them; they have a good quality sound." She likes a teardrop model with walnut sides and a maple top. She also talks with David's luthier Dan Blom to have her old dulcimer repaired as a backup.

Later, she reflects on her new teacher. She is struck by his rock-star presence, understated but very apparent. He lives simply. He only has a few outfits, some old dulcimers hanging on his wall, his cases, and a twin bed in an efficiency apartment, and an armless chair. He sits on the floor when he teaches. He is authentic to the bone, she decides.

As Linda spends more time with her teacher, she appreciates that he tapes every lesson and writes the date and topic on the cassette for her. At home, she listens to the cassette over and over and to practice the song, measure by measure. She finally feels content; she has found her instrument. And David is the most patient teacher she has ever studied with. It's part of who he is, she decides; he never has to work at it. He is fully engaged in whatever he does, and she appreciates how completely present he is with her. Linda's first encounter with her teacher will be the beginning of a mentorship and friendship with him for rest of their lives.

(113)

## 1993 NASHVILLE, TN: MARY LAWRENCE

Mary Lawrence arrives at David's apartment for her dulcimer lesson. Ever since he taught her "Morning Has Broken," she basks in the warmth of his friendship and the joy of learning to play the instrument she has grown to love. For his part, David appreciates her bubbling enthusiasm and considers her a friend. Chatting with her as she gets ready to leave, David mentions something that piques her curiosity. "I've got a new student who is more like me than I was myself." She doesn't press; she knows him well enough to know that he'll tell her about the new student when he's ready.

(114)

## 1993 NASHVILLE, TN: THE APPRENTICESHIP

Twenty-year old Stephen Seifert moved to Nashville last year on his own personal odyssey. A recommendation that he contact a player named Sandy led him to her door; he agrees to do odd jobs for her in exchange for lessons. As Sandy begins to understand the passion for music within him, she introduces Stephen to David by inviting him to go to the Station Inn to watch David perform.

Stephen can hardly contain his excitement; Sandy had frequently mentioned someone named David, and it suddenly dawns on his that this must be the same David he saw perform in Ohio when he was seventeen.

When they meet for the lesson and David listens to him play, he determines that Stephen is much more skilled than his typical students. Their half-hour, regularly scheduled lessons quickly convert to all-day jam sessions. Stephen is in seventh heaven for the opportunity to learn from and work with his hero. When they go to lunch, he peppers David with questions, and he indulges his curiosity. He tells Stephen's mother Nancy that he likes that "Seifert lick," and he'd like to take him on tour. David meant what he said when he told Mary Lawrence about his new student. He fully understands

Stephen's intense drive to play the dulcimer for all it is worth and to make it yield up its secrets in his hands.

(115, 116, 117)

## 1993 NASHVILLE, TN: LINDA SACK

Linda Sack's dedication to the dulcimer and her gentleness resonate perfectly with David; he loves to make her laugh, and she loves his stories of life on the road. Today, he shares another story with her of an incident that happened at a recent festival:

> Well, I'm in this hotel, and I'm at one end of the hallway with my dulcimer, heading to my room. Suddenly, I see a musician at the other end walking toward me carrying his uilleann pipes. He' wearin' a kilt, and while he's walkin', he starts playin' his pipes. So, what else could I do? I started walking toward him, playin' my dulcimer!

(118)

## 1993 NASHVILLE, TN: AN UNEXPECTED PROPOSITION

On Sunday afternoon, Mark and Debra Wait visit Bill and Ellen Pryor. Everyone's chatting and having a glass of wine when they hear a car pull into the driveway—it's David, who jumps out of the car and comes running up to the house. "I've just gotten back from East Tennessee, and I want to show you something!" he exclaims when Ellen meets him at the door. He apologizes for bursting in, and Ellen, eager to find out what he wants to show them, introduces him to her friends. David runs to the car and returns with a large, old wooden box painted black on the top. It's one of the earliest examples of a Tennessee music box he has found. He is so excited that he hasn't even been home yet. He explains he was on his way back to Nashville with the box and was dying to show it to someone, so decided to stop by. He sits on the floor, puts the box across his lap and starts fingerpicking the strings, coaxing a traditional song to arise as he deftly reawakens the box while everyone sits down to listen.

Mark, the new dean of Vanderbilt's Blair School of Music, listens closely as David shares the history of these unique music boxes. Wait is stunned by this unexpected visitor's knowledge, passion, and playing on what appears to be a very primitive instrument.

Mark asks question after question of David. Ellen, Bill, and Debra sit back on the sofa and listen as the two musicians talk with each other for the next half hour. By the end of their conversation, Ellen isn't surprised when she hears Mark tell David, "I want you to join the faculty of the Blair School of Music at Vanderbilt University. I'm not quite sure I can make this happen quickly, but believe me, I want to make it happen."

(119, 120)

## 1993 NASHVILLE, TN: THE PORTRAIT

Portrait photographer Maria von Mathiessen arrives in Nashville to shoot country music artists for her book, *Songs from the Hills: An Intimate Look at Country Music*. Mathiessen eschews the stereotypical glitzy, posed star shots. Instead, her intent is to create a series of black-and-white portraits that reveal the emotions chronicled in country music by the people who convey those emotions via their songs.

On its surface, her portrait of David is unusual for a Nashville musician who is riding eight years of fame when von Mathiessen arrives in town. The top third of the portrait depicts a wide layer of cloudless sky; underneath thinner lines traverse within the frame: a row of trees, then a thin slice of a farmer's field of dried corn, waiting for harvest. A lone tree stands slightly right of center in front of the corn. In the bottom two-thirds of the image, waves of dried, undulating grass over a deeply furrowed field evoke waves lapping a beach.

At the bottom right frame's corner, a man's shirtless arms and hands reach into the frame, his left holds a traditional Appalachian dulcimer upright in a vertical position, while the fingers of his right hand lie on his left wrist; a triad of the greatest importance to the subject.

The genius of this portrait consists in the photographer's revelation of David's essence without revealing his face. Ego is completely subsumed to life's elements that he esteems most: the natural landscape, the metaphorical waves lapping the field suggesting both the waves he rode as a teen and the waves of sound; the lone tree in the distance; and the wide-open sky. The disembodied hand and arm present the dulcimer to viewer; for David, it is much more important that people see it than him.

## 1994 TELLURIDE, COLORADO: DONE

After the Cactus Brothers first tour, the exhausted band members returned to Nashville for two months to rest and restore themselves. Now, they get ready for another tour, this one planned for five weeks. Unlike the first tour, no one is looking forward to this one. Right before they leave, Sam tells John Lomax, "You may have a band when we get back, but it's not going to be this band." John laughs, thinking it's a joke. He had heard rumors about Paul Kirby's erratic behavior, but doesn't understand the extent of the difficulties.

As soon as they embark on the second tour, the troubles begin. The days are long and rough, and annoyances turn into irritations, then exasperations. All had agreed that whoever was driving would get to pick the radio station to listen to, but music tastes differed wildly between them—from Nine Inch Nails to Frank Sinatra— and the bickering gets on everyone's last nerve. After driving all day, they unpack to do a show, then pack their gear up late after the show, and drive back to a hotel to get a few hours' sleep. In the morning, the same routine starts all over again. Some of their gigs pay well; others barely pay the bills.

Word had spread through Music Row that the Cactus Brothers' front man had a serious alcohol and drug problem. His bandmates know it, but nothing can be done until Kirby acknowledges that he has a serious illness and gets professional help. Sam, responsible for writing out a setlist for each gig, frequently has to endure an inebriated Kirby grabbing the setlist during the show while leaning into his face to hiss at him, "You know, you suck!" Kirby can be just one of the guys one minute, then rub them raw with his arguments and put-downs that arise from nowhere when he's drunk or high. David finds himself growing more and more irritated. He is accustomed to the respect and professionalism of studio musicians and producers, and now he's on his last nerve.

Everyone else's nerves are frayed, too, as they arrive in cold and snowy Telluride during ski season. After driving from one hotel to another, they discover there are no hotel rooms available. Eventually, their road manager finagles a way to get them some rest by putting them up with strangers in separate cabins.

The next morning, Sam wakes up, at first unsure of where he is. He gets dressed and wanders outside, searching for a familiar face because he has no idea where everyone else stayed the night. Eventually, he and Tramp find each other, and Tramp tells him that the manager of the bar where they are scheduled to play that evening doesn't have the $300 he is supposed to pay them for upfront expenses. After they find the rest of their bandmates, everyone agrees they will cancel the gig and move on. To make matters worse, no one knows where David is.

David, it turns out, had had enough. Sometime in the middle of the night, livid after another blow-up with Paul Kirby, he called a cab to take the four and a half hour ride from Telluride to Denver to catch a flight home to Nashville.

(121, 122, 123)

Once back in Nashville, David meets with John to tell he has quit the band. John is dumbfounded. He has always considered the Cactus Brothers a win-win for David, for the band, and for John. From the moment David joined the band, John was impressed by their sheer talent together, the breadth of their repertoire and their ability to excite their audiences. He was equally thrilled by how absolutely terrific their songwriting skills and performances were no matter the music genre. He believes in his heart that together they are close to breaking through and making it big. He begs David to reconsider, to no avail. "I'm just not going to do it anymore."

Once the second tour is over, Tramp seeks out David at the Villager Tavern and at his apartment every time he's in town. He is miserable since David left the band. He misses David personally, and also misses the dulcimer sound and music experience that he brought to the band. Tramp feels David's playing made them unique and even more marketable; his loss to him is devastating. David shares that he misses playing with Sam and Tramp, but he tells a friend in no uncertain terms that he will never, ever play with a band again.

Within a year, Sam Poland, the band's dobroist and pedal steel guitar player, leaves the band as well. He, too, has had enough.

(124, 125, 126)

## 1994 NASHVILLE, TN: A NEW TRANSFORMATION

It is a pull toward Nashville almost as much as a push away from the problems with heavy touring that brought David back to Nashville. He missed his private students, many of whom are close friends, and his mind is now brimming with ideas for a solo career. He and John meet again. John, still reeling, knows he can't afford to continue to manage and produce for a niche instrument player who relies on teaching his students for much of his income. David understands; he longs to be back in control of his life and music.

David is forty-two years old. Despite his having played the dulcimer for twenty-one years, its pull on him is stronger than ever. He feels compelled to find, research, and save vintage dulcimers and music boxes by collecting them, not just to own but to record and save for posterity. He loves their deep, mystic sounds. After a long talk together, David and John decide to part ways as manager and client. John will stay on and manage the Cactus Brothers.

Given their history together, and the special heart within each of them, they put aside their mutual disappointments. Deep down, both of them are grateful for their work and friendship over the last ten years. David understands what John has done for his career and what the two have meant to each other.

(127)

## 1994 NASHVILLE, TN: "THAT'S ME"

David, flat broke after leaving the tour, makes the difficult decision to sell the Koa Dulcimer to a pair of collectors in Texas. He lives in his rusty, beat-up Chevy until he can earn enough money to get another apartment.

He becomes a regular at the local blood donation center for the small compensation they offer to donors. On this visit, after the technician draws his blood, she escorts him to the "juice and cookies" room where donors rest, eat, and drink a little before they leave. While sitting there, he notices another man nearby, also hard up enough to have to donate blood for money.

On a table between them David sees a *Nashville Scene* magazine, open to a feature article about him that had just been published. He contemplates the irony of his situation: Nashville appreciates him enough to write a feature article about him, but he isn't able to earn enough to live on without giving blood. He picks up the article and, holding it up to show the other man, points to the picture and tells him, "Hey buddy, take a look: that's me." The man looks at the article, then looks at David. "Naw, that can't be you. That dude has got his shit together." David replies with a wry chuckle, "No, that's really me."

(128, 129)

## 1994 NASHVILLE, TN: PROFESSOR

While David was on tour, dean Mark Wait was working hard to realize his vision for the Blair School of Music. Always a jewel in the crown of Vanderbilt University, the Blair School has a widespread reputation as an excellent classical music school. As Blair's leader, Mark wants to broaden the school's offerings. He plans to develop a new folk music program for study and performance that will represent the folk music traditions that have been so important to Tennessee's history.

Dean Wait calls David, delivering on the promise he made at Ellen Pryor's home—he extends the formal invitation to become the first dulcimer faculty member, not only at Blair School of Music at Vanderbilt University, but, likely, in the world. The newly minted academic joins his old friend Mark O'Connor, professor of the violin/fiddle, to help build the program.

Prior to the appointments of Mark and David, the entire faculty consisted of classically trained musicians. They welcome their new colleagues, and an exciting sense of possibility permeates the air with the synergy of classical and folk music traditions that now coexist under one roof.

Aside from Mark O'Connor's professional experience as an in-demand soloist and studio musician, he already has experience teaching, having just set up his own summer fiddle camps for students. David contributes his years of experience as a private teacher along with his understanding of the dulcimer's place as a significant instrument in American music history.

Like their colleagues, David and Mark O'Connor will assess, write curricula for, teach undergraduate music majors and nonmajors, and evaluate their progress. They will also participate in Blair's community outreach to elementary and high school students. They will have office hours, teach students one-on-one, plan and promote yearly recitals, attend faculty meetings, and work on scholarship goals they themselves set.

Whenever Dean Wait and David run into each other in the hallway, David shakes his dean's hand and smiles as he acknowledges him with a little bow. Dean Wait is utterly charmed.

(130, 131, 132, 133)

---

### David as Academic Scholar

His many years of collecting and researching nineteenth-century instruments, and the people, songs, and stories behind them establish his place in the long line of song catchers and researchers such a Cecil Sharp, Ralph Lee Smith, L. Allen Smith, and younger people like Lucy Long who will publish her dissertation next year: *The Negotiation of Tradition: Collectors, Community, and the Appalachian Dulcimer in Beech Mountain, North Carolina.*

---

## 1994 NASHVILLE, TN: THE CONSUMMATE EDUCATOR

In addition to his academic work, David takes on more teaching via private lessons in his apartment to help make ends meet. He collects $15 per lesson hour for those willing to go to his house, and $45 for the private students he teaches at Blair since part of that money goes back into the program. He consistently gets high marks from his students for his teaching and his demeanor. He always has a smile on his face, and if he is worried about anything or doesn't feel well, they won't know it.

Each lesson, David gets down to business right away. He prefers to train the ear first, typically organizing each lesson around a song. He starts each lesson by playing a piece at a tempo geared to the student's level. With rare exceptions, David avoids starting with tab, preferring instead that the student develop a feel for the melody by listening to it.

With new students, he starts a lesson slowly and patiently with simple, traditional songs like "Boil Them Cabbage" or "Grey Cat on a Tennessee Farm." Once he plays the song for the student, he plays it a second time, now counting the beat with his foot and/or giving strumming instructions: "down, up, down, down, up," directing the student to pay attention to the variation in strums. Sometimes he sings the words of the song; at other times, if he thinks the student is ready, he'll sing the notes or fret numbers as he plays the melody: "Okay, for the Tennessee Waltz, on *Waltz*, it will go to the D-7..." He plays and sings, "we'll have DDDD, DDDD, to the D-7 and G, back to DD, DDDD A, walk to A-7 ...." The student watches his hands and listens as he weaves his way through the song using first one strategy and then another to lay down the track in the student's mind.

When the learner encounters a difficult part, David breaks it down and works on a measure or two at a time, not moving on until he senses confidence in the student. Or, with a particularly challenging section in a piece, he'll demonstrate and give tips for overcoming the challenge. He excuses himself to get a cup of coffee so the student can work through the part alone. By the time he returns, most are eager to show him that they can now play the part. "I knew you could do it!" he exclaims, his delight palpable.

In essence, Dave approaches his lessons with a variety of aural, visual, cognitive, and physical strategies all at once: the sounds he elicits from the dulcimer; suggestions for finger placement for chords; singing the notes to associate them with the frets, singing fret numbers, raising awareness of rhythm; lyrics, melody, and harmony, strumming reminders and—always—positive feedback. Even with beginning students, he'll demonstrate how to add variety to the song by playing in higher or lower on the fretboard, adding a little harmony, or by using little tricks like a hammer-on for fretting efficiency. When the lesson is over, he hands over a cassette tape of his demonstrations of the week's song. If he is going to give the student tab to accompany the song, he does it at the end of the lesson.

Perhaps one of the most challenging but important skills he teaches is to "read hands." The student sits facing David and, while listening, watches his hands: the left moves up and down the fretboard fretting as the right strums or picks the strings. "Developing the skill to read a player's hands is challenging at first," he tells them. "You have to interpret a mirror image of your own hands as they move on the fretboard, but it's one of the best ways to help you learn the timing of a song and the sounds of the fretboard." There's another benefit to being able to read hands. When a new player is in a jam circle, especially with more advanced players who don't use tab, some of the songs may be new to him or her. One way to pick up the song is to study another player's hands to follow where their fretting hand is moving on the fretboard. A new player has the best vantage point for watching by looking at the hands of a skilled dulcimer player directly across from him or her. Or, if a new player understands guitar fretting and can watch a guitar player in the group, the dulcimer player can see the chord changes by watching the guitarist's hand on the guitar neck and, thus, follow along.

David reminds everyone that to really play a song well, they have to play the song until it becomes part of them. "You want to know the song so well, you can play it with your toes," he jokes.

Whether his students are conscious of his teaching method or not, they leave each week with three enormous gifts: a little more understanding of the language that musicians use when they talk about playing; a rich, personal lesson designed to help them play songs with feeling and expression on their own; and an appreciation of the historic roots of the songs they learn to play.

Occasionally, David will call Wanda O'Guin, one of his favorites: "I'm tired of sitting in the office; how about we do a lesson at your house?" Wanda now is the nursing manager for the surgical intensive care unit, so he gives her time to get home and set up her living room so she and her friend Priscilla can have a lesson together. He loves that the warm, motherly Wanda always sets out a little plate of cookies with a fresh pot of coffee on the stove for him. Over the years, the two of them have become close friends. Wanda wants him to be proud of her dulcimer playing, and, indeed, he is.

(134, 135)

## 1994 NASHVILLE, TN: SARAH ELIZABETH AT THREE

David gets ready to perform in concert at Blair, his first as a faculty member. Linda Sack is one of his many student friends who attends.

Concert manager Jennifer Musgrave attends every performance. She always takes her small daughter Sarah Elizabeth with her to expose her to a variety of musical genres and instruments.

As the lights lower in the elegant auditorium, David walks to the center of the large stage and sits, alone, in an armless chair and begins to play. Linda, in the front row but sitting a little off to the side, has a perfect close-up view of him. She later recalls, "I had never seen anything like his performance in my life. Not just the instrument, but the deftness with which he played it. His fingers danced over the fretboard. He had complete command of that instrument. Someone whispered to me, 'He plays the dulcimer like a grand piano player.'"

"At that concert, I sat there, enraptured, my mouth open. I was already in lessons with him, but it was that moment I realized what a master musician he was and what a treasure it was to study under him."

After the concert, Linda smiles as she watches Jennifer, holding her daughter's tiny hand, slowly walk her up to the stage so that Sarah Elizabeth can see his dulcimer up close. As the curly haired redhead approaches, David smiles and kneels down to say hello. She greets him; then, looking into his eyes, solemnly pronounces:

"I have seen a lot of musical performances in my life and a lot of instruments, but the dulcimer is the one I want to play along with the tuba." David bursts out laughing, absolutely tickled by her. He tells her she will have to wait until she is a little bit older before she can play a dulcimer.

The toddler is not to be deterred, however. Now that she has decided that she wants to play the dulcimer, she regularly sends messages to David via her mother: "When can I take lessons with you?" By the time she is in kindergarten, he will finally relent and agree to take her on. When he does, he'll lose any misgivings about teaching such a young student when he recognizes he has a genuine music prodigy under his wing.

(136, 137, 138, 139)

## 1994 CORYDON, INDIANA: BOB AND SHERRI

Bob King and his wife Sherri are new to the dulcimer world. Bob had grown up exposed to plenty of old-time music as he listened to his brother and dad play guitar. One day, a coworker brought a dulcimer to work, and he played it. He was hooked immediately, so ordered his first dulcimer from Sears. Sherri said she wished she could play, too. The first chance they got, they drove to Mountain Made Music in Nashville, Indiana, and bought her one.

They attend their first dulcimer festival at Corydon and find their way to seats in front of the stage to listen to the next performer. Bob takes one look at the long-haired skinny guy as he walks on stage and finds himself annoyed; he hadn't planned to sit through some hippie music performance.

As soon as he hears David's electric opening to the traditional song "Wildwood Flower," Bob nearly falls off his chair. He was not expecting this kind of rendition of the old-time song from his youth. After the performance, he approaches David and introduces himself. They end up sharing each other's background and then swapping stories. David tells Bob that when he first came to

Nashville he was so poor he had slept in his car on two different occasions after he had arrived in the city. He tried to get a $20 money order cashed and had the hardest time because he didn't have a bank account. But he laughs and recalls, "I was sitting in Brown's Diner, and looked at Phil Everly on one side and John Prine on the other, and I thought, this might just work out after all!"

He tells Bob that he had been to the Ohio Valley Gathering Festival earlier this year where he had gotten wind of the possibility of an antique dulcimer that might be for sale in a museum in Davis County, Indiana. Bob volunteers to go look for it after the festival and even promises to deliver it to David in Nashville if he finds it.

Later, when Bob and Sherri take a ride to the museum, they never find the dulcimer David is looking for. Nevertheless, they stay in touch, and reconnect again and again at Midwest festivals like old friends.

(140)

## 1994 NASHVILLE, TN: MARY LAWRENCE AND WANDA

Blair faculty present a yearly student recital. David's first Christmas recital will take place in the stunning Turner Hall with its gleaming stage and paneled walls that provide perfect acoustics.

David always carefully selects the song or songs for each student to perform, picking the simpler tunes for the beginners so they can feel confident. He sits down with his recital students beforehand to explain how the event will take place. "You can invite all the friends and family you like; the concert will be free to the public. You'll take turns on stage, and the lineup will move from least experienced to most experienced students. I'll sit next to you on stage while you perform in case help you need help. I want you to have a good time up there." After the recital, his assistant Sandy and others will have a refreshment area set up in the lobby for students and their guests.

"It's scary—oh my ..." thinks Mary Lawrence upon arriving at Blair's Turner Hall to see the large crowd of people looking for their seats. She has been practicing every day for her turn when she will play and sing "In the Bleak Midwinter." She bolsters her confidence in the knowledge that this 1872 British carol is the perfect dulcimer song for the season. Also, she takes comfort that David will sit on stage with her, so she won't have to feel alone.

Wanda has a case of the nerves, too. She approaches David shortly before her turn to play "Old Joe Clark" to confess she is scared to death of playing in front of others. He whispers to her, "Don't worry about it; it's not going to kill nobody if you make a mistake. I restart songs a lot of times when I start on the wrong note." She listens and grows a bit calmer. As she walks up the stairs to the stage, she recalls his words and remembers how he laughed it off in the past when he made a mistake. He would start over and say, "Well, let's try this one more time!" When she finishes her song, the fear long gone, she looks at David's face beaming at her.

(141, 142)

## 1995 CORYDON, INDIANA: BOB AND SHERRI

The next time Bob and Sherri return to the Corydon festival they know all about many of the professional musicians David has played with. Although suitably impressed, Bob really loves David for David, the teacher and the man he considers his friend. He takes a morning class in which David teaches the twenty students how to play the somewhat challenging tune, "Liberty." First demonstrating a slower version of the song in front of the class, David works through the song measure by measure as the students play with him. Occasionally, he moves around the room to give individual help until the group can finally play a recognizable version. Near the end of the class, David listens to them play together. "Well, if the best of Nashville was playing really bad, and we were a little better, we might just be able to keep up with them!" he tells them with a note of pride. The students explode with laughter.

On the way home, Bob tells Sherri that David inspires him so much that he feels they have a spiritual connection. He tells his son Gabe stories about David that are either firsthand stories or the stories that David has told him. "He is not into status symbols. His philosophy on automobiles is never pay more than $500 on a car, and make friends with a good mechanic. Over the years I saw two different cars he drove. One time he drove an old Oldsmobile from Nashville up to Indiana that was so dilapidated, I wouldn't drive it around the block! Later, he had a 1960 blue Buick that was falling apart. At least it got him here and back."

Another story he tells Gabe has to do with David's performance of "Brush Arbor." The song was inspired by an arbor in Bea Jordan's garden where a teenage David spent hours with his buddy and Bea's son Norman. Both Bob and Sherri had fallen in love with the song and the way he sang it at the festival. Bob explains what happened after he heard him play it the first time. "I remembered every word to the first two verses, but couldn't remember the rest. After his performance, he sat down with us both by reciting each verse slowly so your mom could write them down."

Bob recalls one more thing for Gabe: "The last time your mom and I saw him, he told me, 'There's just one thing I can't abide, Bob...'The Black Mountain Rag" should be played in the key of A, not D!'"

(143)

## 1995 NASHVILLE, TN: NOW FEATURING THE TENNESSEE MUSIC BOX

Music producer Jim Sales tells his friends that his buddy David is the "Chet Atkins of dulcimer players." David knows what he needs and wants on any song he's ever played for Jim. All Jim has to do is start the tapes.

The two have talked off and on about doing an album of old gospel hymns that Jim had heard growing up. Jim has the idea to record the songs in one of several old empty churches in Cades Cove near Townsend, in the Smokey Mountains National Park. Jim has one in mind and tells David about his visit to assess the building. "The acoustics were like being inside a guitar," he tells David. "What a wonderful place to capture the dulcimer!" David buys into it immediately. Jim contacts the Park's public affairs office and gets permission to use the building on the date and time he requests so to avoid the sounds of noisy cars and visitors walking in during their recording session.

What neither of them anticipate is how events in Washington, DC, would have an impact on their plans. President Clinton and Speaker of the House Newt Gingrich come to an impasse over which version of the federal budget will be approved. With time running out, the government shuts down. Suddenly, all National Park Service offices close on the day they are scheduled to record.

David may have been having second thoughts anyway about the plan to record at Cave's Cove due to the physical logistics. They would have had to haul heavy recording equipment and a source of power to the building since the historic church had no power source of its own. (Laptops with microphones are still in the future.)

The two come up with a new concept: feature the Tennessee music box on a CD. Jim has always been fascinated with the way David plays with a feather quill and a bow on the box to draw out the haunting notes that make it sound like a bagpipe. The two agree to switch their focus.

They will produce this album at their own expense in Jim's home studio. Jim sees this as an important project for his career as well as for David's. Jim has recorded thousands of songs and produced song writers' demos day after day, but this project is a recording first for him, and thanks to David's participation he considers it special. Jim wants the listeners to feel like they are sitting in the room with David, listening to the sounds Jim hears. David's goal is to evoke the music and the spirit of the mountains.

Whenever their schedules permit, the two get together to record a song or two until they get it just right. Jim likes to try different microphone placements, and that is the only experimenting that slows them down. David rarely requires two or more takes. As Jim listens to the recordings after each session, he feels very proud of the work. David, he decides, had made it easy for him. He does his straight ahead, live performance in the studio without the need for tweaking the audio. Jim decides to add a little reverb, but he feels there's no need to edit his performances.

When all recordings are mastered, Jim has the CDs pressed, and arranges for a photo shoot at one of the Oak Ridge Boys' historic houses in Hendersonville.

They have produced a special, niche-type product rather than a mainstream country music album. Satisfied and proud of their work, they sell it through David's channels: Neal's Gourd Music on the West Coast; in the Smokies (Clemmer's Wood-in-Strings dulcimer shop in Townsend), and in Arkansas (McSpadden's). Initially Jim handles sales, but then David takes it over.

*Tennessee Music Box Dulcimer Solos* is David's introduction of this unique instrument to the world. He showcases all the ways to elicit the sounds he wants from the box: fingerpicking the first song, All the Good Times" [are Past and Gone]" and strumming the old fashioned way with a turkey quill on a "Redwing" and "Golden Slippers" medley. David had just learned "Redwing" last year from Lawrence Gamble, the only known living traditional player of the music box. "Golden Slippers" harks back to his competition at Winfield twenty-two years ago; perhaps it encapsulates for him the stretch of time that leads him here. He plays with the fiddle bow on the last piece, a southern hymn called "Ten Thousand Charms."

David knows he won't make much from this CD and may even lose money. Despite the cachet of working as a session musician, he has never earned much during his career. Guitar magnate George Gruhn once told David in the early years in Nashville that he was one of the most ambitious musicians he had ever met. Yet, in his best earning year, he only made thirteen thousand dollars. He has spent many a night in his car when he had to, even in Nashville, because his primary goal has never been money. The ambition is all on behalf of the instruments and their music—first, the dulcimer, and now, the Tennessee music box. The laying down the figurative and literal tracks is all that matters to him. Leaving a legacy for the dulcimer's importance in the history of traditional music is what it is all about.

(144, 145)

## The Dedication

David dedicated *Tennessee Music Box* to two people who were important to him: Anne Romaine and Richard Cotten.

Anne Romaine was a folksinger, songwriter, activist, and history professor. Born Dorothy Anne Cooke in 1942 in Atlanta, Ga., she grew up in rural North Carolina. She attended Queen's College in Charlotte, N.C., and traveled as a missionary to Mexico. This missionary work opened her eyes to the social injustices that she would spend her life fighting.

When she returned to the United States, Romaine enrolled in a graduate program in history at the University of Virginia, where she met and, in 1965, married Howard Romaine, who had participated in the Mississippi Democratic Freedom Party's attempt to register African American voters in rural Mississippi. For her master's thesis, she conducted interviews with many of those involved in this project.

Later, Romaine continued her historical work, taking courses at Vanderbilt University. She eventually cofounded the Southern Folk Cultural Revival Project, a group of artists of different races who performed traditional southern music. The group traveled around the South performing most frequently at colleges and festivals, such as Georgia Sea Island Days and Tennessee Grassroots Days.

After a full life dedicated to her causes, Romaine died at age fifty-two, the same year David and Jim recorded the music box album. Her vast collection of papers is held in the South-ern Folklife Collection of the University of North Carolina at Chapel Hill.

The list of guitar players that Richard Cotten knew and played alongside is well known among Nashville musicians. Countless guitarists from Chet Atkins to the most obscure players found their instruments and supplies at Cotten Music with Richard's help. It was a clerk at Cotten Music who sent Mary Lawrence to seek out David. He frequently bought strings, picks, and other items at Cotten, and counted Richard as a good friend. In 2012, Cotten Music moved from Hillsboro Village to its current home in Nashville's Wedge-wood-Houston, and is now known as the North American Guitar.

(146, 147)

## 1995 NASHVILLE, TN: (IM)BALANCE

In his role as adjunct professor, David is well underway in the goal to build an academic dulcimer program at Blair. In addition, he keeps a roster of up to thirty private students, including Mary Lawrence, Wanda, and many others.

Many students count him as a friend as well as a teacher, includ-ing Marilyn Konriff and Caroline Wick. Along with their friend Brenda and Carolyn's husband Don on guitar, the quartet calls themselves "Mountain Laurel" whenever they perform traditional music at local gigs. Their exceptional talent and passion for playing impresses David enough that he is thrilled when they ask him to become their mentor and help them improve their playing. He begins work with them by creating three-part arrangements for the dulcimers so that they can play harmony for a CD they plan to record.

David has always maintained a hectic schedule, and this year is no exception. In February, he was in Fort Worth for its Winter Festival of Acoustic Music to conduct a workshop and perform; in March, he traveled to Paris, Texas, to perform with his friend Debbie Porter. In April, he to drove to the Western Illinois University Radio Station for an on-air performance, and also proudly appeared as both professor and performer at the Bluebird Café for the annual faculty Showcase Dinner to raise money for the Blair Scholarship Fund. In July he reunited with Jean Ritchie, Tom Chapin, and others for the twentieth reunion of Nancy Barker's Kentucky Music Weekend to perform and conduct his workshop. He appeared as a character in sci-fi author Spider Robinson's book, *Callahan's Touch*, the sixth in his series of Callahan books about a zany world of humans and aliens centered on Callahan's bar. Robinson's choice of David for a character in his book is no accident. He is the embodiment of the author's take on the key to universal happiness: "Be kind and generous."

However, Robinson's hope for his readers that—"as they finish each book in the series, they come to understand 'shared pain is diminished, shared joy is increased'"—is only partly true in David's case. Throughout all of his busy activity schedule, perhaps only Darrel knows the true extent to which David finds living with brittle diabetes a constant drain on him physically and mentally. He does his best, but it's almost impossible for him to control his blood sugar. He feels more and more tired and often too sick to eat. He has chronic and worsening pain in his neck, and begins to notice occasional small, unwelcome changes in his ability to control the fretboard with the same deftness for which he is well-known.

David has always had trouble saying "no" to the constant demands on his time. To cope, he occasionally disappears, withdrawing to his apartment to find respite. The phone messages pile up, the door knocks go unanswered, the lights are off, and if any sounds make their way through the spartan apartment's walls they will have arisen from a softly played dulcimer or Tennessee music box. He reappears without notice or explanation upon return.

David has always had to juggle his basic nature as a highly sensitive introvert with the need to earn a living in a business that never guarantees a paycheck or health insurance; the need to discover, create, and connect with other creative artists while coping with his constant physical challenges. If he weren't already susceptible to depression, he would have plenty to be depressed about. Nevertheless, he gathers the strength of his will during his self-imposed retreats. By sheer determination, he chooses joy when he reappears. For a man who considers himself an atheist, he knows better than most the value of his many blessings.

(148, 149, 150, 151, 152, 153, 154, 155, 156, 157, 158, 159)

## 1995 NASHVILLE, TN: STEVE STUBBLEFIELD

Young Steve Stubblefield hails from Shreveport, Louisiana, and is a member of the punk rock group Roadside Monuments. He is one of the first of his tight cluster of friends to take the yellow brick road to Nashville. Steve's musical friendships were forged primarily in Ruston, a city in the rich, cultural stew of the eastern Texas-Louisiana-Arkansas region and home to two universities—Louisiana Tech and Grambling State University. Between the two universities, thousands of college students regularly show up for the dozens of bands in the region as they perform in the many clubs in the area, always giving the crowds more than their money's worth.

Steve is a seeker of skills, new insights and experiences who is infused with a passion for music and learning. Last year he was on fire to record a proper sounding album of songs he composed. Ever since he was a teenager, his modern music education was self-directed and included recording his own compositions at home on a four-track recording machine. His buddy Mike Dickinson had introduced him to his friend Mike Manning, a record store owner and the only person Dickinson knew who had a digital audio tape (DAT) machine; Steve needed one to convert his home audio recordings into digital format and to work on sound leveling for a split seven-inch single record he intended to produce. In the process, Mike Manning became another good friend. Such sharing of knowledge and ties was one of the many benefits accrued by members of this tight Shreveport tribe of musician friends no matter the type of music focus they each pursued.

On August 9 (the day Jerry Garcia of the Grateful Dead dies), Steve drives to Nashville to attend Belmont University. He has been accepted as a student in the sound recording program of the Mike Curb College of Entertainment & Music Business. He turned the key in the ignition of his packed car with some trepidation; his friends already knew he hated country music. "I am scared to death of going to Nashville and getting immersed in 'country'. I am a punk rocker!" he asserted. A preacher's kid who loves his parents but doesn't share their feelings about religion, Steve is also frightened by Belmont's identity as a Baptist University and its prominence in the Christian music industry. When his dad told him that Belmont recently had done away with the weekly chapel requirement, Steve relented and agreed to attend.

His initial concerns soon forgotten, Steve throws himself into the university experience. He and his fellow students scratch the itch to perform by starting The Methadone Actors, an avant-garde, moody punk band that Steve describes to his buddies back home as "Radiohead meets Pink Floyd meets Punk Rock meets British Psychedelics." His talented band is about as far from Nashville's popular country music scene as one could get before leaving the planet. He has no interest whatsoever in the current performers at the top of the Nashville game like George Strait, Reba McEntire, and Toby Keith. He's even further from the traditional roots music of David Schnaufer.

Yet, Steve, like David, has always had the desire to grow by pushing music boundaries. It's no surprise that the Muse will ensure that these two seekers eventually cross paths.

(160)

## 1995 NASHVILLE, TN: MAKE ROOM FOR THE NEW STUDENT

Mark O'Connor takes a phone call in his office at Blair. A woman with a marked Brooklyn accent inquires about taking fiddle lessons with him. During their discussion, she learns that Blair has a folk program that includes David Schnaufer, a professor of the dulcimer. After the call, Mark stops by David's office to let him know that he is going to hear from a new student soon. "She already plays the dulcimer, but she is eager to broaden her skills," he teases; "her name is Cyndi Lauper."

(161)

## 1995 NASHVILLE, TN: JAN AND CYNDI

Jan Pulsford, a Welsh woman with a passion for music and high tech, is hosting friend and collaborator Cyndi Lauper who has come to town to work on a project with her. While she's in Nashville, Lauper intends to meet with David to learn some advanced chording; she uses the dulcimer both on stage and to write songs. Both women know of his reputation and of his instrument; both first took up the dulcimer after hearing Joni Mitchell play it in the seventies.

As she grew up, Jan broadened her music skills in London during the eighties where she worked as a keyboard player, programmer, and composer. After working on various artists' tours, she joined the Thompson Twins as the keyboard player on their Future Days Tour. While on tour, Jan contemplated putting down musical roots in the U.S. On a trip to Nashville, she was struck by the sign, "Welcome to Music City, U.S.A" at the airport. After learning of its rich, musically diverse environment, from the hill music of the East to the blues of Memphis, all mixed with gospel and soul, she made up her mind that Tennessee would be her new home.

When Jan and Cyndi Lauper arrive at Blair, they make their way to David's classroom and sit down in the back. He begins with some background history of the dulcimer, and much to the students' delight, he introduces his guests and even invites Cyndi up to the front to play a duet with him. David had always admired Cyndi Lauper not only for her singing but for her songwriting. He had her voice in mind when he wrote "Twilight Eyes," and he is impressed by how she creates such beautiful songs from simple beginnings, often using single notes to convey the melody. Always eager to learn and collaborate, he is looking forward to working with her.

After the class, David invites both women to his apartment so they can talk. When they walk in the door, they are instantly struck by the dulcimers everywhere. Dulcimers of all shapes and sizes— many of them clearly antiques— hang on the walls of his otherwise small apartment. As his guests scan the hanging instruments, Cyndi asks about the peculiar old boxes leaning against the walls. He explains that he has been researching and collecting and researching Tennessee music boxes for several years now since they, too, are on the dulcimer family tree. Cyndi asks him to play one for her and is instantly smitten with the sound.

As they visit, David learns more about the two women. "When I arrived in Nashville," Jan explains, "the only advice I got from anybody on Music Row was to move...no one could understand what I was doing here. Every time I tried to do something downtown, I got kicked back out." As a result, she built her own studio, English Valley Music, in nearby Hendersonville. She created her own indie label *Collecting Dust* to take advantage of the nascent internet. She plans to take part in building a worldwide music community, and Collecting Dust will allow her to market her productions directly to consumers. And she has worked with Lauper as a cowriter, producer, and touring musical director. Cyndi is here to record at Jan's the next day for her new album.

As they share their common interests, David mentions another topic he has been researching: the Melungeons with their history of denigrated social status. The two women feel a growing connection between David's ideas and their current work on Cyndi's upcoming fifth album, *Sisters of Avalon*. The album will address a variety of timely subjects such as the issue of complacency and ignorance in popular culture and discrimination against minorities, gays, and women. Before they leave, Jan and Cyndi invite him out to Jan's studio to record on a track titled "Fearless" for *Sisters of Avalon;* Cyndi would like Jan to record him bowing the Tennessee music box

David has been looking for a country artist who would be interested in including the music box on one or more recordings. He is also intrigued by Jan's experience and interest in new opportunities and means for sharing music directly with listeners rather than going through the intermediary of Nashville record companies. He agrees to meet them the next day.

(162, 163, 164, 165)


## 1995 NASHVILLE, TN: NATASHA

PhD candidate Natasha Deane, her husband, and their two children moved to Nashville in part so she can work on her doctorate in microbiology and immunology at Vanderbilt University.

One afternoon she takes a break from the lab to browse around in a music store. When Natasha was an undergraduate, she became friends with a fellow student who was a "dulcimer evangelist" who wouldn't rest until he taught her to play the mountain dulcimer. She carried her dulcimer with her ever since. While walking through in the music store that afternoon she recognizes the instrument immediately when she sees a dulcimer for sale. She is so delighted at the sight of the beautiful instrument she tells her husband about it, and he surprises her with that dulcimer as a birthday gift.

Playing dulcimer music provides a nice alternative to the intensity of her work at the university. One day she notices an ad for a four-week Elder Hostel dulcimer class at Blair, every Saturday morning, to be taught by Professor David Schnaufer. Since it won't be a major time commitment, she signs up for the class.

When Natasha arrives for the first class, she notices twenty-or-so people waiting with their dulcimers for the professor.

Later that evening, Natasha explains to her husband what happened. "In the back of the room, the singer Cyndi Lauper and another woman with her were there, too! When David arrived, he played a bit, then told a little of the story of the dulcimer's history. Then, David introduced Cyndi Lauper to us and the two of them played some songs together. We were blown away!"

(166)

## 1995 HENDERSONVILLE, TN: CLEO AND JOE

On the coldest night of the year, David meets his two new friends at English Valley Studio. Inspired by David's description of the Melungeons, Cyndi and Jan begin with the dance tune "The Ballad of Cleo and Joe," a tip of the hat to those people who possess the courage to dress up to become whomever they want to be out on the town on Saturday nights. Jan and Cyndi approach the song as a kind of "Melungeon Stomp," and record David bowing on the music box to accompany the dance beat and provide a counterpoint to Cyndi's singing.

In the coming days, Jan and Cyndi also record "Fearless" with Cyndi's strummed dulcimer and delicate soprano on top of David's droning music box, a study in contrasts that works exquisitely to express the human motivations of fear and desire. The drone of the music box provides a kind of gravitas rarely heard in popular music.

When "Cleo and Joe" is released it will become a huge club hit. It will do its part to breathe new life into the Tennessee music box and enable it to sustain its reason for being: to sing out the earthy affirmation of its historic makers and players: *We were here, and we made music.*

(167, 168)

*David's Reading and Research Interests*

David was a voracious reader. While the dulcimer, its history and traditional music were his passions, his interests were widespread and his taste in music knew no bounds. He read and researched topics about marginalized people, explored other musicians' and musicologists takes on their work and society in books like *Notes on Tones* and *Noise*. He could be found almost every morning on the front porch of Bongo Java café on Belmont, reading the *New York Times* and sipping coffee. And when he wasn't reading, he was seeking out new as well as traditional music to listen to.

(169)

## 1995 NASHVILLE, TN: NATASHA

When David's four-week dulcimer class is finished, Natasha is beside herself with the prospect of losing dulcimer lesson time with David. She makes arrangements to take private lessons once a week at his new second floor apartment in an old house on Belmont Avenue.

One day as she climbs the stairs, she passes the Bill West painting next to a dulcimer made by West and reaches the door to the apartment just as musician Peter Frampton passes by her, holding his dulcimer. She looks at Frampton, then at David. "I never know who I'll see coming and going around you!" David just grins.

(170, 171)

*David and Alan Freeman at Frozen Sound Studio in West Virginia to record for David's demo record to take to Nashville. Courtesy of Kim Monday.*

*Demo sleeve for Rosie's Arms and Other Retreats. David's demo contained three original songs by David and one by David and Alan Friends Vince Farsetta, Frank Beall, studio owner Kim Monday, and drummer Rick Ravenscroft recorded for David as well.*

*Fellow Texas songwriter Johnny Mears became one of David's early Nashville friends along with Drew Ponder in 1984. Courtesy of Johnny Mears.*

*Vince wearing a halo to keep his neck immobile after falling from a scaffold during construction work. David would later wear a similar rig twice after each of two surgeries to repair an old neck injury sustained in a swimming accident. Neither Vince nor David let the halo get in the way of performing. Courtesy of Vince Farsetta.*

*David at the renowned Shreveport, Louisiana club Enoch's where he played solo and with Vince. Courtesy of Stan Carpenter, with thanks to Alan Dyson.*

*Joann and Herb McCullough with David out for a Nashville evening in the early eighties. Courtesy of Joann McCullough.*

*David with friend Toni Price who sang "Colors", the song that David wrote with two elementary school children through the Country Music Hall of Fame's educational program. Courtesy of John Lomax III.*

*David, producer and sound engineer Mark Miller and John Lomax III at Jack's
Tracks where they worked on Dulcimer Player, Dulcimer Deluxe, Dulcimer
Player Deluxe and Dulcimer Sessions. Courtesy of John Lomax III.*

*David laughing during the photo shoot for his second album with John Lomax.
Vince Farsetta designed this jacket that was David's favorite. Courtesy of the Estate
of Alan L. Mayor, photojournalist.*

*David sits on the floor in Vince's Nashville apartment playing "air banjo". David loved and admired Vince not only as a multi-talented and artistic friend, but as a multi-instrument virtuoso, songwriter, arranger, and part-time luthier. Courtesy of Vince Farsetta.*

*David with friend and luthier Moses Scrivenor. David holds the koa dulcimer that Moses made for him under David's guidance. Courtesy of Melanie Wells Lomax.*

*David working on an antique dulcimer at Moses's workbench. Courtesy of Vince Farsetta.*

*David and Bluesman Johnny Shines trade instruments for fun in this snapshot while both were on tour. Courtesy of John Lomax III.*

*David in San Francisco on tour as the opening act for the Everly Brothers. David took advantage of the opportunity to reconnect with Neal Hellman on this trip. Courtesy of Melanie Wells Lomax*

*Director Jim Brown directs David and Emmylou Harris on stage at the Ryman Auditorium for their performance in a 1989 Hank Williams special for television. Courtesy of John Lomax III.*

*Roscoe Russell jams with a young admirer. During David's 1990 East coast tour, Roscoe Russell was the father of Bonnie, the young girl whose music inspired David throughout his life. David and Nova Lomax took a side trip to visit the Russells in Galax. He once told his friend Nova, "I want my music to sound like Bonnie Russell's." Courtesy of Rick Freimuth.*

*David considered the invitation to Johnny and June Carter Cash's 1991 anniversary party one of the highlights of his life. The Cashes invited David, bluegrass legend Bill Monroe, singer Charley Pride, and guitarist Norman Blake to jam in their living room with them. Courtesy of John Lomax III.*

*John Lomax and the Cactus Brothers on the set of the 1992 film, "Pure Country." L to R: David Schnaufer, Tramp Lawing, Dave Kennedy, Paul Kirby, John Goleman, William Goleman, Sam Poland; In front of stage: John Lomax III. Courtesy of Houston Folk Music Archive/Rice University/Norie Guthrie and John Lomax III.*

*David loved the graphic art created by his long-time friend Mack White. The graphic artist designed the quirky "Billy the Id" logo and The Cactus Brothers Comix. Courtesy of Mack White.*

*David on the 1993 set of the music video shoot for the wildly popular "Fisher's Hornpipe" traditional fiddle tune. Courtesy of John Lomax III.*

*Twenty-year-old Stephen Seifert in 1993, first David's protégé and then quickly his partner and collaborator. Stephen holds his chromatic dulcimer on his lap during a visit with his parents to meet David. Courtesy of Nancy Seifert.*

*Cyndi Lauper, David and Jan Pulsford. Jan and David produced Delcimore at English Valley Music, Jan's studio, in Hendersonville a suburb of Nashville. Courtesy of Jan Pulsford.*

# MOVEMENT 6:
# TRANSITIONS

In creative work — creative work of all kinds—those who are the world's working artists are not trying to help the world go around, but forward.

—Mary Oliver, *Upstream: Selected Essays*

The best and only thing that one artist can do for another is to serve as an example and an inspiration.

—Steven Pressfield, *The War of Art*

# 1996 HENDERSONVILLE, TENNESSEE: NEW WAYS, NEW MEANS

David finds English Valley a stimulating place to work and learn. Jan Pulsford's tech saavy impresses him as she shares her thoughts on a recent phenomenon called "the internet." "It will open up everything for independent musicians and provide a new form of music compression via mp3 files. We can send these mp3s off without going through record companies to get our CDs pressed." David likes that idea just fine.

In between finishing his *Tennessee Music Box* CD with Jim, David and Jan meet to plan a new album. *Delcimore* will reflect his reverence for his instrument; he shares a story to illustrate how meaningful the word is to him:

> All the old-timers never called it a dulcimer. It was always 'delcimer' or 'delcimore'. Back in 1979 or so I went to Dublin, Virginia where they have the oldest fiddle contest in America, with a delcimore contest that's been going on since 1930. I won 5th place one year, and the ribbon [was printed with] Delcimore... and I came back the next year and won second place; they had changed [the ribbon name] to Dulcimer. And it broke my heart.

With David's love of history and dulcimers as the context for the album, Jan proposes that *Delcimore* be presented as if it were a field recording similar to those made by the early song catchers. The beginning can suggest a time long ago in the deep woods using traditional tracks like "Brush Arbor" and "Bonaparte's Retreat." From there, she imagines a walk up to the front porch where players sit and explore different music genres via the dulcimer—traditional, classical, jazz, and popular songs. They discuss going full circle at the end with a move from the front porch back to nature with David and Townes's 1987 song "Waltz of the Waters." David tells Jan the song is unfinished, so they put it on the backburner for now.

Later, he learns that Cyndi Lauper offered to sing his and Herb's "Twilight Eyes," so they add it to the track list. He gives Stephen Seifert a call; "Hey Steve, how would you like to play on an album with me?"

(1, 2, 3, 4)

## 1996 HENDERSONVILLE, TN: NIGEL PULSFORD

English Valley Music is an oasis of tranquility that draws in visitors. Jan's brother Nigel takes a break from touring with his British band, Bush, and heads to Hendersonville for a visit with his sister.

When David pops in one day, Jan introduces him to her brother. Nigel finds him very friendly; above all, David's voice captivates him. He makes a mental note to keep it in mind for future work.

(5)

## 1996 NASHVILLE, TN: CONCERTO

Nashville Chamber Orchestra (NCO) Conductor Paul Gambill approaches David with the idea of a concerto for dulcimer and strings. He commissions Conni Ellisor, a violinist with the NCO to compose the concerto with David's help, and he'd like David to perform as the featured artist. It is exactly the kind of cross-fertilization that Dean Mark Wait had envisioned when he took the leadership position at Blair: folk music meets classical music.

Ellisor knows almost nothing about the dulcimer or its canon of mountain music, so she begins by listening: David spends countless hours at her home playing live, traditional music for her to record to listen to for inspiration. He teaches her the history of the songs, answers her questions, and brainstorms ideas for the concerto's three movements.

When he plays the old Appalachian song, "Blackberry Blossom," something resonates. Conni asks David if he was familiar with Margaret Mead's autobiography, *Blackberry Winter*, the title being a farm term for the time of year when a sudden cold snap appears after the initial rising temperatures of spring. Mead chose *Blackberry Winter* as the title for her book because the late frost triggers the growth of lusher blackberries on the canes. Mead uses the metaphor of a blackberry winter for her life: the negativities of her early life became a source of drive and energy for her later world-wide success in anthropology. David remarks that Paul Gambill had originally called him to let him know he had secured a grant for developing the concerto a few months ago during the cold snap that triggered a late spring frost.

And with that, *Blackberry Winter*, will premiere in November of this year.

(6, 7, 8)

## 1996 NASHVILLE, TN: KINDRED SPIRITS

Jerome Henry Baldassari "knows how to pick the splinters out of a mandolin" as they say. As a teenager, he played guitar in rock bands but succumbed to the lure of the mandolin twenty-one years ago when he watched the supremely funny Bottle Hill Boys playing bluegrass tunes at the Philadelphia Folk Festival.

Nashville musicians, regardless of their chosen instrument, are a tight group. Because most have an insatiable curiosity about all genres of music, Baldassari knows the music of the Cactus Brothers. He was especially impressed by the versatility of their dulcimer player as he watched their "Fisher's Hornpipe" hootenanny on TNN; he could play both traditional and rock music as easily as he breathed.

David, too, is impressed more and more as he hears talk of Baldassari who had founded the Nashville Mandolin Ensemble. The well-known Ensemble's repertoire ranges from Bill Monroe's bluegrass to the music of Vivaldi and O'Carolan. David is also intrigued to learn that he has his own company, Sound Art Recordings, through which he has recorded dozens of albums including collections of Christmas, jazz, bluegrass, and classical music. David recognizes that Baldassari, like Mark O'Connor, is another kindred spirit: someone who explores relationships between different genres of music and likes to push boundaries.

Dean Wait hires Jerome, known by his friends as "Butch," to become the third professor of traditional folk music to join Mark O'Connor and David at Blair. Upon welcoming his new teaching colleague to their shared office, David and Butch exchange niceties and then pick up their instruments, sit down and play together. They start with the beautiful, "crooked" gem of a tune from West Virginia, "Wild Rose of the Mountain."

Butch is surprised to learn that David is not from West Virginia like he had assumed, given the traditional way he talks and looks. David laughs and tells him that growing up, he was a ding boy and surfer on the Texas Gulf Coast. When Butch shares that he had worked as a ski instructor and croupier in Las Vegas before turning to music, David is just as surprised. The more they talk, the more they discover the many things they have in common. Their easy laughter can be heard all the way down the hallway at Blair and all the way up to the Muse.

(9, 10, 11)

---

### A "Crooked Tune": Wild Rose of the Mountain

The standard format for American and European folk traditional tunes like jigs and reels consists of two eight bar sections that repeat for thirty-two bars total. The eight-bar length works well for tunes with a simple song structure. However, many tunes diverge from the standard: there maybe be five sections, or three sections, or no repetitions. Some tunes have asymmetrical parts, for example, the A part doesn't repeat, but the B part does, or there may be an odd number

---

of bars, or fractions of bars added or omitted. In others, there may be forty or forty-eight bars. Tunes with variations like these or others that are more unusual are called "crooked" tunes.

Like many of the American roots/tradition songs, "Wild Rose of the Mountain" started as a fiddle tune first popularized by Kentucky fiddler J. P. Fraley (1924–2011). When sung, the lyrics tell the story of a beautiful girl who strayed from one man to the next at local Kentucky dances.

(12)

## 1996 HENDERSONVILLE, TN: PUSHING ON

As Jan and David continue their work on *Delcimore*, she becomes aware that he is in a period of debilitating ill health. She watches as he frequently injects himself with insulin throughout the day to try to control the diabetes. To make matters worse, he expresses frustration with occasional loss of his finger dexterity as he plays. Nevertheless, he pushes on, summoning the effort to make this project meet his typical high standards.

(13)

## 1996 NASHVILLE, TN: SARAH ELIZABETH AT FIVE

By age five, Sarah Elizabeth's pleading has paid off; David agreed to take the kindergartner on as a student. Jennifer takes her to meet David once a week at his Blair office for lessons. Occasionally, when David goes to Jennifer's home to teach, there's always room for one more at her dinner table, so he accepts their invitation to stay for dinner. At other times, Jennifer drops Sarah off at his apartment down the street from Belmont University.

Sarah takes to the dulcimer like a fish to water; she loves her lessons and soon grows to love David. However, when she arrives back home, her mother has to ask her to run around and flap her arms to help get rid of the smell of David's cigarette smoke that permeates her clothing.

It bothers her that he smokes cigarettes. When she gets a little bit older, she will feel close enough to him to tell him—frequently—that he needs to quit.

(14, 15)

## 1996 NASHVILLE, TN: SARAH ELIZABETH AT SIX.

Sarah's dulcimer skills have grown enough that David and Jennifer decide she is ready to experience a dulcimer festival. He takes her with him to Illinois, and, for the first time, Sarah observes the crowd's reaction to him as a performance artist. Although only six, she begins to comprehend that there are two sides to David: the teacher whom she and her family know and love; the one who spends time with her and her mom for holiday picnics and dinners; and "The" David Schnaufer. She is very comfortable with the former, and only mildly interested in the latter.

(16, 17)

## 1996 NASHVILLE, TN: WORN OUT

Since his diabetes diagnosis, David has used strategies to help him in his battle with diabetes, and it always has been easier for him to cope when he's not touring. For exercise, he walks to Blair for his teaching sessions, regularly handing out coffee or a little breakfast to some of the homeless people he passes on his way. He does his best to eat low-glycemic foods and to drink light beer when socializing with friends.

Nevertheless, by October, he is worn out by the disease's physical toll on him. Several extreme flare-ups of diabetes make it almost impossible for him to function. Getting up in the morning, eating, answering his phone, and meeting his schedule are tasks that feel overwhelming. His voicemail box is crammed for weeks. His neck bothers him all the time; he feels his hands won't do what he wants them to do, and his mood is dark more often than not. By sheer force of his will, he does his best at English Valley to finish the recordings for *Delcimore*.

Finally, his diabetes completely out of control, he ends up in the hospital. It takes time, but eventually the treatment succeeds in lowering his blood sugar. Exhausted and discouraged, David calls Gena and explains what happened, desperate for some time away. "Do you mind if I spend some time with you in Texas, Gena?" Because of her work as an inpatient diabetes educator at her local hospital, Gena understands issues that affect blood sugar levels and is happy to help her cousin. It's a testimony to his exhaustion and his fear of the growing weakness in his arms and hands that he even asked.

He leaves Nashville for a visit that will turn into a two-month rest. Stephen agrees to teach David's classes at Blair as well as his private students until he returns.

(18, 19, 20, 21)

## 1996 NASHVILLE, TN: THE VIRTUES OF THE DULCIMER

The Nashville Chamber Orchestra has spent weeks rehearsing to perform for the world-premiere of *Blackberry Winter*. It will premiere in one week on November 30 at Blair. Early newspaper accounts highlight that the concerto was composed for David

Schnaufer, national mountain dulcimer champion, historian of the instrument, and faculty member at Blair.

During interviews on the approaching concerto, conductor Paul Gambill explains that the piece takes the form of the standard fast-slow-fast concerto, but Gambill hopes audiences will experience the surprise that unfolds with the unusual instrumentation presented by the mountain dulcimer and an antique Tennessee music box.

Also on the program for Saturday are performances of the Kodaly "Adagio for Cello and String Orchestra," featuring soloist David Hancock on the cello, and the "Introduction and Allegro" by Edward Elgar. David's friend and fellow faculty member John Johns will join the ensemble for a Vivaldi guitar concerto. This premier will realize a significant goal for Dean Mark Wait: his vision of a faculty that fearlessly crosses musical boundaries.

The day after the premiere, the newspaper reviews will be full of glowing praise. "The final piece highlights the virtues of the dulcimer with astounding clarity...The soloist's performance of the middle movement is riveting, and he is a lively colorist in the finale. The NCO also did their best work of the night here: lots of tricky passages navigated with barely a hitch, good dynamics, and a particularly fine approach to phrase in the second movement. The finale, especially the Copeland-esque transition to the final passages, is particularly rich, with a duet between the soloist and concertmaster standing out as a particularly ravishing piece of writing.

The evening before those postconcert reviews, David walked into the kitchen where Gena is preparing dinner. He pauses to lean in the doorway. She looks up at him. "Well, Gena, tonight's the night."

"For what?"

"In about forty-five minutes, Stephen will play the *Blackberry Winter* concerto at Blair."

(22, 23)

## 1996 NASHVILLE, TN: HAPPY BIRTHDAY, STEVE

When David had called Stephen to ask him to step in to teach his students at Blair before leaving for Texas, he also asked him to come over and see him at his apartment. When he arrived, David handed him a manila envelope with "Happy Birthday, love David" scrawled on it. As Stephen opened the envelope, he recognized the score for the concert. When David asked him to perform in his place as soloist. Stephen was stunned. Despite his own unquestionable musicianship and an earlier private wish that he, too, could perform such an important work, he was deeply unsure of himself as he contemplated the enormous implications of taking over as soloist. First, he had only a little over two months before the concerto's premier. He would have to drop out of Murfreesboro State to devote every waking moment to learn and practice the piece. For the first time in his life, he was scared out of his wits.

David, however, assured him he had no doubts about his ability to take his place in the concerto. They had toured across country together frequently, dazzling audiences with their playing.

The two sat down so Stephen could listen to David play sections of the challenging parts; he shared some final advice on the trickier parts of the performance and how to approach them. Finally, he handed him the keys to his apartment: "Stay at my place, work with Conni, and do whatever you need to do. I'm a phone call away if you have questions." And then, the next day, he was gone.

(24)

## 1996 NASHVILLE, TN: THE APPRENTICE

After getting over the initial shock that his dream of playing the concerto would now be a reality, Stephen got to work. He dropped out of Murfreesboro State and moved into David's apartment. At first, he felt a little like The Sorcerer's Apprentice, but, unlike

Goethe's 1797 apprentice, Stephen would have a different outcome; instead of making a mess, he studied the music, thought about the musical directions within the concerto, practiced long hours, and created when necessary. Between day-long practice sessions, he pored through his neatly filed tabs and photographs. He went to his favorite places to eat and to Bongo Java down the street to have coffee every morning like David did. He became a regular at Hillsboro's Villager Tavern to hang out with David's friends, bombarding them with questions, all in hopes of tapping into David's spirit to help him live up to the task ahead of him.

Conni already knew of David's decisions on the essence and direction that would work for the concerto. She lent all of David's work on cassette tapes to Stephen for him to rerecord in digital format. He spent hours listening over and over to each track to discern the themes and flow of the music. Conni gave him the freedom to be creative since she had unfinished parts that were intended for David to improvise.

David had incorporated the classic walk-down segment from the tune, *Blackberry Blossom* in the first movement of the concerto; Stephen already knew it because David was teaching it in workshops. He also knew the traditional tune, "Ruben's Train", also referenced in the first movement; it would be supported by the violins. But he struggled for weeks on the second movement with its opening with the bowing of the Tennessee music box. The box was finicky when it came to staying in tune. Compared to his McSpadden dulcimers, it was very temperamental, so he spent much of his time learning to bow the box.

The third movement was in roughest form. David and Ellisor had tossed around the idea of incorporating an electric dulcimer, but hadn't made a decision. Stephen wasn't ready to play an electric dulcimer, and that suited Conni. For Stephen, the third movement was the biggest challenge and required the most effort.

Despite the doubts he had about himself beforehand, those post-debut reviews on his performance reveal to Stephen just how far he had traveled since the Cincinnati dulcimer lady had handed him a cardboard dulcimer to try out.

(25)

## 1996 FORT STOCKTON, TEXAS: "YOU DO NOT MASTER A MUSICAL INSTRUMENT."

Fort Stockton is a small town in far West Texas region of the Chihuahuan Desert. When David arrives, he is exhausted. He settles in at Gena's and gradually begins to unwind as he finally gets a chance to rest.

He spends his days walking around the flat, open landscape of the rural desert town. He tells Gena that walking helps him write music. "Modern day music follows the rhythm of cars and machines," he tells her. He prefers to write music to the rhythm of walking; it enables him to feel the "sound" of the ground beneath him. One day he goes on a rant about an expression that particularly bothers him: "mastering a musical instrument." "You do not master a musical instrument," he insists. You learn from it. If anything, it masters you!"

(26)

## 1996 FORT STOCKTON, TEXAS: "IT'S HARD ... TO PUT THE WORDS TOGETHER"

During an evening out at a restaurant, David injects himself with insulin while he and Gena wait for their dinner. When the server stops by to inform them that the dinner had to be delayed, they sit and wait some more. Then, Gena notices him looking around somewhat anxiously.

"Gina, I wish I could have some orange juice," he finally tells her, looking distressed.

"David! Why didn't you say anything?"

"I've tried to explain this to you before; when your brain doesn't have any sugar, you can't figure out how to explain what's going on. It's hard for me to put the words together."

(27)

## 1996 FORT STOCKTON, TEXAS: FAMILY REUNION

David doesn't like it that Gena is worried all the time for him. She can't help it; he told her once about his drummer friend who was diabetic and collapsed one day; the paramedics arrived and learned he was diabetic. They assumed he had high blood sugar, so they mistakenly gave him insulin; they didn't test him first to know that he really needed glucagon, so he died.

David is grateful for the time away from the stress of Nashville. He knows what he needs to do to attempt to control the diabetes, but thanks to Gena's health orientation, he finds it easier to take care of himself with her company than he does in Nashville. They have a lot of catching up to do as he settles into the quiet life of the desert. However, he continues to be vexed about having to be hospitalized for his diabetes and the length of time it took the medical staff to get his blood sugar under control. "I have no idea why it happened," he tells her. "What had gone wrong?" After musing on his question, he continues.

"It all started with the chiggers; my blood sugar got out of control after I got bit by the chiggers."

Gena is a bit confused. "What do you mean?"

Well, I was really worried about the skin on my feet, so I went to the pharmacist, and he gave me cortisone cream and I put it all over my feet and legs."

Gena becomes alarmed. She checks the PDR to see what, if any, contraindications are associated with cortisone use by diabetics.

"David, look at this: Cortisone completely cancels out the effect of insulin, and if you put it on a large part of your body and cover it up with an occlusive dressing, which you did with a pair of long socks, the cortisone is absorbed in."

Gena looks at him, seeing the epiphany cross his face.

"That's what caused it! I should have never blamed it on the chiggers—it wasn't their fault! They were just being chiggers!" he exclaims, remorseful for blaming the tiny insects.

As the days pass and they settle into an easy routine, the cousins talk often. One day, David asks her about a handmade clay pot with a slightly tilted, angled opening that sits in the bedroom where he sleeps. She explains it was made by Mexico's Tarahumara indigenous people, and she had bought it as a gift for a friend.

"You should get one for yourself, Gena; the quality of the sound within that pot when I walk past it is impressive."

Gena stops short; how does he pick up sound coming from that pot? She doesn't hear a thing when she walks past it. Nevertheless, she isn't surprised that he does; she trusts his hearing is more sophisticated than her own. She recalls an experience that involved an expensive violin her family inherited from her aunt who was a classical violinist. She and a friend took it to a pro fiddler in Houston, and after he finished a performance they asked him to play her family violin to see what he thought about it. He agreed, picked it up, and played it. After a minute or so, he stopped abruptly and handed it back to her. "There has been a lot of classical music played on this violin, and I just can't handle it. I'm sorry."

They both agree: musical instruments are built to move sound through resonating chambers. Instruments have a life to them; indeed, we are bathed in sound. Later, he tells her about his dream of the Tennessee music box from Lawrenceburg that he bought the day after the dream. "When I played that antique dulcimer," he tells her, "I could hear all the old music of the past inside it."

"Well David, that's pretty important; I think you should tell people that."

"No, Gena, you can't just come out and tell people things like that 'cause they'll think you're crazy."

Gena doesn't think he's crazy or imagining things. She has her own sensitivities to the world around her similar to the way David does with sound and music. For Gena, it seems logical that instruments hold those sounds within them and that someone highly sensitive to sound—like the fiddler, like David—might pick up on that. To Gena, David has learned how to tune in to a larger part of reality.

Thanks to his time in Fort Stockton, his diabetes is finally under better control. However, his physical problems aren't over. Gena is the one of the very few he feels comfortable with talking about his worries over his health, and he talks with her about the chronic pain he feels in his neck. She offers to buy him a neck brace, but he declines. While Gena and her son take holiday visit with her parents, David stays behind.

Worried and without health insurance, he has always put off going to doctors unless it was an emergency. When Gena and his nephew return, David meets them at the airport to tell Gena that he has a reservation for the next flight to Nashville. His arm has become numb, and he needs to get to a doctor.

(27, 28, 29, 30, 31)

## 1996 NASHVILLE, TN: LOOKING FOR RELIEF

The painful consequences of David's teenage dive accident wouldn't bother him much until he left La Marque, but gradually his neck problems had become apparent to anyone who had spent significant time around him. For years, the chronic pain manifested itself in limited neck mobility that prohibited him from turning his head without turning his whole body toward the direction he wished to look.

As soon as David arrives in Nashville from his stay in Fort Stockton, he heads to the emergency room. To David's shock, the doctor shows him his x-ray to point out where his neck is broken. He undergoes surgery in which the surgeon takes a bone plug from his hip to repair the break in his vertebrae. After surgery he assures

Gena he feels much better with respect to his neck; his hip, however, hurts from the excision of the bone plug.

Echoing his buddy Vince's experience, after his neck surgery David has to wear a metal halo screwed into his head to keep it from moving. He doesn't care what it looks like; he wears it everywhere, even during gigs. He and his buddies laugh about it; he calls it his "cage."

After months of wearing the halo, his doctor removes it. Afterward he notices he has more range of motion in his neck, but not as much as he had hoped. Gradually, the numbness in his arms and hands will creep back. In the meantime, he confides to Vince that he has to reteach himself how to play.

(32, 33, 34, 35)

## 1996 NASHVILLE, TN: TIM BRYAN

Like his Louisiana buddy Steve Stubblefield, twenty-seven-year-old Tim Bryan had also played the college clubs in Ruston, Louisiana. Tim and his bandmate Mike Dickinson had been part of the punk rock scene with their band, the Habitual Sex Offenders, a name designed to grab attention (and one that belied their inner goodness). The music scene in Ruston was a tight one; everyone knew everybody else, and the Habitual Sex Offenders often bumped into Steve Stubblefield's Roadside Monuments on the gig circuit. Gradually, Tim, Mike and Steve would become longtime friends.

Tim's band had broken up recently. Upon hearing the news, Steve encourages Tim to move to Nashville; the bass guitar player had quit his college band. "C'mon up, you can room with me to save money, and work with us in the studio." Steve already had full drums and a keyboard player and wants Tim to take over bass so he can focus on composing, arranging, recording, mixing, and producing.

Tim takes him up on his offer. Next—like every other broke musician—he has to find a day job to pay his living expenses. It doesn't take long; he gets hired as a cook at the Pancake Pantry, a popular eatery in the Hillsboro Village neighborhood where everyone from politicians to businessmen to musicians eat breakfast. The job works for him; the Pantry closes by 3 p.m., thus leaving the rest of the day open for music. He's looking forward to working with the Steve's innovative band. Influenced by the British psychedelic music scene, they strive to explore the potential effects of dynamics within a recording studio setting to answer questions such as, "What effect does playing loudly have on listeners? Softly, gently, abrasively? What happens when we experiment with echo and reverb?" They are good enough that the indie Matador Records out of New York had thrown them enough money to produce an album, *Analog Cabin*.

After work at the pantry, Tim usually strolls the short walk across the street to the Villager Tavern to sip a beer before heading home. The Villager's owner Henry Piarrot calls the tiny but venerable bar his home for a "classless society", welcoming to every social class of people: Belmont and Vanderbilt grads and professors rub elbows with neighborhood old-timers, blue-collar workers and the well known and less known in the music business. No one minds the dive atmosphere with its grungy, dim light and the faint smell of stale beer and cigarettes; it has its own charm. The walls, covered from floor to ceiling with patron snapshots confirm the Villager is a popular gathering place, and it's for many reasons, not the least of which is the consensus that newcomers who behave themselves are quickly folded into the Villager "family" of regulars. It also doesn't hurt that they serve the best Po' Boy sandwiches in Nashville. The two-room joint supplies plenty of comic relief, too. Foosball players squeeze in so tightly around the table in the seven-foot-wide space between the short side of the L-shaped bar and the front wall that they're literally back to back with patrons perched on the barstools. Serious league-caliber dart players gather for throwing marathons that take place in the back room on Tuesday and Thursday nights; nonplayers needing to follow nature's call gingerly navigate their way to the back restrooms. Players throwing darts shout "walk behi-iiiiiind" to remind them to stay behind the throw line (the competitors' only worry: interruption of the game.) Piarrot stocks the jukebox hanging on the wall with current CDs, including those of his patrons who feel special when they hear their music making its way down the tiny, narrow interior to the back room. Bartenders Kevin and Donna have a soft spot in their hearts for broke musicians; if they know you, they don't mind the occasional haggle over price of a sandwich.

For the afternoon patrons, the Villager provides a quiet place to wind down after work before the evening crowd arrives. Tim is usually the first person in the door when the tavern opens up in the afternoon, and notices that a long-haired, Amish-looking dude usually arrives shortly after him. Like Tim, he always sits at the long end of the bar and always orders a beer.

For several months the two men sit next to each other on the stools without speaking.

One day, as Tim stands up to leave, he turns toward David: "Well, so long; nice not talking to you." David leans back as he swivels toward Tim and bursts out laughing. In the days and weeks ahead the two begin to talk regularly about anything and everything that piques their interest. Despite their seventeen-year age difference and widely different musical backgrounds, they discover they have a lot in common. Like David, Tim was a surfer as a teenager, and even has a necklace with a shell pendant that he wears to remind him of times on the beach in Florida. The two share a love of music and a reverence for nature; in Tim's case, he explains that his interests come from his Cherokee maternal grandfather. David surprises him when he comments that he knows exactly where Tim's mother's family comes from in Virginia. David has done research on the Cherokee and admires the way they honor the natural world, including even "the ground they walk on."

The two friends meet five or six afternoons a week at the Villager for a beer or two to swap stories and jokes and discuss music or current events during their hour together. Tim looks forward to talking with this guy David very much. He doesn't remember he had once seen him with the Cactus Brothers, nor does he know who David Schnaufer is or what he does. Tim quickly learns that David prefers to listen to others' stories, dreams and plans. He rarely talks about himself.

(36, 37, 38-39)

## 1997 SMYRNA, TN: "NEVER AGAIN SHALL I RAMBLE ...."

On January 1, at age fifty-two and on the fifty-fourth anniversary of Hank Williams's death, John Townes Van Zandt packs up all his unique, impressive talents as he bids farewell to a lifetime of mental torment, tragic addictions, and ill-made decisions.

Many of his friends knew him as someone who often joked about death; it was always on his mind, and he often brought it up in conversation. Van Zandt's last show in Austin took place at Luneberg's popular Cactus Café. Despite the success of his shows, Luneberg was pissed off with Van Zandt after his gig because he knew he was dying from too many drugs, too much drinking, and just not caring to live any more. "Townes," he asked him at that time, "you have so much to share with the world. You have so much to give. Why are you waiting around to die?" Townes looked at him and replied, "I just can't do it anymore."

About a year before Townes passed away, Nova Lomax visited Van Zandt. The two men were reminiscing about old times and special friends. The subject of David came up. "David's a musical cat," said Townes, "one of the most musical people I've ever met." Lomax will later write about their conversation. "Townes's praise was always hard-won, and he seldom co-wrote songs, especially toward the end of his career, but he made exceptions in Schnaufer's case. Their joint effort 'Waltz of the Waters' ... was one of Van Zandt's last compositions."

After Van Zandt's death, David describes Townes as "the rarest of poet musicians that shared the water of his soul from a very deep well." David, like so many others, recognizes the genius of Townes as a "songwriter's songwriter," and he feels deeply about his death. The fact that Townes died so young, however, does not surprise him. He, too, occasionally half-jokes with close friends that he won't make it much past fifty, given his physical problems. Just like his brother Eric, he always believed he would have a shorter life, given their parents' and extended family's endless health problems and untimely deaths.

(40, 41, 42, 43, 44)

## 1997 NASHVILLE, TN: A PAINFUL SNUB

The Nashville Chamber Orchestra preserves *Blackberry Winter* for posterity by recording with Warner Bros. with Stephen reprising his role as dulcimer soloist. David's name is nowhere on the score, nor will it be on the front or back of the resulting CD when it is released in 2006.

(45)

## 1997 HENDERSONVILLE, TENNESSEE: THE MINGUS CHALLENGE

Jan's brother Nigel crossed the pond again, this time to stay with Jan for six months to relax and work with her on one of her projects related to the work of Charles Mingus, the great American jazz bassist and composer. Jan is working with Mingus's daughter Caroline Keikki to explore ways to incorporate hip-hop into the jazz educational programs offered by her family's "Let My Children Hear Music" program.

When David arrives the conversations turn to ways to utilize dulcimer music. Nigel and David propose that Mingus's challenging piece, "Self Portrait in Three Colors" could be the perfect vehicle to meld dulcimer music and jazz. David begins work on it, but when the Mingus program falls through, Nigel suggests they use it on *Delcimore*.

The two men visit often, usually sitting on the back porch facing into the picturesque woods. There, they drink coffee, smoke cigarettes, and chat. Nigel had been around rock musicians most of his career, but David is someone different. They talk about their respective times in California when David was touring with the Cactus Brothers and Nigel was working there; about the past, present, and future of music in general and more specifically about the dulcimer. Nigel is transported by David's slow, meticulous drawl as he recounts the history of the music box and the stories of the people who played them since the earliest settlers arrived in Appalachia. "His is the kind of voice that makes the listener want to ask more questions just to hear him talk," he tells Jan. He likes David's authenticity, an attribute that Nigel, coming from the UK, finds fresh and impressive.

Once the final decision has been made, Nigel agrees to produce the Mingus piece for *Delcimore*. The complex "Self-Portrait in Three Colors" weaves three different melody lines that are meant to be played simultaneously: David will play one, Stephen Seifert, the other, and Nigel flies in a Ukrainian musician named Alex Federiouk ,who plays a cymbolon to play the third. Nigel will play the guitar on the song. One of Nigel and David's most important goals in this recording is to ensure they capture the sound of the two mountain dulcimers to distinguish them from the sound of the guitar. By the time they finish, all collaborators agree that David and Stephen's long, hard work on the track have turned it into something special, another dulcimer boundary pushed further away.

(46, 47, 48. 49, 50, 51)

---

*Charles Mingus and "Self-Portrait in Three Colors"*

Charles Mingus (1922–1979) was an African-American jazz double bassist, pianist, composer and bandleader, is consid-

---

ered one of the most important American composers of the twentieth century.

Mingus's autobiography begins with the phrase, "In other words, I am three", a metaphor for a man who stands forever in the middle, "unconcerned, unmoved ...waiting to be allowed to express what he sees to the other two." The second man within his persona is frightened, and attacks for fear of being attacked. The third aspect of his persona is"... an over-loving gentle person who lets people into the uttermost sacred temple of his being and he'll take insults and ... sign contracts without reading them and get talked down to working cheap or for nothing, and when he realizes what's been done to him he feels like killing and destroying everything around him including himself for being so stupid. But he can't—he goes back inside himself."

Understanding "Self-Portrait in Three Colors" begins with this understanding of Mingus, the three men within him, and their perpetual negotiation with each other to perform as one. Mingus's third persona resonates the most with David. During this period of his life, he was feeling more worn than usual as a result of the constantly recurring health-related battles, his long struggles to earn a living, and his frustration with the commercial music business. The snub he feels for not having been listed as a co-composer on *Blackberry Winter* still fiercely stings.

Once he became emancipated at age seventeen, David made up his mind that he would choose joy as his path in life. However, his intermittent depression forced him to retreat, and, at times, disappoint his friends. Most don't know the troubles inside, but everyone always forgives him as the bright, shining spirit in their lives.

David and Stephen worked six weeks to get the Mingus piece right, taking several days to work through just the first measures of the song. For David, the inclusion of a such a challenging jazz piece on this album continues his personal musical journey into broadening his skills and his repertoire. And Mingus won't be his last attempt to do so.

(52, 53, 54 55, 56)

## 1997 ANTIOCH, TN: "TINA IS IN GOLD..."

Cyndi Lauper opens for Tina Turner on her current tour, and on the evening of June 6, they appear at the Starwood Theater in Antioch, a suburb of Nashville. Cyndi gives David a call, inviting him to perform a song with her. After they perform, David stands in the wings and watches Tina as she heads toward stage. Later, he'll tell an interviewer at WPLN Nashville Public Radio the story of what happened.

> ... Tina is in gold, looking good, she's up those stairs, she's fixing to take that left onto the stage, and my music box is kind of sticking out over the drum case, and I'm down below looking and I see her right hip brush against that music box, and she stopped, turned around, put her arms akimbo and looked like, 'What is that?' She turned around and hit the stage, and I thought, 'That box was made in 1870 and has just had its finest moment!

(57, 58)

## 1998 HENDERSONVILLE, TN: GOOD VIBRATIONS

David has always felt deeply close to nature, whether during the rides on the waves in Galveston when he was a teen, or with his feeling of kinship to the trees that yielded their wood for the dulcimers and the music boxes. One day out at English Valley, he becomes fascinated by the drone of the thirteen-year cicadas just emerging in the surrounding woods.

For some, the cacophony of sound and the abundance of cicadas flying in the air and landing on anything and everything will be a nightmare. When Jan's six-year-old son Merlyn points out, "They sound like a giant rain stick!" Jan and David look at each other and smile for the opportunity that nature just provided. Jan tells sound engineer Neal Merrick to grab the mics, and they run outside to spend the rest of the afternoon recording the incessant vibrations of the insects' buzzing drones in their search for mates.

Back in the studio, Jan lays on the cicada drones at the beginning of the first track, "Brush Arbor" and at the end of the finished "Waltz of the Waters." Now, all tracks are nested within the rhythmic drone of nature, just as they had planned.

(59, 60, 61)

## 1998 HENDERSONVILLE, TN: "DAVID MAKES THE TRACK COME ALIVE...."

Nigel has been working in the studio on his own project at the same time David and Jan were working on *Delcimore*. He asks David to perform the music box for one of his tracks, "Deep in the Water," for his first solo album, *Heavenly Toast on Paradise Road*. Because David's voice intrigues him so much, he also asks him to recite a text Nigel had written for a one minute, fifty-second spoken word piece for the track entitled, "Love is Dying While Washing is Drying." A stark text about his regret over the push and pull of a troubled woman, David's monologue is accompanied by the sound of a tinny piano and punctuated by the jaw harp. "David makes the track come alive," Nigel tells Jan. The recitation will plant a seed for another collaborative first with Jan, which will take place in two short years.

(62, 63)

## 1998 NASHVILLE, TN: THE NASHVILLE QUARTET

David's work at Blair alongside his classical music counterparts has engendered another dream that he wants to turn into reality. He invites four of his students to form a dulcimer-based string quartet. He promises to work closely with them as he had done with Mountain Laurel and provide them with four-part arrangements of different genres of music: traditional mountain music, of course, but also hymns, classical music, Irish music, and anything else they wish.

Natasha, Linda, Lee, and Sandy agree to form the ensemble group, in part to take the skills they've learned to the next level but also for the opportunity to work closely with their mentor. Natasha and Linda started as his students, Sandy has worked as David's assistant for years, and Lee comes to the group as an already-seasoned player.

For Lee especially, the opportunity to work with David means his playing has come full circle. He will describe to an interviewer, "I first saw David in the 'Fisher's Hornpipe' video on TNN." His hunt for his name led him to a record store where he had to order the *Dulcimer Player Deluxe* CD. "The clerk had no idea who I was talking about. She called her supplier and the look on her face was priceless...she is going, 'Really—really—REALLY!' And she hangs up and says, "Do you know he is on tour with the Everly Brothers?" "Yes, I want his CD. So I got the CD, and I took it home, and it was incredible....It was such an inspiration. It completely changed the way I play dulcimer; it changed the way I think about the dulcimer."

As fast as David creates music arrangements for them, the four soak them up. He will meet Tuesday evenings with them at Natasha's house. Many of his arrangements are the classic country favorites, either standalone ones such as "Whiskey Before Breakfast" or as medleys he creates. Inspired by their mentor, and drawing on their long-honed talent, soon they are performing at festivals and other public gigs across the country. They appear on Nashville Public Radio's "Live in Studio C" program, in concert at the Blair School of Music, at the Kentucky Theater, and in many other venues. They work hard to develop their skills with David's guidance and encouragement, and it shows. By 2002, David will produce their first CD, *Four-Part Inventions*. He could not be more proud of them.

(64, 65, 66))


## 1998 NASHVILLE, TN: GUESS WHO SITS NEXT TO ME

Steve Stubblefield's spring graduation at Belmont coincides with the breakup of his Methadone Actors band just when Matador Records had put money on the table to sign the group. The Actor's drummer, a brand-new Belmont student, devout Christian, and younger than the rest of the band, didn't quite know how to handle his older bandmates and their creative pursuits, so he quit. Steve tried to find another player, but when the drummer quit, it was over.

To earn some money. Steve gets a job as a grill cook with Tim at the Pancake Pantry. Their daily routine is to work from 6 a.m. to 3 p.m. flipping pancakes and hamburgers on the flattop grills. Tim, tired of the daily grind and missing music, eventually tells Steven he came to Nashville to be a musician, not a cook, so he's leaving to return to Louisiana. Steve understands; they both agree that working at the Pantry is like getting their asses kicked every day.

Once Tim is gone, Steve also heads over to the Villager after work to have a beer with friends. They play video golf and listen to the old regulars sit and tell stories. One of the quieter regulars is a guy named David. As Steve and David get to know each other, Steve starts looking for David every day after work. A few months pass, when one day, while studying the wall in front of him covered from bottom to top with photographs and music memorabilia, his eyes land on a 1986 "Dulcimer Extraordinaire" poster hanging on the wall near the ceiling that he never noticed before. It reads "David Schnaufer in Concert." He suddenly realizes the identity of the guy he has been sitting next to for the last six months.

(67, 68)

## 1998 NASHVILLE, TN: MY ZEN BUDDHIST FRIEND

To say Steven experienced an unexpected surprise when he found out who his friend was would be an understatement. Back in Louisiana, Steve's grandfather had bought a McSpadden dulcimer kit for him when he was seven; once they put it together, Steve broke every string on it pretending to be Eddie Van Halen. When he was a teenager, his mother often played a cassette tape of *Dulcimer Player Deluxe*.

As Steven and David get to know one another, David learns about his history in Louisiana, his engineering work at Belmont, and his love of songwriting. One of their favorite things to do is to sit around and talk about song ideas; they sit every afternoon at the bar brainstorming and jotting down the best ideas on their "Villager Tavern notebooks," cocktail napkins they carefully fold and pocket to save for later inspiration. One afternoon, another regular approaches them with one of his own song ideas; to David's great amusement, Steve turns it into a tune for him, "It Rained So Hard the Croppy Ate the Corn." When another patron reveals his frustration with the lack of respect for his Confederate ancestor, owner Piarrot writes a set of lyrics he titles "Crackers," later meeting David at his apartment so the two of them can collaborate on the music for their friend. Once they started talking dulcimers, David tells Steve he had undertaken the dulcimer initially to help him write songs. "You ought to try it Steve." David offers to get him started with a couple of lessons, and Steven takes him up on the offer.

Over time, their talks deepen, Steven likes that David thinks about complex topics but expresses himself in simple ways; he describes him to his other friends as a guy with a "Zen Buddhist mentality." He finds himself opening up to David and asking him for advice. Once, when he explains his anguish over breaking up with his girlfriend, David empathizes, sharing his own feelings regarding a recent breakup. "Aren't you upset?" "No, Steve, he drawls…I'm not the marrying type," David smiles. Steven decides, "Maybe I'm not either."

(69, 70)

## 1998 NASHVILLE, TN: DO IT YOURSELF

Largely due to his admiration of David, Steve Stubblefield decides to learn to play the dulcimer. He uses his tax refund to buy the Walnut McSpadden teardrop dulcimer that David had used on *Delcimore*. Their weekly lessons quickly turn into weekly jam sessions, and David soon considers Steve a fellow songwriter and musician rather than his student.

The two friends share a certain disillusionment with the music business. David admires Steve's do-it-yourself attitude that is implicit in all his work. Occasionally, their discussions turn to Music Row down the road where demos are made in multimillion-dollar studios. David and Steve are already experimenting with making records on a four-track in Steve's dark basement apartment in Hillsboro village; they both enjoy the experience of going back to the basics.

Whenever David tells him how good he is, Steven appreciates it, but he never believes it's all just him. Instead, he calls the work a "collaboration with the song fairies" who trust him to stay out of the way and gift him with some truly beautiful words and melodies; he is merely their vehicle.

David and Steven will shape each other's thinking as they continue to jam weekly; their playing leads them to do what both like to do best: keep traditions while pushing boundaries.

(71, 72)


## 1999 NASHVILLE, TN: THE GRAND OLD DULCIMER CLUB

For a while, several of David's longtime friends including Wanda O'Guin, Mary Lawrence, Carolyn Wick, Zada Law, Sandy, Marilyn Konriff and several others have talked about meeting together to socialize, play music, learn new songs, and share tips for playing. For a year now, the group has met informally, usually on the third Sunday of each month, for a get-together they call "Dulcimer Sundays." David attends as often as he can to play with them. Their playing always goes up several notches when he is there leading the group.

Starting in January of this year, members discuss that it's time to create a more formal club. Organized by Sandy, the structure is loose and open; everyone at any skill level is welcome. Anyone who wants to play with any acoustic musical instrument is also welcome. No dues will be collected, and they'll keep the third Sunday of the month as a meeting time to help people to remember the date. Carolyn and her husband Don volunteer to coordinate gigs for the Club, including their first at the McKendree Senior Living Center. The youngest in attendance is Sarah Elizabeth, now almost eight.

Despite the lack of official structure, Club members divvy up to volunteer for jobs to keep the Club going. One member volunteers to start a club newsletter, another to write profiles of members so they can get to know one another. Zada writes the first profile for the newsletter, highlighting Wanda O'Guin, one of David's favorites. ("*He loves her tremolo!*") Everyone agrees to chip in postage money to have the newsletters sent to their homes.

At the February meeting, members brainstorm a name for the club. Options include Music City Dulcimer Club, Dulce Vita, Cumberland Dulcimer Club and several others. Mary Lawrence suggests "The Grand Ole Dulcimer Club", and, by March, with a slight change from "ole" to "old", members vote it the favorite. The Grand Old Dulcimer Club is now official.

The Club's songs appear every month in the new newsletter. The old Carter family song, "Wildwood Flower," "Angelina the Baker" (by Stephen Foster), "Grey Cat on a Tennessee Farm," "Bile Them Cabbage," and "Amazing Grace" are among the dozen songs posted in the first newsletter. "Tennessee Waltz", also on the list, is the most modern song, written in 1946.

By March, members begin planning for a dulcimer-centered festival, a first in Nashville. If all goes well, David hopes it will become an annual festival maximizing the dulcimer's exposure so more people will consider learning to play. Sponsored by Metro Parks, the Blair School of Music, and the Grand Old Dulcimer Club, "Dulcimer Day" will take place in June on the grounds of the Historic Two Rivers Mansion in Nashville.

( 73, 74, 75, 76, 77, 78)

## 1999 HURON, TN: DAN AND MARY

Professors Dan Pfeifer and Mary Nichols at Middle Tennessee State University (MTSU) enter the dulcimer world for the first time after a friend invites them to attend a unique gathering at Ellis Truett's home. Truett, one of the first collectors to appreciate the cultural significance of Tennessee music boxes, hosts a quarterly gathering of acoustic music friends. This weekend, some seventy-five people have made their way to Truett's home for one of the most intensive and exciting playing many of them will ever experience. After initial greetings and invitations to help themselves to a refreshment and have a bowl of the community stew, players fan out to play in his house, on the lawn, and within a schoolhouse replica Truett built on his farm. Both pro and amateur musicians jam together, spark connections, and learn bits of history.

Before joining the faculty at MTSU, Dan worked in the music industry as a sound engineer and producer on the road and in the studio. Mary is a documentarian with expertise in video and photography. When they heard about the unusual nature of Truett's gathering, they were intrigued. Mary grabbed an 8mm camera on her way out the door.

When they arrive, Dan and Mary are astonished. Ellis' house is like a musical museum filled with instruments and books and now packed with people playing acoustic instruments everywhere. Dan, a musician himself on piano and tuba, is captivated with the authenticity of the sounds. They hit it off with Ellis immediately. When Mary laments that she has no music experience and wishes she could play along, Ellis walks to another room and returns to present her with a handmade dulcimer. "If you can play a song on this before you leave; you can take this home." He introduces her to Lucille Parker who teaches her to play "Little Liza Jane." The next morning she plays it for Ellis, and he is good to his word: "Okay, it's yours!"

Dan and Mary leave that experience with a passion to document what they had just experienced. Mary will ultimately produce two documentaries featuring players from that night, *School House Sessions I* and *School House Sessions II* with funds from MTSU, the Tennessee Arts Council, and monies she had received when a grant proposal was approved. They also left that night intrigued with learning to play the Truett dulcimer. Mary works at it, tapping into Dan's knowledge of music so much so that he decided to learn to play it, too. That day at Truett's will lead them right to David's door.

(79, 80, 81, 82)

# 1999 CHARLESTON, WEST VIRGINIA: DAVE HAAS CAPTURES MAGIC

Dave Haas has played the dulcimer for six years; he had found a good teacher in fellow club member Bob Webb who has invited David Schnaufer to their club this April day for a workshop and follow-up concert.

Dave knows plenty about David Schnaufer's teaching. He took classes from David at the annual week-long Mountain Dulcimer University in Boone, North Carolina. A year later he attended a prefestival workshop taught by David in Winfield, Kansas. Dave is bubbling with anticipation for the visit.

The workshop takes place in the basement of Christ Church in downtown Charleston. Sixteen members of Dave's club file into the church basement to attend the morning and afternoon sessions. Their goal is to learn David's techniques for playing smoothly and creatively on the dulcimer. They work hard on the song "Elk River Blues" in the morning. After a lunch break, David leads them through "My Pretty Quadrille" in the afternoon. David's position has always been, "learn the melody, learn the chords, then add techniques to move beyond playing a song the same way three times in a row."

With the workshops over, it is time to move upstairs for the evening concert. A sudden storm threatens to cancel the event, especially when the power goes out. But David is unperturbed and wants to perform, despite having worked all day. There are no lights, no microphones nor amplifiers. Just David, several dulcimers and a Tennessee music box, with an audience of eighty people who have gathered to listen to him perform.

Haas brought his video camera to record the performance so he can study it at home and asks David if he would mind if he videotaped the concert. "Sure, Dave, that's perfectly fine" he replies. It's a decision that will turn out to be an extraordinary stroke of luck for David Schnaufer's legacy, although neither realizes it at the time.

Dave, in a front row center seat and just six feet away from his idol, sets up his video camera and locks it onto its tripod. Fortunately, the lack of lights doesn't matter; he records a compelling hour and a half long concert of David playing some of his favorite instruments and chatting easily with the audience, a close-up, priceless historic videotape of a genius at work.

(83)

---

### Dave Haas on the Schnaufer Teaching Style

In 2008, ten years after the original recording of David's concert, Dave Haas asked friend Bob Webb to digitized his high-8 mm tape of the recording. Bob did improve the sound by evening out the ambient noises—such as audience clapping—to match the sound level of David's talking and playing. Despite the lack of lighting and without the distracting jump cuts that often interfere with concert watching, the resulting digital DVD is perhaps the clearest and best-sounding extensive amateur video ever taken of David Schnaufer performing in front of a live audience. David's unique look, personality, and style of playing are exceptionally easy to see for those who never experienced him playing live.

After retiring in 2020 as a chemistry teacher, Dave Haas has devoted his time to performing as a musician, workshop teacher, composer, and writer. He has fond, vivid memories of David's teaching style. "The way he strummed and his right hand techniques had a big influence on me. He used a lot of two finger chords, and taught me to move the melody around the fretboard, from the melody line to the bass and then to the upper octave. I still teach that way. He inspired me to stretch myself."

Because he had been a professional educator, Dave was always keenly aware of David's teaching techniques while taking his classes. "David had a lot of patience with people, and a laid-back personality. He knew how to make everyone feel successful. There are always plenty of mistakes when first

---

learning a song, but he never criticized. Instead, he would respond in a slow drawl, 'Well, that's all right, we'll do it again.' Students never worried about being intimidated because he was patient, kind, encouraging and accepting of people."

Eleven years after his friend digitized Dave's tape, it made its way to a mutual friend named Debbie Porter. She used it as a fundraiser for her "Dulcimers for David" program in Texas.

Dave Haas still uses a similar approach to teaching that he learned from David Schnaufer years ago.

To learn more about Dave Haas and/or order a DVD of the Schnaufer concert, visit his website at *https://www.dave-haasmusic.com/*

(84)

## 1999 WINFIELD, KANSAS: DOUG THOMASON'S BANJO-MER

California luthier Doug Thomson has spent the last twenty-two years developing and refining his "Banjo-mer," an instrument first inspired by the Bacon and Day banjo he saw long ago in a music store. The hybrid instrument's combined elements of both the mountain dulcimer and the banjo allow the ease of learning the dulcimer with the sound of the banjo. His signature sound-hole design is a star.

Doug attends Winfield every other year to perform and man a booth to sell his instruments. He had never met David before, but he was well aware of his reputation. When he learned David would be here this year, he decided to make a Banjo-mer for him. Doug studied the cover of the CD *Dulcimer Player Deluxe* and noticed the half-moon sound holes, so made the hybrid instrument with that sound hole design rather than the usual star-shapes.

David and Stephen Siefert will play concerts ever day of the festival in one of the big barns that also housed the vendors. After each concert, David sells his CDs and talks to people, so Doug watches and waits for the opportunity to approach him, hoping to make a sale. Doug introduces himself and presents the Banjo-mer. David looks at it, curious. He notices that it looks very similar to a dulcimer, but has a smallish, round, Remo banjo head in place of the strum hollow on a traditional dulcimer.

"Wow, this is unusual ...."

Doug explains, "It just has the three strings, without the dual treble strings that many dulcimers have since they don't work as well with a banjo sound. So, it sounds like a banjo, but it's easier to play. It opens up a whole new way of playing. People can play it in any tuning, but my preference is D-A-D."

Given the one octave distance between the bass and the treble string, he notes "it allows a player to get a banjo-like sound: you pluck the top, then strum, and come in on the treble string with your thumb. And it sounds like the old-time banjo frailing style that way; it gives you that nice octave when you pick, mimicking the octave that the fifth string of the banjo gives you."

David listens. When he picks it up and starts to play it, a big smile grows on his face, "This is great, I could get into this!"

"I made this one with the half-moons, thought you might like that."

"No, no, I like the stars like on yours!" David replies. "I want to order a Banjo-mer with the star sound holes, Doug. But I owe everybody money right now, so I can't pay you until a little later."

"Don't worry about that, I'll make you one and we'll settle up later."

After a long talk together, Doug is so struck by David's warmth and friendliness, he decides then and there to invite him to come out to the next "Claremont Spring Folk Festival." Doug is co-director and tells him, "We'll pay you and put you up at a hotel; would you do a workshop and perform?"

"Well, I'd love that Doug," and the two plan to meet again next May in California. Doug promises to send him his custom-built Banjo-mer by January at the latest.

(85)

## 1999 NASHVILLE, TN: JONI BISHOP

The obituary reads: "Master fiddler Randy Howard, winner of more than 300 instrumental competitions, died Tuesday at his home in Nashville. He was 38."

As is often the case in the musician community, Howard's peers plan a musical celebration for his family at the Station Inn. When David's friend Joni mentions to him that she plans to attend the benefit, he tells her he'll be there, too. She is surprised; lately, much to her concern, David has seemed ill and weak.

The evening of the memorial concert, Joni watches David with concern. However, the minute he starts playing, he is transformed. A thought occurs to her: As long as he is making music, he's back with all his own energy.

(86, 87)

## 1999 RUSTON, LOUISIANA: "NO PRESSURE AT ALL!"

One Friday afternoon—Tim Bryan, back in Louisiana—gets a call from David;

"You need to come back right now; you and Steve are going to start a new band and I'll help. We need you to come back; you're gonna be the bowman on a dulcimer."

Tim can't believe what he's hearing. "Are you kidding me?" David had sworn to Tim many times he'd never play in a band again.

"You know I've never played a dulcimer a day in my life, nor do I know a lick of bluegrass."

"C'mon back; it's just for fun, no pressure at all."

Finally, Tim relents, mostly because of "Uncle Dave's" involvement. "All right; cool man, give me a month to close things up here and I'll be back."

(88)

## 1999 COLUMBUS, GEORGIA: BLACKBERRY WINTER REDUX

The first time David was in Columbus, it was to stand up to his brother Eric's wedding. Now he is back, this time as a soloist for the Columbus Georgia Symphony's performance of *Blackberry Winter* at the Three Arts Theater. Stephen Seifert will play the first and third movement with David bowing his beloved nineteenth-century Tennessee music box in the second.

(89)

## 1999 GREENVILLE, SOUTH CAROLINA: A SELF-ACTUALIZED MAN

In December, a newspaper profile appears of the man whom his admirers call a "seeker." He has worked with everyone from the top people in his field to the humblest. He feels strongly about social justice, civil rights, feminism, and he is against war. His friends consider him an open-minded leader. He finds the divine in art, music, the theater, reading and nature to nourish his soul. He loves the ocean. During a reflective moment, he admits to the reporter that he has an exaggerated sense of responsibility, and sometimes becomes captive to it. Admirers consider him a mentor but someone who never pulls rank; "it would never occur to him," says one.

Eric Schnaufer's profile is published after fourteen years of hard work as rector of St. Peter's Episcopal Church in Greenville. Despite having mostly parted ways after the troubles of their La Marque youth, Eric and his brother still mistakenly believe that they have little in common.

(90)

## 2000 NASHVILLE, TN: STUMPING THE MASTER

With Tim Bryan back in Nashville, he and Steve Stubblefield join David for a weekly Friday afternoon dulcimer "lesson" at David's apartment. They use the term "lesson" loosely; their meetings include moments of teaching from time to time, but Tim and Steve are skilled musicians and therefore quick studies on the dulcimer. Mostly, the three jam two or three hours every Friday, then head to the Villager to talk about practice over a beer.

Tim takes additional lessons on learning to bow. Each week David cues Tim to play by asking him, "What did you work on this week, Tim?" Tim plays, and David then jumps in to accompany him.

Occasionally, Tim likes messing with David. He creates novel songs with bits and pieces of traditional music to challenge him when he starts to play along. It's tough though; David is so good he can jump right in anywhere and start playing.

Eventually, the day Tim has been waiting for arrives. Tim sits down on the chair in front of David and starts playing a crooked song of his own arrangement. His rearrangement is full of time signature changes popping in and out. David bemused, just sits and listens as Tim plays.

"Nope; can't do it. Can't do it. Not even trying."

"Yes!!!"

Later, Tim laughs as he tells Steve the story of finally stumping the master. "It was my crowning achievement in life!"

Steve and Tim talk about David all the time. They decide that he wants to play with them because he's a natural teacher; he has two musicians who are buddies and are hungry to learn whatever he teaches them. But more than anything else, they believe he's ready to do something different. Some of their Villager discussions revealed that he feels pigeonholed into doing festivals and playing the same songs he has played for years. Nashville music had already begun to change yet again thanks to Garth Brooks's astonishing success with "New Country" during the last decade. David treasures the traditional yet longs to break out of the traditional chrysalis that contains him to stretch himself. Like the old timers' spirits inhabiting the instruments they left behind, he, too, wants people to hear his music. But he doesn't want to do it the slick way that has taken over Nashville. He wants to do it his own way.

(91)

## Garth Brooks Brings It On: New Country

While David may have grown to disdain aspects of the commercial music business, living in Nashville meant that he was well aware of the latest changing of the guard as the younger generation of songwriters, singers, and musicians made themselves known, most prominently by Garth Brooks who led the style of music referred to as New Country through the 1990s.

New Country's heritage was an amalgam of traditional country music and sounds of rock bands playing to stadium-sized crowds along with influences from gospel and R&B. Brooks introduced aggressive vocal performances, more prominent drums, and electric guitar solos. The homespun feel of the country music stage is gone. His performances were characterized by his energetic movements on stage and pyrotechnics that had become commonplace with the rock bands of the previous decade. Other performers, including a new generation of women, were making waves as well. Country music began to bear little resemblance to its humble, rural roots typified by the Appalachian dulcimer canon.

(92, 93)

## 2000 NASHVILLE, TN: SARAH ELIZABETH AT NINE.

Always mature for her age, Sarah takes in everything she sees and hears, and she thinks and feels deeply. She loves the ease with which David has become part of her family. Her great-grandmother loves him, and he even played for her at her eightieth birthday. She feels touched that he saves all the Christmas cards from her grandmother. David is so quietly attentive to her young cousin who was diagnosed with autism that the two get along beautifully. Her family throws a party for David's birthday at their home every year, and they always bake him his favorite chocolate cake to celebrate. Not because he is a celebrity; it's because he feels like a member of their family. He has taken her with him to perform in Nashville and at several festivals, and frequently shares his pride of her with his many friends.

Jennifer has raised Sarah Elizabeth with a marked respect for her intellect; the two often share their observations and feelings about the people whom they know and love.

But Sarah Elizabeth and David don't talk about those subjects. They play together. Song, after song, after song. And this year, as a result of their work, he takes her to Chattanooga, where she wins the first Tennessee Mountain Dulcimer championship.

(94, 95, 96)

Ever since Doug Thomas sent him his Banjo-mer, David has included playing it as part of his performances. And, wherever he plays it, Doug gets at least one order for a Banjo-mer.

When David arrives in Claremont for the Spring Music Festival and settles in, he and Doug have a talk.

"David, after you went to two festivals, I sold four Banjo-mers. I don't want to charge you anything for your instrument, but, I wonder if you would consider instead writing an agreement that I can use your pictures and your music on the Banjo-mer in exchange for the one I made you? I don't want to infringe on your rights".

"You can use whatever you want Doug, it's yours to use," David replies, and sits down to hand write their agreement: in exchange for the Banjo-mer, Doug can use photos from the festival, his music, and a recording for a CD Doug plans.

At the Claremont festival, David plays Banjo-mer on stage for an audience of two thousand attendees. The excitement is palpable; everyone loves it. From now on, everywhere David goes to perform, people will call Doug to tell him, "I saw David playing one of these—I want one!" The agreement paid for itself, Doug says.

David often called Doug after a festival. "Hey Doug, good buddy, I'm playing your Banjo-mer everywhere and a lot of people are copying you, but let me tell you, yours is still top of the wood-pile!"

(97)


## 2000 NASHVILLE, TN: TWO MORE JOIN THE CLUB

Georgia Hobb first heard dulcimer music at a festival she attended and loved the sound so much she bought one from a luthier who had a booth there. It stayed under her bed for two or three years.

One day her good friend Jane asked, "When are you going to learn to play that thing?" Georgia laughs. "When I can find a good teacher."

Soon, she reads a notice in the paper about something called the "Grand Old Dulcimer Day." A few days later, she pulls into the grounds of the historic Two Rivers Mansion on Saturday morning.

Much to David's delight, the festival "Dulcimer Day" was such a success last year that it looks like it will become the annual festival he hoped for. This year, with support from the Board of Parks and Recreation and Blair, the festival continues the tradition of providing all-day performances, educating the public about its history and music via hands-on workshops, displays of vintage instruments including the Tennessee Music Box, and small-group demonstrations. In addition, informal jamming and sing-a-longs with Tennessee musicians dot the grounds.

Georgia wanders throughout the park-like setting when she arrives, enjoying the educational table and listening to the music from small jams occurring everywhere. Toward the end of the day, she makes her way over to the main stage to see a man wearing blue jeans, a shirt buttoned up the neck, suspenders and wearing a straw hat. His performance on the dulcimer stuns her. She thinks to herself, "If I could ever play like that, I'd love it."

When the applause dies down after his performance, the man announces, "And by the way, I'm teaching classes over at Vanderbilt and you're welcome any time;" He adds, "It doesn't cost as much as the regular classes because they're meant for everyone, not just the Vanderbilt students."

Georgia learns his name is David Schnaufer, and signs up for lessons. After the first one she is enthralled and tells all her friends about it.

A friend from her bridge club named Lela calls her after hearing of her recent lessons.

"Georgia, I have a wooden psaltry I bought at a craft fair at Centennial Park. I bought it on a whim because the man playing one at the booth where they were selling them was making such beautiful music. I asked him, "Is that hard to play?" "Oh, no; it's very easy" he told me. And I, like a sucker, bought one!" she laughs.

"Lela, why don't you take it to David ... he'll know what to do with it."

Lela likes the idea so she makes an appointment to see him at Blair. David plays a bit on the psaltry, then shares his opinion. "You'll never be able to keep this in tune; it's not built right." Lela looks at him and smiles. "Well, then, get me a dulcimer." David smiles right back.

(98, 99)

## 2000 LOUISVILLE, KENTUCKY: DAN EVANS

Dan Evans, England's premier fingerstyle dulcimer player, first heard David Schnaufer last year on a CD while he stayed with a Florida couple during his US tour.

The second time he encounters David, the two meet in person during this year's Kentucky Music Week. Nancy Barker invited Dan to teach and perform for the festival. Being very new, Dan doesn't know anybody, is unsure of where rooms are located and how things work. He finds his way to the library of the college where a lunch buffet is provided for the instructors. He selects pizza and a drink at the buffet and then looks for a seat, but all are taken. He finally finds an empty table and sits down alone. David appears, and asks, "Hey, Dan, welcome to Kentucky! Do you mind if I set with you?" Dan, who knows David's legendary status in the dulcimer world, feels the question should have been the other way around. "What a gent," he thinks as he pulls up a chair for David, and the two spend some quality time sharing stories.

The third time Dan encounters David is at the end-of-festival concert performed by the instructors. Dan selects Roger Nicholson's "Spring Season" for his short performance piece and is well received. After he takes his bow, and on the way back to his seat, he passes by the one everyone has nicknamed "the professor." David, smiling and applauding enthusiastically, tells him, "Excellent!"

"Praise from Caesar indeed," thinks Dan to himself smiling warmly back.

(100)

## Dan Evans, David, and Roger Nicholson

David certainly recognized "Spring Sessions" when Dan performed it. Nicholson's recordings were some of the first David listened to, studied, and attempted to play back in 1973 after buying his dulcimer. "I tried to show all the different styles and sounds you can get with the instrument," Nicholson once said. His skills ranged from the baroque to more traditional, drone-based pieces. He became an authority on musical modes and had great understanding of the roots of music and in Eastern influences. Dan Evans writes, "His original (mock) Elizabethan compositions and transcriptions of ancient lute tunes have yet to be surpassed on the dulcimer."

"I was hugely influenced (and still am) by Roger's dulcimer work," says Dan. Evans has built a career as a world-class musician and composer on both the mountain dulcimer and acoustic guitar. On tour in 2018, he appeared in concert at Vanderbilt University's Blair School of Music as a soloist, and with Stephen Seifert in the second half of the concert.

If you would like to learn more about Dan Evans, visit this renowned musician, composer and producer at his website, "*https://www.english-dulcimer.com/* where you can also watch the full concert at Blair's beautiful Turner Hall.

After Roger Nicholson passed away in 2009, Dan Evans rightly accepted the mantle as England's premier dulcimer musician.

(101, 102, 103, 104, 105)

Growing up on a farm, Rocky Alvey not only learned farming but also how to be an engineer. Like most farm families, his had to be able to take apart, build, or repair anything on the farm whether structural, electric, hydraulic or mechanical. Rocky learned by doing: building grain bins, barns, machine sheds; he could modify tractors and water systems ... he learned it all.

When he was young, he spent many an evening alone or with his friends camping out next to a little pond on the hill behind his house, gazing at the night sky. One night, a bright shiny light crossing above caught the friends' attention. Later, they learned it was a satellite, and Rocky was hooked. For the rest of his life, he wanted to contemplate the stars and see as far as he could into infinity. In seventh grade, he sold so many *Grit* newspapers in town on the weekends in pursuit of the sales prize, he won: it was a telescope.

Rocky grew up, got married and had kids. During his family's child rearing years, money was tight, so he couldn't buy the kind of telescope he wanted. He had the mechanical skills and the knowledge of telescope anatomy by then, so he built one and continued to pursue his passion to explore the cosmos.

Thanks to his lifelong interest in astronomy and his expertise in the technological side of the field, Vanderbilt University hires him this year to supervise their Dyer Observatory. Located in Brentwood, one of the most beautiful places in Nashville, Dyer is surrounded by Radnor Lake and by forest.

Once hired, Rocky learns that Dyer has become somewhat of a white elephant for Vanderbilt after NASA's launch of the Hubble Space Telescope into low-earth orbit ten years ago. Suddenly, Hubble became one of NASA's most vital tools for space exploration and a publicity boon for astronomy. The growing internet and new software development resulted in a flurry of building new observatories much larger than Dyer across the globe. Vanderbilt astronomers could no longer do the kind of research at Dyer that could be done with the newer, larger, and more sophisticated telescopes being built.

Rocky savors the ability to peer into the night sky through the Dyer telescope and thinks long and hard about ways to ensure the observatory's future. For the next two years, he will work as one of the key figures in the ongoing discussions regarding a new purpose and identity for the observatory he has grown to love.

During his time off from work, he partakes in another pastime he enjoys. He writes little songs and records them on a cassette recorder, just for his own enjoyment.

(106, 107)

## 2000 MITCHELL, INDIANA: A MIGHTY FINE DRESS

David heads to Mitchell to headline the annual gathering at Spring Mill Festival for concerts, dulcimer workshops, lessons, and jam sessions all day long. The festival concludes with an evening concert from 7 to 10 p.m. He's looking forward to seeing his old friend Nancy Barker, the director of Kentucky Music Week, who is there to appear with her Kentucky Standard Band.

During a break they finally meet to catch up with each other. As they stand talking, a woman in her mid-thirties walks up to David in a cape and dress made out of fabric covered in David's photos. She carries her matching bag of the same fabric. Clearly excited by this chance to meet him, she gushes, "David! David! What do you think of my dress?" as she smiles from ear to ear and twirls for him. David, always polite, tells her "Why, that's mighty fine!" and chats with her a few minutes.

When the fan finally leaves them alone again, he turns toward Nancy.

"Nancy Lou, what would you do with something like that? I can't wrap my head around it!"

"I can't imagine," Nancy replies, struck once again by how grace-fully David handled the encounter, giving his fan some of the rare time he had available that day without a single complaint.

(108)

## 2000 NASHVILLE, TN: *LEAPER'S FORK* AND *UNCLE DULCIMER* SESSIONS

David's connection with them is all the fuel Tim Bryan and Steve Stubblefield need to launch their new band, Starlings, TN, a name they chose not as a reference to birds, but to beings from the greater universe. Soon they are gigging all over Nashville with mutual gui-tarist friend T.J. Larkin and other friends who drop in from time to time, including David. He began as their instructor but serves more as their coach and collaborator for writing, arranging, and record-ing music that pushes boundaries forward.

One night Tim and Steve overhear David break out singing "The Way You Move the Air" to himself. As a result, Steve starts bugging David to do his own vocal album. David had sung occasionally but considered himself a songwriter and musician first. He was always a little self-conscious about his voice, so he says he'll think about it.

As the Starlings develop under David's influence, Tim and Steve—the latter having once loathed traditional country music—find themselves expanding their repertoire; they keep aspects of their beloved psychedelic rock but now look to work toward some-thing new while incorporating their own preferred roots. They study country music by Bill Monroe, the Stanley Brothers, the Del-more Brothers; banjoist Dock Boggs, and bluesman Charley Patton all rolled in to one, "with Appalachia as a backdrop."

They regularly record their works on a four-track cassette recorder, sometimes at Tim's, at other times in Steven's basement apartment in Nashville. They share their recordings with "Uncle Dave" while still pressing him to start that new vocal album of his own. The authenticity of their songs resonates within him. "Dang,

Steve, I want to sound just like that. But I don't want to do any of that fancy, ping-pong, track recording. Everything has to be done in four tracks."

The Starlings work one afternoon a week, recording songs they will turn into their first album, *Leaper's Fork*, dedicating the album to "All those who have looked for, found, and lost love; thanks for taking that leap." David works on arrangements with Steve, Tim, and T.J. Larkin to help them meld traditional songs with the band's own, unique style, pushing musical boundaries yet again: "Grey Cat on a Tennessee Farm," "Red Rocking Chair," "Nothing but the Blood of Jesus" and their own rollicking, kitchen-table version of "Whiskey Before Breakfast," a song David recorded some twenty years ago on his and Alan's first cassette, *Hogfiddler's Fancy*. Whenever they ask, he plays dulcimer, Tennessee music box, Banjo-mer, and jaw harp on to support them.

Of all the songs on *Leaper's Fork*, Tim and Steve consider their cover of "Sarah" as one of their finest, as do their fans when they perform it in public. Written by David and Herb McCullough in David's early years in Nashville, the Starlings' version slows it down and turns it into a captivating, swinging jazzy piece, perhaps even more memorable than the original.

At the same time they work on their own recordings, Steve and Tim record tracks for David after he finally relented to Steven's urging: he agrees to sing on eight of the ten songs that will appear on his self-produced, *Uncle Dulcimer*, a term of affection bestowed upon him by his friend Zada's little niece.

Steve will say in retrospect, "What I love most about David: he is as genuinely into us and our work as we are into him. Nothing seems to stop him, and he's not ever afraid to cross boundaries to try something new."

Yet, for some time now beginning with his work on *Delcimore*, Jan Pulsford, Tim and Steve along with and other friends have noticed an increase in David's "bad days." During recording for *Uncle Dulcimer*. David pushes on, despite the intense physical pain in his neck yet again. During the last song they record, "Spotted Pony," he can barely play the Banjo-mer through the song. For the first time, the guys witness him fumble through several spots. Steve asks him, "Do you want me to recut it?" "Nope," he replies, "it's going to live the way it is with the imperfection." People closest to him note his increasing withdrawals to his apartment. He occasionally misses prearranged get-togethers with friends like Sarah and her Mom and even an occasional performance, sometimes apologizing profusely afterward; at other times, he reappears as if nothing untoward had happened.

When he and the Starlings finish their recordings for their respective albums, David disappears yet again, later telling Gena he had to undergo a second surgery on his neck. This time, they inserted a titanium rod to help alleviate the excruciating pain.

( 109, 110, 111, 112)


## 2000 NEW ORLEANS, LOUISIANA: A TIP OF THE HAT TO AN OLD FRIEND

It had been years since Leo Kretzner had thought about his visit long ago with David beside the creek at the Antioch Nature Center. By the end of the seventies, he had traveled and performed a great deal but had gradually left public performing behind him as he turned toward his work as a research biologist. The last time Leo saw David in person was at his Cactus Brothers gig in Seattle.

This year he'll attend the annual Mardi Gras Dulcimer Festival in Louisiana. He first watches Karen Mueller perform and is blown away by her playing. David and Stephen Seifert follow. When the two mount the stage, Leo leans back in his chair at the back of the room to listen, the sheer enjoyment washing over him. The music triggers old memories, taking him back to the time when he and David first met back in the seventies when they were young. There was Rabbit Junction, and the time with Al Freeman and David at the reservoir that summer of 1981, and at the many festivals they attended over the years of the Dulcimer Boom.

Leo suddenly snaps out of his thoughts when he realizes that the music has stopped, and everyone is looking at him.

"You know, I want to say it's really good to see Leo Kretzner out and about again," says David into the mic, looking at him with a big smile.

"I first met Leo when I visited him at an outdoor education center back in the seventies ... I remember him showing me the hawks and owls in the clinic they had there; they were pretty impressive. He had a beautiful red-tailed hawk named Haki that you could pet on his chest. That day was when Leo showed me how to play in D-A-D and across the strings, and I want to thank him for that."

Leo is deeply moved by this unexpected compliment from his well-traveled, longtime friend.

(113, 114)

## 2000 PULASKI, TENNESSEE

David is on a mission. He and T.J. Larkin are driving to Pulaski to examine an old dulcimer owned by a man named Lawrence Gamble for what David considers his biggest and most important project of his career: he wants to build a multimedia archive of historic dulcimers and music boxes that includes their photos, their provenance and the music played on them. He understands the importance of work like this to museums and universities and the urgency involved. Time is short; each year that passes, another old-timer musician who has one foot in the now and one in the past will pass away, taking the stories and music with him or her. For the instruments, some will be lucky enough to be passed down in the family; others will be lost forever.

David's blue car is packed with his mono Marantz field recorder, a small camera and a gooseneck light, flashlights, tape measures and notebooks for recording dimensions, and an SM50 microphone. Looking at the pile packed inside his rickety car, he laughs "Look at all this, T.J.! This is how you win a Grammy!"

T.J. finds David's visual literacy for old instruments fascinating. For many years now his interest in the works of early song catchers and musicologists like Cecil Sharp, John Lomax I, and his son Alan have become his own. He also admires the work of instrument historians like Ralph Lee Smith, Keith Young's old friend from Annandale, Virginia. By combining his two interests in one project, he continues and expands the scope of documenting and cataloguing the instruments, collecting information on the backstory of each instrument and their current and previous owners, and the music they played.

Like an experienced archeologist, David can pick up an old dulcimer or music box for the first time and explore it for clues to learn its history and folk context. Most instrument makers in the nineteenth and early twentieth centuries were not luthiers but backyard craftsmen or woodworkers of various skill levels who fashioned the instrument at home. Wood choice, body shape, body dimensions, sound-hole designs, and traces of paint tell him about the region and sometimes even the county where the instrument was birthed. String wear reveals how often the instrument was played, whether it was strummed with a plectrum or with fingers. Minute traces of rosin in the cracks of the old wood are a clue that reveals the instrument was bowed. Old frets yield their secrets, too. Usually made of fence wire or staples, under David's gaze the number of frets, placement, and wear reveal the instrument's region of origin. Consistently even wear along the edge of the fretboard tells him the owner used a noter. David would explain to T.J. that on this instrument, this song was possible, and somebody played it this way. A hundred miles away, they did it differently.

While searching for dulcimer people in the hills and hollows of Appalachia, David was not only interested in the instruments themselves and songs but was equally dedicated to recording the oral histories of the instrument's owners over time. T.J., his partner in this project, considers the details about old songs incredible. David counts on T.J.'s engineering and recording skills along with his facility with technology to preserve the music they collect.

When they arrive at Gamble's, David and Lawrence greet each other warmly; T.J. is struck by how easily David makes small talk: the southern politeness takes over, and Gamble welcomes them both. T.J. has a sense he's experiencing something very special that very few outsiders will ever see or know about.

The old man considers David a friend he can trust after having met him once before on an earlier fieldwork visit. In fact, to David's surprise and delight, he found an old poplar music box lying on a woodpile in Gamble's barn during that last visit; Gamble agreed to sell it to him. On this visit, he assesses and documents everything in his notebook about Gamble's dulcimer before another surprise.

"You know, David, I got an old record of me playing that thing from way back."

David and T.J.'s eyes widen as they look first at Gamble, then at each other and smile.

"Well, any chance you have it handy? If you like, we could play it and record it for you today so T.J. here can preserve your music for you on a CD. We'll bring your record back and a CD for you next month so you can hear yourself play again."

Mrs. Gamble disappears for a minute, then returns with a small, fragile acetate disk. He and T.J. examine it, and David concludes, "This is one of those we're only going to get one chance to play; it's liable to crumble after we play it, so we have to do it right." Gamble gives them permission to borrow the disk to take to T.J.'s home studio. That evening he gently places the rare disk on the turntable, hits "record," and sets the needle upon the disk to release the sound that had been locked in long ago. T.J. is mesmerized by what he hears.

(115)

## 2000 NASHVILLE, TN: A WORTHY ROAD

When English Valley Music releases *Delcimore*, thoughtful students of David Schnaufer's music could wonder at both the personal and the professional trajectory he laid down since his 1983 recording of *Hogfiddler's Fancy* with Alan Freeman.

It has been only seventeen years since Alan and David parted ways. He chooses the music to play now and decides who will produce his work.

One of his admirers believes that the most significant aspect of his personal journey is happening now. He has traveled from apprentice to professional to generous mentor and teacher, not only of the hardest-working and most gifted of players but with scores of newcomers who are intrigued by his opinion that anyone can play this simplest of instruments if they want to make music. His generosity is well-known among his thousands of fans at festivals around the country and by his Nashville students, many of whom play in the Grand Old Dulcimer Club.

In his forty-eighth year, by sheer force of his will to learn, create, perform, nurture, teach and befriend, he always seems to manage to bounce back from his constant struggles with ill health. His friends are so used to it that they believe he'll be around forever.

*David with his tiny protégé and musical prodigy Sarah Elizabeth during her first public performance with him in the late nineties. Courtesy of Sarah McWhirt-Toler.*

*Steve Stubblefield and Tim Bryan, musicians in their own right, started out as David's students and ended up as friends, and collaborators. David mentored the two as they began the Starlings, TN band and occasionally joined the band in jams and for performances and recordings. Photo courtesy of Kelly Love.*

*A glimpse of David's 2001 Performance at Kentucky Music Weekend at Louisville's
Iroquois Amphitheater. Courtesy of Nancy Barker.*

*David and Sarah in performance at the Blair School of Music, Vanderbilt
University in 2001. Courtesy of Sarah McWhirt-Toler.*

*David and Mary Carty met through Nancy Barker at Kentucky Music Weekend.
David loved Mary's boys and admired her many crafting skills, especially her
basketmaking. Nancy asked Mary to make sure David got the proper meal for
diabetics during her festivals. Courtesy of Mary Carty.*

*Page from a birthday scrapbook that Sarah Elizabeth made for David for his 50th
birthday. She poses between David and Jean Ritchie at the Dulcimer Chautauqua
Festival in New Harmony, Indiana. Courtesy of Sarah McWhirt Toler.*

The honor
of
your presence
is requested
at
the wedding
of
Sarah Elisabeth
on
a date
to be announced
approximately
fifteen years from today


Music to be provided
by
David Schnaufer, dulcimer

March Down to Old Tennessee
Sarah

First Dance:  My Tennessee Valentine

*Although only twelve, Sarah enclosed an invitation in David's 50th birthday scrapbook in which she invites him to perform at her "future wedding" in fifteen years. Sadly, he would not live to see her marry.. Courtesy of Sarah McWhirt-Toler.*

*David's 2004 Letter to the Editor of Dulcimer Players News: Despite twenty-eight years of awards and accolades, David never rested on his laurels. Besides being a voracious reader, he continued to grow his understanding of music across genres and time by exploring the past as well as pushing boundaries for the future. Courtesy of Dulcimer Players News/Ashley Ernst.*

*David cracks up with Stephen Seifert as they perform "Black Mountain Rag" at the Augusta Heritage Center in Elkins, West Virginia. Courtesy of the Augusta Heritage Center.*

*A shot from the Pfeiffer/Nichols educational documentary, Stories and Songs of the Tennessee Music Box. Decades after Cecil Sharp, Olive Campbell and John Lomax III's grandfather John Avery traveled the United States as song catchers, David picked up the mantle. He worked with T.J. Larkin and others for years to collect, document and analyze old dulcimers and Tennessee music boxes and record the music of these rapidly disappearing instruments for posterity. David and T.J. were still constructing their online archive when David passed away. Courtesy of Mary Nichols.*

*Only in Music City! The 2006 "Dulci-marathon": For several years, David and many of his friends and members of the Grand Old Dulcimer Club played their dulcimers on the sidewalk to cheer Nashville Marathon runners on Belmont Boulevard. Courtesy of Kelly Love.*

*T.J. Larkin and David jamming on the porch of the Belmont house where David had a tiny third floor apartment in 2006. Courtesy of Kelly Love.*

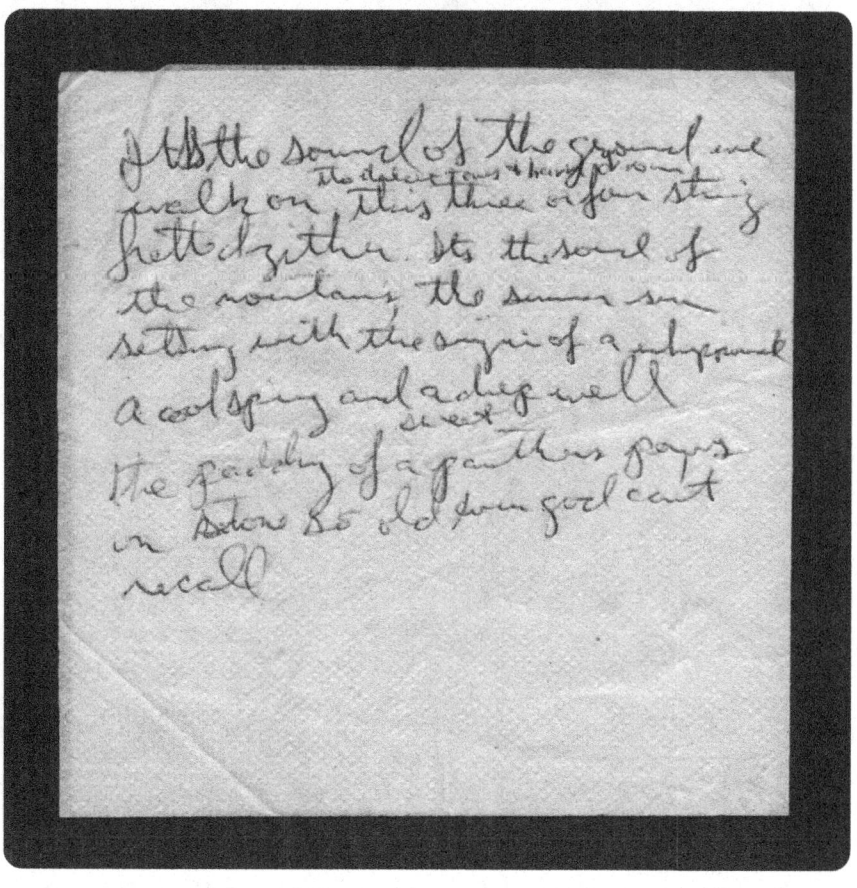

*One of twenty-nine "Villager Notebooks" that were found and saved after David passed away.
David would jot down thoughts, song ideas and word-plays on cocktail napkins whenever he
was at one of his favorite watering holes and carefully tuck them away in his pocket for later
inspiration. This poetic note reads: Its the sound of the ground we walk on this three or four
string fretted zither. Its the sound of the mountains, the summer sun setting with the singin of a
whippoorwill A cool spring and a (sweet) deep well the padding of a panthers paws on the stone
so old even god can't recall. Courtesy of Vanderbilt University/Special Collections and Archives.*

*Dulcimer Quartet member Linda Sack poses with her mentor and friend: "Itinerant musician" describes him; he traveled a lot and lived day to day financially. The car he drove was a gift to him by a friend. He lived simply. He only had a few outfits, the dulcimers on his wall, and his cases, and a twin bed in an efficiency apartment. He would sit on the floor. There was not a disingenuous bone in his body. He had integrity, He made me feel safe. He would fight for what was important to him. He never sold out. He didn't kowtow to anyone. He was the most grounded person whom I knew. He was not a big man—all of this was his spirit.*
*Courtesy of Linda Sack.*

# MOVEMENT 7:
# JOURNEY'S END

Rest not till you rivet and publish yourself of your own personality.

—Walt Whitman

In D-A-D dulcimer tuning, "D" is home.

For the last sixteen years, Darrel Ellis has met with his good friend for lessons as well as for social visits. Today they're at David's apartment, and Darrel watches him get ready to record himself putting down two songs on an antique dulcimer for a historical sound archive he is excited about.

Darrel notices there is a groove knocked out of the fretboard, then watches as David hits "record" and starts to play really hard. When he finishes, Darrel asks him,

"David, what are you doing playing that so hard?"

He stops, and shows Darrel the groove.

" A hundred years ago, someone played it really hard so I'm playing it really hard to get the same sound as its owner." He smiles and adds, and "I'm going to leave my signature mistake in it, too."

(1)

*David's "Signature" Mistakes by T.J. Larkin*

When David referred to his "signature mistake," he didn't mean a deliberate error but a "happy accident" in the recording of a song that makes the work special or unique. One of the most famous "mistakes" in commercial music was Merry Clayton's voice cracking twice during a second take as she belted out the refrain in the apocalyptic antiwar song, "Gimme Shelter." The Rolling Stones knew magic when they heard it, and they kept it in. Many consider it the greatest backup vocal of all time.

David's happy accidents were usually instrumental and would result from not quite fingering a note the way he intended, or from having a note do its own thing in an unexpected way. In every recording in which he left the signature mistake rather than remove it, he did it because it made the song organic and unique—his preference—rather than a work of perfection created in a studio.

(2,3)

## 2001 NASHVILLE, TN: "I'M DOING IT MYSELF"

Once Steve Stubblefield and David finish recording *Uncle Dulcimer*, they approach a producer who rejects the idea of using a four-track recorder for a professional album, insisting that the quality wouldn't be up to it. When David gets the news, he tells Steve, "Fuck it; I'm doing it myself." He pays for his own production costs that include hiring Steve for engineering time. Steve declines, reminding David that he never collected for a single lesson after the first two and even played dulcimer gratis on a rap album project Steve had worked on. But David insists and tells him he'll pay him in increments of four hundred dollars over time. Steven finally relents knowing that David "[is] always hell bent on doing things professionally."

(4)

## 2001 NASHVILLE, TN: SOMETHING BRAND NEW

Old friend Rattlesnake Annie is back in the States recording at the Muscle Shoals studio in Alabama for her next album, *Southern Discomfort*.

One day, Maureen Sellers, a fellow dulcimer performer and teacher makes her way to David's office at Blair carrying a music box that his friend Don Neuhauser sent with her to give to him during her visit.

As David sees Maureen walk in, he lights up. "Maureen! Come here, I got something I want you to hear!" He had just received the completed track for Rattlesnake Annie's cover of "House of the Rising Sun" for the *Southern Discomfort* album. As Maureen listens to the track, she deems that the mournful bowing on the music box takes the traditional blues song to a whole new level.

(5, 6)

## 2001 HENDERSONVILLE, TN: *TWANGIN' DUDE*

In 2001, the internet is just penetrating worldwide consciousness; the vast majority of people don't have internet access yet, and those who do have dial-up connections. YouTube is still four years away; there is no social media yet: no Zoom, no Facebook, no apps like TikTok.

Nevertheless, Jan Pulsford has started working on the Rocket Network, a little-known global internet platform for audio professionals that enables them to upload music files to share, edit, rework, and collaborate with other professionals almost in real time. One evening, she's chatting with Vesa, a guitar player from Finland. She mentions David as she explains she's working on a dance track to mix David's instruments and voice with synths and beats, and she needs some inspiration.

Vesa asks Jan, "How's this for a title: 'Twangin' Dude'? If we get your friend to do some talking, he could go like,

> I don't care for girls and such, I don't care for cars that
> much...
> I just care for the moon and stars, I'm a twangin' dude.

She runs the idea by David, and he loves the suggestion. He also finds the idea of being involved in online collaboration very exciting, not the least of which is because it will give artists more autonomy. After David writes the lyrics, Jan records him speaking the lines:

> My name is Ebenezer.
> I heard that sound when I was in the womb. It was my
>     father's father's father
> calling from the mountain,
> howling at the moon.
> I was electric before electricity,
> the twang of the bow and the land before the city. And I
>     learned to dance before I could walk
> and I could twang before I could talk.
> I play the sound of the ground I walk on,
> I wasn't born to play it smooth.
> I'll play the thunder and the mountain Dew. I'll play the
>     sound of the ground I walk on rough and rocky.
> I'm a twanging dude.
> I'll twang on the banjo
> I'll twang on the harp.
> I'll twang on zither strings and I'll twang on your heart.
>     I'm a twanging dude
> I'm the twanging dude.
> I'm the twanging dude
> This ain't no violin.
> I wasn't born to play it smooth.
> I play the sound of the ground I walk on rough and rocky.
> I'm a twanging dude
> twanging dude
> twang, twang,
> twang, twang.

(7)

> ### "I Play the Sound of the Ground I Walk On" by T.J. Larkin
>
> T.J. believes that David's frequent affirmation, "I play the sound of the ground I walk on" is one of his most memorable. It's a hint at how he sees himself as a musician: an interface between the sounds of the earth itself and the unique, culture-bound musical sounds inherent in every place. Each musician contributes his or her own vibrations and waves to perpetuate the process; these resonate over, around and through the air, gradually settling into the earth.
>
> His choice of the name "Ebenezer" is likely no accident. Derived from the Hebrew אבן ('*eben*), stone, and עזר (*azar*), to help or support, he affirms his connection to the earth and as a support for those he counts as friends and family. By recording "Twanging Dude," David leaves his mark in the new world of synthesized dance music as a bridge between old and new in his mission to push musical boundaries. The result sounds like nothing he has ever created before.
>
> (8, 9)

## 2001 NASHVILLE, TN: DAN AND MARY

As a result of their introduction to the dulcimer at Ellis Truett's weekend party, Mary Nichols and Dan Pfeifer begin lessons with David. Every two weeks during the semester, the two make the hour and a half drive from Woodbury to Blair. Mary's lesson takes place first; David plays a new song with her, working her through it bit by bit. After her hour, Dan has his lesson. Because he is a musician, he picks up the instrument quickly, so David usually works with him on the harmony for the same song he just taught Mary so the two can play together back at home.

David recommends Mary order a dulcimer from McSpadden, and a short time after she orders it he calls her to tell her it arrived. "Well, Mary, I've been playing your dulcimer and I tell ya, it can pump some air!" he laughs. He will play it day after day to break it in for her, and when he hands it over, it will be love at first sight and sound.

(10, 11, 12, 13)

## 2001 NASHVILLE, TN: THEIR OBI-WAN

Mike Dickinson is in town to attend Tim Bryan's upcoming wedding, but first there's a celebration at Tim's house for all his friends to get together and jam. Tim, Steve Stubblefield, and Mike Manning are longtime Louisiana friends. Mike had left Ruston for Austin about the same time that Steve went to Nashville to attend Belmont. In Austin Mike started his own music business and indie label, Chicken Ranch Records.

Mike had heard about David when Steve told him a story of David demonstrating how a dulcimer sounds when played on a table. "When you play it like this," he told them, demonstrating, "the dulcimer sounds like this, like crap." Then, after pulling one of the drawers out of a dresser, he turns it upside down and places the dulcimer on his lap, bottom-side-up, and plays a short piece. "We all heard the difference, the impressive sound amplification. It was fascinating!" When Tim and Steve introduce David to Mike, understands: David is their Obi-wan Kenobi of the Starlings band, and as they talk, he decides he likes the sage, chilled-out guy, too.

After watching David jam with the others, and seeing David's impact on Tim and Steve's playing, Mike thinks to himself what his friends have told him all along: David is a dulcimer pioneer and a groundbreaking artist. They get a chance to talk again at Tim's wedding about videotaping David performing at an upcoming Starlings launch party.

At the wedding reception at the Hermitage Hotel, David sings his composition, "Tennessee Valentine" to the newlyweds while everyone enjoys a piece of the dulcimer-shaped cake.

(14)

## 2001 NASHVILLE, TN: *UNCLE DULCIMER*

*Delcimore* receives a 2001 Nashville Music Award nomination. Again, reviewers are impressed by the unexpected pairing of a wide range of music with the dulcimer in a natural setting suggested by the sound of the cicadas. One reviewer notes that the "Blackberry Winter" track on the CD often accompanies figure-skater Ekaterina Gordeeva's performance on ice.

Blair faculty buddy Butch Baldassari will pen a review of *Uncle Dulcimer* in which he notes "David is one of the greatest dulcimer players ever...for being largely responsible for bringing the instrument into the modern age and developing a good portion of the technique and repertoire we use today." He goes on to point out that *Uncle Dulcimer* "could easily have been called, *The Other Sides of David Schnaufer*" since it showcases not only his Banjo-mer, Tennessee music box bowing, and electric playing, but his fingerpicking, singing, and most importantly, his songwriting." David includes "Tennessee Valentine," cowritten with Rachel Dennison (Dolly Parton's sister) and "Brush Arbor," another original song but for the first time recorded with lyrics.

One of the most remarkable tracks on the album, the historic "Shavin' a Dead Man," puts to rest any argument that a home recording can't capture lightning in a bottle. Recorded around the table in Steve Stubblefield's kitchen immediately after David taught him and Tim the song, Steve hit the record button to capture David leading on the Banjo-mer along with some postrecording talk around the table. Their recording of "Shaving a Dead Man" is an impressive piece that captures the musicians' skills and joy, and the kitchen session takes David and friends full circle to the mountain tradition of jamming with friends and family, not in a studio, but at home.

(15, 16)

## 2001 NASHVILLE, TN: HE IS THE CONCEPT

Starlings Steve, Tim, T.J. and José accepted the Pancake Pantry's owner's invitation to hold a double CD launch party at the Pantry on a December Saturday night. Their own *Leaper's Fork* CD won't be released until early next year, but they want to honor "Uncle Dave" at the same time since the *Uncle Dulcimer* CD has just been released.

Steven and David like to joke that *Leaper's Fork* and *Uncle Dulcimer* are sister albums in the same way that people consider the Beatles albums *Rubber Soul* and *Revolver* as sister albums—you can't have one without the other. The two albums will be forever entwined in that the tracks for both were recorded sequentially with their combined creative input drawn from the same vein. The Starlings' influence on David is clear; if it hadn't been for Steve pushing David not only to create *Uncle Dulcimer* but to sing on it, he may have never done it. David himself is the concept for this aptly named album.

The Pancake Pantry, normally a breakfast joint, hosts a legendary party this night. By invitation only, neighborhood friends pack into the venue in anticipation of some great music. Girlfriends volunteer to waitress, and the food is excellent. David sits in once or twice when the Starlings play and enjoys the hoopla.

When David gets up to play solo, suddenly, the room goes quiet, and everyone leans forward to listen as he starts off with "Norwegian Wood" and his own "Tennessee Valentine." Mike Dickinson had the forethought to bring a video camera, and T.J. has brought along his DAT to record audio. Later, Mike will release two of David's party performance videos on his Chicken Ranch Records

YouTube channel, thereby allowing everyone in the world who wants to experience a bit of the party to enjoy David's playing.

(17, 18, 19, 20)

## 2001 NASHVILLE, TN: HIS FATHER'S LESSON

Those who know him best understand that David has always fully inhabited several different worlds simultaneously; on rare occasions, a few of those worlds intersect.

A treasured element in his orbit consists of the Starlings band. Despite their relative youth, David considers them collaborative peers. He understands and shares their interest in pushing music boundaries as they experiment with genres. They draw inspiration not only from a wide and deep well of inspiring musicians but from Appalachia. He's the football coach who occasionally jumps in to play and who sees his role as one of encouraging them to believe in their talents and follow their musical bliss. His expertise is never imposed but always available whenever they ask.

Another world David moves within just as smoothly consists of his students, both through Blair and private instruction. They range in age from professional musicians to semiprofessionals to amateurs, seniors to the youngest students he teaches (Jan Pulsford's son Merlyn, "six years old going on 30" takes lessons and adores David.) Most of these students tend to immerse themselves in traditional songs and hymns, and he happily plays with and mentors them to help them develop their skills.

A few friends feel particularly protective of him, and their disapproval of his friendship and collaboration with the Starlings is palpable. The Starlings sense their judgment, knowing that they are disliked for their lifestyle and their nontraditional approach to music.

David, like his old friend Townes, has little respect for those to whom Townes once referred as the "more authentic than thou, stick-in-the-mud traditionalists in the crowd." He keeps his feelings on the matter mostly private. Nor does he reveal his disappointment with those who don't trust his values. He refuses to pass judgment on either group for their tastes in music or for their lifestyles. His own inspiration for playing music began with admiration for his brother's and father's band skills, along with his harmonica-playing teenage surfing buddies. Later, pop music, Tex-Mex, country, and rock informed his taste. Since the time he was the same age as the Starlings members are now, he fed his hunger to develop his playing and explore musical boundaries by seeking out every genre and style of playing he could, criss-crossing the country to find mentors. His appreciation for the endless variety and value of music grew rapidly as he spent with mountain people, West Coast folkies, hippies, outsiders, original thinkers, dreamers, inventors, and countless musicians of other instruments with whom he played over the years. Everything he reads, everyone he knows, and the world around him inspire him to think, to work on new lyrics, to play. Everything—especially when it is new—captures his imagination. These days, he'll often joke with T.J., "It's time to take a break from the dulcet tones of the dulcimer," and off they go, listening to or playing something else, like Coltrane's jazz to classical. David's musical comfort zone leaves nothing behind and embraces everything new, no matter where it is rooted.

Long, long ago, Frank Schnaufer imparted important input to his young son about the value of differing perspectives. David learned that lesson. As a result, he welcomes the Starlings to every dulcimer event, whether it be the Dulcimer Days festival or his students' recitals.

At this year's Christmas recital, those in his traditional world and the those of the avant-garde world come together; anyone troubled by the other side keeps their feelings to themselves. Most are thankfully unaware of any tension underneath the surface. David is above it all, so everyone does his or her best to harmonize tonight for the man who brought them together. Their respect and admiration for him is one thing they all have in common.

(23, 24, 25)

469

## 2002 NASHVILLE, TN: MUTUAL ADMIRATION

When *Leaper's Fork* is released, one reviewer describes it as "a shimmering blend of traditional and winsome originals played with shambling, entrancing spirit on bouzouki, mandolin, electric dulcimer, and other rootsy instruments." Another calls it "soothing to the Southern soul from the first twang ... a gravelly, aggregate of rock and bluegrass with a heavy spoon of psychedelia that slides through your mind like well-aged moonshine." She acknowledges the lo-fi, four-track recordings, but adds, "For those who can appreciate it, the roughness of the recording accompanies the music perfectly."

The Starlings have had a profound influence on David, and their debut album is a testimony to David's influence on them as their identity evolved from British psychedelic band to the modern, eclectic sound palette they embrace today. Another reviewer pegs them as a band that "brings new flavor ... a revelry of traditional songs in the most untraditional way.'"

David could not be more proud of their work.

(26, 27, 28, 29)

## 2002 NASHVILLE, TN: LET'S PLAY IT

At Darrel's, David kicks off the lesson by asking him, "So, what do you want to learn today?"

"Well, I heard "I'll Fly Away" on the *Oh Brother Where Art Thou?* soundtrack; I wanted to learn that."

"Okay, do you have the CD? Well, get it out and let's play it."

Darrel plays the song through once and watches as David chords around a little bit.

"Play it again." The second time through, David stops to tune his dulcimer.

"What are you doing?"

"I cannot believe that this is a Grammy award-winning CD and these guys are all out of tune. I cannot stand to play with people out of tune." He tunes down the dulcimer until he's satisfied.

"Play it again." He listens for a moment, then starts to play along perfectly with the song. "That's it; okay, let's go learn it."

(30)

## 2002 NASHVILLE, TN: FAMILY REUNION: GENA

Since the eighties, Gena's interest in traditional medicine has grown steadily. In 2001 she enrolled in acupuncture college and graduated in 2001. Her parents are now living in Tennessee. Right after obtaining her license, she found herself on the way to Nashville to visit her father who had been hospitalized due to a sudden illness. During one their visits, she opened a newspaper; on the page in front of her was an ad for a position as an acupuncturist in a new office in the Baptist Hospital professional building. Intrigued, she stayed an extra day to interview, and got the job. Back in Texas, Gena packs up and makes the move that she had not planned for, very happy with the thought of living closer to her family and David.

Once she settled in, David invites Gena over to his apartment on Belmont and to his concerts. When Karen, Gena's sister is in town, the three cousins have dinner together. David assures them both that his blood sugar has been at a healthy, lower level ever since he visited Gena in Fort Stockton. He tells them he's certain it was because of all the laughing they did together.

Despite the fact that she doesn't play the dulcimer, the cousins still feel a strong connection due to the thread of tradition that binds them: David's, with his traditional music, and Gena, with her conviction that traditional medicine has much to offer her patients.

Each has found a way to reconnect with a deep past that had been lost to them growing up.

(31)

## 2002 NASHVILLE, TN: CLICKETY-CLACKING WITH T.J.

On T.J.'s latest visit to Blair, David shows him some authentic bones from minstrel times that are housed in a display case. David loves playing the bones. He takes them out of the case and solemnly announces that these were some of the best ever made; after letting T.J. take a look at them, he demonstrates how to play the rhythm instruments.

T.J. is hooked. David borrows them to take to a woodworking friend who creates a jig that will enable him to make an exact copy out of rosewood for both of them.

One of their favorite pastimes becomes playing the bones together. Everywhere. The woodworking buddy makes them more replicas out of walnut, then pine, and even lignum vitae. They take gleeful delight in playing them, oblivious to their being the most annoying people in the room as they have their fun clacking the bones. Walking on the sidewalk, in the car, sitting around David's office, even at the Sportsman's Bar and Grill, they pull them out to play. After repeated, exasperated attempts by the manager to get them to lay off the bones—"Will you guys stop playing?"— he finally lays down the law; "That's it! I don't want to hear no more bones in this bar, no more bones!" He temporarily bans them until they reform.

As a result of their banishment, the two become more circumspect in their playing. One night over at his place, T.J. picks up an old, decrepit resonator guitar to accompany David on the bones. With the circular resonator barely hanging from the guitar, T.J. plays and starts laughing as the resonator flaps, adding its own sound to the notes of the guitar and the clackety-clackety-clack of the bones. David, too, cracks up laughing at the joy of the sounds. A couple more minutes of playing and David stops and pronounces, "This is it man! We're doing it! This is our new band: Reso-Bones!" T.J. records them: rickety guitar, bones, and jaw harp. The resulting tape contains twenty minutes of music and an hour of their hilarious laughter.

(32)

*What are musical "Bones"?*

Rhythm bones are a folk music concussion instrument that dates back to the earliest recorded human history in many places around the world. Originally crafted from animal bones and later wood, Shakespeare mentions them in Act IV, Scene I of *A Midsummer Night's Dream*. Nick Bottom says, "I have a reasonable good ear in music. Let's have the tongs and bones." Early English and Irish immigrants brought them to North American and played them to keep the beat steady on their jigs and reels. Historian Sue Barber notes that the bones were part of the musical tradition of the slave quarters of the United States in the eighteenth and nineteenth centuries, and co-opted by white musicians who performed in blackface during the minstrel show performances.

The bones enjoy periodic revivals throughout history, especially among folk musicians. They can be heard on many modern folk recordings such as those of the Irish group The Chieftains or of The Carolina Chocolate Drops in the US, the latter of whom have an excellent tutorial on the bones on YouTube.

(33)

## 2002 NASHVILLE, TN: SARAH ELIZABETH AT ELEVEN

As Sarah Elizabeth's confidence and playing skills grew under David's tutelage and family friendship, she felt more at ease expressing her opinions to him. For a number of years, she has worried about his heavy smoking. She never liked the smell of cigarettes since the times she first took lessons with him. As she got older, she would inform him from time to time that it was bad for him; "I know, I know," was all he would answer, or he'd brush off her concerns with a little joke. She tried reasoning with him the way her mother reasoned with her, but to no avail.

To her delight, after enjoying his chocolate cake at his fiftieth birthday party this year, he tells Sarah he has decided to quit smoking. The eleven-year-old feels a sense of relief flood through her as her worries lift from her shoulders.

Steven Stubblefield gets the word, too. David tells him he has left the Villager Tavern with its ever-present layers of smoke hanging in the air. Now, his friends look for him at Bongo Java on Belmont where he sits with his morning coffee and newspaper. The later afternoons or early evenings are reserved for hanging out with friends who followed him over to the Sportsman's Bar and Grill where he has an occasional light beer or a glass of white wine with Vince and his wide circle of friends.

Steve and Tim share their worries that his quitting smoking may really be about health problems catching up with him. Nashville was changing. David was changing. On some level, they sense the writing is on the wall.

(34)


## 2002 NASHVILLE, TN: LAYING GROUNDWORK

Dan Pfeifer and collector Ellis Truett have become close friends. Whenever Dan visits, the two men sit up until 3 a.m. talking. Dan absorbs everything he can about old-time music, dulcimers, music boxes and Truett's work, similar to David's, of collecting and documenting the boxes. Dan learns to make a dulcimer with his friend, then he builds more on his own. Mary Nichols begins making them, too.

(35, 36, 37, 38)


## 2002 NASHVILLE, TN: SARAH, ALMOST TWELVE

By the time she turns twelve, Sara Elizabeth has also helped David with his fieldwork to chronicle the history and evolution of dulcimers over time. He shows her how to take measurements, collect stories and photos, and catalogue the information. The two take turns playing the boxes so he can record their voices. A story for her future grandchildren some day, this modern young girl gets the rare opportunity to play period songs on period instruments with the best dulcimer musician in the world.

(39)


## 2003 NASHVILLE, TN: CONTEMPLATING ETERNITY

After two years of solicitation from multiple sources of input and research, Vanderbilt makes the decision to move the Dyer Observatory from the under the aegis of the Physics and Astronomy program to the Public Affairs office. The idea behind the move: use the Observatory as a promotional tool to marry the arts and sciences to educate and entertain the public.

The Public Affairs people reach out to Dean Mark Wait to ask if he would like Blair to participate by holding concerts in front of the Observatory.

"What kind of concerts would you like to have?" asks Dean Wait

"You tell us."

"How about an evening concert by two of our professors, David Schnaufer and Butch Baldassari?"

It will be a splendid occasion for everyone involved. David and Butch along with Nashville Symphony oboist Bobby Taylor open the new series on April 27 with a concert entitled "Music on the Mountain." Butch jokes that the three musicians are "a string band with an oboe." The concert will be free, and the public is invited to bring picnic baskets, blankets, and friends. After the concert, the public will have the opportunity to tour the Observatory and look through the telescope until 10 p.m.

During the afternoon, Dyer director Rocky and his event staff set up a tent, sound system, lights, and three hundred chairs.

David takes his dulcimers and the Tennessee music box from Lawrence Gamble's barn. During his solo turn, he demonstrates how he makes music on the box, first using a turkey quill and then a bow. As the sun sets, David weaves the history of the music box in between his songs. Rocky is spell-bound, and so is the audience; the concert is a huge success.

After the concert and tours are over, Rocky sees David and T.J. Larkin, so walks over to introduce himself, asking, "Would you like to have a private viewing of Saturn?"

David had visited the Dyer grounds a few days earlier to scope out the location of the concert. Now, he is excited to get a private tour to see the telescope. The two musicians walk along as Rocky explains the history of the Observatory. Once inside, David and T.J. follow Rocky up the staircase to the platform at the viewer end of the giant telescope. Rocky notices that halfway up the stairs, David stops talking, and his head starting to hang. Now, at the top of the stairs and no longer smiling, he stares at the telescope, silent. Rocky wonders what is going on; he senses a big emotional change in him. Rocky shows them how to look through the viewfinder of the telescope to see the ringed planet. David looks into the viewfinder for quite some time without saying a word. "Something has changed about him," Rocky thinks to himself as he watches David contemplate Saturn. From the side, he notices David's eyes start to well up.

Finally, David turns to leave, and says very little as he descends the stairs and walks out the door. Later, he calls Rocky to invite him to get together with him at the Sportsman's Bar and Grill. After David orders his white wine and Rocky orders a beer, he looks at Rocky. "I want to thank you for what you did for me the other night after the concert. I couldn't tell you what that meant to me that night because I was pretty choked up when I looked out at Saturn. It took me back to one of the last times I saw my father. We looked through a telescope at Saturn. He died not too long after that."

David and Rocky will meet several times at Dyer over the next two years to sit outside and talk about music and life and other topics, but, with a couple of exceptions, he turns down Rocky's invitation to look through the telescope again; it's just too emotionally difficult for him. Nevertheless, the Dyer Observatory, surrounded by its idyllic beauty, will become one of David's favorite places in Nashville. Whenever he needs to be alone, he'll go up the hill with his dulcimer, just to play for himself.

(40, 41, 42, 43, 44)

## 2003 NASHVILLE, TN: SPIRALING BACK, FULL CIRCLE

The year winds down with two especially significant projects in David's life. First, Miramax releases the film *Cold Mountain*, a story of three people: two women, mirror opposites of each other, who become close friends and do their best to survive in the waning days of the Civil War. The sweetheart of one of them—now a wounded Confederate soldier—becomes disillusioned with war and the Southern cause. He deserts the crippled army and struggles to make his way back to Cold Mountain, North Carolina, to his true love.

Given Hollywood's usual sorry depiction of Appalachia, nine Appalachian scholars, writers and teachers convene to assess the accuracy of the film's depiction of Appalachia after the film's release. They generally agree that "failures in authenticity great and small occur" surrounded the book's adaptation, location, screenplay, and casting. However, most compliment the "beautiful score" by T. Bone Burnett and his team. They offer praise for Burnett's presentation of traditional nineteenth- and twentieth-century tunes whose emotional truths have been largely out of earshot of average listeners. One in particular praises Burnett for demonstrating "a working knowledge of recent developments in the Southern mountains' rural music traditions by employing the talents [of] many of Nashville's most noted acoustic players." One of those acoustic musicians is David, who plays the dulcimer on "You Will Be My Ain True Love" ("ain" derived from Scottish, "own") to back Allison Kraus and Sting's singing. He is so proud of his work that he will later add their names to a list on notebook paper he has started of the professional musicians with whom he has worked over the course of his career. "You Will Be My Ain True Love" will be nominated for a Grammy and an Oscar.

The second work he considers significant this year is an academic paper he plans to publish. Back in 1998, David cowrote and published a scholarly paper with his assistant entitled "Tennessee Music Box: History, Mystery and Revival." The two outlined the results of their study of the Tennessee music box to categorize, describe, and write about its history. The Tennessee Folklore Society Bulletin published it, building upon the previously written works by Jean Ritchie, Ralph Lee Smith, and many others.

This year he pens a second article that is emblematic of his work with T.J. on the Dulcimer Archive Project to preserve a written, visual, and audio record of the origins and development of the dulcimer across space and time. In his paper, "A Brief History of the Appalachian Dulcimer" he writes of the earliest known artistic depiction of the dulcimer's ancestor, an angel painted on the ceiling of Denmark's Rynkeby Church sometime in the sixteenth century. In effect, this paper expands upon the history he first read in Jean Ritchie's *The Dulcimer Book* in 1974.

*Since the sixties, the Appalachian dulcimer has staked a claim in the American orchestra of rock, pop, jazz, country, blues and classical and is now more popular than ever. Its sweet voice will be heard for centuries to come because it's the sound of the ground we walk on.*

Typically, there's not even a hint to suggest that the claim he describes owes much to his own considerable efforts to stake that claim.

(45, 46)

## 2003 NASHVILLE, TN: THAT'S WHAT FRIENDS ARE FOR

David, Vince, the Starlings band members, Rocky, and a host of whoever else drops by meet weekly for a glass of white wine and discussions that range from current events to music, philosophy to history, and always include plenty of wit and laughter. Rocky loves listening to David's takes on the world. He feels like he is in the presence of a living legend: the world's only dulcimer professor. He learns that David is a little jaded about politics, and his early hippy/folk persona shows through. He believes in freedom of speech, live and let live, and he loves women. He has just as much respect for women artists as for male artists.

Rocky does not consider himself a musician, and—especially in Nashville—he would never tell a soul he writes songs in his free time, even though he believes he can write a pretty good lyric. He considers himself a bit of a hack guitar player. He can play keyboard and guitar only enough to figure out a little bit of the melody of the tunes that arise in his mind. Back in the seventies, he had written four little songs he saved to cassette.

Now that he has started writing songs again, he shares his work with his new friend during one of the evening get-togethers. "David, I've written some songs, and I don't know what to do with them;

would you mind just giving me some advice?" Rocky leaves him a cassette to listen to.

About a week later, David calls him. "Rocky, you have to record these; this is spectacular. You've got some really good songs here. I know just the person who can help you record this: T.J. Larkin, my buddy from the Starlings, TN. band. T.J. can play anything, and he has a studio."

Encouraged by David's assessment, Rocky will go to T.J.'s studio every Monday with his new lyrics and ideas, and T.J. will help him turn each one into a professional track. David, too, comes to the studio periodically to play the dulcimer, music box, and jaw harp on several of Rocky's songs.

Rocky watches one day, awestruck, as David prepare to lay down one of his tracks for the album title tune, "Blackberry Jam." David sets up to play the jaw harp, and T.J. mics him while the two talk through how they will record. As Rocky watches this side of David at work, he suddenly thinks, *He's a genius.* "Blackberry Jam" had been planned for a duration of two minutes, fifty-three seconds; to Rocky's surprise, David doesn't stop playing where Rocky planned the song to end. Not only does he keep playing the jaw harp, but he ramps it up and gets into the zone. He's on fire, so T.J. just keeps recording. The energy in the room reminds Rocky of a sports car taking off; the fiddle flies, the guitar steps up to keep up, and David plays the jaw harp at warp speed for another two minutes and thirteen seconds. Finally, they end it at the perfect place with a burst of laughter and jokes about calling the fire department. Rocky has never had so much fun in his life. Later, he can only describe the session to his wife as "magic unfolding."

For another track, David reads a sober, voiceover introduction to Rocky's "Sarah." With the mournful bowing of the Tennessee music box in the background, David reads a letter from Civil War soldier Sullivan Ballou to his wife. A week after he wrote the letter, Ballou was killed at the Battle of Bull Run. The voiceover provides a moving contrast and perfect introduction to Rocky's love song that follows it.

David especially likes Rocky's "Shawnee Town," a hilarious folk tune that evokes the earliest times of traditional music when isolated mountain people created their own entertainment for rowdy singing and dancing. The song begins with an assertive introduction by David on the jaw harp and leads the listener into Rocky's lyrics about a gal he has in Shawneetown: "She can fight like a man,/she can spit and chew/got a red-bone hound and a mustache, too!"

"Nobody could have written that but you, Rocky!" David laughs. The final track provokes not only happy rocking and foot-tapping but hilarious laughter and appreciation for the clever lyrics, and T.J. records it all.

(47, 48, 49)


## 2003 NASHVILLE, TN: A WARNING

Like Vince and others close to David, Rocky worries about David's seeming lack of interest in the business side of his work. To his friends, he only seems to care about the music itself these days and doesn't even have an agent or a manager. He seems most comfortable taking a cue from his younger colleagues' footsteps, producing and recording himself.

David had grown cynical over the years about the mainstream music business. When Rocky asks him for advice for to setting up his own music label, Muddy Sunshine, David warns him: "Well, you're steppin' in shit, Rocky, and you get that all over your shoes in the music business."

(50)

## 2003 NASHVILLE, TN: SARAH ELIZABETH AT TWELVE

Sarah Elizabeth tells her mother that she is considering a career as a folk artist. The last two years she had attended Western Carolina University's annual Dulcimer University, a week of classes, jams, and performances headed by Lois Hornbostel. She took classes from additional dulcimer teachers while at Dulcimer U. including Robert Force, Don Pedi, and Janita Baker, and he has befriended many in the tight-knit dulcimer community in addition to David in her desire to grow as a musician. This year she releases her first CD, *Beyond the Limits.*

A number of years ago when Jennifer lost her father and then grandfather, she worried about the impact on her daughter. She explained to Sarah that if she wanted to work with older people long enough to feel strong ties with them, the reality was that she would likely know them when they died. It would be her choice to continue or not. If she didn't want to face that kind of loss, she could stop working with them and focus on other ways to grow her love of music. "Either way is okay with me" her mother explained. Death hadn't been scary for Jennifer's daughter, but it was enormously sad for her.

Sarah faces a personal loss once again this year. She felt particularly fond of the world-class luthier and dulcimer player Robert Mize. Mize was an old man by the time Sarah Elizabeth met him; he had been profiled for his dulcimer work in the 1975 *Foxfire* books; his dulcimers were in the Smithsonian and frequently given as gifts by the Tennessee governor to foreign dignitaries. Sarah held him in her heart dearly after studying with him, and she believes he felt the same about her; he had even made her a dulcimer.

When Mize passes away at the age of eighty-two, it breaks Sarah's heart. At first, she doesn't want to go to his funeral. After reflection, she tells her mother, "You be there for people when they are living, so you should be there when they die." Sarah does attend and plays the dulcimer at his funeral.

Her daughter had always spent a great deal of her music learning with adults; most were younger than Mize but all decades older than she was. After the funeral, she tells her mother that she will deal with the sadness when it came, and that she wanted to continue working with David and all her other mentor friends.

(51, 52, 53)

## 2003 WOODBURY, TN: THEY'VE DONE IT FOR HIM

David accompanies the Dulcimer Quartet for "Dulci-Mania/An Evening of Dulcimer Music" at the Cannon Count Arts Center in Woodbury Tennessee. Billed as an evening with the best contemporary mountain dulcimer players, David and his guests the Gallier Brothers perform, but David's mind is firmly on his quartet with their intricate strumming and picking conversations between Linda, Natasha, Sandy, and Lee. To the audience, their sparkling performance appears effortless. David knows better; he knows the countless hours the four have put in to perform flawlessly. They've done it for him.

(54)

## 2003 NASHVILLE, TN: THE MUSIC BOX BUG

Rocky has caught the music box bug from David, so he decides to try his hand at building one. He and David meet in his Blair office to take measurements from the several of his old music boxes David has displayed around the room. As the two measure the boxes, Rocky can't contain his excitement with his ideas on the theory of sound.

"You know, if we expand it this way, I can get standing waves, and if it's a bigger box and I change the sound holes, and if I try a different material on it, the vibration will be different in this part of the instrument and..."

David quietly listens, then raises his palm toward Rocky to stop. With a big smile and his best professorial tone, he tells him: "Rocky! It's *just* a box. You're overthinking!"

(55)

## 2004 NASHVILLE, TN: THE FIRST PITCH

Inspired by the Truett tradition, Dan and Mary occasionally host hoe-downs on their farm in Woodbury, and David attends when time permits. Dan and Mary's fascination with David's ability to coax songs from the music boxes leads them to begin discussions on a documentary project about the boxes. Such a film would reveal their unique characteristics and provenances and feature David playing songs on them.

Mary and Dan are excited with the idea of providing their expertise for such a project so approach David about it. His fear that his name might be exploited in a commercial DVD leads him to say no.

(56, 57, 58, 59)

## 2004 LOS ANGELES, CA: LETDOWN

When scholars assessed last year's *Cold Mountain* soundtrack for "failures in authenticity great and small," they found none and praised the recording,

However, the live performance of "You Will Be My Ain* True Love" by Sting and Alison Krauss at the Oscars show this year includes a great failure to acknowledge Appalachia as far as David is concerned. During the performance, Sting plays a hurdy-gurdy in his attempt to reproduce the Tennessee music box drone heard on the original recorded track of the song. David is disappointed that the worldwide audience was not able to experience the unique, earthy drone of the music box that would have been more culturally and musically appropriate for the song. It deeply matters to him, not for his sake, but for the sake of the instrument.

(60, 61)

## 2004 NASHVILLE, TN: UPLIFT

Windham Hill Records producer Steve Buckingham asks David to contribute to the upcoming album, *Appalachian Picking Society*, a concept album devoted to traditional old-time country, bluegrass, and folk tunes that will feature a who's who of acoustic pickers, such as Chris Thile, Bela Fleck, Abigail Washburn, Dan Tyminski, and several others. The album features thirteen tracks and four interludes, with each track reflecting the taste of the contributing musician and performed in a range of styles that complement each other.

David chooses "When Silence Was Golden," an instrumental tune he composed in 1989 with buddy Herb McCullough that made its debut on his first Nashville album, *Dulcimer Player*. He takes his McSpadden "Schnaufer Model" to the studio to record the song. And since Buckingham also had asked him to contribute two of the four interlude tracks, he also takes along his 1870 Tennessee music box to bow on the first interlude track.

A Canadian critic pronounces the album superb; he writes, "David Schnaufer's 'When Silence Was Golden' is drop-dead gorgeous, meditative playing." A British reviewer years later will write on Amazon, "I can't rave about this album enough. The virtuosity of every musician on it, from Union Station's Dan Tyminski...David Schnaufer...to the incredibly versatile Bela Fleck is nothing short of breathtaking."

(62)

## 2005 NASHVILLE, TN: TITAN

> January 14, 2005 ... the Huygens spacecraft descended
> through Titan's murky atmosphere and touched down –
> if a bit precariously – by bouncing, sliding and wobbling
> across the surface of Saturn's largest moon Titan. This was
> the first time a probe had touched down on an alien
> world in the outer Solar System.
>
> *—Astrobiology Magazine*

Rocky has been close friends with David long enough now to expect the unexpected from him, and always delivered with his dry sense of humor. Yet he still makes Rocky laugh out loud every time. When he and David sit down at the Sportsman's Bar to catch up with each other, David drawls, "Well, Rocky, I read they landed a probe down on Titan."

"Yes, that's right."

"And I see they found a bunch of lacquer thinner up there."

Rocky bursts out laughing; his was a pretty close characterization of the soup of chemicals that they found on Saturn's largest moon.

(63, 64, 65)

## 2005 NASHVILLE, TN: DOCUMENTARY'S A GO

Over the past year, David has been thinking about Dan and Mary's documentary idea centered on his research on Tennessee music boxes. Dan continues to discuss the idea with him, proposing a collaboration that includes David and Ellis Truett, with Dan as producer and sound engineer and Mary as videographer. Under the aegis of Middle Tennessee State University, they could produce a not-for-profit documentary for the public good. Dan would write the grant proposal to find the funds to cover all expenses. When

Dan explains that the goal of their project would be to educate the public—especially schoolchildren—on their music heritage, and that the DVD would be dispersed for free to institutions such as schools, libraries, archives, and museums, David finally relents. It will be a good complement to the work he's doing with T.J. for the future online dulcimer archive.

(66, 67, 68)

## 2005 NASHVILLE, TN: *WAX*

It's the seventh year of the annual Grand Old Dulcimer Day festival at Two Rivers Mansion. In addition to the all-day concerts, jams on the lawn, displays, demonstrations, "The Tradition Continues" stage for young performers and free introductory group lessons, David has a new demonstration for those who appreciate history.

This demonstration is the result of David's collaboration with Martin Fisher. Fisher met David when the television program *Tennessee Crossroads* was scheduled to shoot a feature about Martin's hobby of cylinder recording, an interest which had developed as a sideline of his lifelong passion for music, record collecting and his study of the technology of recording and playback of grooved media. He owns one of the first recording mediums, the Edison wax cylinder recorder. Martin invited David to his home to play some traditional songs on the day that the Crossroads producer and crew were due to shoot.

The vintage technology gave David an idea. He invited Martin to bring his Edison machine to record a performance by the Grand Old Dulcimer Club and friends at Two Rivers Mansion. When television, newspapers, and the local radio stations got wind of the unusual project, they planned to attend as well.

On the day Martin arrived, forty dulcimers played "Grey Cat on a Tennessee Farm" into the large horn of the Edison with David leading on a Tennessee music box. The Edison cylinder, the first established recording apparatus, allowed the participants to hear the reproduction of their playing as it would have been heard by listeners between 1890 and 1924. The best part was getting to listen to the playback immediately after they performed. T.J. Larkin had the forethought to ask his friend Andra Butler to video the performance, one he describes as "pretty primitive and pretty cool" after watching Butler's video.

Martin Fisher mans a booth to demonstrate the Edison Cylinder and play the recording at this year's Grand Old Dulcimer Day festival; attendees will listen firsthand to the grandaddy of modern vinyl records, CDs, and MP3s.

(69, 70, 71, 72, 73)

### Historic Acoustic Recording by Martin Fisher

The "wax" cylinder we used for David's event was actually composed of a metallic soap compound. Thomas Edison's first experiments were conducted with various wax or waxlike substances such as ceresin and beeswax, but these were deemed unsuitable. The subsequent formulas used in cylinder manufacture consisted of very little or no wax at all; a metallic soap formula was developed within a very short time. Variants of this formula continued to be used by both "wax" cylinder manufacturers as well as in the blanks used for commercial disc recording right up to the development of the lacquer disc blank in the 1930s: the latter is still used to cut most master discs used in record production today.

Acoustic recording began to be replaced by electric processes in 1925. Two of the big three labels (Victor and Columbia) had largely made the transition either before or by mid-year, except in special cases. Edison was the holdout but made the transition to electric recording around 1928. Although he eventually embraced electric recording, the old man himself was of the opinion that the acoustic process just sounded better, and he had a point. Certainly *his* acoustic recording process could be argued to be one of the best at the time.

*The Butler video*

After the recording session and viewing Andra Butler's video recording, David and friends discussed the creation of a DVD for posterity. Rocky Alvey agrees to release the video through his new label, Muddy Sunshine, with half the sales proceeds to benefit a fund at Blair for the purpose of research and edu cation on the mountain dulcimer that David established in 1995. You can watch a brief portion of the session here on YouTube, and see other recordings Martin has done by search-ing "Martin Fisher and wax cylinder" on YouTube. If you wish to purchase a copy of the resultant documentary, *Wax*, you can buy one here: https://www.tullglazener.com

## 2005 NASHVILLE, TN: APPALACHIAN MANDOLIN AND DULCIMER

On May 13, Dave and Butch appear on the WoodSongs Old-Time Radio Hour program for an interview and to perform songs together from their first album, *Appalachian Mandolin and Dul-cimer*. The two perform an electric rendition of the old American reel, "June Apple," followed by "Drunken Hiccups," "Wild Rose of the Mountain," and "Fisher's Hornpipe." In between songs, the host chats with the two friends and colleagues. When he remarks that a dulcimer looks like a silly-putty mandolin that has been stretched lengthwise, David quips, "That's right, like a roadkill fiddle!"

Butch and David are justifiably proud of their work on the CD; Butch asserts "No overdubs here!!! Just straight-ahead live playing!" David describes it as "a musical conversation performed on vintage and contemporary instruments in settings to showcase the rare archaic harmonies of these joyful, lonesome and eternal themes."

Their brilliant collaboration on *Appalachian Mandolin and Dulcimer* will be Butch and David's last completed CD.

(74, 75)

---

### The Old Time Radio Hour Interview

You can access Butch and David's delightful interview on the WoodSongs Old-Time Radio Hour via the show's archives at https://www.woodsongs.com/show-archives/. Scroll down the list that appears to Show Number 377, and click the link on the right. The music plus interview starts at approximately 7:28 into the show.

You can also find the show easily via the website, *the-grandolddulcimerclub.com*. See the pull-down menu at the top of the page titled "Listen and Watch", then click on "Podcasts" and scroll down to the WoodSongs podcast. Stay around long enough and you'll hear the Peasall Sisters who played George Clooney's children in the film, *Oh Brother Where Art Thou?*

---

## 2005 MURFRESSBORO, TN: FAMILY REUNION: DAVID AND ERIC

Gena and Karen's father passed away at eighty-five and will be buried in his home state of Texas shortly after the memorial service.

Their uncle's passing brings David and Eric together to attend his service. The ceremony and family gathering provide an opportunity for the two brothers to reflect on the distance between them that has marked much of their lives since they were young. At their respective ages of fifty-seven and fifty-one, both overcome their pride and mutual hurts and welcome each other's careful steps toward rapprochement.

(76, 77, 78)

## 2005 NASHVILLE, TN: TAMING SATAN

Work on the Tennessee music box documentary with Dan and Mary is in full swing. After much brainstorming and many planning discussions, Dan, Mary, Ellis, and David settle on a focus and format: David and Ellis will select seven music boxes—most from the Truett collection—that exemplify the variations in craftsmanship and tonal range.

Their end-product DVD will entail a dual format. It will include a profile each of the boxes via an informal discussion between David and his assistant during the first feature. Mary will shoot these 'Discovery" features in Truett's home where David discusses the provenance of each box demonstrate his assessment of its unique physical and tonal characteristics. She also shoots previous owners of two of the boxes, one of whom is Lawrence Gamble, who relates how he purchased two of his own boxes from friends, one box for a dollar and the other for a quarter. The "Performance" segment will feature David performing a song on each dulcimer in Truett's vintage schoolhouse to provide authentic period ambience and a good acoustic setting.

Shooting and recording takes place over the next eight months. In between recording sessions, they learn firsthand how David conducts his research. He spends hours getting to know the instruments and, when necessary, restoring them to playing capability. He sits cross-legged on Truett's living room floor to discern not only its voice and personality but also the type of song it plays best. Certain boxes don't play well in certain keys (major or minor) and are finicky about their cooperation with respect to music genre, e.g., hymns vs the blues. Each box gets a name according to its previous owner, origin, or a particularly unique characteristic.

Mary shoots David's initial physical assessment to determine heft, length, wood type, metalwork, sound-hole placement and design, décor, and fret material (usually wire found on the farm), the likely plectrum used by its owner, and any evidence of the frequency of use. He walks the viewer through unusual characteristics; one box has recessed end pieces; another a recycled fretboard, evidence suggesting that the first version had flaws in fret placement, so the builder turned it on its side to redo the fretwork.

One unusual, all-black box with distinctive carvings along the fretboard gives him some trouble. "Nope, nope, not going to let me play that note. Won't let me play old hymns, it won't intonate well in a major key" he tells them as he tries to coax it to release its music. Everything about the box is angular, dark, and unwelcoming. It breaks strings and fights being played. Initially referred to as Hole-In-Back, the team nicknames it "Satan." Eventually David discovers it's willing to play if he uses a noter. Later, Mary and Dan agree that watching David figure out how to tame it was remarkable.

Dan plans a day and a half to shoot the six Performance segments. The entire team moves to Truett's schoolhouse for the shoot. Dan's goal is to capture the highest quality audio and video for each instrument within the traditional authenticity supplied by the schoolhouse, certainly different from his work in a studio setting. He sets up a digital eight track with high-quality mics, three around David and the boxes and two farther out to hear the reverb in the room.

Occasionally, all three stay over at Truett's during their project. Usually, Mary bids everyone goodnight early and Dan, David, and Ellis stay up all hours of the night talking about traditional players they knew and Ellis's large collection of old-time music recordings that he plays for his friends. They analyze his old cassettes and reel-to-reel recordings, each one suggesting how to do this or capture that the next time around. Dan and Mary love how David always thinks, always connects, and always creates. He loves people, yet is very private about himself. He isn't a big talker about his personal life, but that doesn't matter; they always have plenty to talk about.

On the day they shoot the Performance segments, they are forced to deal with the smothering heat and an unexpected nest of hornets inside the schoolhouse. Dan also faces unwelcome outside ambient noise during his recordings: first crowing roosters, then tractor and trucks passing by make for a very long day. During the recording of "Hot Corn, Cold Corn" on the box they refer to as the "Crump" box, the chirping of a bird aggravates David at first, but he finally accepts the inevitable: "Okay, If he wants to be on my recording, I guess he's going to be in it."

(79, 80 81, 82)

## 2005 LA MARQUE, TEXAS: A VISIT WITH AN OLD FRIEND

David takes a quick time-out to revisit the past. He travels to La Marque to look up his childhood friends who still live there. In his typical fashion, he arrives unannounced to knock on the door of his old surfing buddy Terry Theobald. After the initial laughter and hugs, Terry notices that his old friend seems somewhat "off center, out of balance, but not crazy," he decides.

As they talk, Terry has the sense that David is looking for something he hasn't found, but whatever it is, he doesn't reveal it. Instead, the two return to memories of their youth and, for the duration of his visit, talk about treasured old times at school and at the beach, surfing, and music.

(83)

## 2005 NASHVILLE, TN: BUTCH

Butch is at home this afternoon, cooking up some red beets. He knows David loves red beets, so he calls him up and tells him to come over. When he arrives, David follows Butch into the kitchen and sits down at the table where Butch serves him a nice-sized bowl of brown rice with the beets. David doesn't eat any more than two or three bites. Suddenly, Butch fully realizes how much diabetes has ravaged his fragile frame over the last ten years.

David and Butch have been talking about doing a new album together called *Appalachian Christmas*. Despite Butch's concerns about David's health, on this visit it doesn't occur to him that David might not have enough time.

(84)

## 2005 NASHVILLE, TN: PASSING THE TORCH

After meeting at Blair for a lesson with one of his young students, David sits back to listen to him play his own dulcimer arrangement of Hank Williams's "I'm So Lonesome, I Could Cry." When he finishes the piece, he looks up at his tutor as David sits quietly, leaning toward him, his face thoughtful. Then, he breaks his silence. "I'm going to start playing it like you do. Makes more sense."

(85)

## 2006 NASHVILLE, TN: SESSIONS CALLS

David gets the call for more session work: he records a track for Faith Hill's Christmas album, *Joy to the World*. Linda Ronstadt wants him for three tracks on her upcoming album, *Adieu, False Heart*. And he plays the dulcimer on Simone White's *I Am the Man*. This is the kind of work he dreamed of thirty-five years ago as he planned to take his dulcimer to Nashville, and he doesn't take them for granted, but there is much more in his heart and soul today.

## MAY 2006 NASHVILLE, TN: NO DOUBT, NO DENIAL

Dean Mark Wait is walking to his car after work this hot afternoon when he suddenly bumps into David in the parking lot. He stops to say hello and make some small talk, but David says he has to tell him something. "I've been having trouble with my vision lately, and went to the doctor, and they've found some 'boogers' on my brain: I've got cancer." Mark is stunned, especially by the matter-of-fact way David just explained his situation. "He didn't sound fearful; in fact, he almost seemed dismissive," he tells Ellen Pryor when he calls her about it. Fear and uncertainty take hold of them even before they hang up.

(86)

## 2006 NASHVILLE, TN: DARREL

Shortly after David talked with Dean Wait about his diagnosis, he and Darrel go out to lunch. As a physician, Darrel has no illusions about the implication of his situation. Both know he has limited time.

"What do you think you should do?" he asks David.

David explains the work that he has done with both his MTSU friends and T.J. "I want to make sure my dulcimers and music boxes go to the Tennessee State Museum."

"Okay, then you need to focus on that," Darrel tells him.

(87)

## 2006 NASHVILLE, TN: THE BLUEPRINT

Through their times together in lessons, in playing together, and during the Tennessee Music Box project, Dan Pfeifer and Mary

Nichols have grown to look forward to their times with David. Once, after a lesson, Mary tells him, "My music just sounds like I'm playing the notes. It's missing that special quality I hear when you play. "Mary, you have to feel it to play it" he tells her. Over the last few years of their get-togethers, the three of them have had many talks about feeling the music.

When Dan and Mary hear the news that David is ill, they both suddenly feel a sense of urgency to accelerate their work to finish the *Songs and Stories of the Tennessee Music Box* DVD project. Dan focuses on the CD that will accompany the DVD, and Mary focuses on the film editing. They want to show both to David as soon as possible.

The finished DVD is remarkable in that not only does it enable the viewer take a listen and a peek into the past, but it also reveals the evaluation process of these antique instruments. In essence, it becomes David's blueprint for the next generation of researchers who will follow him.

(88, 89, 90, 91)

## 2006 NASHVILLE, TN: DARREL, MARK AND ELLEN

Mark Wait calls Ellen with more news. "David is sick and in the hospital at Vanderbilt Medical Center. The house where he lives is being sold, so the owner wants his apartment vacated. Some friends are going to move him out of the apartment and into the Residents Inn near you while the doctors try treating his cancer."

Darrel gets the call: Can he help Zada and David's friend Sandy clear out his apartment? The house's owner needs David's things out by 5 p.m. the next day. The three quickly meet up and do what needs to be done; there isn't much. Each carries away a little piece of David's life; Sandy and Zada take his books, papers, and clothing, Darrel takes his two armless lesson chairs, his grief lightened for a moment as he recalls the look of horror on David's face the time they arrived to play at a company Christmas party. "What's wrong, David?" Darrel had asked him. "Look! All the chairs have arms!" he responded, exasperated.

In the meantime, Vanderbilt doctors attempt a last-ditch effort to beat back the cancer.

Mark and Ellen visit David before he leaves the hospital. They feel helpless, but know how he likes to start his day. Mark takes him the *New York Times* and Ellen takes him his daily espresso.

(92, 93, 94, 95)


## 2006 NASHVILLE, TN: SARAH ELIZABETH AT FIFTEEN

Sarah Elizabeth's mother Jennifer gets the call: David is in the hospital at Vanderbilt and has just been diagnosed with cancer. His assistant passes a message to Jennifer from David: he wants to be the one to tell Sarah.

Jennifer thinks back on the earlier talks about losing loved ones with Sarah as they drive to the hospital. When they arrive, they are told that David is in the middle of an especially bad episode right now, and it is impossible for them to see him.

The next day, they return. Despite his diagnosis that the cancer has metastasized, David tells Sarah Elizabeth he is going to be fine. Sarah, however, is too perceptive to take him at his word. She will return on a subsequent visit to the hospital to acknowledge what he cannot bear to tell her, and she will give him her own message to him to tuck away in his heart.

(96, 97)

## 2006 GREENVILLE, SOUTH CAROLINA: ERIC SCHNAUFER

Jennifer calls Eric Schnaufer with the news. His first, anguished thought: "No...no...no....Not again." His own early family life in La Marque had been suffused with family illness and tragedies, and over his long career he had dealt with both countless times during his pastoral work. Nevertheless, he is not prepared for the thought of losing David now. Heavy with sorrow, he packs a suitcase and catches a plane to Nashville.

When he walks into David's hospital room and sees his frail, younger brother in the bed, Eric does his best not to let his shock show on his face. The two greet each other with a smile, neither one acknowledging that Eric recognizes the situation.

The doctors inform Eric that David's cancer is in the brain and the lungs. They want to do a biopsy to determine how to treat it, but it has already spread quickly and extensively.

Eric asks David what he can do for him. Any remaining resentments left between them evaporate, a welcome reconciliation for both of them that began back in August of last year when they reconnected at their uncle's funeral. The two brothers go on to discuss what to do to take care of David's personal affairs. David asks Eric and his close friend Zada to share duties as his medical power of attorney, so while Eric is in town, Zada and Eric bundle him up in a wheelchair and take him to Zada's bank to have the paperwork drawn up. Zada agrees to serve as executrix of his tiny estate. David tells Eric that he has arranged to gift his collection of antique dulcimers and music boxes to the Tennessee State Museum in Nashville. His papers and documents relevant to his career will go to the Anne Potts Library as the *David Schnaufer Collection;* he wants the extensive sound files he and T.J. Larkin created for each instrument in his collection donated there as well.

He has some personal instruments that he wants to give to Eric for him and his son and to Butch and Sarah Elizabeth. He has not had the time to give the gifts, but everyone understands the time is now.

(98, 99)

## 2006 NASHVILLE, TN: T.J. AND ROCKY

Rocky Alvey is one of many in David's circle of friends whom T.J. Larkin dreads calling.

"Dude, Schnaufer is sick. He has been having problems, and he has been diagnosed with brain cancer. "

Rocky listens; suddenly, he feels his heart sinking fast. Choking up, he whispers into the phone, "What can I do, T.J.?"

"Nothing, Rocky. It's pretty bad. I'll keep you informed."

(100, 101)

## 2006 NASHVILLE, TN: ALAN FREEMAN

News of David's diagnosis makes its way to West Virginia and Alan Freeman. Alan had nursed a longtime disappointment with David since 1984 that wasn't helped by a failed foray to Nashville years afterward to try and make it in the music business. But underneath all the brash, rough exterior is a big heart and a sense of deep awe and respect for what David had accomplished. It's time to tell him what he really feels and makes the call to talk with his old friend while he can.

(102, 103)

## 2006 NASHVILLE, TN: ELLEN

Once David moves into the Residents Inn, he and his friend Ellen Pryor often talk by phone. However, as the days pass, he finds it more and more difficult to dial or talk on the phone. Communication is better in person, so Ellen visits him frequently. "David, how can I help? What can I bring you?" Sensitive to her friend's condition, she understands immediately that David is embarrassed because he can't communicate very well with her. She decides to refrain from asking about his difficulties and keeps the conversations centered on what he needs. Whatever he tells her, she takes him for his little refrigerator: bread, cheese, fruit, milk, fruit juice. And coffee, always coffee.

His doctors soon realize that they are out of time to plan any systemic treatments in addition to the radiation: the cancer is spreading so fast there is no time. Eric gets the call and approves David's move to Alive Hospice.

(104, 105, 106)

## 2006 NASHVILLE, TN: SARAH ELIZABETH AT FIFTEEN

Sarah and David had already said their goodbyes in the hospital, after which she made several visits to hospice. David invites her for one last visit. She brings him his favorite three-layer chocolate cake she baked for him to eat while she plays the dulcimer for him. Because she wants to remember David while he is still himself, she has decided this will be her last visit with her friend and mentor.

When she returns home, she stares at the chestnut Civil War–era music box that David had recently given her. It suddenly occurs to her that he must have known his illness was terminal the day he gave it to her.

Many months after his death she will find a postcard tucked inside a little sock that she keeps in her dulcimer case to hold smaller things. The postcard was from David; he had slipped it into the sock without her noticing during her last visit. On it, she reads a note in which he shares how proud he was of her and, for the first time, expressed his deepest feelings to her: "I love you."

(107, 108)

## 2006 NASHVILLE, TN: ELLEN

Even after his move to Alive Hospice, Ellen continues to pass by Starbucks every morning to take him his favorite double-shot espresso on her way to work. Ellen, despite being a strong woman, feels her heart break one morning when the hospice caretakers have to put a special powder in his coffee to help him swallow it.

(109)

## 2006 NASHVILLE, TN: HERB MCCULLOUGH

When David is moved to hospice, his chief caretaking companion guards his privacy, turning away the many requests by others who wish to visit him. One of those turned away is Herb McCullough, his co-composer and one of David's best friends. Nobody will stop him from seeing his friend, he decides, so Herb flies from Florida into Nashville right after hearing the news.

Herb slips in one evening when the others are gone to pay his last respects to the man he considered his kindred spirit. Herb tells David all the reasons he has admired him over the years, not the least of which being that he always seemed to know what he wanted to make of his life, rather than be swayed by what others expected of him.

Herb reminisces about the old days and the many good times they had before retiring to Florida. Herb dearly loved David's oft-said reminder every time they composed together: "You never know where a song will go." The two of them had seen that happen time and time again during their careers. Songs seem to take on a life of their own, and Herb tells David about the joy that he felt every time he sang their "Starry Lullaby" to his grandchildren.

In the days after Herb's visit, other friends within his circle begin to slip in, too. Always together, Georgia and Lela stop by, with Lela taking him his favorite vegetarian food cooked with vegetables from her garden. One friend and admirer, John Renwick, drives all the way from Charlotte, North Carolina. He first "met" David when he borrowed the Happy Traum video *Learning Mountain Dulcimer* from the library to teach himself how to play the dulcimer he made. After working his way through the video, John took David's classes at every festival he could. He was heartbroken to hear the news and took off two days of work to make the trip to see the man who made such a difference in his life and to tell him he loved him.

(110, 111, 112)

## 2006 NASHVILLE, TN: DARREL

Darrel frequently drops by to see David between nine and ten at night. On this latest visit, he has brought his dulcimer with him.

"Do you want to play?" David shakes his head no.

"Do you want me to play?" He shakes his head yes.

So Darrel sits alongside his friend and begins to play one soft, soothing song, and then another.

Upon hearing the music, a nurse walks in. When she asks about his instrument Darrel tells her that this instrument is called a dulcimer. Surprised and appreciative of the music, she looks over at David and asks, "Do you play, too?"

(113)

## 2006 NASHVILLE, TN: VINCE

Calm on the outside, devastated on the inside, Vince Farsetta spends his last visit with David, feeding his life-long buddy the last food he will eat.

(114)


## FRIDAY, 8.18.2006 NASHVILLE, TN: TIM BRYAN

Tim Bryan enters the building and walks in the door at 2:00 p.m., his usual weekly lesson time. He is determined not to cry. Everything is sterile, quiet, and serene in the Alive Hospice room. Jan Pulsford is reading at the end of the bed, and David is asleep. Jan, who has been a rock for Zada during these last days, has watched over David frequently like a guardian spirit. When she sees Tim's stricken face, she tells him she'll step out for a couple of hours so he can have time alone with David.

Tim hasn't seen David since he was diagnosed in June. He is shocked at the emaciated figure lying on the bed, his mentor and friend. The man he had always known as energetic, witty, and passionate despite his many physical ailments over the years, a man who gave everything he had to everyone dear to him, lies still and asleep. Tim sits on a chair next to David's side, drowning in grief.

When David's eyes slowly open, Tim realizes he is unable to speak. He reaches over to clasp his hand and talks softly to him. He understands that David is still there when he feels David's now frail fingers give a weak squeeze within his own. Tim decides to remind him of their good times together. He whispers about all the fun they had, the learning, the teaching, the performing, the recording, the laughing, the pranks they would play on him...how much he and Steven loved the faces he would make, his hand gestures, and how he would rock and wiggle on the bar stool as he expressed himself and when he had to readjust his ponytail to clean the steam from his glasses, how they'd all be in stitches. He promises David he will be a part of his life every single day for the rest of his own life. His shoulders become heavier and heavier as he fights off the grief. David's body is almost done, and all that is left in this world, in this room, in this bed is his gradually fading spirit. Turning slightly away, Tim can't fight off the tears anymore and starts to cry. He tells him he's sorry he wouldn't get to die the Cherokee way, the way David had told him he wanted to go—alone in the woods, embraced by Nature. He tells David he loves him and that he hopes he is proud of his legacy. He thanks him again for the gift of the black dulcimer that David had played at Johnny Cash's house, and promises he will treasure it for the rest of his life.

"You will not be forgotten. None of us will ever forget you, nor will the world. Your story and your songs will live forever, and people will talk about you long after you are gone from this world. You have meant everything to me, to us in your Starlings family." Tears well up gently in David's eyes as he looks at Tim and gives him one last little squeeze of his hand, his eyes closing as he falls back to sleep.

(115, 116, 117)

## 2006, 23 AUGUST NASHVILLE, TN: ERIC AND DAVID

Eric Schnaufer receives the call. The phone rings again, and yet again within the space of the short time it takes for him to pack a small suitcase.

Within a few hours from the initial call, Eric takes the last of his flights to Nashville this summer. He makes his way to Alive Hospice, down the hall to the room, and approaches David's bedside, a tidal wave of grief washing over him as he learns that David has just passed away.

Eric stands watch over his younger brother as he lies sleeping in his final repose.

(118)

# REQUIEM

And yet we should not grieve for those who have gone from us in the primes of their lives after happy and fruitful years of activity, and who have been privileged to accomplish in full measure their task in life.

—Albert Einstein, from a consolation letter to a friend.

The sole purpose of human existence is to kindle a light in the darkness of mere being.

—Carl Jung, Memories, Dreams, Reflections, Ch. 11

The recollections of those who attended David's memorial service have grown faint over time. Yet many recall images that made indelible impressions: miles of cars parked along the road to the Dyer Observatory for the open air service. A standing-room-only crowd. The famous sitting next to the homeless. Dulcimer music played by friends, and a flower-arrangement in the shape of a dulcimer. A red-tailed hawk that swooped unusually low over the service led by Eric prompted wonder among many; so did a butterfly that alighted on a string of a dulcimer placed on stage, its wings gently opening and closing in a slow, mesmerizing rhythm. Those who were there tell of laughter mixed with plenty of tears for the sendoff of a man who was privileged "to accomplish in full measure his primary task in life[1]." According to Joseph Campbell, that task is a human universal one, depicted in stories across all cultures: to

---

1. Einstein, Albert.

undertake a spiritual and psychological journey that will result in an understanding of our true nature and the meaning of our lives. The traveler must meet tests and challenges with the help of guides along the way; if successful, he or she returns from the journey to bestow divine blessings upon the surrounding community, and live as an enlightened being who has experienced not only the ordinary but the extraordinary.

Throughout his life, David met the unwelcome challenges head on: his family tragedies, the vicissitudes and economic insecurity of a professional musician's life; his own hidden insecurities and fears, and his life-long health struggles. There's a temptation to speak of David's life in a mundane sense that belies the way he approached life: Yes, he did perform with very famous people, but he equally valued the many "regular" people he met on his journey. Yes, he suffered both physically and psychologically from never earning what he was worth, yet he never allowed the lack of earnings commensurate with his work and talent to sway him from his path. Himself a recipient of charity during the hard times in his life, he paid that charity forward in countless ways. He regularly donated his talent to others without cost, and gave lessons or extended lesson time gratis, just for the pleasure of participating in a music community. This beloved musician and teacher was acutely aware that his journey benefitted from the grace and camaraderie of others he met along the way who helped shaped him. Just as he was mentored by many other dedicated musicians, songwriters and luthiers, he paid their gifts forward, mentoring many aspiring artists on their own life journeys. In addition to his timeless music, he left a legacy of influence that can be read in the posture of his former students who adopted aspects of his unique style of playing the dulcimer; his spirit is evident in their teaching for those who know how to look for it. All these experiences and his impact blossomed from two simple goals: the first he revealed to Nova Lomax: "I want my music to feel like Bonnie Russell's did." And the second grew out of the first: he wanted to be a catalyst for the dulcimer's appreciation and evolution.

His curiosity and meticulous nature led him to conduct worthy historical work; his friend and fellow musician Fred Meyer points out that he single-handedly saved the Tennessee music box from extinction[2]. And in 2012, The Appalachian Dulcimer Archive went online at Vanderbilt University thanks to his research.[3] Today, Nashville's Tennessee State Museum houses his collection of antique dulcimers, and the David Schnaufer Collection is housed at Vanderbilt's Special Collections and Archives in the Blair School of Music.

One of the blessings that resulted from David's life's journey was that he did succeed at making his life meaningful: He took an obscure instrument gathering dust under America's bed and revealed its rightful place in the world's musical heritage. He derived joy in seeing professionals and amateurs alike give the dulcimer its due respect and in transporting others outside of their ordinary selves and into the world as he perceived it could be: a music community free of judgement and bound by a love of craft; a world where learning and laughter accompany that music; a world made up of people who value the traditional and the new at the same time; a world of people who understand the benefits and contributions bestowed upon us not only by our immigrant ancestors but by the diverse peoples we meet in our lives and by those who give us shoulders to stand on.

By adjusting our scope's focus on his life, we may revel in his wit, his talent, his gentleness and the joy he generated, and contemplate the choices we make on our own personal journey. Perhaps the most important lesson he left us is to think carefully about our choices and how well they align with our values. David's values convey a deep and vital cultural meaning for a world increasingly filled with people who often feel abandoned, depressed, angry or alone, who long for a sense of community, and who have lost touch with nature. In his 1995 doctoral thesis, *The darker side of Dixie: the seamier side*

2. Fred Meyer, E-mail message to author. February 21, 2021.
3. Jim Patterson, "Online Archive Extends Legacy of Dulcimer Legend David Schnaufer." Vanderbilt University. November 29, 2012. Accessed May 27, 2020. https://news.vanderbilt.edu/2012/11/29/dulcimer/.

*of the rural south*, Cecil Kirk posits that southern music has always reflected, promoted and reinforced southern values and behavior; however, Kirk asserts that a significant portion of the genre referred to as "southern music" includes "pervasive darker themes and topics: racism, domestic violence, male control over women, drunkenness, brutality, murder, gun ownership, Confederate symbolism, and folk justice in response to perceived violation of family honor."

David, like Jean Ritchie and those toward whom they both gravitated were certainly aware of these darker components given their lifetime immersion in southern music. Significantly, both chose to draw their water from a different, richer southern well. In the case of Jean Ritchie, she grew to understood the dangers of unfettered capitalism for the environment and its effect on the working man; she spoke her feelings about it via her music. It is no small irony that David, a man whose basic nature was that of an introvert, chose his music for its ability to sing to the better angels of our nature, thus building bonds between people and across communities.

And, what of the dulcimer's own journey? Well, when a string is plucked or strummed it creates energy in the form of vibration that creates an effect that musicians refer to as *sustain*, meaning how long that pitch resonates across time. Both David and the dulcimer—thanks their profound impact on all who knew them and know of them—will always demonstrate an exceptional sustain together.

# ACKNOWLEDGEMENTS

This book could not have been written without the generous cooperation of David's family and friends who shared their memories, insights, music expertise, teaching expertise, photos and images, audio and video files, primary source documents and encouragement. I am especially grateful to Eric and Thiela Schnaufer for sharing private memories of Eric and David as brothers and to Gena Fleming for the gift of her unique insights into the development of David's philosophy and values over the entire course of his life. Special gratitude also goes to Linda Sack whose directive—*Go and tell David's story*—gave me the courage to knock on John and Melanie Lomax's door in February 2020. John invited me into their home and wove remarkable tales of the Lomax family, Nashville in the nineteen-eighties and early nineties, and of their work and friendship with David. To my astonishment, John even insisted I copy hundreds of documents from his files on his copy machine the first day we met! Despite the passage of time, John's wonder and admiration for David's talent conveys a sense of excitement that no written or audio source can provide. I can't thank him enough for his ongoing encouragement and the connections he made for me throughout the research and writing. Additional special gratitude for their patience with endless questions, for sharing primary sources and/or additional text goes to: Doug Berch, Sinclair Baldassari, Nancy Barker, Dan Blom, Mary Lawrence Breinig, Linda Brockinton, Tim Bryan, Bonnie Carol, Natasha Dean, Dan Evans, Ron Ewing, Vince Farsetta, Robert Force, Rick Freimuth, Dave Haas, Neal Hellman, Lois Hornbostel, Norman Jordan, Jon Kay, Leo Kretzner, T.J. Larkin, Zada Law, Tramp Lawing, John Nova Lomax, Kelly Love, Sarah McWhirt-Toler, Joann McCullough, Mark Miller, Mary Nichols, Wanda O'Guin, Dan Pfeifer,

Henry Piarrot, Sam Poland, Ellen Pryor, Jan Pulsford, Rattlesnake Annie, Stephen Seifert, Maureen Sellers, Holling Smith-Borne, Steven Stubblefield, Doug Thomson, Mark Wait, and Mack White, all of whom generously participated in multiple conversations to help with insight into David's public and private sides and/or into the music business. A very special thank you to Darrel Ellis for his expertise on David's medical challenges and for sharing the impact of those challenges on his dear friend. Thanks, also, to Paul Shekelle and Carl Paulus for leading me to a deeper understanding of the many medical issues David faced. I also owe an incredible debt to the late Madeleine MacNeil and Ralph Lee Smith for leaving an invaluable, historical record of the dulcimer and its community via *Dulcimer Players News,* their books and music. I reached out almost too late to Mr. Smith, and just too late by a few days to interview Ms. MacNeil, much to my sorrow.

For their ongoing feedback on the manuscript and unwavering encouragement, I am indebted to Cynthia Dunn, Claudia Estep, Kathleen Homel, Kelly Love, and Twilla McClellan. My sincere thanks as well to Paul Wachter for sticking through endless revisions on the *Pluck* cover, and to Phillip Gessert of gessertbooks.com for *Pluck*'s beautiful interior.

To everyone who shared primary source materials, stories and/or research and writings, there would be no book without your contributions. Thank you from the bottom of my heart for helping me get to know this remarkable man.

- Rocky Alvey
- Anonymous 1
- Anonymous 2
- Amy Appleby
- Virginia Arouh
- Duck Baker
- Harry Beall
- Olivia Beaudry
- Judy Beier
- Melleta Bell
- Aaron Bentley
- Tim Binckley
- Joni Bishop
- Jim Brown
- Loretta Callens
- Cade J. Campbell
- Al and Emily Cantrell
- Rich and Mary Carty
- Stan Carpenter
- Greg Crutcher
- Donna Czubernat
- Natasha Dean

- Ashley Ernst
- George Del Gobbo
- Mike Dickinson
- Andreas Peter Dornonville de la Cour
- Alan Dyson
- Harrison Eppright
- Steve Eulberg
- Ron Ewing
- Martin Fisher
- Jim French
- Hannah Fuller
- George Gills
- Rev. Keith Gordon
- Nelda Green
- Debbie Grizzell
- George Gruhn
- Norie Guthrie
- Julie Harston
- Georgia Hobb
- Joe Hobbs
- Lela Hollabaugh
- Doyle Jeeter
- John Kay
- Bob and Sherri King
- Marilyn Konriff
- John Macrini
- John Manion
- Mike Manning
- Theresa Mayor Smith
- John McEuen
- Señor McGuire (Jim McGuire)
- Jennifer McWhirt
- Johnny Mears
- Fred Meyer
- Rob Meyer
- Gerry Milnes
- Kim Monday
- Karen Mueller
- Douglas Naselroad
- Joe Nolan
- Robert Oermann
- Mark O'Connor
- Rebecca Percoco
- Francisco Pérez
- Andrew Piarrot
- Henry Piarrot
- Laura Pils
- Sam Poland
- Drew Ponder
- Nigel Pulsford,
- John Renwick
- Jerry Rockwell
- Toni Sager
- Jim Sales
- Nathan Salsburg
- Ronda Savage
- Pam Setser
- Gary Skarke
- Terry Theobald
- Doug Thomson
- Hank Tilbury
- Vip Vipperman
- Carolyn Wick
- Anna Lomax Wood
- Jim Woods
- The late Jerry Wright
- David Young
- Mary Young
- Radim Zenkl

# BODY OF WORK

I discovered the following books, published recordings and videos during the research for *Pluck*. They consist of work that David created and/or collaborated on with others. This list is likely incomplete. Readers who have knowledge of missing items or corrections: please send comments to the contact page on DavidSchnauferPluck.com and I will update the list with acknowledgement to you.

## BOOKS/BOOKS WITH CDS

*1980*

*Finger Dances for Dulcimer* | Bonnie Carol/Kicking Mule Records

*1982*

*Anthology for the Fretted Dulcimer* | Lois Hornbostel/Mel Bay Productions

*1994*

*Swing Nine Yards of Calico*/Book and CD |David Schnaufer/Delcimore

## MUSIC AND LYRICS

*1981*

*Out of the Cold* | Sidetrack (Grantsville W. Va.)/Alan Freeman

## *1983*

*West Virginia Woman* | Karen Mackay /West Virginia Woman Records/Produced by Alan
    Freeman

*Who's Yer Boy?* | Midwest Coast Records (JH) w Fred Meyer/Jerry Rockwell (Jaw Harp)

*Hog Fiddlers Fancy* |Produced by Alan Freeman

## *1984*

*Rosies Arms and Other Retreats* | Boy Howdy Records/Produced by David Schnaufer

## *1985*

*Rockin' with the Rhythm* | The Judds/RCA/Ariola International (dulcimer/jews harp)

## *1987*

*Heartland* | The Judds/RCA/Curb Records

*Kathy Mattea: Untasted Honey* | Kathy Mattea/Mercury Records (Plays dulcimer on "Life
    as we knew it".)

*Christmas Time with the Judds* | The Judds/Curb Records (dulcimer)

## *1988*

*Smokey Mountain Christmas* | Various Artists/Brentwood Music

## *1989*

"Tennessee Morning" |Co-writer w Harry Beall, Kyle Fredericks

*Dulcimer Deluxe* | David Schnaufer/S.F.L (Sounds from Lomax)

*Dulcimer Player* | David Schnaufer/S.F.L (Sounds from Lomax)

*Dulcimer Player Deluxe* | David Schnaufer/S.F.L (Sounds from Lomax) |Combined songs
    from previous two

albums minus two songs due to CD track limit

*Smokey Mountain Hymns* | Jack Jezioro & Co. /Brentwood Music (dulcimer)

*Wagoneers Good Fortune* | A&M Records (Germany). Dulcimer

*Michael Johnson: Life's a Bitch* | BMG/Germany and RCA/UK (Jaw Harp)

## *1990*

Music Video: *Get Rhythm* |Martin Delray/Atlantic Records (Played Jaw Harp)

*Smokey Mountain Hits* | Brentwood Music

*World Sampler 6* | Adventures in Music (Played "When Silence Was Golden")

## *1991*

*The New Nashville Cats* | Mark O'Connor /Warner Bros. (Played dulcimer on "Traveler's Ridge")

*Cowboy Christmas Songs* | Michael M. Murphy/Warner Bros. (includes Vince Farsetta on banjo) *Pure Hank* | Hank Williams Jr./Warner Curb

## *1992*

*Dulcimer Sessions* | S.F.L. (Lomax-first cassette/album/CD release)

*Country & Western Sampler*| Adventures in Music (Played "Fishers Hornpipe")

*KLBJ's Local Licks Live*| KLBJ-FM ("Run, Run, Run"; written by D. Schnaufer, H.McCullough, Paul Kirby)

1993 *The Cactus Brothers* | Cactus Brothers/Liberty Records

1994

*Church in the Wildwood* | Cumberland Records (various tracks)

*David Schnaufer: One Man, Two Hands, Four Strings* | David/The Massive Recording Company\S.F.L. (Australian Release)

## *1995*

*Best Of All Possible Worlds* |Chris Vallillo/Gin Ridge Records. (Mountain dulcimer)

*The Great Shunga River* | Jim Curley/5th Gear (Plays dulcimer on "Oh, Susannah" Disc 1 Track 2

*Old time, vocal week & festival* |Elkins, W.Va. Augusta Heritage Center

Recordings from various concerts at Davis & Elkins College

## *1996*

*Tennessee Music Box Dulcimer Solos* |David Schnaufer/Rivertime Records/Jim Sales

*Reality Weeping* | Sam Sistler/Primavera

## *1997*

*Conversations in Silence* | Uncredited

*Sisters of Avalon* | Cindi Lauper/Epic (David Plays Dulcimer and Tennessee Music Box)

*Grandpa's Advice* | Adie Grey/Hey Baby Records (U.S.)/Demon Records (UK). (Plays dulcimer.)

*The Cat's Cradle Songs, Volume One* | Sidney Plays "Starry Lullaby" (David, Herb McCullough)

*Masters of the Mountain Dulcimer I* |Newtonville, NY: Susan Trump Music Instrumental Selections

*Celebrations of the American Farm* | Almanac Recording Co. (Plays "In the Bleak Midwinter".)

## *1998*

*Under a Southern Moon* | Al and Emily Cantrell/ Sombrero Records. (dulcimer on "Riddle of the Fiddle")

*Old Dogs* | Waylon Jennings, Mel Tillis, Bobby Bare, Jerry Reed/Atlantic (Jaw Harp)

*Pure Hank* | Blackout/Lumberjack (Vol. 19 of Curb's Bocephus series)

*Heavenly Toast on Paradise Road* | Nigel Pulsford (One minute fifty-second spoken monologue; jaw harp on "Love is Dying while the washing is drying")

*Line Dance Fever 5* | Curb Records (Europe) Fishers Hornpipe (dulcimer)

*Merry Christmas ... Have a Nice Life* | Cindi Lauper/Epic Records ( David plays the Tennessee Music Box on "Three Ships" and "In the Bleak Midwinter"/rereleased in 2019)

## *1999*

*Delcimore* | David Schnaufer with Stephen Seifert/Collecting Dust

*Reluctant Daughter* | Sally Barris/Wrensong

## *2000*

*A dulcimer for you, Darlin'* | Debbie Porter/Lyric's Mama Music/ (Plays on "I Will Too", "Tennessee Waltz" and "Tennessee Valentine".)

*Grace is Amazing* | Debbie Porter/Lyric's Mama Music (Guest artist)

*Tin Roof Tango* Mark Shelton Productions, Lewisville, Tx

*Twilight Eyes* | Forerunner Music Group, Nashville, Tn

## *2001*

*Uncle Dulcimer* | David Schnaufer/Analog Cabin, Steven Stubblefield prod.

*Breakin' Up Winter: An Old Time Music Gathering* | Martin Fischer/Vintaphone Record-ings/Cylinder Recordings"2001 Plus". ("Grey Cat on a Tennessee Farm" and "Brush Arbor".)*

*Leaper's Fork* | Starlings TN/Chicken Ranch Records

## *2002*

*Southern Discomfort* | Rattlesnake Annie/Rattlesnake Records (David bows Tennessee music box on "House of The Rising Sun")

*No Summer Storm* | Liberty Pike Musical Group

*NPR All Songs Considered 2* | National Public Radio/ (Plays dulcimer on "All I Have to Do is Dream")

*Sentimental Journey* | Debbie Porter/Lyric's Mama Music

*Spirit of the Wood* | Dulcilirium Enterprises

*Four Part Inventions* | Nashville Dulcimer Quartet, David Schnaufer, Producer

## *2003*

*Cold Mountain Soundtrack* | DMZ/Sony (w Sting and Alison Krauss: "You Will Be My Ain True Love")

*In the Bleak Midwinter* | Earwave Label

*Masters of the Mountain Dulcimer II*|Newtonville, NY: Susan Trump Music

*The Best of "Nashville Unlimited" Christmas Benefit Concert, Vol. I* | Earwave/Live "In the Bleak Midwinter"

*Burning the Dulcimer* | Aaron Thornton

*Old Fashioned Christmas* | Nashville, Tenn.Village Square Music, 2003.

*Palestine Old Time Music Festival* |Various arts/No label (David plays "I'm So Lonesome I Could Cry"; "Elk River Blues")

*Journey* | Alan Rhody/John Prine/MauraO'Connell/Ashwood Recordings

*https://www.discogs.com/release/14384303-Various-Breakin-Up-Winter-An-Old-Time-Music-Gathering

## 2004

*Appalachian Picking Society* | Various/BMG Music (David plays "When Silence was Golden" and two interludes on dulcimer and Tennessee music box.)

*Live from Blair* | Blair School of Music

*All Songs Considered* | 4CD collection/NPR Classics/National Public Radio

*A Tribute Concert for Bob Mize and Mama Maude* |Susan Trump/East Bay's Mountain Dulcimer Society CD/DVD *Memories, Ghost Stories & Second Chances* | Lee Rowe

*It's Dulcimer Time! Rockin' Around the Clock* | Jeff Hames/CD Baby (Produces and performs)

## 2006

*Adieu False Heart* | Linda Ronstadt/Vanguard (Plays dulcimer on three tracks as Derek Schnaufer)

*Arkansas Traveler: Music from Little House on the Prairie* | Pa's Fiddle Recordings (David and Butch Baldissari play "The Devil's Dream")

*Songs of the Tennessee Music Box* |Dan Pfeiffer and Middle Tennessee State University

*The Many Sounds of the Banjo-Mer* | Doug Thomas and various artists/Stinky Dog Studiosn(David plays with Starlings, TN on "Sarah" and solo on "Cumberland Gap")

*Dulcimers for David* | Debbie Porter and T.J. Larkin

*Dulcimers for David, Too!* | Debbie Porter

## 2007

*I am the Man* | Simone White/Honest Jon's Records (plays dulcimer on title song)

*The Nashville Dulcimer Quartet* | David Schnaufer and the Quartet/Appearance on *The Nashville Nobody Knows*

*A Hundred Miles or More* | Allison Kraus/Rounder Records/(Dulcimer on "You Will Be My Ain True Love")

## 2008

*Delcimore Revisited* | David Schnaufer with Stephen Seifert/Collecting Dust

## 2011

*Erin* | David Schnaufer and Rocky Alvey/Muddy Sunshine

## *2014*

*Duets* | Linda Ronstadt/Rhino Records Compilation. (Dulcimer on "Adieu False Heart" credited to Derek Schnaufer)

*Appalachian Mandolin & Dulcimer* | Butch Baldassri and David Schnaufer/Sound Art Recordings

# DVDS

## *1990*

*Learning Mountain Dulcimer* | David Schnaufer/Homespun Music. Video/Tab

## *2000*

*Under Kentucky Skies: 25 Years of Kentucky Music Weekend*/Ruffian Pictures/KET (Interviews and performances)

## *2004*

*A Tribute Concert for Bob Mize and Mama Maude* |Susan Trump/East Bay's Mountain Dulcimer Society CD/DVD

## *2006*

*Stories and Songs of the Tennessee Music Box* | Daniel Pfeiffer and Middle Tennessee State University

2007 *The Nashville Dulcimer Quartet* | David Schnaufer and the Quartet/Appearance on *The Nashville Nobody Knows* television show

*Ballad of Nashville 1864* (contributor)

## *2008*

*Wax* | David Schnaufer/Muddy Sunshine

## *2019*

*David Schnaufer in Concert* | Filmed by Dave Haas in 1999/Distributed by Lyric Mama's Music in 2019

## UNPUBLISHED MUSIC

Countless hours of music by David and his contemporaries from the dulcimer boom of the seventies were recorded but never released, and are waiting to be discovered in closets and storage sheds. If you have these rare recordings, please contact the Wilson Library at the Blair School of Music, Vanderbilt University to inquire about donating your find to the David Schnaufer Collection for the benefit of future scholars of American Roots Music.

## SONGS DAVID WROTE:

### with Herb McCullough

Mr. Snow

When Silence Was Golden

The Way You Move The Air

Starry Lullaby

'O' Pony

Sarah

Run, Run, Run (also Paul Kirby)

### with Townes Van Zandt, Jan Pulsford

Waltz of the Waters

### with Vince Farsetta

Dapper John's Reel

## DULCIMERS MADE BY DAVID

*Tres Ríos* Dulcimers by David Schnaufer (two known instruments; others out there somewhere!)

Three McSpadden Models in collaboration with Lynn McSpadden: Schnaufer Special,
   Schnaufer Model 6, the Schnaufer Baritone

# TEN *PLUCK* DISCUSSION STARTERS FOR
# BOOK CLUBS

1. What does it mean to have a "good life," and who should define what a good life entails? In what ways do we make meaning of our own lives?

2. What obstacles might get in our way in of determining our own paths in life? What options do we have to overcome those obstacles?

3. What would you be willing to give up to walk your own path in life?

4. How has this story shaped your own thinking about whether there is such a thing as a self-made man or woman?

5. What does David's story reveal about the nature of our relationships with family and friends? Do you believe we can truly know one another? If not, what conditions have to be present for love to grow between people?

6. If we define our "comfort zones" by a place, or by the people who surround us, how do we change when we leave our comfort zones?

7. Why is music so important in culture? What does music do for us as individuals? As members of a community? What is the true cost to society when we cut funding for music and the arts in schools, or when it is absent from our lives?

8. How might our lives be changed if more people were *producers* of music rather than *consumers* of music? What personal and social obstacles keep us from making our own music? How can we eliminate those obstacles in our lives?

9. What does it say about cultural values that most of David's obituaries focused almost entirely on the famous people with whom he played? If he had written his own obituary, what do you think he would have put front and center in the story of

his life?

10. Many people characterize others' success as "magical," or something that occurred because they were lucky. How might such thinking get in the way of pursuing our own path in life, or in defining "success" for ourselves?

# SOURCES

## MOVEMENT 1: ORIGINS

1. Dornonville de la Cour, Andreas Peter. Personal communication. February 23, 2021.
2. Schnaufer, David. "A Brief History of the Mountain Dulcimer." The Grand Old Dulcimer Club. January 4, 2016. Accessed 25 August 2020. http://www.thegrandolddulcimerclub.com/#/a-brief-history-of-the-mountain-dulcimer/
3. Shackelford, Laurel, and Bill Weinberg. *Our Appalachia: An Oral History*. Lexington: University Press of Kentucky, 1977.
4. Harrison, Lowell H. *A New History of Kentucky*. Lexington: University Press of Kentucky, 1997.
5. Kleber, John E. *The Kentucky Encyclopedia*. Lexington: University Press of Kentucky, 1978.
6. Lewis, Helen M., Linda Johnson, and Donald Askins. *Colonialism in Modern America: The Appalachian Case*. 2017.
7. Smith, Ralph Lee. *The Story of the Dulcimer*, 2nd. ed. Knoxville: The University of Tennessee Press, 2016.
8. McGregor, Robert Kuhn. "Cultural Adaptation in Colonial New York: The Palatine Germans of the Mohawk Valley." *New York History* 69, no. 1 (1988): 4-34. Accessed 6 August 2020. www.jstor.org/stable/23178485.
9. Mielnik, Tara Mitchell, Ph.D., and Carol Bucy, Ph.D. "Nashville's Historical Timeline." Nashville > Play > History > Timeline. Accessed 4 March 2020. https://www.nashville.gov/Play/History/Timeline.aspx.
10. Ancestry® | Genealogy, Family Trees & Family History Records. Accessed 23 July 2020. https://www.ancestry.com/family-tree/tree/166801642/family?cfpid=322167075295.
11. Jordan, Terry G. "GERMANS." *The Handbook of Texas Online* | Texas State Historical Association (TSHA). June 15, 2010. Accessed 23 March 2020. https://tshaonline.org/handbook/online/articles/png02.
12. Jordan, Terry G. *The German Element in Texas: An Overview*. Rice University. Accessed 3 March 2020. https://scholarship.rice.edu/bitstream/handle/1911/63280/article_RIP633_part1.pdf?sequence=1&isAllowed=y.
13. Jordan, Terry G. *The German Element in Texas: An Overview*. Rice University. Accessed 30 March 2020. https://scholarship.rice.edu/bitstream/handle/1911/63280/article_RIP633_part1.pdf?sequence=1&isAllowed=y.

14. "TENNESSEE COLONY, TX" | *The Handbook of Texas Online* | Texas State Historical Association (TSHA)." Texas State Historical Association. Accessed 30 March 2020. https://tshaonline.org/handbook/online/articles/hlt08#.

15. Ancestry® | Genealogy, Family Trees & Family History Records. Accessed 24 July 2020. https://www.ancestry.com/imageviewer/collections/2272/images/40394_b062353-02632.

16. Dick, David. *Let There Be Light: the Story of Rural Electrification in Kentucky.* Plum Lick Publications, 2008.

17. Linn, Karen. *That Half-barbaric Twang: The Banjo in American Popular Culture.* 1994. Urbana and Chicago: The University of Illinois Press.

18. Ancestry® | Genealogy, Family Trees & Family History Records. Accessed 24 July 2020. https://www.ancestry.com/imageviewer/collections/2272/images/40394_b062353-02632

19. Ritchie, Jean. *Dulcimer People.* Oak Publications, 1975.

20. "Uncle Ed Thomas Dulcimer." Ritchie, Jean. *The Dulcimer Book.* New York: Oak Publications, 1974.

21. Yates, Mike. "Cecil Sharp in America." Musical Traditions Internet Magazine Home Page. June 30, 2000. Accessed 31 July 2020. http://www.mustrad.org.uk/articles/sharp.htm.

22. Hajdu, David. *Positively 4th Street: The Lives and Times of Joan Baez, Bob Dylan, Mimi Baez Fariña, and Richard Fariña.* New York: Picador, 2011.

23. Lomax Hawes, Bess. "American Folk Music, Teaching Course Outline", San Fernando State College Fall 1958. to 1974, 1958. Manuscript/Mixed Material. https://www.loc.gov/item/afc2014008ms1503/.

24. Walls, David. "On the Naming of Appalachia." David Walls Professor Emeritus of Sociology. Accessed 7 March 2020. https://web.sonoma.edu/users/w/wallsd/on-the-naming-of-appalachia.html.

25. 10 Sep 1900, El Paso Daily Herald, "Great Destruction of Life and Property". Newspapers.com. Accessed 7 March 2020. https://www.newspapers.com/image/77766839/.

26. Jordan, Terry G. "GERMANS." *The Handbook of Texas Online* | Texas State Historical Association (TSHA). June 15, 2010. Accessed 23 March 2020. https://tshaonline.org/handbook/online/articles/png02.

27. Stoddart, Jess. "Challenge and Change in Appalachia: The Story of Hindman Settlement School" (2002). *Education in Appalachian Region 3.*

28. Smith, Ralph Lee. *Appalachian Dulcimer Traditions.* Lanham, MD and London: Scarecrow Press, 2002.

29. Ritchie, Jean. *The Dulcimer Book.* New York: Oak Publications, 1974.

30. Linn, Karen. *That Half-barbaric Twang: The Banjo in American Popular Culture.* Urbana and Chicago: University of Illinois Press, 1994.

31. Kleber, John E., and Thomas D. Clark. *The Kentucky Encyclopedia,* 1992.

32. Campbell, John C. *The Southern Highlander and His Homeland.* New York: The Russell Sage Foundation. 1921.

33. Yates, Mike. "Cecil Sharp in America." *Musical Traditions Internet Magazine* Home Page. June 30, 2000. Accessed 16 March 2020. http://www.mustrad.org.uk/articles/sharp.htm.

34. Miles, Suzannah Smith. "Finding Barbara Allen: The Songcatchers Olive Dame Campbell and Cecil Sharp." Earl Scruggs Center. August 2, 2014. Accessed 21. March 2020. http://earlscruggscenter.org/?s=Finding Barbara Allen.

35. Yates, Mike. "Cecil Sharp in America." *Musical Traditions Internet Magazine* Home Page. June 30, 2000. Accessed March 16, 2020. http://www.mustrad.org.uk/articles/sharp.htm.

36. Schnaufer, D. Eric. "Schnaufer Family History." Interviewed by author. February 21, 2020.

37. "U.S., World War I Draft Registration Cards, 1917-1918 for Chris Schnaufer."Accessed 7 August 2020. https://www.ancestry.com/imageviewer/collections/6482/images/005152508_02493?pId=16873715.

38. "Texas, Select County Marriage Records, 1837-2015 for C. Schnaufer." Accessed 7 August 2020. https://www.ancestry.com/imageviewer/collections/9168/images/45607_b298996-01847?pId=26391650.

39. Greene, Andy. "Readers' Poll: The 10 Best Protest Songs of All Time." *Rolling Stone*. June 25, 2018. Accessed August 07, 2020. https://www.rollingstone.com/music/music-lists/readers-poll-the-10-best-protest-songs-of-all-time-141706/bob-dylan-masters-of-war-172547/.

40. McGuinn, R., 1999. "Fair Nottamun Town". [online] Folk Den. Accessed 5 May 2020. https://www.ibiblio.org/jimmy/folkden-wp/?cat=17%22&paged=8.

41. Staff. "Maud Karpeles Biography." Cecil Sharp in Appalachia. Accessed 7 August 2020. http://cecilsharpinappalachia.org/MaudKarpelesBiography.html.

42. Winick, Steven. ""Jean Ritchie: 1922-2015"." Library of Congress Blogs. June 11, 2015. Accessed 2 August 2020. https://blogs.loc.gov/folklife/2015/06/jean-ritchie-1922-2015/.

43. Pynchon, Thomas. "Richard Farina." Accessed 24 March 2020. http://www.pynchon.pomona.edu/uncollected/farina.html.

44. Hajdu, David. *Positively 4th Street*, 2011.

45. Winick, Stephen. "Jean Ritchie, 1922-2015." *Folklife Today*. June 11, 2015. Accessed 13 February 2020. https://blogs.loc.gov/folklife/2015/06/jean-ritchie-1922-2015/.

46. Ritchie, Jean. *Singing Home of the Cumberlands*. Lexington, Ky: U of Kentucky Press. 1988. p. 252.

47. Frank C Schnaufer in the U.S., World War II Army Enlistment Records, 1938-1946. Accessed 7 August 2020. https://search.ancestry.com/cgi-bin/sse.dll?indiv=1&dbid=8939&h=981244&ssrc=pt&tid=166801642 &pid=322167075296.

48. Schnaufer, D. Eric. Personal communication August 17, 2020.

49. Schnaufer, D. Eric. Interviewed by author. February 21, 2020.

50. National Archives and Records Administration; Hospital Admission Card Files, ca. 1970; NAI: 570973; Record Group Number: Records of the Office of the Surgeon General (Army), 1775-1994; Record Group Title: 112.

51. Office of Medical History. Accessed 7 August 2020. https://history.amedd. army.mil/booksdocs/wwii/PM4/CH14.Tuberculosis.htm.

52. Long, Esmond R., MD. "Chapter 14: Tuberculosis in World War I." U.S. Army Medical Department: Office of Medical History. Accessed 28 February 2020. https://history.amedd.army.mil/booksdocs/wwii/PM4/CH14.Tuberculosis. htm.

53. Rosenblatt, M. B. "Pulmonary Tuberculosis: Evolution of Modern Therapy." *Bulletin of the New York Academy of Medicine.* March 1973. Accessed 7 August 2020. https://www.ncbi.nlm.nih.gov/pmc/articles/PMC1806933/?page=5.

54. Arnold, Marc. *Disease, Class and Social Change.* Newcastle upon Tyne: Cambridge Scholars Publishing 2012.

55. Kelly, Susan. Vol. 39, No. 1, *DISCRIMINATION* (SPRING 2011) Published by Oral History Society. 2011.

56. "Rosemary Kennedy, 1918-2005." The Autism History Project. Accessed 3 April 2020. https://blogs.uoregon.edu/autismhistoryproject/people/ rosemary-kennedy/.

57. Digital Images. California, County Birth, Marriage, and Death Records, 1849-1980. Ancestry.com. Lehi, UT, USA. 2017.

58. Kruth, John. To Live's to Fly: The Ballad of the Late, Great Townes Van Zandt. Cambridge, MA: Da Capo, 2008.

59. "Scrub Typhus." Centers for Disease Control and Prevention. October 03, 2019. Accessed 15 March 2020. https://www.cdc.gov/typhus/scrub/index. html.

60. Schnaufer, D. Eric. Interviewed by author. February 12, 2020.

61. Nevin, Remington L., and Ashley M. Croft. "Psychiatric Effects of Malaria and Anti-malarial Drugs: Historical and Modern Perspectives." *Malaria Journal.* June 22, 2016. Accessed 2 August 2020. https://www.ncbi.nlm.nih.gov/pmc/ articles/PMC4918116/.

62. Grob, Gerald N. "Mental Health Policy in America: Myths and Realities. " *Health Affairs* 11, no. 3 (March 1992): 7-22. doi:10.1377/hlthaff.11.3.7.

63. Anderson County Genealogical Society, and Kay Wolf. "The Tracings, Volume 16, Number 03, November 1997." The Portal to Texas History. May 20, 2008. Accessed 17 March 2020. https://texashistory.unt.edu/ark:/67531/ metapth37949/m1/9/?q=Schnaufer.

64. "U.S. WWII Hospital Admission Card Files, 1942-1954." Ancestry.com. 2019. Accessed 20 March 2020. http://catalog.archives.gov/advancedsearch.

65. "Our History." Henry Street Settlement. December 31, 2020. Accessed 3 January 2021. https://www.henrystreet.org/about/our-history/.

66. Ritchie, Jean. *Singing Home of the Cumberlands.* 1988.

67. Winick, Stephen. "Jean Ritchie, 1922-2015." Jean Ritchie, 1922-2015 | *Folklife Today.* June 11, 2015. Accessed 13 February 2020. https://blogs.loc.gov/ folklife/2015/06/jean-ritchie-1922-2015/.

68. AmNY. "Jean Ritchie, 92, the Village's 'Mother of Folk'." *AmNewYork.* June 18, 2015. Accessed 2 August 2020. https://www.amny.com/news/jean- ritchie-92-the-villages-mother-of-folk/.

69. Szwed, John F. *Alan Lomax: The Man Who Recorded the World.* New York:

Penguin Books, 2011.

70. Herald-Leader, and John Cheves. "Jean Ritchie, 92, Introduced Mountain Dulcimer Music to the World." Kentucky.com Accessed 25 February 2020. https://www.kentucky.com/entertainment/music-news-reviews/ article44602842.html.

71. Szwed, John F. *Alan Lomax: The Man Who Recorded the World*. New York: Penguin Books, 2011.

72. "Why Is Nashville Called Music City?" *Nashville Scene*. August 22, 2002. Accessed 2 April 2020. https://www.nashvillescene.com/arts-culture/article/ 13007578/why-is-nashville-called-music-city.

73. Reports, Staff. "Why Is Nashville Called Music City? The Fisk Jubilee Singers and Queen Victoria Get the Credit." *The Tennessean*. February 19, 2019. Accessed August 02, 2020. https://www.tennessean.com/story/life/2019/02/ 19/why-nashville-called-music-city/2906635002/.

74. Lomax, John, III. Interviewed by author. February 3, 2020.

75. Schnaufer, D. Eric. Interviewed by author. February 12, 2020.

76. Schnaufer family documents, courtesy of D. Eric Schnaufer.

77. AmNY. "Jean Ritchie, 92, the Village's 'Mother of Folk'." *AmNewYork*. June 18, 2015. Accessed 2 August 2020. https://www.amny.com/news/ jean-ritchie-92-the-villages-mother-of-folk/.

78. Farsetta, Vincent. Interviewed by author. March 2, 2020.

79. Schnaufer, D. Eric. Personal communication. January 17, 2021.

80. Schnaufer, D. Eric. Interviewed by author. February 12, 2020.

81. Schnaufer family documents, courtesy of D. Eric Schnaufer.

82. Kruth, John. *To Live's to Fly: The Ballad of the Late, Great Townes Van Zandt*. Cambridge, MA: Da Capo, 2008.

83. Jordan, Norman. Interviewed by author. March 30, 2021.

84. Schnaufer, D. Eric. Personal communication. 2021.

85. Dean, Natasha. Interviewed by author. July 22, 2020.

86. Schnaufer, D. Eric. Interviewed by author. February 12, 2020.

87. "Hundreds Killed, Thousands Injured in Texas City Disaster of 1947." ABC13 Houston. April 16, 2020. Accessed 18 April 2020. https://abc13.com/ disaster-fire-explosion-texas-city/1865491/.

88. "Three Men Die in Texas City Blast." *Lubbock Morning Avalanche*. March 31, 1958. Accessed 30 March 2021. https://www.newspapers.com/image/ 78312380/?terms=Union Carbide explosion.

89. Schnaufer, D. Eric. Personal communication. 2021.

90. Hellman, Neal. Personal communication. February 15, 2021.

91. Hellman, Neal. "Liberating Richard: Some Thoughts on the Richard Farina Dulcimer Book." Accessed 4 January 2021. http://www.richardandmimi.com/ liberatingrichard.html.

92. Lawing, Tramp. Interviewed by author. June 13, 2020.

93. Schnaufer, D.Eric. Interviewed by author. February 12, 2020.

94. Wright, Jerry, and David Schnaufer. "Jerry Wright Interviews David Schnaufer. " Accessed 10 February 2020. http://www.jerrywrightfamily.com/interviews. htm.

95. "Jew's Harp Jaw's Harp". Accessed 14 October 2020. http://www. antropodium.nl/Duizend Namen Mhp.htm.
96. YouTube. December 7, 2012. Accessed 14 October 2020. https://www. youtube.com/watch?v=4SpWuseQGys.
97. La Maignan, Catherine. "Fred Crane in His Own Words 1927-2011." http://www.maultrommelverein.at/wp-content/uploads/2011/12/In-his-0.
98. Seeger, Charles. "The Appalachian Dulcimer." *The Journal of American Folklore* 71, no. 279 (1958): 40-51.

# MOVEMENT 2: CROSSING THRESHOLDS

1. Orleans, Susan. "To My First Time". *Airmail: Women of Letters*. Compiled by Michaela McGuire. Scoresby: Penguin Group Australia., 2015.
2. Robison, Jennifer. "Decades of Drug Use: Data From the '60s and '70s." Gallup.com. November 18, 2020. Accessed March 06, 2021. https://news. gallup.com/poll/6331/decades-drug-use-data-from-60s-70s.aspx.
3. 1960s Flashback-Economy / Prices. Accessed August 03, 2020. http://www. 1960sflashback.com/1960/economy.asp.
4. History.com Editors. "The 1960s History." History.com. May 25, 2010. Accessed April 03, 2020. https://www.history.com/topics/1960s/ 1960s-history.
5. "18 Nov 1960, Page 6 - *The La Marque Times* " Newspapers.com. Accessed August 03, 2020. https://www.newspapers.com/image/6018269/?terms=Cub Scouts Visit Newspaper Office.
6. Schnaufer, D.Eric. Interviewed by author. February 12, 2020.
7. Hajdu, David. *Positively 4th Street*. New York: Farrar, Straus & Giroux, 2001.
8. "Carolyn Hester." Will Marston. October 26, 1984. Accessed August 03, 2020. https://www.willmarston.com/carolyn-hester.
9. "Monotony and the Sacred: A Brief History of Drone Music." ABC Radio National. May 06, 2015. Accessed August 14, 2020. https://www.abc.net.au/ radionational/programs/earshot/monotony-and-the-sacred/6448906.
10. Emerick, Geoff. Here, *There and Everywhere: My Life Recording the Music of The Beatles*. New York: Avery, 2007.
11. Sheff, David. *"All We Are Saying ..." The Philosophy of the New Left*. New York: Putnam, 1971.
12. Barker, Nancy. Interviewed by author. April 16, 2020.
13. Blosser, John. "Terry Hennessy: Luthier of the Fariña Legend." http://richardandmimi.com. Accessed August 03, 2020. http://richardandmimi.com/hennessy.
14. Hajdu, David. *Positively 4th Street*. New York: Farrar, Straus & Giroux, 2001.
15. Lawing, Tramp. Interviewed by author. June 13, 2020.
16. Madame La Pulse Productions. "David Schnaufer—Delcimore". Hendersonville, TN: Collecting Dust, 2000. Promotion brochure for the Collecting Dust/Schnaufer production of the CD, *Delcimore*.

17. League, The Broadway. "IBDB.com." Internet Broadway Database. Accessed August 03, 2020. https://www.ibdb.com/broadway-cast-staff/edith-kessler-3948 12#Credits.

18. Farsetta, Vincent. Interviewed by author. March 2, 2020.

19. Hajdu, David. *Positively 4th Street.* New York: Farrar, Straus & Giroux, 2001.

20. "Oral History of John Lomax III." Interview by Norie Guthrie. Scholarship. Rice.edu. November 10, 2017. Accessed July 2, 2020. https://scholarship.rice. edu/ohms/viewer.php?cachefile=file_88b611df-70e4-4167-b1d1-6815e5d56de6_wrc09160_ohms.ohms. Interview conducted on behalf of the Houston Folk Music Archive.

21. Clemens, Christopher. "The Jester Lounge: Calabasas, CA 91302." Accessed August 04, 2020. http://www.thejesterlounge.com/.

22. "Mountain Dulcimers - Mountain View Arkansas - McSpadden." Dulcimer Shoppe. Accessed 3 March 2020. https://mcspaddendulcimers.com/about/

23. Attoun, Marti. "Making Mountain Dulcimers." American Profile. January 20, 2011. Accessed 3 March 2020. https://americanprofile.com/articles/mcspadden-dulcimer-factory-video/.

24. Staff. "Artist Spurs Revival of Folk Instrument." Newspapers.com. Accessed June 11, 2020. https://www.newspapers.com/image/31500506/?terms=Lynn McSpadden.

25. Lomax, John, III. Interviewed by author. February 3, 2020.

26. Fleming, Gena. Personal communication. January 15, 2021.

27. Fleming, Gena. Interviewed by author. September 6, 2020.

28. "Appendicitis." Mayo Clinic. May 24, 2019. Accessed March 28, 2021. https://www.mayoclinic.org/diseases-conditions/appendicitis/symptoms-causes/syc-20369543.

29. Schnaufer, D. Eric. Personal communication. March 28, 2021.

30. "Patients in Hospital." *The Mainland Times* (La Marque, Texas), January 23, 1963.

31. Theobald, Terry. Interviewed by author. October 23, 2020.

32. *No Direction Home Bob Dylan.* Directed by Martin Scorsese. France: Paramount, 2006. DVD.

33. Hajdu, David. *Positively 4th Street.* New York: Farrar, Straus & Giroux, 2001.

34. Winick, Steven. ""Jean Ritchie: 1922-2015"." Library of Congress Blogs. June 11, 2015. Accessed August 12, 2020. https://blogs.loc.gov/folklife/2015/06/jean-ritchie-1922-2015/.

35. Cheves, J. 2015, 6.2. "Jean Ritchie, 92, introduced mountain dulcimer music to the world". *Lexington Herald-Leader* online. Retrieved 2020, 2.25, from https://www.kentucky.com/entertainment/music-news-reviews/article44602842.html.

36. "Newport Folk Festival" Accessed 13 March 2020 from: https://www.britannica.com/art/Newport-Folk-Festival.

37. Macrini, John. Interviewed by author. October 10, 2020.

38. "H.M.Dansby Heads United Fund Drive." *The Mainland Times* (La Marque, Texas), August 25, 1960. newspapers.com. Accessed October 11, 2020.

39. Schnaufer, D. Eric. Personal communication. January 6, 2021.

40. Alvey, Rocky. Interviewed by author. November 7, 2020.

41. Ellis, Darrel. Interviewed by author. July 8, 2020.

42. Schnaufer, D. Eric. Interviewed by author. February 12, 2020.

43. Staff. "Schnaufer Is Tops in Bible Reading." Https://www.newspapers.com/image/386399765/?terms=Schnaufer Is Tops in Bible Reading. Accessed August 08, 2020.

44. Hellman, Neal. "Driving with the Beach Boys: The Golden Light from the West" Unpublished memoir.

45. Turner, Rick. "Richard and Mimi Farina and the 6 1/2 Fret." Rickturnerblog (blog), December 14, 2016. Accessed July 9, 2020. https://rickturnerblog.com/2016/12/14/richard-and-mimi-farina-and-the-6-12th-fret/.

46. "Mountain Dulcimers - Mountain View Arkansas - McSpadden." Dulcimer Shoppe. Accessed March 03, 2020. https://mcspaddendulcimers.com/about/.

47. Attoun, Marti. "Making Mountain Dulcimers." American Profile. January 20, 2011. Accessed March 03, 2020. https://americanprofile.com/articles/mcspadden-dulcimer-factory-video/.

48. Staff. "Artist Spurs Revival of Folk Instrument." *The Camden News.* Newspapers.com. Accessed June 11, 2020. https://www.newspapers.com/image/31500506/?terms=Lynn McSpadden.

49. Force, Robert. Interviewed by author. January 30, 2021.

50. "Force Tracks Down His Wild Dulcimer Roots." *The Port Townsend Leader*, 13 July 2010, https://www.ptleader.com/stories/force-tracks-down-his-wild-dulcimer-roots,54749. Accessed April 12, 2020.

51. Farsetta, Vince. Personal communication. May 1, 2020.

52. Farsetta, Vince. Interviewed by author. February 29, 2020.

53. Havers, Richard. "Why Brian Jones Was So Important To The Rolling Stones: UDiscover." *UDiscover Music.* July 03, 2020. Accessed May 13, 2020. https://www.udiscovermusic.com/stories/just-why-was-brian-jones-so-important-to-the-rolling-stones/.

54. Wawzenek, Bryan. "Top 10 Brian Jones Rolling Stones Multi-Instrumentalist Songs." December 05, 2014. Accessed May 13, 2020. https://ultimateclassicrock.com/brian-jones-multi-instrumentalist-songs/.

55. Kruth, John. "The Secret Genius Behind The Rolling Stones' Classic 'Between the Buttons'." Observer. January 20, 2017. Accessed May 13, 2020. https://observer.com/2017/01/brian-jones-rolling-stones-between-the-buttons-anniversary/.

56. "The Rolling Stones." Ed Sullivan Show. January 05, 2021. Accessed February 16, 2021. https://www.edsullivan.com/artists/the-rolling-stones/#:~:text=The Rolling Stones first appeared,both halves of the show.

57. Pies, Don. "Regency TR-1 Transistor Radio History." Regency TR-1 Transistor Radio History. Accessed August 12, 2020. http://www.regencytr1.com/.

58. Jaime Espensen-Sturges, "XERF," *Handbook of Texas Online*, accessed August 24, 2020, https://www.tshaonline.org/handbook/entries/xerf.

59. Malone, Bill C., and Tracey E. W. Laird. *Country Music USA.* Austin:

University of Texas Press, 2018.

60. Madame La Pulse Productions. "David Schnaufer—Delcimore". Hendersonville, TN: Collecting Dust, 2000. Promotion brochure for the Collecting Dust/Schnaufer production of the CD, *Delcimore*.

61. Hajdu, David. *Positively 4th Street*. New York: Farrar, Straus & Giroux, 2001.

62. Marcus, Greil. "Tombstone Blues." *Los Angeles Times*. May 20, 2001. Accessed March 24, 2020. https://www.latimes.com/archives/la-xpm-2001-may-20-bk-142-story.html

63. Pynchon, Thomas. "Richard Farina."Accessed March 24, 2020. http://www.pynchon.pomona.edu/uncollected/farina.html.

64. Lomax, John, III. Interviewed by author. February 3, 2020.

65. Mankad, Raj. "Houston Alternative Media : Telling It Like It Was." *The Rag Blog*. August 05, 2014. Accessed April 04, 2020. http://www.theragblog.com/houston-alternative-media-telling-it-like-it-was/.

66. Jordan, Norman. Interviewed by author. March 30, 2021.

67. Theobald, Terry. Interviewed by author. October 23, 2020.

68. Macrini, John. Interviewed by author. October 10, 2020

69. Fleming, Gena. Personal communication. September 10, 2020.

70. Baldassari, Sinclair. Interviewed by author. July 6, 2020.

71. Lomax, Nova. Interviewed by author. May 31, 2020.

72. Schnaufer, D. Eric. Interviewed by author. February 12, 2020.

73. Jordan, Norman. Interviewed by author. March 30, 2021.

74. Theobald, Terry. Interviewed by author. October 23, 2020.

75. Lomax, Nova. Interviewed by author. May 31, 2020.

76. Schnaufer, D. Eric. Interviewed by author. February 12, 2020.

77. Staff. 1968 "La Marque High School Yearbook." Classmates.com. Accessed August 09, 2020. https://www.classmates.com/siteui/yearbooks/182072.

78. Hoffman, David, and Ken Adderson. "1968 Was a Very, Very Tense Year in America." Youtube.com, March 28, 2020. Adderson's film "Confrontation" was unreleased until David Hoffman published it on youtube.com.

79. Schnaufer, D. Eric. Personal communication.

80. Schnaufer, D. Eric. Interviewed by author. February 12, 2020.

81. Harmon, John. "Jean Ritchie, Folk, Mountain Music Legend: An Appreciation from the AJC Archives." AJC June 06, 2015. Accessed April 3, 2020.

82. Lomax, John, III. Interviewed by author. February 3, 2020.

83. "Oral History of John Lomax III." Interview by Norie Guthrie. Scholarship. Rice.edu. November 10, 2017. Accessed July 2, 2020. https://scholarship.rice.edu/ohms/viewer.php?cachefile=file_88b611df-70e4-4167-b1d1-6815e5d56de6_wrc09160_ohms.ohms. Interview conducted on behalf of the Houston Folk Music Archive oral history project.

84. Bryan, Tim. Interviewed by author. July 20, 2020.

85. Ellis, Darrel. Interviewed by author. July 8, 2020

86. Lomax, Nova. Interviewed by author. May 31, 2020.

87. Farsetta, Vincent. Interviewed by author. March 2, 2020.

88. McEuen, John. Interviewed by author. December 3, 2020.

89. "How the Nitty Gritty Dirt Band's 'Will the Circle Be Unbroken' Saved

Traditional Country Music." *Wide Open Country*. May 12, 2018. Accessed June 1, 2020. https://www.wideopencountry.com/will-the-circle-be-unbroken-nitty-gritty/.

90. Amorosino, Brad. "The Circle, Unbroken: 50 Years of The Nitty Gritty Dirt Band." *Acoustic Guitar*. February 03, 2016. Accessed June 6, 2020. http://acousticguitar.com/the-circle-unbroken-50-years-of-the-nitty-gritty-dirt-band/.

91. Jordan, Norman. Interviewed by author. March 30, 2021.

92. "Three Men Die in Texas City Blast." Newspapers.com. March 31, 1958. Accessed March 30, 2021. https://www.newspapers.com/image/78312380/?terms=Union Carbide explosion.

93. Schnaufer, D. Eric. Interview by author. January 4, 2021.

94. Schnaufer, D. Eric. Interview by author. August 17, 2020.

95. Schnaufer, D. Eric. Personal communication. July 30, 2020.

96. Schnaufer, D. Eric. Interviewed by author. February 29, 2020.

97. Schnaufer, D. Eric. Personal communication. January 6, 2020.

98. Theobald, Terry. Interviewed by author. October 23, 2021.

99. Schnaufer, D. Eric. Interviewed by author. February 29, 2020.

100. Staff. "1969 La Marque High School Year Book." Classmates.com. Accessed August 09, 2020. https://www.classmates.com/siteui/yearbooks/180465?page=45.

101. Schnaufer, D. Eric. Interviewed by author. February 29, 2020. Documents courtesy of D. Eric Schnaufer.

102. Urbanski, Dave. *The Man Comes Around: The Spiritual Journey of Johnny Cash*. Lake Mary, FL: Relevant Media Group, 2004.

103. Mastropolo, Frank. "When Bob Dylan, Joni Mitchell Performed on Johnny Cash's TV Show." *Ultimate Classic Rock*. May 30, 2020. Accessed August 09, 2020. https://ultimateclassicrock.com/bob-dylan-joni-mitchell-johnny-cash-show/.

104. ClassicTVHits.com: TV Ratings 1960's. Accessed August 09, 2020. https://www.classictvhits.com/tvratings/1969.htm.

105. Jordan, Norman. Interviewed by author. March 30, 2021.

106. Theobald, Terry. Interviewed by author. October 23, 2020.

107. Schnaufer, D. Eric. Personal communication August 8, 2020.

108. Schnaufer, D. Eric. Personal communication. July 30, 2020.

109. Shekelle, Paul, MD. Personal communication. February 29, 2020.

110. "Edith Schnaufer Death Certificate". Ancestry.com. 2019. Accessed March 20, 2020. https://www.ancestry.com/imageviewer/collections/2272/images/.

111. Jordan, Norman. Interviewed by author. March 30, 2021.

112. Schnaufer, D. Eric. Personal communication. January 6, 2020.

113. Schnaufer, D. Eric. Interviewed by author. August 17, 2020.

114. "Austin Episcopal Seminary to Graduate 22 Tuesday." 18 May 1970, 16 - *The Austin American* at Newspapers.com. Accessed September 28, 2020. https://www.newspapers.com/image/386479610/.

115. "Officers 'The Greatest, Cadets Top Level'." *Victoria Advocate*. August 9, 1970. Accessed August 09, 2020. https://www.newspapers.com/clip/50052182/

dennis-works-on-maritime-academy-ship.

116. Jordan, Norman . Interviewed by author. March 30, 2021.

117. Kay, Jon . Interviewed by author. February 5, 2021.

118. Schnaufer, Eric. Personal communication. January 17, 2021.

119. Hellman, Neal. Personal communication. January 28, 2021.

120. Hellman, Neal. "When I Saw My First Dulcimer" unpublished manuscript. July 2, 2020.

121. Hellman, Neal. Personal communication. July 2, 2020.

122. McCullough, Joann. Interviewed by author. March 17, 2020

# MOVEMENT 3: ODYSSEYS

1. Schnaufer, D. Eric. Personal communication. July 30, 2020.

2. "Concerning the Mountain Dulcimer." John Kay.February 5, 2021. From unpublished transcript of October 9,1995 interview of David Schnaufer.

3. Fitzpatrick, James C. "Rare Dulcimer at Show." *Kansas City Times*. Accessed 10 August, 2020. https://www.newspapers.com/image/59525369/?terms=Rare Dulcimer at Show.

4. The Dulcimer Shoppe. Advertisement. *Mugwump's*, Spring 1979,13.

5. Carol, Bonnie. Personal communication. February 2, 2021.

6. Carol, Bonnie. Personal communication. January 27, 2021.

7. Bonnie Carol Biography. Accessed 12 April 2020. http://bonniecarol.com/BonnieBio.html.

8. Carol, Bonnie. Interviewed by author. April 6, 2020.

9. Force, Robert. Interviewed by author. January 30, 2021.

10. Staff. "Force Tracks down His Wild Dulcimer Roots." *Port Townsend Leader*. July 13, 2010. Accessed 9 August 2020. https://www.ptleader.com/stories/force-tracks-down-his-wild-dulcimer-roots,54749.

11. "Welcome." Robertforce.com. Accessed 15 January 2020. https://robertforce.com/SongsAndInstruction/SongsAndInstruction.html.

12. Force, Robert and Albert D'Ossché. *In Search of the Wild Dulcimer*. New York: Random House, 1974.

13. Young, David. Interviewed by author. April 12, 2020.

14. Young, Mary. Interviewed by author. April 10, 2020.

15. Freimuth, Rick. Interviewed by author. April 6, 2020.

16. Crouse, Timothy. "Blue." *Rolling Stone*. June 25, 2018. Accessed 10 August 2020. https://www.rollingstone.com/music/music-album-reviews/blue-104415/.

17. Joni Mitchell Library - "Blue: Rolling Stone, August 5, 1971." Joni Mitchell. Accessed 10 April 2020. https://jonimitchell.com/library/view.cfm?id=252.

18. Young, David. Interviewed by author. April 17, 2020.

19. Freimuth, Rick. Personal communication. April 12, 2020.

20. Young, Mary. Interviewed by author. April 10, 2020.

21. Hellman, Neal. Personal communication. February 4, 2021.

22. Macrini, John. Interviewed by the author. October 10, 2020.

23. Freimuth, Rick. Personal communication. April 12, 2020.

24. Farsetta, Vince. Personal communication. April 8, 2020.

25. Amorosino, Brad. "The Circle, Unbroken: 50 Years of the Nitty Gritty Dirt Band." Acoustic Guitar. February 03, 2016. Accessed 8 June 2020. http://acousticguitar.com/the-circle-unbroken-50-years-of-the-nitty-gritty-dirt-band/.

26. Barker, Nancy (Johnson). Interviewed by author. March 22, 2020.

27. Goddard, Peter. "No Mariposa like This One: Dylan, Lightfoot, Young, Mitchell." *Toronto Star* (Toronto, Canada), July 17, 1972.

28. Farsetta, Vince. Personal communication April 26, 2020.

29. Freimuth, Rick. Personal communication. April 20, 2020.

30. "Dance All Night—The Highwoods Stringband Story." Online via folkstreams.net. USA: Piggysnout Productions and Mudthumper Music, 2018. Accessed 6 September 2020. https://www.folkstreams.net/film-detail.php?id=435.

31. Lomax, John, III. Interviewed by author. February 3, 2020.

32. Schnaufer. D. Eric. Personal communication. January 17, 2021.

33. Schinder, Scott, and Andy Schwartz. *Icons of Rock: An Encyclopedia of the Legends Who Changed Music Forever*. Westport, CT: Greenwood Press, 2008.

34. Madame La Pulse Productions. David Schnaufer–Delcimore. Hendersonville, TN: Collecting Dust, 2000. Promotion brochure for the Collecting Dust/Schnaufer production of the CD, *Delcimore*.

35. "Concerning the Mountain Dulcimer." John Kay.February 5, 2021. From unpublished transcript of October 9,1995 interview of David Schnaufer.

36. "David Schnaufer." Interview by Jerry Rockwell. "Contemporary Mountain Dulcimers and the People Who Pick 'em." Accessed 15 February 2020. https://www.jcrmusic.com/. contemp.md.1.html. Originally published in *Dirty Linen* #34 June/July 1991.

37. Staff. "Marriage Announcement." *La Marque Times,* February 1, 1973.

38. Fleming, Gena. Interviewed by author. September 6, 2020.

39. Schnaufer, D. Eric. Personal communication, July 30, 2020.

40. "Texas, Death Certificates, 1903-1982 for Frank Cleaver Schnaufer." Ancestry.com Accessed 2 February 2020. https://www.ancestry.com/imageviewer/collections/2272/images/33154_b062892-00083?pId=80474.

41. Thiela Schnaufer. Interviewed by author. August 17, 2020.

42. Schnaufer, D. Eric. Personal communication, February 29, 2020.

43. Fleming, Gena. Personal communication. September 6, 2020.

44. Freimuth, Rick. Personal communication. May 8, 2020.

45. Green, Nelda. Interviewed by author. January 3, 2021.

46. Hobbs, Joe. Interviewed by author. January 4, 2021.

47. Bentley, Aaron. Personal communication. November 28, 2020.

48. Campbell, Cade J. Interviewed by author. September 12, 2020.

49. White, Mack. Personal communication. June 9, 2020.

50. Hobbs, Joe. Interviewed by author. January 4, 2021.

51. Green, Nelda. Interviewed by author. January 3, 2021.

52. Bentley, Aaron. Interviewed by author. November.28.2020.

53. Campbell, Cade J. Interview by author. September 12, 2020.

54. Callens, Loretta. Personal communication, September 11, 2020.

55. Schnaufer, D. Eric. Personal communication, February 29, 2020.

56. Bentley, Aaron. Interviewed by author. November, 28. 2020.

57. Sul Ross State University Yearbook 1973-74. Courtesy of Sul Ross State University.

58. Hines, Chet. *How to Make and Play the Dulcimore*. Harrisburg, Pa: Stackpole Books, 1973.

59. "Concerning the Mountain Dulcimer." John Kay.February 5, 2021. From unpublished transcript of October 9,1995 interview of David Schnaufer.

60. Thomas, Dana. "THE DULCET DULCIMER." The Washington Post. October 07, 1990. Accessed 25 August 2020. https://www.washingtonpost.com/archive/lifestyle/style/1990/10/07/the-dulcet-dulcimer/14c0410f-983a-457d-be6c-f5c71673b340/.

61. Jarvey, Paul. "Pulling His Heart Strings." Worcester Telegram & Gazette, September 26, 1990.

62. Eppright, Harrison. "1973 Austin, J.R. Music." Interviewed by author. April 14, 2020.

63. Elliott, Tom. "Roger Nicholson: Britain's Most Influential Dulcimer Player." *Independent*. October 23, 2011. Accessed 16 June 2020. https://www.independent.co.uk/news/obituaries/roger-nicholson-britain-s-most-influential-dulcimer-player-1908238.html.

64. "Concerning the Mountain Dulcimer." John Kay.February 5, 2021. From unpublished transcript of October 9,1995 interview of David Schnaufer.

65. "Concerning the Mountain Dulcimer." John Kay.February 5, 2021. From unpublished transcript of October 9,1995 interview of David Schnaufer.

66. Schnaufer, D. Eric. Personal communication, July 30, 2020.

67. Wright, Jerry, and David Schnaufer. "Jerry Wright Interviews David Schnaufer." Interview. Http://www.jerrywrightfamily.com. Accessed 10 February 2012. http://www.jerrywrightfamily.com/interviews.

68. Macrini, John. "Harmonicas and Dulcimers". Interviewed by author. October 10, 2020.

69. Schnaufer, D. Eric. Personal communication. January 17, 2021.

70. Schnaufer, D. Eric. Personal communication. January 6, 2021.

71. Bentley, Aaron. Interviewed by author. November 28, 2020.

72. Schnaufer, D. Eric. Personal communication. February 29, 2020.

73. Lomax, John, III. Interview by author. February 3, 2020.

74. Lomax, John, III. *Nashville: Music City USA*. New York: Harry N. Abrams, 1985.

75. Young, Mary. Interviewed by author. April 5, 2020.

76. "Oral History of John Lomax III." Interview by Norie Guthrie. Scholarship. Rice.edu. November 10, 2017. Accessed 2 July 2020. https://scholarship.rice.edu/ohms/viewer.php?cachefile=file_88b611df-70e4-4167-b1d1-6815e5d56de6_wrc09160_ohms.ohms. Interview conducted on behalf of the Houston Folk Music Archive oral history project.

77. Kruth, John. *To Lives to Fly: The Ballad of the Late, Great Townes Van Zandt.* Cambridge, MA: Da Capo, 2008.

78. Schnaufer, D. Eric. Personal communication. January 6, 2021.

79. Setser, Pam. Interviewed by author. April 3, 2020.

80. "Oral History Interview with Jean Jennings." Accessed 9 April 2019.Oral History Project - Interview with Jean Jennings, Lyon College Regional Study Center, 13 June 2003, mslibrary/rcol/jennings.html.

81. Dark, Harry, and Phil Dark. "Folk Traditions Flourish in Ozarks." *Chicago Tribune* (Chicago, Illinois), April 30, 1978, sec. 4.

82. "David Schnaufer." Interviewed by Jerry Rockwell. "Contemporary Mountain Dulcimers and the People Who Pick 'em." Accessed 15 February 2020. https://www.jcrmusic.com/contemp.md.1.html. Originally published in *Dirty Linen* #34 June/July 1991.

83. "Jean Bonds Jennings (1934-2005)." Find a Grave. Accessed 3 October 2020. https://www.findagrave.com/memorial/24797637/jean-jennings.

84. Beall, Harry. Interviewed by author. January 23, 2021.

85. Milnes, Gerry. Interviewed by author. December 5, 2020.

86. Hornbostel, Lois. Interviewed by author. April 22, 2020.

87. "An Interview with Alan Freeman." Interview by Bob Cox. *Dulcimer Player News*,1987,17-19. Accessed 5 April 2020. issuu.com.

88. Staff. "Hurdy-Gurdy Coffeehouse to Reopen at New Location." Newspapers.com/Shoppers News at Paramus, NJ. October 2, 1985. Accessed 27 April 2020. https://www.newspapers.com/image/543013320/?terms=Alan Freeman dulcimer player.

89. Bean, Covey. "Jimmy Driftwood Drifts to OCC." Newspapers.com. *Daily Oklahoman*. October 11, 2011. Accessed 27 April 2020. https://www.newspapers.com/image/452396909/?terms=Alan Freeman dulcimer player.

90. Buckley, Daniel. "Musical Gold in the Hills." Newspapers.com/*Tucson Citizen*. October 12, 1990. Accessed 27 August 2020. https://www.newspapers.com/image/579344412/?erms=Alan Freeman dulcimer player.

91. Mason, Phil, ed. "Periodical or Newspaper The Dulcimer Players News." Volume 1. LC Catalog - Item Information (Full Record). January 1975. Accessed 8 April 2020. https://catalog.loc.gov/vwebv/search?searchCode=STNO&searchType=1&recCount=25&searchArg=0098-3527.

92. Beall, Harry. Interviewed by author. January 23, 2021.

93. "Oral History of John Lomax III." Interview by Norie Guthrie. Scholarship. Rice.edu. November 10, 2017. Accessed 2 July 2020. https://scholarship.rice.edu/ohms/viewer.php?cachefile=file_88b611df-70e4-4167-b1d1-6815e5d56de6_wrc09160_ohms.ohms. Interview conducted on behalf of the Houston Folk Music Archive oral history project.

94. Force, Robert. "The Mud Bug Boogie." Robertforce.com. Accessed 8 April 2021. https://robertforce.com/SongsAndInstruction/Songs/TheMudbugBoogie.html.

95. Staff. "Thomas Hart Benton's Final Gift." NEA. June 18, 2018. Accessed 2 September 2020. https://www.arts.gov/about/40th-anniversary-highlights/thomas-hart-bentons-final-gift.

96. Thomson. Doug. Interviewed by author. July 15, 2020.

97. Force, Robert. Personal Communication. January 30, 2021.

98. Force, Robert. Personal Communication. January 30, 2021.

99. Force, Robert. Personal Communication. January 30, 2021.

100. Carol, Bonnie. "Bonnie: A Brief Bio." Bonnie Carol. Accessed 17 February 2020. http://. bonniecarol.com/BonnieBio.html.

101. Carol, Bonnie. Interviewed by the author. March 3, 2020.

102. Hellman, Neal. "Some Thoughts on the Pacific Rim Dulcimer Gathering." *Dulcimer Player News*, Jan. & Feb. 1976, vol 2: 21.

103. Mason, Phil, ed. *The Dulcimer Players News* 1976. Vol. 2 No. 2.

104. Mason, Phil, and Mason-MacNeil, Madeline eds. *Dulcimer Players News* 1976. Vol. 2 No. 3.

105. Meyer, Fred. Interviewed by author. February 24, 2021.

106. French, Jim. "On Winning Winfield." Interviewed by author. August 28, 2020.

107. Bate, Seth Stephen. "Coming Home to Winfield: The History of the Walnut Valley Festival." Https://soar.wichita.edu. May 2018. Accessed 30 August 2020. https://soar.wichita.edu/bitstream/handle/10057/15473/t18005_Bate. pdf?isAllowed=y&sequence=1. Master's Thesis online.

108. McCarty, David. "Exclusive: Inside Winfield's National Flatpicking Guitar Championships." Fretboard Journal. October 09, 2018. Accessed 26 August 2020.https://www.fretboardjournal.com/features/ exclusive-inside-winfields-national-flatpicking-guitar-championships/.

109. "WALNUT VALLEY CHAMPIONS and PRIZES WON 1972 Thru PRESENT." Walnut Valley Festival. Accessed 31 January 2020. https://www. wvfest.com/wp-content/uploads/ALPHA-ALL-WINNERS- ARCHIVE-1972-PRESENT-compressed.pdf.

110. Wright, Jerry, and David Schnaufer. "Jerry Wright Interviews David Schnaufer. " Interview. Accessed 10 February 2012. http://www.jerrywrightfamily.com/ interviews.

111. Staff. "Breathing Life into the Dulcimer." *Frets Magazine*, December 1988, 46-488.

112. Ward, Kendra. "David Schnaufer." *Dulcimer Times*, 1977,14.

113. Brockinton, Linda. Interviewed by author. November 2, 2020.

114. White, Mack. Interviewed by author. June 9, 2020.

115. Ewing, Ron. Personal Correspondence. May 24, 2020.

116. Hornbostel, Lois. Interviewed by author. April 22, 2020.

117. Jetton, Susan. "They Travel Nation with Mountain Tunes." Newspapers. com/*Charlotte Observer*. September 27, 1970. Accessed 27 April 2020. https://www.newspapers.com/ image/621277618/?terms=.

118. MacNeil, Madeline, and Dulcimerplayersnewsinc. "Jean and Lee Schilling." Issuu.com. Accessed 15 April 2020. https://issuu.com/ dulcimerplayersnewsinc/docs Vol. 5:1 Winter, 1979.

119. Carol, Bonnie. Personal correspondence. April 6, 2020.

120. Carol, Bonnie. Personal communication.

121. White, Mack. Interviewed by author. June 9, 2020.

122. "Oral History of John Lomax III." Interview by Norie Guthrie. Scholarship.

Rice.edu. November 10, 2017. Accessed July 2, 2020. https://scholarship.rice. edu/ohms/viewer.php?cachefile=file_ 88b611df-70e4-4167-b1d1-6815e5d56de6_wrc09160_ohms.ohms. Interview conducted on behalf of the Houston Folk Music Archive oral history project.

123. Kruth, John. *To Lives to Fly: The Ballad of the Late, Great Townes Van Zandt.* Cambridge, MA: Da Capo, 2008.

124. Hall, Michael. "The Great, Late Townes Van Zandt".*Texas Monthly*. March 01,1998. Accessed 25 May 25, 2020. https://www.texasmonthly.com/articles/ the-great-late-townes-van-zandt/.

125. Carol, Bonnie. Personal communication. April 11, 2020.

126. Berch, Doug. Personal communication. April 14, 2020.

127. Carol, Bonnie. Personal communication. April 11, 2020.

128. Schnaufer, David. "Harris Picking." *Dulcimer Players News*, 1979, Fall Issue, 24-25.

129. White, Mack. Personal correspondence. June 9, 2020.

130. Kretzner, Leo. Interviewed by author. April 14, 2020.

131. Kretzner, Leo. Calendar notes. May 25, 1977.

132. Kretzner, Leo. Personal communication.

133. Kretzner, Leo. Personal communication.

134. "Concerning the Mountain Dulcimer." Interview by Jon Kay. February 5, 2021. From unpublished transcript of October 9,1995 interview of David Schnaufer by John Kay.

135. Lomax, John Nova. Interviewed by author. May 31, 2020.

136. Smith, Ralph Lee. *Appalachian Dulcimer Traditions.* Lanham: Scarecrow Press, 2010.

137. Smith, Ralph Lee. "Jacob Ray Melton: An Appreciation." *Dulcimer Players News*, 2001.

138. "David Schnaufer." Interview by Jerry Rockwell. "Contemporary Mountain Dulcimers and the People Who Pick 'em." Accessed 15 February 2020. https://www.jcrmusic.com/. contemp.md.1.html. Originally published in *Dirty Linen* #34 June/July 1991.

139. Padgett, Woody. "Dulcimers: Virginia Style! Roscoe Russell." *Dulcimer Players News*, 1979.

140. Woods, William C. "A Family's "North Carolina Dance Music"." *Washington Post*, March 15, 1970, Accessed 23 July 2020.

141. Cox, Lelia Carson. "Music Comes Naturally to the People of Galax." *New York Times*, July 5, 1970. Accessed 23 July 2020. https://www.nytimes.com/1970/ 07/05/archives/music-comes-naturally-to-the-people-of-galax.html.

142. Freimuth, Rick. Personal Communication. April 12, 2020.

143. Freimuth, Rick. Personal Communication. April 7, 2020.

144. Young, David. Interviewed by author. April 13, 2020.

145. Young, Mary. Interviewed by author. April 5, 2020.

146. Freimuth, Rick. Personal Communication. April 7, 2020.

147. Young, David. Interviewed by author. April 13, 2020.

148. Young, Mary. Interviewed by author. April 5, 2020.

149. Ellis, Darrel. Interviewed by author. July 8, 2020.

150. Carol, Bonnie. Personal communication.

151. Galax Lodge #733 Loyal Order of the Moose. *41st Annual Old Fiddlers' Convention*. Galax, Virginia: Galax Lodge #733, 1976.

152. Freimuth, Rick. Personal communication.

153. History of the Old Fiddler's Convention." Old Fiddler's Convention. Accessed 5 January 2021. http://www.oldfiddlersconvention.com/history.htm.

154. Carol, Bonnie. Personal communication. February 5, 2021.

155. Carol, Bonnie. Personal communication. April 6, 2020.

156. Carol, Bonnie. "Events Calendar." *Dulcimer Player News*, 1979, 4.

157. Beall, Harry. Interviewed by author. January 23, 2021.

158. Hornbostel, Lois. Personal correspondence. April 29, 2020.

159. Carol, Bonnie. Personal correspondence. April 28, 2020.

160. Buckley, Daniel. "Musical Gold in the Hills." *Tucson Citizen* (Tucson, Arizona), December 12, 1990.

161. Hornbostel, Lois. "An Interview with Alan Freeman, Mountain Dulcimer Player." Interview. Yumpu.com. Accessed 22 April 2020. https://www.yumpu.com/en/document/read/18728557/print-this-article.

162. Bean, Covey. "Jimmy Driftwood Drifts to OCC." Newspapers.com/The Daily Oklahoman. October 11, 2011. Accessed 27 April 2020. 452396909/?terms=Alan Freeman dulcimer player/.

163. Bryant, Roger. "Mountain Music Maverick." *Rocky Mount Telegram* (Rocky Mount, North Carolina), September 13, 1996.

164. Staff. "Hurdy-Gurdy Coffeehouse to Reopen at New Location." Newspapers.com/Shoppers News at Paramus, NJ. October 2, 1985. Accessed 27 April 2020. https://www.newspapers.com/image/543013320/?terms=Alan Freeman dulcimer player.

165. "An Interview with Alan Freeman." Interview by Bob Cox. *Dulcimer Player News*, 1987, 17-19. Accessed 5 April 2020. issuu.com.

166. "An Interview with Alan Freeman." Interview by Bob Cox. *Dulcimer Player News*, 1987, 13-2. Accessed 5 April 2020. issuu.com.

167. Freimuth, Rick. Personal communication. April 12, 2020.

168. Farsetta, Vince. Personal communication. April 16, 2021.

169. Farsetta, Vince. Interviewed by author. April 8, 2020.

170. Freimuth, Rick. Personal communication. April 7, 2020.

171. Young, Mary. Interviewed by author. April 6, 2020.

172. MacNeil, Madeleine, ed. Cover Photo Summer 1979. *Dulcimer Players News*. Accessed 5 September 2020. https://issuu.com/dulcimerplayersnewsinc/docs/120823173214-a39cb13eafde48a491f6e305991dd608.

173. Carol, Bonnie. Personal communication. February 18, 2021.

174. Lomax, Alan. Recording Details: "The White Cockade". The Association for Cultural Equity. Culturalequity.org. Accessed September 13, 2020. http://research.culturalequity.org/rc-b2/get-audio-detailed-recording.do?recordingId=12317. Accessed on 4.9.2020.

175. Hafner, Donald. "Musician Got Paid More." Prof. Donald Hafner Home Page. Accessed September 13, 2020. https://sites.google.com/bc.edu/donald-hafner/imm/colonial-music/musician-got-paid-more.

176. Schnaufer, David. "Harris Picking." *Dulcimer Players News*, 1979, Fall Issue, 24-25.

177. Force, Robert. Interviewed by author. January 30, 2021.

178. Weiss, Piero, and Richard Taruskin. *Music in the Western World: A History in Documents*. Belmont, CA: Thomson Schirmer, 2008.

179. Arnold, Chris. "Music Industry Goes After Guitar Tablature Sites." NPR. August 07, 2006. Accessed 5 September 2020. https://www.npr.org/templates/story/story.php?storyId=5622879.

180. Force, Robert, Albert d'Ossché, Neal Hellman, Bonnie Carol, Michael Rugg, and Michael Hubbert. *Pacific Rim Dulcimer Songbook Companion to the Record Album*. Pacific Rim Dulcimer Project. Felton, CA: Capritaurus/Dusty Moose Publishers, 1977.

181. Carol, Bonnie. Interviewed by author. June 6, 2020.

182. Hellman, Neal. Interviewed by author. May 12, 2020.

183. Kretzner, Leo. Interviewed by author. April 22, 2020.

184. Farsetta, Vince. Personal communication.

185. MacNeil, Madeline. "Letter from the Editor." *Dulcimer Players News*. Accessed 2 May 2020. 120823172719-1b3f36eb1c06449f964fd039fa802e2c. Vol 1.No.5 Winter 1979.

186. Freimuth, Rick. Interviewed by author. April 7, 2020.

187. Freimuth, Rick. "Ten Steps to Building a Dulcimer (Simplified.)" Paeonia, Colorado. May 3, 2020.

188. Ewing, Ron. Personal communication. January 27, 2021.

189. Ewing, Ron. Interviewed by author. May 28, 2020.

190. Fleming, Gena. Personal communication.

191. Seida, Linda. "Bluestein Family." Fresnofolklore.org. Accessed 4 September 2020. https://fresnofolklore.org/artist_profile_bluestein_family.html.

192. Hornbostel, Lois. Interviewed by by author. April 29, 2020.

193. Gene Bluestein Collection 1910-2002 (1955-1995). University of North Carolina. Lib.unc.edu. Accessed September 4, 2020. https://finding-aids.lib.unc.edu/20379/.

194. Osegueda, Mike. "Friends Will Gather for Bluestein." Newspapers.com/*The Fresno Bee*. March 25, 2005. Accessed September 05, 2020. https://www.newspapers.com/image/658440541/?terms=Jean Ritchie.

195. Berch, Doug. Interviewed by author. June 6, 2020.

196. Ewing, Ron. Interviewed by author. May 28, 2020.

197. Barker, Nancy. Interviewed by author. April 16, 2020.

198. Barker, Nancy. Interviewed by author. March 22, 2020.

199. MacNeil, Maddie, ed. "Kentucky Music Weekend." *Dulcimer Players News*, 1980, 6:4.135.

200. Beebe, Greg. "Taking the Dull Out of Dulcimer." Newspapers.com. Accessed 1 April 2020. *Santa Cruz Sentinel*, July 11, 1980, www.newspapers.com/image/62669965/.

201. Osler, Jack M. "Make Yourself at home down on the Farm." *Dayton Daily News*, 5 Oct. 1980, https://www.newspapers.com/image/406313850/?terms=Bob+Evans+Farm+Festival.

202. Beall, Harry. Interviewed by author. January 23, 2021.

203. Sellers, Maureen. Interviewed by author. April 24, 2020.

204. Kretzner, Leo. "Leo Remembers David." Interview by author. April 20, 2020.

205. Camp, Ann. "Leo Kretzner: An Interview." *Dulcimer Players News/Spring*, 16-18.

206. White, Mack. Personal communication. August 30, 2020.

207. Sellers, Maureen. Interviewed by author. April 24, 2020.

208. Lomax, John, III. Interviewed by author. February 3, 2020.

209. Staff. "Historical Museums." Newspapers.com/*Austin American-Statesman*. September 26, 1982.Accessed 30 August 2020. https://www.newspapers.com/image/379576361/?terms=Lomax Exhibit.

210. Miller, Townsend "Country Music" Newspapers.com/*Austin American-Statesman*. October 1, 1982. Accessed 30 August 2020. https://www.newspapers.com/image/379511135/?terms=Lomax%2BExhibit.

211. Huey, Steve. "The Judds: Biography & History." AllMusic. Accessed 14 May 2020. https://www.allmusic.com/artist/the-judds-mn0000086312/biography.

212. Staff. "Breathing Life into the Dulcimer." *Frets Magazine*, December 1988, 46-488.

213. Leahey, Andrew. "Flashback: CMT Airs First Country Music Video." *Rolling Stone*. June 25, 2018. Accessed 14 May 2020. https://www.rollingstone.com/music/music-country/flashback-cmt-airs-first-country-music-video-37213/.

214. Carol, Bonnie. *Dust off That Dulcimer & Dance! A Mountain Dulcimer Instruction Book*. Sherman Oaks, CA: Alfred Publishing,1983.

215. Beall, Harry. Interviewed by author. January 23, 2021.

216. Farsetta, Vince. "Vince and David". Interviewed by author. May 23, 2020.

217. Sellers, Maureen. Interviewed by author. April 24, 2020.

218. Kretzner, Leo. Personal communication. April 29, 2020.

219. Hellman, Neal. Personal communication.

220. Carol, Bonnie. Interviewed by author. February 9, 2020.

221. Hornbostel, Lois. "An Interview with Alan Freeman, Mountain Dulcimer Player." Yumpu.com. Accessed June 20, 2020. https://www.yumpu.com/en/document/read/18728557/.

222. Bryant, Roger. "Alan Freeman: Mountain Music Maverick!" *Rocky Mount NC Telegram*, September 13, 1996. Accessed December 2, 2020. Newspapers.com.

223. Beall, Harry. Interviewed by author. January 23, 2021.

224. Wright, Jerry, and David Schnaufer. "Jerry Wright Interviews David Schnaufer." Interview. Http://www.jerrywrightfamily.com. Accessed 10 February 2012. http://www.jerrywrightfamily.com/interviews.

# MOVEMENT 4: ARRIVALS

1. Farsetta, Vince. Personal communication. May 8, 2021.

2. Farsetta, Vince. Interviewed by author. May 1, 2020.

3. Howard, Wayne. "West Virginia's Hammons Family." Goldenseal, 2014.

Accessed 11 September 2020. http://www.wvculture.org/goldenseal/winter14/Hammons.html.

4. "Vince Farsetta." ARTISTdirect. February 2, 2018. Accessed 16 August 2020. https://www.artistdirect.com/artists/vince-farsetta/429363.

5. Ward, Kendra. "David Schnaufer". *The Dulcimer Times*, Fall, 1977.

6. Monday, Kim. Interviewed by author. February 11, 2021.

7. Farsetta, Vince. Interviewed by author. May 1, 2020.

8. Staff. "Nashville Then: Best of 1984." *The Tennessean*. January 06, 2015. Accessed 2 February 2021. https://www.tennessean.com/picture-gallery/news/local/2015/01/06/nashville-then-best-of-1984/21330391/.

9. Lomax, John, III. *Nashville: Music City USA*. Harry N. Abrams, 1985 p35.

10. Millard, Bob. *The Judds*. Doubleday, 1988.

11. Lomax, John, III. *Nashville: Music City USA*. Harry N. Abrams, 1985 p35.

12. Uppuluri, Ram. "Murals Make City's Past Come to Life." Newspapers.com. November 12, 1984. Accessed 8 September 2020. https://www.newspapers.com/image/111527081/?terms=Nashville Parthenon.

13. Ponder, Drew. Interviewed by author. May 11, 2020.

14. O'Neal, Lee Ann. "Historic Burger Joint Opens after Fire." Newspapers.com. December 29, 2004. Accessed 8 September 2020. https://www.newspapers.com/image/245254676/?terms=Browns Diner.

15. Pulsford, Jan. Personal communication. May 5, 2020.

16. "Brown's Diner Where I Swing." Review. Chefpaulette.net (blog), March 2, 2017. Accessed 11 September 2020. https://chefpaulette.net/2017/03/02/browns-diner-where-i-swing/.

17. Vipperman, Vip. Interviewed by author. May 22, 2020.

18. Oermann, Robert K. "Down Home Dulcimer Champ Finally Takes on Music City." *The Tennessean,* December 16, 1984. https://www.newspapers.com/image/112200867/.

19. Mears, Johnny. Interviewed by author. January 21, 2021.

20. Ponder, Drew. Interviewed by author. May 11, 2020.

21. O'Conner, Mark. Interviewed by author. May 23, 2020.

22. "Breathing Life Into The Dulcimer." *Frets Magazine*, December 1988, 46-48.

23. "Walnut Valley Champions and Prizes Won." Wvfest.com. https://www.wvfest.com/wp-content/uploads/ALPHA-ALL-WINNERS-ARCHIVE-1972-PRESENT-compressed.pdf?x91140.

24. Miller, Mark. Interviewed by author. May 29, 2020.

25. Mears, Johnny. Interviewed by author. January 21, 2021.

26. Ponder, Drew. Interviewed by author. May 11, 2020.

27. Thomson, Doug. Interviewed by author. July 15, 2020.

28. Vipperman, Vip. Interviewed by author. May 22, 2020.

29. David Schnaufer "Here Comes the Sun". Performed by David Schnaufer. October 22, 2011. Accessed 12 September 2020. https://www.youtube.com/watch v=fV7FUwcmK5A&list=RDkwT7baKB2rc&index=12.

30. Farsetta, Vince. Interviewed by author. May 1, 2020.

31. Carol, Bonnie. Personal communication. April 29, 2020.

32. Ellis, Darrel. Interviewed by author. July 8, 2020.

33. Tilbury, Hank. Interviewed by author. May 4, 2020.
34. Farsetta, Vince. Personal communication. May 1, 2020.
35. McCullough, Joann. Interviewed by author. March 17, 2020.
36. McCullough, Herb. "Writing with David." Http://herbsongs.com (blog), September 16, 2000. Accessed 23 March 2020. http://herbsongs.com/ST_david.htm.
37. Tilbury, Hank. Interviewed by author. May 4, 2020.
38. Lomax, John, III. Interviewed by author. February 3, 2020.
39. DeLaney, Kelly. "Interviews with David Schnaufer and Karen Ashbrook." *Dulcimer Player News*, 1989.
40. "David Schnaufer." Interview with David by Virginia Arouh. 1999. Unpublished interview courtesy of Jan Pulsford.
41. Moraine Music: "Brent Maher." Morainemusic.com. Accessed 6 July 2020. https://www.morainemusic.com/brentmaher.
42. Staff. "Maher to Address Tunesmiths." *The Tennessean* (Nashville, Tennessee), May 11, 1986.
43. "Moraine Music: Brent Maher." Morainemusic. Accessed July 6, 2020. https://www.morainemusic.com/brentmaher.
44. Staff. "Maher to Address Tunesmiths." *The Tennessean* (Nashville, Tennessee), May 11, 1986.
45. Goldsmith, Thomas. "Dulcimer Virtuoso Picks for the Stars." *The Tennessean* (Nashville, Tn.), October 26, 1986, Sunday ed.
46. "David Schnaufer." Interview with David by Virginia Arouh. 1999. Unpublished interview courtesy of Jan Pulsford.
47. "David Schnaufer." Interview with David by Virginia Arouh. 1999. Unpublished interview courtesy of Jan Pulsford.
48. Lawing, Tramp. Interviewed by author. June 13, 2020.
49. Boehm, Mike. "A Pure Mix : Paul Kirby and His Cactus Brothers Don't Compromise Sense of Adventure in Country-Rock Hybrid." *The Los Angeles Times*. September 30, 1993.
50. Farsetta, Vincent. Interviewed by author. April 2, 2020.
51. Farsetta, Vincent. Personal communication.
52. Lomax, John, III. Interviewed by author. February 3, 2020.
53. Rattlesnake Annie. Personal communication. December 13, 2020.
54. Hellman, Neal. Interviewed by author. November 22, 2020.
55. MacNeil, Madeline. "The MacNeil-Hellman Report." *Dulcimer Player News*, Fall 1991, 20-22.
56. Gilbert, Andrew. "Telling Tales and Making Music." *Santa Cruz Sentinel*, January 19, 1990. Accessed 22 November 2020. https://www.newspapers.com/image/68116013/?terms=Gourd Music.
57. Breinig, Mary Lawrence. Interviewed by author. March 3, 2020.
58. Smith, R.T. "Dulcimer Redux." Shenandoahliterary.org. July 18, 2016. Accessed 4 February 2021. https://shenandoahliterary.org/snopes/2016/07/18/dulcimer-redux/.
59. Smith, Ralph Lee. "July 2013." Musical Fun in a Golden Time (VIDEO) - Swarthmore College Bulletin. Accessed 4 February 2021. https://www.

swarthmore.edu/bulletin/archive/wp/july-2013_musical-fun-in-a-golden-time-video.html.

60. Sabol, Cathy. "Ralph Lee Smith." *Dulcimer Player News*, 1982.

61. Breinig, Mary Lawrence. Interviewed by author. March 3, 2020.

62. Vipperman, Vip. Interviewed by author. May 22, 2020.

63. Rattlesnake Annie. Interviewed by author. April 22, 2020.

64. O'Guin, Wanda. Interviewed by author. February 17, 2020.

65. Kuntz, Andrew. "Grey Cat on a Tennessee Farm." Traditional Tune Archive. May 06, 2019. Accessed 18 November 2020. https://tunearch.org/wiki/Annotation:Grey_Cat_on_a_Tennessee_Farm.

66. Miller, Mark. Interviewed by author. May 29, 2020.

67. Glazener, Tull. "Waltz of the Waters". September 02, 2012. Accessed 3 January 2020. https://www.tullglazener.com/remembering-david/september-2012-waltz-of-the-waters.

68. McCullough, Joann. Interviewed by author. March 17, 2020.

69. McCullough, Herb. "The First Time I Wrote with David Schnaufer." Herbsongs.com (blog), May 15, 2000. Accessed 11 September 2020.

70. Miller, Mark. Interviewed by author. May 29, 2020.

71. Lomax, John, III. Personal communication.

72. McCullough, Herb. "The First Time I Wrote with David Schnaufer." Herbsongs.com (blog), May 15, 2000. Accessed 11 September 2020.

73. Kienzle, Rich. "Chet Atkins." Country Music Hall of Fame. Accessed September 18, 2020. https://countrymusichalloffame.org/artist/chet-atkins/.

74. O'Conner, Mark. "Mark O'Connor: Memories of David Schnaufer." Interviewed by author. May 23, 2020.

75. Lomax, Melanie. Interviewed by author. May 19, 2020.

76. Farsetta, Vincent. Interviewed by author. April 2, 2020.

77. Lawing, Tramp. Interviewed by author. June 13, 2020.

78. Seifert, Stephen. Interviewed by author. August 11, 2020.

79. Thompson, Doug. Interviewed by author. July 15, 2020.

80. "Breathing Life Into The Dulcimer." *Frets Magazine*, December 1988, 48.

81. McCullough, Herb. "Writing with David." Http://herbsongs.com (blog), September 16, 2000. Accessed 21 June 2020. http://herbsongs.com/ST_david.htm.

82. Lawing, Tramp. Interviewed by author. June 13, 2020.

83. Poland, Sam. Interviewed by author. June 20, 2020.

84. Woodward, Brian. "Cactus Brothers Return with Eclectic Sound." *The Daily Sentinel* (Grand Junction, Co.), June 20, 1993.

85. Lomax, John, III. Interviewed by author. May 4, 2020.

86. Miller, Mark. Interviewed by author. May 29, 2020.

87. Lomax, John, III. Interviewed by author. May 4, 2020.

88. Wolfe, Charles. "Hank Snow." Country Music Hall of Fame. Accessed 18 September 2020. https://countrymusichalloffame.org/artist/hank-snow/.

89. Farsetta, Vincent. Interviewed by author. April 2, 2020.

90. Wolfe, Charles K. "Macon, Uncle Dave (1870-1952), Banjoist and Singer." Accessed 12 September 2020. American National Biography Online, 2000.

doi:10.1093/anb/9780198606697.article.1803150.

91. Malone, Bill C., and Tracey E.W. Laird. *Country Music USA: A 50-year History*. Austin: University of Texas Press, 1968.

92. Lawing, Tramp. Interviewed by author. June 13, 2020.

93. Miller, Mark. "Recording with David Schnaufer". Interviewed by author. May 29, 2020.

94. Lomax, John, III. Personal communication. April 13, 2020.

95. Lomax, Melanie. Personal communication. April 13, 2020.

96. Creative Commons. "Fisher's Hornpipe." Traditional Tune Archive. May 12, 2020. Accessed 15 September 2020. https://tunearch.org/wiki/Annotation: Fisher's_Hornpipe.

97. Jabbour, Alan. "Fisher's Hornpipe [in D]." The Library of Congress. Accessed 15 September 2020. https://www.loc.gov/item/afcreed000143/.

98. Miller, Mark. Interviewed by author. May 29, 2020.

99. Hellman, Neal. Interviewed by author. November 22, 2020.

100. Lomax, John, III. Interviewed by author. May 4, 2020.

101. "*Dulcimer Deluxe* David Schnaufer." Review of *Dulcimer Deluxe. Country Song Roundup*, August 1988.

102. "*Dulcimer Deluxe*." Review of *Dulcimer Deluxe* Cassette. *Dulcimer Players News*, 1988.

103. Hellman, Neal. Interviewed by author. November 22, 2020.

104. Lomax, John, III. Interviewed by author. May 4, 2020.

105. *Dulcimer Players News* 1988. Vol. 14 No. 4.

106. Lomax, John, III. Interviewed by author. May 4, 2020.

107. Gaubeaux, Rob. "Digital Dulcimer." *Dulcimer Players News*, 1988,12-13.

108. Seifert, Nancy. Interviewed by author. March 24, 2020.

109. Lomax, John Nova. "Starry Lullabye." *Houston Press*. April 02, 2016. Accessed 20 September 2020. https://www.houstonpress.com/music/starry-lullabye-6545543.

110. Staff. "The Fret Pack: Unorthodox Acoustic Players Pushing Musical Boundaries." *Nashville Banner Lifestyles* (Nashville, Tennessee), March 18, 1989.

111. David Schnaufer Plays "Sarah" with Vince Farsetta. Performed by David Schnaufer and Vince Farsetta on Oct. 22, 1989. Uploaded to YouTube 2011. Accessed 19 September 2020. https://youtu.be/kwT7baKB2rc.

112. Staff. "Tons of Tunes." *Austin-American Statesman* (Austin, Texas), August 18, 1989. Accessed 19 September 2020.

113. Stubblefield, Steve. Interviewed by author. December 24, 2020.

114. Prime, John Andrew. "Dulcimer player dabbles in music variety." *The Times*, Shreveport, Louisiana. October 23, 1989.

115. McCleod, Jerry. "Enoch's a Café, a Nightclub and a Melting Pot." *The Shreveport Journal* (Shreveport, Louisiana), July 10, 1989.

116. "David Schnaufer: Dulcimer Player." Review of *Dulcimer Player. Billboard Magazine*, November 25, 1989.

117. Staff. "The Fret Pack: Unorthodox Acoustic Players Pushing Musical Boundaries." *Nashville Banner Lifestyles* (Nashville, Tennessee), March 18,

1989.

118. SFL Tapes and Discs. "David Schnaufer Dulcimer Player Deluxe." News release, Nashville, TN, 1989. SFL.

119. Delaney, Kelly. "Interview with David Schnaufer." *Dulcimer Players News*, Winter 1989.Vol. 15,116.

120. Baker, Duck. Interview by author. November 15, 2020.

121. Berch, Doug. Interviewed by author. June 6, 2020.

122. Barker, Nancy. Interviewed by author. April 16, 2020.

123. Lundy, Ronni. "Muster Your Pluck and Make Some Dulcet Tones." *The Courier-Journal* (Louisville, Ky), June 17, 1989.

124. Fleming, Gena. Interviewed by author. September 6, 2020.

125. Breinig, Mary Lawrence. Personal communication. February 9, 2021.

126. Breinig, Mary Lawrence. Interviewed by author. March 15, 2020.

127. Brown, Jim. Interviewed by author. July 8, 2020.

128. "Smithsonian Folkways Recordings." Liner Notes. 1962. Accessed 30 November 2020. https://folkways-media.si.edu/liner_notes/folk-legacy/FLG00005-LP.pdf.

129. Farsetta, Vince. Interviewed by author. May 1, 2020.

130. BMI Music. December 5, 1989. Invitation to release party for *Dulcimer Player Deluxe*, 10 Music Square East, Nashville. Courtesy of John Lomax III.

131. SFL Tapes and Discs. "David Schnaufer Dulcimer Player Deluxe." News release, Nashville, TN, 1989. SFL.

132. Seifert, Stephen. Interviewed by author. July 28, 2020.

133. Seifert, Stephen. Interviewed by author. July 28, 2020.

134. Lomax, John Nova. Interviewed by author. May 31, 2020.

135. Lomax, John, III. Interviewed by author. May 4, 2020.

136. Farsetta, Vince. Interviewed by author. May 1, 2020.

137. Lomax, John Nova. Interviewed by author. May 31, 2020.

138. Smith, Ralph Lee. *Appalachian Dulcimer Traditions*. Lanham: Scarecrow Press, 2010.

139. Smith, Ralph Lee. "Jacob Ray Melton: An Appreciation." *Dulcimer Players News*, 2001.

140. Rockwell, Jerry. "Contemporary Mountain Dulcimers and the People Who Pick 'em". Accessed 2 February2020. https://www.jcrmusic.com/contemp.md.2.html.

141. Woods, William C. "A Family's "North Carolina Dance Music"."*Washington Post*, March 15, 1970.

142. Cox, Lelia Carson. "Music Comes Naturally to the People of Galax." The New York Times, July 5, 1970. Accessed July 23, 2020. https://www.nytimes.com/1970/07/05/archives/music-comes-naturally-to-the-people-of-galax.html.

143. Padgett, Woody. "Dulcimers: Virginia Style! Roscoe Russell." *Dulcimer Players News*, 1979.

144. Lomax, John Nova. Interviewed by author. May 31, 2020.

145. "Parents of Murdered Children to Meet." Fosters.com. June 28, 2010. Accessed January 04, 2021. https://www.fosters.com/article/20100628/GJNEWS02/706289924.

# MOVEMENT 5: METAMORPHOSIS

1. Boehm, Mike. "He's Tied to the Strings." *Los Angeles Times* (Los Angeles), January 23, 1992. Accessed September 28, 2020. https://www.newspapers.com/image/177387298/.

2. SFL Tapes and Discs. "David Schnaufer Films Instructional Video." 1990 News release, Nashville, Tn.

3. Blom, Dan. Interviewed by author. June 25, 2020.

4. Brockinton, Linda. Interviewed by author. October 16, 2020.

5. Lomax, Nova. Personal communication.

6. Lomax III, John. Dulcimer Delux [sic] Fan and Retailer Newsletter. 1990.

7. Crutcher, Greg. Interviewed by author. December 7, 2020.

8. Lomax III, John and Lomax, Melanie. Interviewed by author. February 3, 2020.

9. SFL Tapes and Discs. "David Schnaufer: 1 Man, 2 Hands, and 4 Wires." 1991 News release, Nashville, Tn.

10. "Hank Williams Sr. Permission Agreement." Beth Vahle to John Lomax III/ SFL Discs and Tapes. June 1, 1990. In The Curtis Publishing Company. Indianapolis, Ind, 1990. Hank Williams Sr. Agreement granted by the Estate of Hank Williams c/o The Curtis Management Group. Courtesy of John Lomax III.

11. Ellis, Darrel. Interviewed by author. July 8, 2020.

12. Farsetta, Vince. Personal communication.

13. Glazener, Tull. "Colors." September 01, 2019. Accessed September 29, 2020. https://www.tullglazener.com/remembering-david/september-2019-colors.

14. Orr, Jay. "Colors: Kids Learn about Life through Music". *Nashville Banner*. March 22, 1991. C1, C5.

15. O'Connor, Mark. Interviewed by author. May 22, 2020.

16. Glazener, Tull. "Colors." September 01, 2019. Accessed September 29, 2020. https://www.tullglazener.com/remembering-david/september-2019-colors.

17. Lomax, John III. Interviewed by author. May 19, 2020.

18. "Flaco & Santiago Jimenez" Folk ArtsTexas Cultural Trust. https://txculturaltrust.org/bio/flaco-santiago-jimenez/. Accessed September 26, 2020.

19. "Santiago Jiménez, Jr." National Endowment for the Arts. https://www.arts.gov/honors/heritage/santiago-jimenez-jr. Accessed September 26, 2020.

20. Patterson, Rob. "The Chief of *Conjunto*." *Dallas Observer*, November 2, 1995. Accessed October 11, 2020. https://www.dallasobserver.com/music/the-chief-of-conjunto-6404162.

21. Staff. "Santiago Jiménez, Jr." National Endowment for the Arts. August 19, 2013. Accessed September 27, 2020. https://www.arts.gov/honors/heritage/fellows/santiago-jiménez-jr.

22. Ellis, Darrel. Interviewed by author. July 8, 2020.

23. Hellman, Neal. Interviewed by author. February 1, 2020.

24. Hellman, Neal. Personal communication. January 28, 2021.

25. Lomax, Melanie. Interviewed by author. April 2, 2020.

26. Staff. "National Dulcimer Champion Coming to Mineola." *Tyler Courier-Times* (Tyler, Texas), November 8, 1991.

27. Redmond, Mike. "Oh, Brother, The Everlys Can Sing." *Indianapolis Star* (Indianapolis, Indiana), August 2, 1990, "On Music" sec.

28. David Schnaufer. Interview by Jerry Rockwell. "Contemporary Mountain Dulcimers and the People Who Pick 'em." Accessed February 15, 2020. https://www.jcrmusic.com/contemp.md.1.html. Originally published in *Dirty Linen* #34 June/July 1991.

29. Bentley, Aaron. Interviewed by author. November 28, 2020.

30. White, Mack. Interviewed by author. June 9, 2020.

31. Staff. "Wednesday." *Austin American-Statesman* (Austin, Texas), October 18, 1990.

32. Staff. "Performances" *Austin American-Statesman* (Austin, Texas), October 24, 1990.

33. Blackstock, Peter. "Surprise CNJ success thrills Donovan." *Austin American-Statesman* (Austin, Texas), October 25, 1990.

34. Staff "Folk Craft Music Workshop Set in Wilmington." *Brattleboro Reformer* (Brattleboro, Vermont), September 27, 1990.

35. Genovese, Peter. "A Sound Not Like Any Other." *Central New Jersey Home News*. New Brunswick, New Jersey. July 19, 1990. p. 15. Accessed September 24, 2020.

36. Carty, Mary. Interviewed by author. July 24, 2020.

37. Hornbostel, Lois. Interviewed by author. April 29, 2020.

38. Breinig, Mary Lawrence. Interviewed by author. June 11, 2020.

39. McEuen, John. Interviewed by author. December 3, 2020.

40. Fleming, Gena. Interviewed by author. September 20, 2020.

41. Lomax, John III. Interviewed by author. February 3, 2020.

42. "Past Performers." Winnipeg Folk Festival. June 21, 2020. Accessed October 01, 2020. https://www.winnipegfolkfestival.ca/lineup/past-performers/.

43. Poland, Sam. Interviewed by author. June 20, 2020.

44. Staff. "Dulcimer Concert at Blue Mt. Lake." *The Post-Star* (Glens Falls, New York), June 19, 1991.

45. Lomax, John III. Interviewed by author. February 3, 2020.

46. Pryor, Ellen. Interviewed by author. June 18, 2020.

47. Heil, Alan L. *Voice of America: A History*. New York: Columbia University Press, 2003

48. Bishop, Joni. Interviewed by author. May 4, 2020.

49. Carty, Mary. Interviewed by author. July 24, 2020.

50. Grizzell, Debbie. Interviewed by author. June 25, 2020.

51. Poland, Sam. Interviewed by author. June 20, 2020.

52. Farsetta, Vince. Interviewed by author. May 1, 2020.

53. Setser, Pam. Interviewed by author. April 20, 2020.

54. Barker, Nancy. Interviewed by author. March 22, 2020.

55. Crutcher, Greg. Interviewed by author. December 7, 2020.

56. Lomax, John Nova. Interviewed by author. October 19, 2020.

57. Lawing, Tramp. Interviewed by author. June 13, 2020.

58. Lomax, John III. Interviewed by author. February 2, 2020.

59. SFL Tapes & Discs PR. "Schnaufer Set for Second Video." 1991 News release, Nashville, TN, July 31.

60. Puckett, Jeffrey Lee. "The Cactus Brothers Will Cut Loose at Phoenix Hill." *The Courier-Journal* (Louisville, Ky), December 4, 1993.

61. Lomax, John III. Release and video courtesy of John Lomax III.

62. Crutcher, Greg. Interviewed by author. December 7, 2020.

63. Lomax, John III. Interviewed by author. February 3, 2020.

64. Kinetic Management. PR. "Cactus Brothers Mount Fall Offensive." News release, Nashville, TN, October 10, 1991.

65. Sellers, Maureen. Interviewed by author. April 24, 2020.

66. "Walnut Valley Celebrates 20 Years!" *Walnut Valley Occasional* (Winfield, Kansas), July 1, 1991. Accessed April 4, 2020. Newspapers.com.

67. Carty, Mary. Interviewed by author. July 24, 2020.

68. Ellis, Darrel. Interviewed by author. July 8, 2020.

69. Poland, Sam. Interviewed by author. June 20, 2020.

70. Grizzell, Debbie. Interviewed by author. June 25, 2020.

71. Barker, Nancy. Interviewed by author. April 16, 2020.

72. Ellis, Darrel. Interviewed by author. July 8, 2020.

73. Editor. "Brittle Diabetes Mellitus (or Labile Diabetes) Is a Term Used to Describe Particularly Hard to Control Type 1 Diabetes." Diabetes. March 09, 2020. Accessed October 02, 2020. https://www.diabetes.co.uk/ brittle-diabetes.html.

74. "Mary Emily Schnaufer Death Certificate." Ancestry.com. Accessed February 04, 2020. https://www.ancestry.com/imageviewer/collections/2272/images/ 40394_b062422-00791?pId=23473888.

75. Ellis, Darrel. Interviewed by author. January 8, 2020.

76. Staff. "Funeral Benefit for Nashville Guitar Maker." *Tennessean* (Nashville, TN. ), December 1, 1991.

77. Lomax, John Nova. Interviewed by author. October 19, 2020.

78. Lomax, John Nova. Personal communication. October 18, 2020.

79. Lomax, John Nova. Personal communication. September 30, 2020.

80. Farsettta, Vince. Personal communication. October 5, 2020.

81. Lomax, John, III. Interviewed by author. February 3, 2020.

82. Metcalfe, Jean. "Super David Schnaufer." *Louisville Music News*, May 1992. Accessed May 24, 2020. http://www.louisvillemusicnews.net/webmanager/ index.php. WEB_CAT_ID=50&storyid=13310&headline=Super_Dave_ Schnaufer&issueid=39.

83. McCullough, Joann. Personal communication. June 12, 2021.

84. Lawing, Tramp. Interviewed by author. June 13, 2020.

85. Lomax, John, III. Interviewed by author. February 3, 2020.

86. Communications, Vanderbilt Division of. "'Ignore Boundaries' Dean Mark Wait Reflects on His Decades at the Blair School of Music." *News Vanderbilt University*. July 17, 2020. Accessed December 11, 2020. https://news. vanderbilt.edu/2020/07/17/ignore-boundaries-dean-mark-wait-reflects-on- his-decades-at-the-blair-school-of-music/.

87. Pryor, Ellen. Interviewed by author. June 18, 2020.

88. Wait, Mark. Interviewed by author. March 27, 2020.

89. McEuen, John. Interviewed by author. December 3, 2020.

90. Lomax, John III. Personal communication.

91. Hurst, Jack. "Country Music." *Chicago Tribune* (Chicago, Illinois), December 1, 1991.

92. Fleming, Gena. Interviewed by author. September 6, 2020.

93. King, Bob. Interviewed by author. May 20, 2020.

94. Bentley, Aaron. Interviewed by author. November 28, 2020.

95. White, Mack. Interviewed by author. June 9, 2020.

96. Staff. "Buzz (Mack White)." *Fort Worth Star-Telegram* (Fort Worth, Texas), May 30, 1993.

97. Lomax, John III. Interviewed by author. February 3, 2020.

98. MacQueen, Steve. "Lotsa Music." *Tallahassee Democrat* (Tallahassee, Florida), January 15, 1993.

99. Boehm, Mike. "A Pure Mix: Paul Kirby and His Cactus Brothers Don't Compromise a Sense of Adventure in Country-Rock Hybrid." *Los Angeles Times* (Los Angeles, CA), September 30, 1993.

100. Jinkins, Shirley. "They're Prickly, But Fun." *Fort Worth Star-Telegram*, May 28, 1993.

101. MacQueen, Steve. "Lotsa Music." *Tallahassee Democrat* (Tallahassee, Florida), January 15, 1993.

102. Bryan, Tim. Interviewed by author. July 20, 2020.

103. Poland, Sam. Interviewed by author. June 20, 2020.

104. Stubblefield, Steve. Interviewed by author. June 11, 2020.

105. Liberty Records. Monterey Artists (booking). "Cactus Brothers 1993 Tour Dates." Itinerary, Nashville, TN.

106. Poland, Sam. Interviewed by author. June 20, 2020.

107. Kretzner, Leo. Personal correspondence with author. April 20, 2020.

108. Liberty Records. Monterey Artists (booking). "Cactus Brothers 1993 Tour Dates." Itinerary, Nashville, TN.

109. Poland, Sam. Interviewed by author. June 20, 2020.

110. Lomax III, John. Interviewed by author. April 16, 2020.

111. Liberty Records. Monterey Artists (booking). "Cactus Brothers 1993 Tour Dates." Itinerary, Nashville, TN.

112. Sack, Linda. Interviewed by author. February 2, 2020.

113. Sack, Linda. Interviewed by author. February 2, 2020.

114. Breinig, Mary Lawrence. Interviewed by author. April 9, 2020.

115. Seifert, Stephen. Interviewed by author. July 28, 2020.

116. Seifert, Nancy. Interviewed by author. April 9, 2020.

117. Breinig, Mary Lawrence. Interviewed by author. April 9, 2020.

118. Sack, Linda. Interviewed by author. February 2, 2020.

119. Pryor, Ellen. Interviewed by author. June 18, 2020.

120. Wait, Mark. Interviewed by author. March 27, 2020.

121. Poland, Sam. Interviewed by author. June 20, 2020.

122. Lawing, Tramp. Interviewed by author. June 13, 2020.

123. Lomax, John, III. Interviewed by author. February 3, 2020.

124. Poland, Sam. Interviewed by author. June 20, 2020.

125. Lawing, Tramp. Interviewed by author. June 13, 2020.

126. Lomax, John, III. Interviewed by author. February 3, 2020.

127. Lomax III, John. Interviewed by author. April 16, 2020.

128. Fleming, Gena. Personal communication. December 17, 2020.

129. Seifert, Stephen. Personal communication.

130. Pryor, Ellen. Interviewed by author. June 18, 2020.

131. O'Connor, Mark. Interviewed by author. May 22, 2020.

132. Wait, Mark. Interviewed by author. March 27, 2020

133. Long, Lucy Margaret, "The Negotiation of Tradition: Collectors, Community, and the Appalachian Dulcimer in Beech Mountain, North Carolina" (1995). *Dissertations available from ProQuest*. AAI9532237. https://repository.upenn.edu/dissertations/AAI9532237.

134. O'Guin, Wanda. Personal communications. Spring 2020.

135. Breinig, Mary Lawrence. Personal communications. Summer 2020.

136. Schnaufer, David, and Judy Beier, student. *My Lessons with David*. Date unknown, CD recorded from original cassette.

137. McWhirt, Jennifer. Interviewed by author. July 22, 2020.

138. McWhirt-Toler, Sarah. Interviewed by author. June 25, 2020.

139. Sack, Linda. Interviewed by author. February 2, 2020.

140. King, Bob. Interviewed by author. May 20, 2020.

141. Breinig, Mary Lawrence. Personal communication. December 7, 2020

142. O'Guin, Wanda. Personal communication. Spring 2020.

143. King, Bob. Interviewed by author. May 20, 2020.

144. Seifert, Stephen. Interviewed by author. July 28, 2020

145. Sales, Jim. Interviewed by author. July 28, 2020.

146. Gruhn, George. Interviewed by author. July 22, 2020.

147. "Overview of Collection", in the Anne Romaine Papers #20304, Southern Folklife Collection, The Wilson Library, University of North Carolina at Chapel Hill.

148. Sherman, Kim. "The History of Cotten Music Center." The North American Guitar. Accessed August 07, 2020. https://thenorthamericanguitar.com/pages/the-history-of-cotten-music-center.

149. Fleming, Gina. Personal communication. September 6, 2020.

150. Pulsford, Jan. Personal communication. July 1, 2020.

151. McWhirt-Toler, Sarah. Personal Communication. June 25, 2020.

152. McWhirt, Jennifer. Personal Communication. July 22, 2020.

153. Farsetta, Vince. Personal communication. May 20, 2020.

154. Stubblefield, Stephen. Personal communication. July 15, 2020.

155. Konriff, Marilyn. Personal correspondence. February 10, 2020.

156. Wick, Carolyn. Personal communications. 2019-2020.

157. Ellis, Frances. "Miss Belle's House Makes Fun Outing." *Paris News* (Paris, Texas), March 5, 1995.

158. Pike, Bill. "Now Hear This: Iroquois Amphitheater Will Showcase Kentucky Music." *Courier Journal* (Louisville, Kentucky), July 26, 1995.

159. Guest. "The Callahan Touch - PDF Free Download." Epdf.pub. Accessed October 06, 2020. https://epdf.pub/queue/the-callahan-touch07323 7e3bfd5834c360f96ef210273e515692.html#.

160. Staff. "Festivals." *Fort Worth Star-Telegram* (Fort Worth, Texas), February 10, 1995.

161. Stubblefield, Steven. Interviewed by author. December 23, 2020.

162. O'Connor, Mark. Interviewed by author. May 22, 2020.

163. Meyer, Fred. Personal communication. February 24, 2021

164. Dean, Natasha. Interviewed by author. July 22, 2021.

165. Pulsford, Jan. Interviewed by author. July 1, 2020.

166. Dean, Natasha. Interviewed by author. July 22, 2021.

167. Auroh, Virginia. Unpublished interview transcript courtesy of Jan Pulsford. July 5, 1999.

168. Pulsford, Jan. Interviewed by author. July 1, 2020.

169. Rogers, John. "Music Man David Schnaufer." *Nashville Scene*, August 31, 2006.

170. Deane, Natasha. Interviewed by author.. July 22, 2020.

171. Larkin, T.J. Personal communication with images.

# MOVEMENT 6: TRANSITIONS

1. Seifert, Stephen. Interviewed by author. July 28, 2020.

2. Pulsford, Jan. Interviewed by author. July 1, 2020.

3. Arouh, Virginia. Interview transcript courtesy of Jan Pulsford. July 5, 1999.

4. Kruth, John. *To Live's to Fly: The Ballad of the Late, Great Townes Van Zandt.* Cambridge, MA: Da Capo, 2008.

5. Pulsford, Nigel. Interviewed by author. August 3, 2020.

6. Seifert, Stephen. Interviewed by author. July 28, 2020.

7. Banner, Lois W. *Intertwined Lives: Margaret Mead, Ruth Benedict, and Their Circle.* New York: Vintage, 2004.

8. Adams, Larry. "Open Chamber." *Nashville Scene.* November 28, 1996. Accessed October 13, 2020. https://www.nashvillescene.com/news/article/13001047/open-chamber.

9. Baldassari, Sinclair. Interviewed by author. July 6, 2020.

10. "Butch Baldassari: Home." Research Guides. Accessed October 06, 2020. https://researchguides.library.vanderbilt.edu/baldassari.

11. Weiss, Roger. "The Bottle Hill Boys - 1971-1972 - Roger Weiss - Music and Dance." Roger Weiss. May 18, 2020. Accessed October 06, 2020. https://rogerweiss.com/bottle-hill-boys-1971-1972/.

12. "Wild Rose of the Mountain 1" Traditional Tune Archive. May 06, 2019. Accessed October 25, 2020. https://tunearch.org/wiki/Annotation:Wild_Rose_of_the_Mountain_(1)

13. Pulsford, Jan. Interviewed by author. July 1, 2020.

14. McWhirt, Jennifer. Interviewed by author. July 22, 2020.

15. McWhirt-Toler, Sarah. Interviewed by author. June 26, 2020.

16. McWhirt, Jennifer. Interviewed by author. July 22, 2020.

17. McWhirt-Toler, Sarah. Interviewed by author. June 26, 2020.

18. Fleming, Gena. Personal communication. December 17, 2020.

19. Pulsford, Jan. Interviewed by author. July 20, 2020.

20. Fleming, Gena. Interviewed by author. October 4, 2020.

21. Seifert, Stephen. Interviewed by author. July 28, 2020.

22. Fleming, Gena. Personal communication. October 4, 2020.

23. Adams, Larry. "Open Chamber." Nashville Scene. November 28, 1996. Accessed July 20, 2020. http://www.nashvillescene.com/news/article/13001047/open-chamber.

24. Seifert, Stephen. Interviewed by author. July 28, 2020.

25. Seifert, Stephen. Interviewed by author. October 1, 2020.

26. Fleming, Gena. Personal communication. June 20, 2021.

27. Fleming, Gena. Personal communication. October 4, 2020.

28. Fleming, Gena. Interviewed by author. September 20, 2020.

29. Fleming, Gena. Interviewed by author. September 6, 2020.

30. Farsetta, Vince. Interviewed by author. May 1, 2020.

31. Stubblefield, Steven. Interviewed by author. July 11, 2020.

32. Farsetta, Vince. Interviewed by author. May 1, 2020.

33. Fleming, Gena. Personal conversation.

34. Stubblefield, Steven. Interviewed by author. July 11, 2020.

35. Pulsford, Jan. Interviewed by author July 20, 2020.

36. Bryan, Tim. Interviewed by author. July 20, 2020.

37. Stubblefield, Steven. Interviewed by author. July 11, 2020.

38. Piarrot, Andrew. Interviewed by author. June 17, 2021.

39. Piarrot, Henry. Interviewed by author. June 21, 2021.

40. Lomax, John Nova. Interviewed by author. October 19, 2020.

41. McWhirt-Toler, Sarah. Interviewed by author. June 25, 2020.

42. Glazener, Tull. ""Waltz of the Waters"." Tull Glazener. September 02, 2012. Accessed January 3, 2020. https://www.tullglazener.com/remembering-david/september-2012-waltz-of-the-waters.

43. Kruth, John. *To Live's to Fly: The Ballad of the Late, Great Townes Van Zandt.* Cambridge, MA: Da Capo, 2008.

44. Lomax, John Nova. "Starry Lullabye." *Nashville Scene*, August 24, 2006. Accessed June 6, 2020. https://www.nashvillescene.com/music/article/13013646/starry-lullabye.

45. *Blackberry Winter.* Conni Ellisor. Accessed August 25, 2020. http://ellisormusic.com/compositions/blackberry-winter/.

46. "About Let My Children Hear Music." CHARLES MINGUS. Accessed March 14, 2021. https://www.charlesmingus.com/about-mingus-institute.

47. Pulsford, Jan. Personal communication. March 13, 2021.

48. Pulsford, Jan. Interviewed by author. July 1, 2020.

49. Pulsford, Nigel. Interviewed by author. August 3, 2020.

50. "Nigel Pulsford Biography." OneSecondBush.com RSS. Accessed September 21, 2020. http://onesecondbush.com/bush/biography/.

51. Mingus, Charles, and Nel King. *Beneath the Underdog: His World as Composed*

*by Mingus*. New York: Vintage Books, 1991.

52. Seifert, Stephen. Personal communication.
53. Pulsford, Jan. Personal communication. March 13, 2021.
54. Pulsford, Jan. Interviewed by author. July 1, 2020.
55. Pulsford, Nigel. Interviewed by author. August 3, 2020.
56. Mingus, Charles, and Nel King. *Beneath the Underdog: His World as Composed by Mingus*. New York: Vintage Books, 1991.
57. Ponder, Drew. Interviewed by author. May 11, 2020
58. Cardona, Nina. "Dulcimer Master Dies." WPLN News - Nashville Public Radio. August 24, 2006. Accessed February 16, 2021. https://wpln.org/transcripts/.
59. Arouh, Virginia. Interview with David Schnaufer. July 5, 1999. Courtesy of Jan Pulsford.
60. Pulsford, Nigel. Interviewed by author. August 3, 2020.
61. Pulsford, Jan. "David Schnaufer *Delcimore*", p. 4.
62. Pulsford, Nigel. Personal communication. March 9, 2021.
63. Pulsford, Nigel. Interviewed by author. August 3, 2020.
64. Deane, Natasha. Interviewed by author. July 22, 2020.
65. "Interview with Lee Rowe." http://www.jerrywrightfamily.com. 2001. Accessed July 22, 2020. http://www.jerrywrightfamily.com/.
66. Sack, Linda. Interviewed by author. February 2, 2020.
67. Stubblefield, Steven. Interviewed by author. July 11, 2020.
68. Stubblefield, Steven. Interviewed by author. December 23, 2020.
69. Stubblefield, Steven. Interviewed by author. July 11, 2020
70. Howard, Jessica. "Texas-born Virtuoso Finds Harmony, Sophistication in Appalachian Instrument." Vanderbilt University Register: Texas-born Virtuoso Finds Harmony, Sophistication in Appalachian Instrument. April 1, 2002. Accessed December 30, 2020. https://web.archive.org/web/20160117085555/http://www.vanderbilt.edu/News/register/Apr01_02/story9.html.
71. Stubblefield, Steven. Personal communication. December 30, 2020.
72. Stubblefield, Steven. Interviewed by author. July 11, 2020.
73. Law, Zada. Personal communication.
74. Breinig, Mary Lawrence. Personal communication.
75. O'Guin, Wanda. Personal communication.
76. Wick, Carolyin. Personal communication.
77. Konriff, Marilyn. Personal communication.
78. Beier, Judy. GODC History Compilation. March 14, 2010. Nashville, Tennessee.
79. Nichols, Mary. Personal communication. March 14, 2021.
80. Pfeifer, Dan. Personal communication. March 14, 2021.
81. Nichols, Mary. Interviewed by author. March 7, 2021.
82. Pfeifer, Dan. Interviewed by author. March 7, 2021.
83. Haas, Dave. Interviewed by author. October 31, 2020.
84. Haas, Dave. Interviewed by author. October 31, 2020.
85. Thomson, Doug. Interviewed by author. July 15, 2020.

86. Bishop, Joni. Interviewed by author. May 4, 2020.

87. Orr, Jay. "Randy Howard, Master Fiddler, Dies of Cancer." *The Tennessean* (Nashville, Tn), July 1, 1999.

88. Bryan, Tim. Interviewed by author. July 20, 2020.

89. Del Gobbo, George. Interviewed by author. February 22, 2021.

90. Lundeen, Nan. "Marriage of the Earthly and the Divine." *Greenville News* (Greenville, South Carolina), December 8, 1999.

91. Bryan, Tim. Interviewed by author. July 20, 2020.

92. Neal, Jocelyn. "Garth Brooks, New Country and Rock's Influence." norton. com. Accessed March 3, 2021. https://wwnorton.com/college/music/ whats-that-sound4/assets/garth-brooks-new-country.pdf.

93. Malone, Bill C., and Tracey E. W. Laird. *Country Music USA*. Austin: University of Texas Press, 2018.

94. McWhirt-Toler, Sarah. Interviewed by author. June 25, 2020.

95. "News and Notes." *Dulcimer Player News*, Autumn 2000.

96. Piarrot, Henry. Interviewed by author. June 21, 2021.

97. Thomson, Doug. Interviewed by author. July 15, 2020. http://banjomer.com.

98. Hobbs, Georgia and Hollabaugh, Lela. Interviewed together by author. July 4, 2020.

99. Blackwood, Suzanne Normand. "Grand Old Dulcimer Day Features Music, Education." *The Tennessean* (Nashville, Tennessee), May 2, 2005.

100. Evans, Dan. Personal communication. March 21, 2020.

101. Kay, John. Interviewed by author. February 5, 2021.

102. Evans, Dan. Personal communication. December 22, 2020.

103. Evans, Dan. Personal communication. March 21, 2020.

104. Elliott, Tom. "Roger Nicholson: Britain's Most Influential Dulcimer Player." *The Independent*. October 23, 2011. Accessed March 21, 2020. https://www. independent.co.uk/news/obituaries/ roger-nicholson-britain-s-most-influential-dulcimer-player-1908238.html.

105. "Dan Evans - Dulcimer, Guitar & Composer." English Dulcimer. June 22, 2020. Accessed December 21, 2020. https://www.english-dulcimer.com/.

106. Alvey, Rocky. Interviewed by author. November 7, 2020.

107. "Hubble Marks 30 Years in Space with Tapestry of Blazing Starbirth." HubbleSite.org. April 24, 2020. Accessed November 29, 2020. https://hubblesite.org/contents/news-releases/2020/news-2020-16.

108. Barker, Nancy. Interviewed by author. March 22, 2020.

109. Law, Zada. Personal communication.

110. Musgrave, Jennifer. Interviewed by author. July 22, 2020.

111. Bryan, Tim. Interviewed by author July 20, 2020.

112. Stubblefield, Steven. Online post. February 14, 2018.

113. Kretzner, Leo. Personal communication. January 27, 2021.

114. Kretzner, Leo. Interviewed by author. August 29, 2020.

115. Larkin, T.J. Interviewed by author. March 11, 2021.

# MOVEMENT 7: JOURNEY'S END

1. Ellis, Darrell. Interviewed by author. July 8, 2020.
2. Saunders, Luke. "Listen to the Isolated Vocals of These 6 Classic Tracks." *Happy Mag*. February 11, 2020. Accessed March 12, 2021. https://happymag. tv/listen-to-the-isolated-vocals-of-these-6-classic-tracks/.
3. Larkin, T.J. Personal communication. March 11, 2021.
4. Stubblefield, Steven. Interviewed by author. July 11, 2020.
5. Rattlesnake Annie. Personal communication. April 26, 2020.
6. Sellers, Maureen. Interview by author. April 20, 2020.
7. Pulsford, Jan. Personal communication. July 8, 2020.
8. Larkin, T.J. Personal communication. March 11, 2021.
9. "The Amazing Name Ebenezer: Meaning and Etymology." Abarim Publications. Accessed March 15, 2021. https://www.abarim-publications. com/Meaning/Ebenezer.html.
10. Nichols, Mary. Personal communication. March 14, 2021.
11. Pfeifer, Dan. Personal communication. March 14, 2021.
12. Nichols, Mary. Interviewed by author. March 7, 2021.
13. Pfeifer, Dan. Interviewed by author. March 7, 2021.
14. Dickinson, Mike. Interviewed by author. March 16, 2020.
15. Baldissari, Butch. "Uncle Dulcimer" (Review). *Dulcimer Player News*, 2008, 45.
16. Howard, Jessica. "Texas-born Virtuoso Finds Harmony, Sophistication in Appalachian Instrument" Vanderbilt University Register. April 1, 2002. Accessed September 18, 2020. https://web.archive.org/web/ 20160117085555/http://www.vanderbilt.edu/News/register/Apr01_02/ story9.html.
17. Larkin, T.J. Personal communication. March 11, 2021.
18. Bryan, Tim. Interviewed by author. July 20, 2020.
19. Stubblefield, Steven. Interview by author. July 10, 2020.
20. Dickinson, Mike. Interview by author. March 16, 2020.
21. Bryan, Tim. Interviewed by author. July 20, 2020.
22. "Starlings, Tn. at the Pancake Pantry." *Nashville Scene*. December 6, 2001. Accessed May 18, 2020. https://www.nashvillescene.com/arts-culture/article/ 13006485/nicholas-payton-thursday-126.
23. Larkin, T.J. Interviewed by author. February 28, 2021.
24. Stubblefied, Steven. Personal communication. December 23, 2020.
25. Howard, Jessica. "Texas-born Virtuoso Finds Harmony, Sophistication in Appalachian Instrument." Vanderbilt University Register: Texas-born Virtuoso Finds Harmony, Sophistication in Appalachian Instrument. April 1, 2002. Accessed December 30, 2020. https://web.archive.org/web/ 20160117085555/http://www.vanderbilt.edu/News/register/Apr01_02/ story9.html.
26. Robbins, Beth. "Hayseed Rock: Starlings Flock to the Hills with First Album. " *The News-Star* (Monroe, Louisiana), July 12, 2002.
27. "Leaper's Fork Review." *The Daily Advertiser* (Lafayette, Louisiana), July 12,

2002.

28. Wallace, Ann. "Come Out to Kick Off a Summer Musical Tradition at the Farmer's Market." *The Leaf-Chronicle* (Clarksville, TN), June 28, 2002.

29. Piarrot, Henry. "Starlings, TN Brings Beautiful Sounds of the Dulcimer into Mainstream Music." *The Tennessean* (Nashville, TN), May 19, 2002.

30. Ellis, Darrel. Interviewed by author. July 8, 2020.

31. Fleming, Gena. Personal communication.

32. Larkin, T.J. Personal communication. March 11, 2021.

33. "Rhythm Bones History." Rhythm Bones History. Accessed March 12, 2021. https://www.rhythmbones.com/bonesHistory.html.

34. Stubblefield, Steven. Personal communication. December 23, 2020.

35. Nichols, Mary. Personal communication. March 14, 2021.

36. Pfeifer, Dan. Personal communication. March 14, 2021.

37. Nichols, Mary. Interviewed by author. March 7, 2021.

38. Pfeifer, Dan. Interviewed by author. March 7, 2021.

39. McWhirt, Sara Elizabeth. Personal communication. December 13, 2020.

40. Larkin, T.J. Interviewed by author. February 28, 2021.

41. Alvey, Rocky. Interviewed by author. November 7, 2020.

42. Wait, Mark. Interviewed by author. March 27, 2020.

43. W.,J. ""Music on the Mountain" W/Butch Baldassari, David Schnaufer & Bobby Taylor." Nashville Scene. April 24, 2003. Accessed May 28, 2020. https://www.nashvillescene.com/arts-culture/article/13008492/mccoy-tyner-thursday-24th.

44. "New 'Music on the Mountain' Community Event Launched at Dyer Observatory." Vanderbilt University. April 27, 2003. Accessed December 30, 2020. https://news.vanderbilt.edu/2003/04/27/new-quotmusic-on-the-mountainquot-community-event-launched-at-dyer-observatory-60012/.

45. Arnold, Edwin T., Tyler Blethen, Amy Tipton Cortner, Anna Creadick, John Crutchfield, Silas House, John C. Inscoe, Gordon B. McKinney, and Jack Wright. ""APPALJ" Roundtable Discussion: "Cold Mountain", the Film." *Appalachian Journal* 31, no. 3/4 (2004): 316-53. Accessed February 19, 2021. http://www.jstor.org/stable/40934797.

46. MacNeil, Madeline, ed. "News and Notes." *Dulcimer Player News*, 2004.

47. Larkin, T.J. Interviewed by author. February 28, 2021.

48. Larkin, T.J. Interviewed by author. February 17, 2021.

49. Alvey, Rocky. Interviewed by author. November 7, 2020.

50. Alvey, Rocky. Interviewed by author. November 7, 2020.

51. McWhirt, Jennifer. Personal communication. March 29, 2021.

52. McWhirt-Toler, Sarah. Personal communication. March 29, 2021.

53. McWhirt, Jennifer. Interviewed by author. July 22, 2020.

54. L., B. "Dulci-Mania/An Evening of Dulcimer Music." *Nashville Scene*. April 3, 2003. Accessed October 30, 2020. https://www.nashvillescene.com/arts-culture/article/13008396/altered-spaces-video-art-physical-world-opening-friday-april-4.

55. Alvey, Rocky. Interviewed by author. 11.7.2020.

56. Nichols, Mary. Personal communication. March 14, 2021.

57. Pfeifer, Dan. Personal communication. March 14, 2021.
58. Nichols, Mary. Interviewed by author. March 7, 2021.
59. Pfeifer, Dan. Interviewed by author. March 7, 2021.
60. Larkin, T.J. Personal communication. March 10, 2021.
61. Strange, Benjamin. "Talk Bass Forum." TalkBass.com. March 1, 2004. Accessed March 12, 2021. https://www.talkbass.com/threads/what-did-sting-play-at-the-oscar-awards.118590/.
62. The Province (Vancouver, British Columbia, Canada). "Quickspins." Review of "When Silence Was Golden". November 23, 2004. Accessed December 29, 2020. https://www.newspapers.com/image/504993249.
63. Alvey, Rocky. Interviewed by author. November 7, 2020.
64. "What Happened When Huygens Landed on Titan Eight Years Ago." *Astrobiology Magazine*. January 15, 2013. Accessed November 11, 2020. https://www.astrobio.net/titan/what-happened-when-huygens-landed-on-titan-eight-years-ago/.
65. Staff. "The Huygens Landing: One Year on." ESA. January 13, 2006. Accessed November 27, 2020. http://www.esa.int/Science_Exploration/Space_Science/Cassini-Huygens/The_Huygens_landing_br_one_year_on.
66. Nichols, Mary. Personal communication. March 14, 2021.
67. Pfeifer, Dan. Personal communication. March 14, 2021.
68. Nichols, Mary. Interviewed by author. March 7, 2021.
69. Fisher, Martin. Personal communication. March 17, 2021.
70. Fisher, Martin. Interviewed by author. March 15, 2021.
71. Larkin, T.J. Personal communication.
72. Alvey, Rocky. Interviewed by author. November 7, 2020.
73. Humbles, Andy. "Festival Chance to Try a Dulcimer." *The Tennessean* (Nashville, Tn.), May 13, 2005.
74. Baldissari, Butch. "Remembering David Schnaufer." *Nashville Scene*. August 30, 2006. Accessed January 03, 2020. https://www.nashvillescene.com/music/article/13026850/remembering-david-schnaufer.
75. Brance. "Appalachian Mandolin and Dulcimer." *Bluegrass Today*. October 4, 2005. Accessed December 12, 2020. https://bluegrasstoday.com/appalachian-mandolin-and-dulcimer/.
76. D. Eric Schnaufer. Interviewed by author. January 6, 2021.
77. Fleming, Gena. Personal communication.
78. "Obituaries: Kenneth Charles Fleming." *The Daily-News Journal* (Murfreesboro, Tennessee), August 7, 2005. Accessed September 7, 2020.
79. Nichols, Mary. Personal communication. March 14, 2021.
80. Pfeifer, Dan. Personal communication. March 14, 2021.
81. Nichols, Mary. Interviewed by author. March 7, 2021.
82. Pfeifer, Dan. Interviewed by author. March 7, 2021.
83. Theobald, Terry. Interviewed by author. October 23, 2020.
84. McCullough, Joann. Interviewed by author. October 23, 2020.
85. Anonymous. Accessed on March 18, 2020.
86. Wait, Mark. Interviewed by author. March 27, 2020.
87. Ellis, Darrel. Interviewed by author. July 8, 2020.

88. Nichols, Mary. Personal communication. March 14, 2021.
89. Pfeifer, Dan. Personal communication. March 14, 2021.
90. Nichols, Mary. Interviewed by author. March 7, 2021.
91. Pfeifer, Dan. Interviewed by author. March 7, 2021.
92. Ellis, Darrel. Interviewed by author. July 8, 2020.
93. Law, Zada. Personal communication. August 30, 2020.
94. Pryor, Ellen. Interviewed by author. June 18, 2020.
95. Wait, Mark. Interviewed by author. March 27, 2020.
96. McWhirt, Jennifer. Interviewed by author. July 22, 2020.
97. McWhirt-Toler, Sarah. Personal communication. March 29, 2021.
98. McWhirt, Jennifer. Interviewed by author. July 22, 2020.
99. Schnaufer, D. Eric. Interviewed by author January 6, 2020.
100. Larkin, T.J. Personal communication. February 28, 2021.
101. Alvey, Rocky. Interviewed by author. November 7, 2020.
102. Hornbostel, Lois. Interviewed by author. April 29, 2020.
103. Beall, Harry. Interviewed by author. January 23, 2021.
104. Schnaufer, D. Eric. Personal communication.
105. Ellis, Darrel. Interviewed by author. July 8, 2020.
106. Pryor, Ellen. Interviewed by author. June 18, 2020.
107. McWhirt-Toler, Sara Elizabeth. Interviewed by author. June 25, 2020.
108. McWhirt-Toler, Sara Elizabeth. Personal communication. March 29, 2020.
109. Pryor, Ellen. Interviewed by author. June 18, 2020.
110. Renwick, John. Interviewed by author. February 28, 2021.
111. Hobb, Georgia and Hollabaugh, Lela. Interviewed by author.
112. McCullough, Joann. Personal correspondence. February 11, 2020.
113. Ellis, Darrel. Interviewed by author. July 8, 2020.
114. Farsetta, Vince. Personal communication.
115. Stubblefield, Steven. Personal communication. February 28, 2021.
116. Law, Zada. Personal communication. August 30,3020.
117. Bryan, Tim. Interviewed by author. July 20, 2020.
118. Schnaufer, Eric D. Personal communication.

Made in the USA
Las Vegas, NV
12 December 2023

82603125R00315